READER BONUS!

Dear Reader,

As a thank you for your support, Action Takers Publishing would like to offer you a special reader bonus: a free download of our course, "How to Write, Publish, Market & Monetize Your Book the Fast, Fun & Easy Way." This comprehensive course is designed to provide you with the tools and knowledge you need to bring your book to life and turn it into a successful venture.

The course typically **retails for $499,** but as a valued reader, you can access it for free. To claim your free download, simply follow this link <u>ActionTakersPublishing.com/workshops</u> - use the discount code "coursefree" to get a 100% discount and start writing your book today.

If we are still giving away this course by the time you're reading this book, head straight over to your computer and start the course now. It's absolutely free.

READER BONUS!

<u>ActionTakersPublishing.com/workshops</u>
discount code "coursefree"

The MIND-BODY Connection

THE KEYS TO UNLOCKING YOUR FULL POTENTIAL

Email: lynda@actiontakerspublishing.com

Website: www.actiontakerspublishing.com

ISBN # (paperback) 978-1-956665-50-5
ISBN # (Kindle) 978-1-956665-51-2
Published by Action Takers Publishing™

Table of Contents

It takes awareness to effect change.
~Lynda Sunshine West

Introduction

In the journey of life, we often find ourselves at crossroads, facing choices that define not just our paths but who we are and who we become. "*The Mind-Body Connection: The Keys to Unlocking Your Full Potential*" is a book that offers guidance, wisdom, and profound insights into this intricate journey. It's not just a book; it's a beacon of light for those navigating the sometimes-turbulent waters of existence.

In this compelling anthology, 14 voices come together, each bringing their unique perspective and expertise on the vital interplay between our minds, bodies, and spirits. Their collective wisdom, borne from personal experiences and professional insights, illuminates the path to achieving a harmonious, fulfilled, and purpose-driven life.

As you turn these pages, you'll encounter a diverse range of topics, each addressing essential aspects of the mind-body connection. From the transformative power of breathwork, the setting of healthy boundaries, to overcoming deeply ingrained belief systems, each chapter serves as a key to unlock parts of yourself that perhaps have been long forgotten or yet to be discovered.

Chapter 1 begins with a poignant exploration of the power of our thoughts and their profound impact on our physical health. The journey into the mind-body connection starts with understanding how our inner dialogue shapes our external reality. This chapter sets the stage for a deep dive into self-awareness, an essential first step in the process of personal growth and transformation.

As we progress, chapters 2 through 13 unfold a tapestry of experiences and strategies, weaving together elements of spirituality, emotional resilience, and physical wellness. You'll encounter powerful stories of overcoming adversity, insightful techniques for managing stress, and practical advice for cultivating mindfulness and self-compassion.

Each author brings their unique flavor to the table, yet a common thread runs through their narratives: the undeniable truth that our mental, emotional, and physical well-being are inextricably linked. This book is not just about understanding this connection; it's about harnessing it to create a life of balance, fulfillment, and joy.

You will discover how lifestyle choices, from the food we eat to the spaces we inhabit, play a crucial role in shaping our mental state. You'll learn how mindful practices like yoga, Tai Chi, and even dance can be powerful tools for mental and physical well-being. The insights shared here are both practical and profound, offering a holistic approach to wellness that transcends conventional wisdom.

In Chapter 14, the culmination of this journey, you'll encounter a heartfelt message about embracing authenticity, breaking free from limiting beliefs, and the transformative power of self-expression. This chapter is a testament to the incredible journey of self-discovery and the beauty of becoming who you truly are.

"*The Mind-Body Connection: The Keys to Unlocking Your Full Potential*" is more than just a collection of chapters; it's a journey. It invites you to explore, challenge, and nurture every aspect of your being. As you read, you are encouraged to reflect, to pause, and to apply these insights to your life. This book is an invitation to embark on a journey of self-discovery, to unlock your potential, and to embrace the fullness of life with an open heart and mind.

Each chapter in this book is a steppingstone towards a greater understanding of yourself and the world around you. As you read these pages, keep an open mind and heart. Allow the experiences and wisdom of these authors to guide you, inspire you, and challenge you to grow in ways you never thought possible.

"*The Mind-Body Connection: The Keys to Unlocking Your Full Potential*" is more than a book; it's a companion in your journey of growth and self-discovery. It's a source of inspiration and a guide for anyone seeking to deepen their understanding of the intricate dance between mind, body, and spirit. As you turn each page, may you find the keys to unlock your full potential and embark on a journey of transformation, healing, and profound self-realization.

Lynda Sunshine West and Sally Larkin Green

CHAPTER 1

Cultivating Resilience: Beyond Overcoming Fear

by Lynda Sunshine West

Resilience is the ability to bounce back from adversity, and it's closely linked with how we manage our fears. By continuously working on the mind-body connection, we not only face our fears but also build resilience, equipping ourselves to handle future challenges more effectively.

I had no idea when I was five years old and ran away and was gone for an entire week how that would affect my life. When I came home, I was riddled with fears and would live the next 46 years as a scared adult. While my fears stopped me from doing a lot of things, my ability to bounce back is what has kept me going all these years.

In 2015, at the age of 51, I decided to breakthrough one fear every day for a year. You see, I had allowed fear to control my life for many decades. I decided at that time that I was no longer going to allow my fears to control me and, rather, I was going to gain control over my fears.

Imagine waking up every morning asking yourself a simple question, three words that will forever change your life. Those words were, "What scares me?" Sometimes it's the simple things in life that changed the trajectory of our lives forever.

2015 was not only a year of breaking through fears, it was also my first year as an entrepreneur. Boy it was that a scary year. Fear is different for everybody. For me, fear showed up in so many simple things like starting a conversation with a stranger, going to a restaurant by myself, going to a movie by myself, meeting new people, and many more. The greatest discovery I made during that year of breaking through fears was that my greatest fear was the fear of judgment. You see, the fear of judgment stopped me in my tracks from doing something that may embarrass me. By knowing that was my greatest fear, I was now able to focus on one big fear, instead of all of these small fears. With that said, it's not to minimize the small fears because all fears are fear and no matter how big or small the fear is, it can feel debilitating and prevent you from living the life you truly want to live.

I'm excited to share with you a few of the techniques that I have learned along this journey and how they have helped me to become more resilient and to live a life I never imagined I would live.

Building Emotional Resilience

What is emotional resilience and how do you build it? Emotional re-silience

Emotional resilience is an invaluable trait, especially in the unpredictable ebb and flow of life's challenges. It's the ability to bounce back from setbacks, adapt to change, and keep going in the face of adversity. Emotional resilience doesn't mean you don't experience stress, emotional upheaval, or suffering. Rather, it signifies the capacity to endure and emerge from these challenges stronger, wiser, and more capable.

Think of some times in your life when you were under a tremendous amount of stress. How did that feel? Did you feel like you were out of control and that you would never recover? Been there, done that on way too many occasions. I've come to realize that building emotional resilience is like strengthening a muscle; it requires time, effort, and practice. Here are some strategies I use to cultivate this essential quality:

Foster a Positive Outlook

Maintaining a positive outlook is not about ignoring life's pressures but about maintaining a sense of hope and optimism even in difficult times. CAUTION: The practice of living a positive outlook can cause negative people to disappear from your life. Don't worry, though, because eventually you'll be glad they're gone.

Two things you can do to maintain a positive outlook are to 1) practice gratitude by regularly reflecting on and appreciating the good things in life, no matter how small they may seem, can shift your perspective and help you see beyond current challenges and 2) reframe negativity by learning to recognize and challenge pessimistic or catastrophic thoughts. By consciously reframing those thoughts in a more positive or realistic light, you can significantly alter your emotional response to stressful situations.

Embrace Change

Change is a constant in life, and those who are resilient tend to view change as an opportunity rather than a threat. Flexibility and adaptability are key components of emotional resilience. I have always embraced change as fun and exciting (I had 49 jobs in 36 years and have lived in more than 40 houses throughout my time on this earth). I realize that not everyone embraces change, though. Every week for three months, try something new. Learn to embrace that change and you'll see how your life changes. Wrapping your head around it may be a challenge, but it's worth a try, right?

Believe in your ability to learn and grow from your experiences. Viewing challenges as opportunities for growth rather than insurmountable obstacles enhances your resilience. After all, change is inevitable. You might as well enjoy it. I highly recommend being willing to adjust your goals and strategies in response to changing circumstances. Have fun with it.

Build Strong Relationships

A supportive network of friends, family, and colleagues can provide a buffer against life's stressors. Strong, positive relationships are crucial to have emotional resilience. You're not alone. You have people in your life who want to support you. If you don't have a lot of positive influences in your life, it's time to branch out and find some. They are out there; you just need to search for and find them. Don't hesitate to reach out to your people during tough times. Sometimes we don't even need to reach out to them to gain their support. Just knowing they're there can make challenging situations more manageable. Likewise, being there for others can enhance your sense of purpose and connection, and that'll strengthen your own resilience.

Develop Problem-Solving Skills

The ability to solve problems under pressure is a hallmark of emotional resilience. And believe it or not, problem-solving is a skill that can be attained. You don't have to be born with it. When faced with a challenge, focus on finding solutions rather than dwelling on the problem. One of the things I love doing is to tackle my challenges by breaking them into smaller, manageable parts. If I look at the big picture, it makes me want to crawl into a hole and hibernate until it's over, but doing that just makes it worse and it's never over until after I stop hibernating. Brainstorming possible solutions by myself and with other supportive and uplifting people has helped me open up to trying different strategies and that's exciting.

Set Realistic Goals and Take Action

Setting realistic goals and taking the necessary steps to achieve them is empowering. What was the last goal you set that you achieved? Remember that feeling when you sit down to set your goals. Define what you want to achieve and break it down into actionable steps. Then celebrate every step along the journey. You don't have to wait until you finish the big picture in order to celebrate. I pat myself on the back on a regular basis and say, "Great job, Lynda Sunshine. Keep going. You got this." By physically patting myself on the back while I congratulate myself, I am connecting my mind (congratulating myself) with my body (patting myself on the back) with the feeling of accomplishment. It's a good feeling and I want to achieve the feeling more often. By taking that one simple action, I become encouraged to keep going and doing what I'm doing to get the results I'm getting. It may feel weird at first, but it's helped me make tremendous progress in my personal and business life. The more I accomplish, the more confident I become. The more confident I become, the more I encourage and empower others to become more confident. There's nothing quite like empowering others with the tools to become more confident.

Learn from Experience

Resilience is often forged in the fire of adversity, just like a diamond that needs 725,000 pounds per square inch in order to be created. Fortunately, we humans don't need that much weight of pressure to create our resilience. Reflecting on how you've coped with past challenges can help you identify strategies that worked (and those that didn't). Remind yourself of the times you've overcome obstacles in the past and realize that you can do that again. It's not a one-and-done type of life. We get do-overs. Remember that every setback is setup for another opportunity to learn, grow, and improve.

Harness the Power of Storytelling

As a book publisher who helps women and men share their stories, I understand the power of stories in shaping our perceptions and beliefs. What stories are you telling yourself about who you are? Are you repeating stories that you've been told since you were a child? Are those stories actually true? Or are they just stories you've adopted to be the truth? Learn the power of your story and use it to create the life you want to live. Are your life's narratives based on facts or are they based on others' beliefs? This is a question I frequently ask myself. It helps me to know who I really am and live my authentic life.

It's time to write a new story about your past, present and future. Yes, future. Decide today who you want to be tomorrow and then take the actions necessary to make that happen.

Long-Term Strategies for Sustained Mind-Body Harmony

One of the things I've come to love is the ability to learn and grow no matter my age. I started my personal development journey at age 51.

And I don't feel old at all. I feel alive. I firmly believe that the more we are open to growing and learning, the younger we become. Your chronological age isn't necessarily the same as your biological age. I've heard some people age 25 say they feel like they're 70 and I've heard 70-year-olds say they feel like they're 25. It's all relative. How can that be explained? I'm not sure, but I do know that as of the writing of this chapter, I'm age 60 and I feel like I'm in my early 30s. I feel so alive and I know it's because I finally took time to get in touch with who I am, what I'm all about, and why I'm here on this planet. Taking time to listen to my body and mind has created within me a desire to live (one I never experienced before) a long and prosperous life surrounded by loving, caring, giving, positive, uplifting and motivational people who are making a greater impact on the planet. By continually learning about the mind-body connection, I am open to what life has in store for me.

Embracing the Journey

Lastly, embracing this journey of exploring and strengthening the mind-body connection is ongoing. It's not just about overcoming individual fears but about embracing a lifestyle that fosters mental, physical, and emotional well-being. It's a lifelong journey, one where each step is significant.

As you continue to explore and harness this powerful connection, you'll find yourself living a more enriched, balanced life. The mind-body connection is a profound tool for transformation, and by understanding and utilizing it, we can all lead more fulfilled and fearless lives.

Lynda Sunshine West

She ran away at 5 years old and was gone an entire week, came home riddled with fears and, in turn, became a people-pleaser.

At age 51, she decided to break through one fear every day for a year and, in doing so, she gained an exorbitant amount of confidence to share her story.

Her mission is to empower 5 million women and men to write their stories to make a greater impact on the planet.

Lynda Sunshine West is the Founder and CEO of Action Takers Publishing, a Bestseller Book Publishing Expert, Speaker, 38 Time #1 International Bestselling Author, Contributing Writer at Entrepreneur Magazine, Senior Level Executive Contributing Writer at Brainz Magazine, Executive Film Producer, and Red Carpet Interviewer.

Connect with Lynda Sunshine at www.actiontakerspublishing.com.

CHAPTER 2

Healing From the Inside Out!

by Sally Larkin Green

Beloved, I pray that you may prosper in all things and be in health, just as your soul prospers. 3 John 1:2

There is a divine secret that's at the core of our existence. It's the beautiful, God-given connection between our minds and our bodies. This isn't just an idea or a passing thought, it's a reality we live every single day. This connection, this perfect harmony between our physical selves and our spiritual thoughts, is what we call the mind-body connection. It's a powerful force, a testament to God's magnificent design. As we look into understanding and nurturing this bond, we open ourselves to a life overflowing with joy, brimming with health, and rich in fulfillment. Let's talk about how this connection can transform our lives and guide us toward an abundant life.

The bible verse above beautifully encapsulates the essence of the mind-body connection. It's a reminder that our physical well-being and our spiritual and mental health are deeply intertwined. When our mind is filled with positive thoughts, our body responds. Similarly, when we take care of our body, our mind finds peace and clarity.

I remember a time in my life when this connection became particularly evident. I was going through a phase of stress and uncertainty, and it reflected in my physical health. I felt tired and drained most of the time. I'll talk more about that later in this chapter, but when I turned to prayer, meditation, and self-care, not only did my outlook on life change, but I also noticed a remarkable improvement in my physical well-being. It was as if my body was saying "thank you" for taking care of my mind and spirit.

This experience is not unique to me. Many of you might have experienced similar transformations. Perhaps it was through meditation, yoga, or simply spending quiet time in nature. These practices aren't just activities; they are pathways to align our mind and body with our purpose.

Understanding the mind-body connection involves recognizing that our thoughts, feelings, beliefs, and attitudes can positively or negatively affect our bodies. In other words, our minds can affect how healthy our bodies are! On the flip side, what we do with our physical body (what we eat, how much we exercise, even our posture) can impact our mental state.

This dual relationship between mind and body opens up amazing possibilities. It means we have more control over our health and happiness than we might have thought. We can use our thoughts to foster a healthier body, and we can use our physical state to nurture a more positive and productive mind.

Think about the impact of stress or anxiety on your body. These emotions trigger a physical response – maybe a headache, stomach upset, or sleeplessness. Your body tells you something's off balance in your mind. Conversely, when you're joyful, your body tends to feel better too. You might notice more energy, better sleep, or a more robust immune response.

As I navigate through the twists and turns of my life, the connection between my mind and body becomes increasingly clear. My journey, woven with threads of love, responsibility, and personal growth, tells a story that's both challenging and rewarding. This path, filled with deep affection and unwavering commitment, has seen its share of trials that have impacted me both emotionally and physically. Taking care of my mother, who battles Alzheimer's, and my father, who, despite suffering a heart attack, often neglects the advice of his doctors, has been a path filled with emotional turbulence and physical demands. It's a journey that continuously reinforces the deep and undeniable connection between our emotional well-being and physical health.

Watching my mom struggle with Alzheimer's has been heart-wrenching. Alzheimer's is not just a loss of memory; it's a slow fading of the person you once knew. The emotional toll of this can be overwhelming. At the same time, dealing with my dad's stubborn refusal to follow doctor's orders after his heart attack adds to the stress. It's a constant worry, a fear of what might happen next, and a feeling of helplessness that perhaps I'm not doing enough.

The stress and anxiety of caregiving have manifested in various physical symptoms. I often find myself exhausted and overwhelmed by the weight of my responsibilities. Stress headaches have become a common occurrence, throbbing reminders of the constant pressure I'm under. Additionally, I've developed a persistent pain in my hip, causing me to limp – a physical reflection of the emotional burden I carry.

Sleepless nights have become a norm. I frequently wake up in the middle of the night, my mind racing with worries and to-do lists, making it nearly impossible to fall back asleep. The lack of restful sleep only exacerbates my physical ailments and drains my emotional reserves.

In the midst of this, I've had to take over managing my parents' finances and grocery shopping. This added responsibility, while necessary, brings its own set of challenges. The situation becomes particularly stressful when my dad calls, often last minute, to say he's out of food – items he didn't tell me to buy but now urgently needs. These moments are not just about the inconvenience; they symbolize the constant unpredictability and demand of my caregiving role.

Despite these challenges, this journey has also been one of growth and resilience. I've learned to find strength in moments of weakness and hope in times of despair. The love I have for my parents is the driving force that keeps me going, even on the toughest days.

Navigating this path has also taught me the importance of self-care. I've realized that to be there for my parents, I must also take care of myself. This means finding small pockets of time for rest, seeking support when needed, and acknowledging my own physical and emotional limits.

My story is one shared by many caregivers around the world. It's a story that speaks to the challenges, sacrifices, and love that define the caregiving experience. While it's a journey fraught with difficulties, it's also one filled with moments of tenderness, deepening relationships, and an understanding of life's fragile beauty.

As I continue on this path, I carry with me the lessons learned, the strength gained, and the hope that each new day brings. The journey is far from over, but I move forward with a heart full of love and a spirit resolved to face whatever lies ahead.

So, how do we strengthen this mind-body connection? The first step is through awareness. Pay attention to the signals your body sends you. When you're feeling unwell, ask yourself what might be happening in your mental or emotional life that could be contributing to this. Similarly, notice how taking care of your body through exercise, healthy eating, and rest can influence your mood and mindset.

Prayer and meditation are powerful tools for nurturing this connection. They allow us to quiet the mind, connect with God, and find peace. This peace then manifests in our bodies, often as a sense of relaxation and rejuvenation. I often find myself energized and feeling better after my morning and evening meditations.

Physical activity is another key component. Exercise not only strengthens our bodies but also releases endorphins, chemicals in our brains that act as natural painkillers and mood elevators. It's incredible how a simple act like a brisk walk can lift our spirits and improve our health.

Let's also remember the power of laughter and joy. Proverbs 17:22 says, "A merry heart does good, like medicine, but a broken spirit dries the bones." Find joy in your everyday life, laugh often, and your body will respond with vitality and energy. My husband has a wonderful sense of humor, we laugh often.

Another daily habit I am discovering is mindful eating. It's not just what we eat, but how we eat that can strengthen the mind-body connection. Mindful eating involves paying full attention to the experience of eating and drinking. It's about noticing the colors, smells, textures, flavors, temperatures, and even the sounds of our food. By eating mindfully, we become more aware of our body's hunger and satiety signals, leading to a healthier relationship with food. This practice can also involve gratitude for the nourishment food provides, acknowledging the effort taken to prepare the meal, and recognizing how specific foods impact our mood and energy levels.

I want to share with you another powerful way I practice self-care, a way that beautifully aligns with my creative spirit. It's through the joy of Art. When I engage in expressive arts like painting or writing, it's more than just a hobby; it's a profound way to strengthen the connection between my mind and body. These creative pursuits allow me to express feelings and thoughts that sometimes words alone can't capture. Every stroke of the paintbrush, every word I write, becomes a pathway to release stress, to grow in self-awareness, and to find inner peace. By including these activities in my weekly routine, I am not just developing professionally; I am nurturing my soul, caring for the temple that is my body, and walking on a path of wellness.

One of the most transformative practices we can embrace in our lives is developing an attitude of gratitude. This isn't just a feel-good phrase; it's a powerful truth that can profoundly change our mental state. When we begin or end each day by counting our blessings, and acknowledging all that we're grateful for, we do much more than shift our focus. We open our eyes to the incredible abundance that surrounds us. This simple act of gratitude is a gateway to a new perspective, one that allows us to see God's hand in every aspect of our lives.

This change in perspective is not just minor; it's a seismic shift in how we view our world. By focusing on what we have, rather than what we lack, we start to see our lives in a new light. Every small blessing becomes a source of joy, every challenge an opportunity for growth. This shift in mindset is a powerful tool against stress. In moments of gratitude, our worries and tensions seem to melt away, replaced by a sense of peace and contentment.

However, the benefits of an attitude of gratitude extend beyond our mental well-being. Believe it or not, this change in perspective can also have a tangible effect on our physical health. Studies have shown that gratitude can lead to better sleep, lower blood pressure, and a stronger immune system. It's as if our body responds in kind to the positivity we foster in our minds.

When we live with a grateful heart, our mood naturally uplifts. We find joy in the every day, and our outlook becomes one of hope and optimism. This positive mindset can have a ripple effect on those around us, creating an environment of positivity and well-being.

So, I encourage you, as you wake up each morning or as you lay down to sleep at night, to take a moment to count your blessings. Reflect on the goodness in your life, the big things and the small. Thank God for the roof over your head, the food on your table, the people who love you, and even the challenges that make you stronger. As you do this, you'll find that gratitude becomes more than a habit; it becomes a way of life. You'll start to notice the abundance that's always been there, and your heart will overflow with joy and peace.

While caring for my parents and managing the complexities of their health and needs, I've been grappling with personal struggles that have significantly impacted my life. These challenges revolve around my weight, my financial situation, and my deep-seated thoughts about self-worth, particularly about money.

My battle with weight has been an ongoing struggle, exacerbated by the stress and demands of caregiving. The constant pressure, coupled with sleepless nights and irregular eating habits, has led to weight fluctuations that I find hard to control. It's a cycle that seems to feed itself – the more stressed I become, the more my eating habits suffer, and the more my weight fluctuates, the more stressed I feel. It's a physical manifestation of the emotional turmoil within.

Parallel to my weight issues, I've been facing challenges with my finances. Taking over my parents' financial responsibilities while managing my own has stretched me thin. The financial burden is not just about the numbers; it's about the constant worry and the feeling of being overwhelmed. This struggle has been a significant source of stress, contributing to my overall sense of unease and discomfort.

At the core of these struggles lies a deeper issue – my thoughts about self-worth and money. I've come to realize that my financial challenges are intertwined with how I view my worth, especially regarding my ability to create wealth. There's a part of me that feels unworthy, that doubts my capabilities and this mindset has held me back, not just financially but in various aspects of my life.

I believe that the key to overcoming my financial and weight challenges lies in changing my mindset. It's about shifting my thoughts from self-doubt to self-worth, from a mindset of scarcity to one of abundance. I need to embrace the belief that I am worthy and that I can create wealth and a healthy lifestyle for myself.

This journey is about finding balance and being aware of the interconnectedness of my physical health, financial health, and self-worth. I am learning that the way I think about myself and my capabilities directly impacts my physical and financial well-being. It's a process of self-discovery, of peeling back the layers to understand the root causes of my struggles.

I am committed to changing my thinking, to nurturing a mindset that embraces my worth and my ability to create a positive and prosperous life. I know that this change won't happen overnight, but I am ready to take the necessary steps. I am aware that as I work on my mindset, both my financial situation and my weight issues will begin to align with my new perspective.

This segment of my journey is about healing – healing from the inside out. It's about recognizing that my thoughts and beliefs have power and that by changing them, I can change my life. It's a path filled with challenges, but also with hope. I am on a journey to finding balance, embracing my worth, and unlocking the abundance that life has to offer.

The concept of the mind-body connection is more than just an idea; it's a profound truth about our existence. This connection serves as a reminder of our intricate and beautiful complexity as creations of God. We are not just physical beings navigating through the world, nor are we solely spiritual entities disconnected from our earthly bodies. We are a harmonious blend of mind, body, and spirit, each part interwoven in a delicate and purposeful design.

When we talk about nurturing the mind-body connection, we delve into the art of listening and responding to the needs of both our physical and spiritual selves. It's about recognizing the signals our bodies send us – whether it's stress manifesting as a headache or joy expressing itself through a surge of energy. Similarly, it's about understanding how our mental and spiritual states can directly impact our physical health and well-being.

By fostering this connection, we open ourselves to a life that is not just lived but is richly experienced in all its dimensions. A life where health is not merely the absence of illness but a state of complete physical, mental, and spiritual well-being. A life where happiness is found not in fleeting pleasures but in a deep sense of contentment and purpose. This is the life that aligns with God's plan for us, a life where we live out our full potential, embracing every joy and challenge with faith and resilience.

We often forget the power we hold over our health and happiness. It's easy to feel like we are at the mercy of external circumstances, but the truth is, we have significant control over how we respond to life's challenges. By nurturing our mind-body connection, we can choose practices and thoughts that promote health and well-being. We can decide to engage in activities that bring us joy, adopt habits that enhance our physical health, and foster a mindset that strengthens our spiritual connection.

As we embark on this journey, it's important to remember that we are not alone. Faith, hope, and love are our companions along this path. Faith in a higher purpose, hope in the face of adversity, and love for ourselves and others – these are the guiding lights that will lead us to a life of harmony and fulfillment.

Let's embrace this journey with open hearts and minds. Let's commit to taking care of our bodies, enriching our minds, and nurturing our spirits. In doing so, we align ourselves with the divine rhythm of life, experiencing the fullness of what it means to be beautifully and wonderfully made.

The mind-body connection is a gift, a key to unlocking a life of health, happiness, and alignment with God's plan. It's a journey worth embarking on, filled with discoveries, growth, and the joy of living in true harmony. So, let's journey together, with faith, hope, and love, every step of the way.

Sally Larkin Green

Sally Larkin Green is the Vice President of Author Development at Action Takers Publishing. With a background in business and Computers, Sally's passion for storytelling and empowering others has transformed her into a bestselling author and inspirational speaker.

In March 2020, Sally realized that while she was good at caring for everyone else, she was really bad at caring for herself. This revelation sparked a journey of self-care, leading her to invest in herself and contribute to a multi-author book project. That experience ignited Sally's passion for writing and her desire to help others share their stories with the world.

As Vice President of Author Development, Sally guides aspiring writers through the process of transforming their ideas into bestselling books. She provides invaluable feedback, accountability, and encouragement.

Beyond her publishing role, Sally is a sought-after inspirational speaker, sharing her experiences and insights. She motivates individuals to embrace self-care, pursue their passions, and unleash their inner author.

January 2024 marked a new milestone for Sally, as she celebrated the publication of her first children's book, "The Cutest Baby Dragon." This delightful tale reflects her imaginative storytelling ability and passion for engaging young readers.

Connect with Sally at www.ActionTakersPublishing.com.

CHAPTER 3

Connect to Your Mind, Body and Soul

by Amy Stephens, HTCP

---

*Mom, you have always shown me your amazing strength
and I have always loved your sense of humor! Thank you
for being a listening ear, my biggest cheerleader and
keeping me on my toes. I love you!*

Tip: *Take a seat in a chair or your sofa. Option 1 - cross your right
ankle over your left if your hips are tight. Option 2 - put your right
ankle on top of your left thigh for a deeper stretch. Now that I have your
attention and you are settling in, I want you to notice first what you are
feeling. Is there discomfort in your hip, knee, ankle? Are you wiggly
trying to find a more comfortable spot? Are you already frustrated?*

began my yoga journey in 1996 when I was super stressed out in my
interior design career. I was a recent college grad and a new employee

to a mom and pop healthcare design firm. I really didn't have boundaries around work and I didn't understand the concept of 8-5 pm. Instead, I did 8-7 pm because traffic was easier to leave and the office was quiet and I could catch up on the day before heading home.

Take a few rounds of deep breathing here, please. Inhale to 3, Exhale to 6.

The actual word Yoga means to Yoke, or the Union. The idea of yoga was completely foreign to me as a mid-20 something. What I did know was I was always active and suddenly I was sitting for long periods of time and noticed my back and hips were beginning to hurt.

Off to my first yoga class I go. My friend and I were younger than most who were set up in the class already and I felt like I was doing really well and concentrating hard during that first class. Like anything else you do for the first time, I tried to pay attention and move through it all without a blunder or disruption. Class 1 - DONE and accomplished!

When we as humans do something and it feels good and a sense of accomplishment afterward, we have a bit of a high to do it again. So a few days later I went to my second class. After about four weeks, I signed up again and off I went to a third class driving an hour one way to enjoy the time for myself. I loved the practice so much that I quit my interior design job a year and a half later and went to my first yoga teacher training in 1998.

That began my journey of taking my hobby into my career. When a person begins to listen to their intuition more and more, something new begins to guide them. This knowing, the gut feeling, the pull to do something ... it is listening to the breath, to your body, and flowing from one pose to the next. Flowing to a point that you enjoy a time so much you can't wait to get back at it again.

Tip continued: *Now, unwind by putting your right foot on the floor, give a rub to your knees, and tell them "Thank you." And we will move to the second side. Option 1 - left ankle on top of the right. Option 2 - left ankle on top of the right thigh. Take a deep breath and settle in.*

As we get older, we forget to listen to our bodies until our bodies tell us ... "Damn, *I hurt!*" Then the doctor discusses surgery or "take this pill" to cover up the pain. But the reality is that taking the time to move more every day will prevent the pain that becomes present. Desk chairs are not always the best; if you are a digital nomad and looking at places to rent for a while, what does their desk area look like? Working from a bed, kitchen table, outdoor furniture, a sandy beach?

If you have a larger office set up, do you have a walking desk that keeps you moving gradually while you listen to a podcast, webinar or have a work call that allows you to have that freedom to walk some while someone is on the other line? Learn to listen to the calls of your body, your mind and your soul (aka heart).

When I was in another stressful job situation, I used to hear books being dropped in the other room in the middle of the night while I was asleep. It was the wildest thing. I have always been a sound sleeper, but when your guides want you to listen they get creative on the sounds you hear. No books were ever moved, but it was enough to wake me from a deep sleep and to get me out of bed to go check. There was a night when I was just beginning to dream. In my dream, I said "NO" to my boss. When I woke up, I decided it was time for a big change. That week, I quit my job and focused more on teaching yoga like I'd been doing since 1998. Now, with Zoom, I'm able to work with people from all over the world. My students are happy because they don't have to travel to take my classes. They don't even need to take a shower. We meet on Zoom and I start teaching the yoga class.

For many of my clients, moving their bodies is the first way they start feeling more connected back to themselves. This reminds me of how I used to sit at a desk for many hours, and I started having aches and pains that were new to me. Moving around helped me feel better. When you incorporate breathing as a second step of awareness, it is something that becomes the thread to allow movement to occur, be it walking, running, yoga, skiing, gymnastics, etc.

Do you remember finding your freedom as a kid? I was never a long-distance runner; I was a sprinter. I had long legs growing up and could go fast, but those long-distance running sessions were horrible for me. What do you remember from your childhood that made you run like Phoebe in the Friends episode … wild and free! It is liberating and even powerful, no matter how crazy you think you look.

Movement, breath and now let's connect to your soul. *While you ponder that, go ahead and unwind your legs and put both feet flat on the ground.* Envision Oak Tree roots coming out of your feet and into the Earth to give you ample support you need from your body to connect you to your Soul.

I want to ask you a few questions:

1. Do you feel sexy?

2. When was the last time you felt playful?

3. How often in a day do you find yourself laughing?

These may seem like odd questions, but what I find as I get older is that people tend to lose the playfulness that we had when we were younger. Maybe you grew up in a household where you were *the* adult as a child. Maybe you were not to be seen or heard and you lost your voice along the way.

Tip: *Take a moment and put your left hand over the center of your chest (this is your heart center). This connects the feminine side of yourself to your heart. Now place your right hand, the masculine side of yourself, directly on top of the left. Take a deep breath in, to a count of 3, pause, then exhale through your nose, counting slowly to 6. This time, inhale slowly to 4 through your nose, pause, exhale slowly through your nose to 8. Do this for 10 rounds of breath. Pause again. Let your hands come down from your heart.*

This type of breathing is supportive to help you mentally slow down. By placing your hands on your heart, you connect into your Soul. We are not separate, Body, Mind and Soul. We are connected. How you choose to connect is up to you. This is one way I have taught thousands of people and it is the easiest way to slow down. It brings more oxygen into your bloodstream, clarity to your mind, and a new awakening to your soul.

Now, when was the last time you belly laughed? What do you remember from that experience? Write it down, relive that experience and treasure that moment.

If you don't have an example of that, then when was the last time you cried so hard and what triggered those tears? Are you able to feel that in your soul? Sometimes we cry for one reason, but there is an underlying different reason that triggers the tears.

For example, my mom and I were visiting an area that had cooler temperatures than where I lived. My air pressure was low and the lights for each of my tires were lit up. I had forgotten that cooler temperatures trigger the lights on the gauge in my car. I had to find a gas station to fill up my tires. It was not like how it used to be and I couldn't get the tire pressure stick to show the reading of the tires. I was angry. I was frustrated. I cried. I felt alone. "Why did I have to do this all alone – again?" These feelings drew up in me and then I was frustrated with crying at this stupid situation. I wiped my tears on my shirt, pulled myself together, and got through the situation. When I got in the car, I was still frustrated and discouraged and had to take a few rounds of deep breaths so I didn't yell at my mom. Even though she was with me, she knew I had to work through this situation. She sensed my frustration and knew to stay out of the way. What could she do, really?

So when I asked when was the last time you belly laughed, that is why. It is more fun to reflect on a situation that raised your oxytocin levels and brought you joy versus dwelling on a situation that dragged you down.

When you wake up each morning, I invite and encourage you to pause and give thanks for waking another day. This is not a given every day for everyone. So take that moment after the alarm goes off and really give thanks. During the winter months, it is a harder practice for most. So honor what provides you gratitude.

If you are still stirred up on something from the day before or decades before, hit the "Control, Alt, Delete" of your mind and reset for the new day. That may sound crazy, but it does work. Same goes for voicing up how you feel or felt while dealing with a conversation. Talk to that person who triggered you and get to the root of the situation. Don't run away.

Setting boundaries is a bit of a *high*. Find your power, voice your needs and wants. It is an awesome feeling. Sure, it takes some courage to step up and do it, but make it happen. Don't let someone else stifle your voice. Trust me, when you come from a space of wanting to make a change for yourself in a meaningful way, you will do great in setting those boundaries.

Oftentimes our body gives us hints that we are not comfortable with a situation, a person, a subject matter discussed. Maybe you have higher anxiety or maybe you feel a heaviness come over you that prevents you from moving forward. Don't let depression guide your day. Ask yourself, "Is this mine or someone else's?"

When you acknowledge what you are feeling, you find an inner strength that guides you deeper and gives you more A-ha moments, than tears. Find your voice, experience the power of boundaries, and enjoy this newfound guidance that you can trust within you.

Let's pause a moment and take a deep breath. Inhale 3, Exhale 6.

What do you feel in yourself at this moment? Remember, all these changes that you have experienced will begin to move out of you and move you out of your comfort zone. This is a great part of the healing process. Journal more, watch for signs that keep repeating (for example, clock 11:11 or 2:22). My grandmother always shows up on license plates with her initials when I need to know I have support and cheerleaders around me, even when they are not in physical form.

Take another deep breath and release. Inhale 4, Exhale 8.

When you connect stronger to what your Body tells you, you gain that additional strength of how to hear your Mind / your thoughts and be present to your Soul. When these three aspects come together, you be-come Whole and experience a Wholistic approach to healing. Don't numb yourself, listen. Honor yourself. Love yourself.

Always know that you are not alone! Don't let someone tell you … "You're too sensitive" and get away with it. Find your voice and say, "How I feel is mine and it doesn't affect you. If you can't have an honest conversation with me, that is yours." This is a bold and powerful statement, so make yourself taller when you say it. Feel your body take up more space and don't shrink!

You are Whole! You are Amazing! You are Healing!

Enjoy the process, continue to grow and take naps along the way. Naps are like tiny hugs to your nervous system. When you create an atmosphere of awareness for yourself, your intuition (that gut feeling) guides you stronger day to day.

Ask questions of your guides, then ask them for specific guidance. If you go in with an expectation of how it "should" be, you are unlikely to receive the outcome you are looking for. You will fight the brick wall time and time again. "Control, Alt, Delete" each day and pause. Learn to ask your Guides for signs - numbers 11:11, 2:22, 4:44, 10:10. Or maybe you have animals that show up on a regular basis that serve as a guide to you. Or maybe you have a deceased loved one that you feel around you. Learn to ask more questions and get the messages understood better from them. Begin to experiment with what works for you.

Take a deep breath in and count to 4, Pause, Exhale to 8.

You are well on your way to a stronger Mind, Body and Soul Connection. Congratulations and continue on your journey.

Amy Stephens, HTCP

A yoga practitioner and teacher since 1998, Amy Stephens, HTCP realized she is a recovering anxious empath and perfectionist.

Amy's journey of learning about energy healing started in 2001 with the Healing Touch Program, and it just felt so natural and amazing to see the individuals she worked on light up. Amy has worked with over 1,000 individuals on their healing journey.

Amy's goal has always been to make sure her clients create a sense of balance for Mind, Body and Soul. Many of Amy's clients experience depression, anxiety, have physical limitations in their body, such as scoliosis, knee/hip replacements and can't get to the floor. Amy's 1:1 Personal Training sessions have been supportive and motivating to the clients she has worked with for years.

Based in Scottsdale, Arizona, she works with clients remotely all over the world. And when not working, she can be found in her kayak surrounded by Water!

Connect with Amy at www.AmyStephens.net.

CHAPTER 4

Are You Outta Your Mind?: Breaking Free From an Organized Cult

by ChristianeAnna Rodriguez

Carolyn Kelly - your wisdom and vision of Heaven on Earth and your motherly love during my time of awakening will forever live with me. I love you dear child of the Universe. Can't wait to hear what you're up to.

There was a time in my life when my panties would bunch up if you asked me the above question. This became an inquiry from a Shamanic Practitioner and wise crone that I trusted.

"Are you outta your mind?" was most often posed to me after engaging with my past troubles, worries and emotional demise that hurt my body and spirit from growing up in a family cult system. The unraveling had layers and deserved deep inquiry.

There were evenings of tossing and turning like a rotisserie chicken with one thought spinning the next into an onslaught of stories and more suffering. This led me to heartache, mistrust with life and others.

This place was the "norm" many years. One misinterpreted diagnosis after another came with this mindset: PTSD, anxiety, depression, bi-polar, fibromyalgia, chronic fatigue syndrome, borderline personality, lyme disease, insomnia, weight gain, weight loss, addictions and suicidal ideation. I never once said to any doctor, "Hey, I'm pretty certain I'm being abused by a cult and its organization." When you are so deep in it and trained from a young age, this is not your main thought. That would feel like betrayal.

These labels lived within my body in a deafening silence while maintaining a mask that allowed me to appear seamlessly stable and happy within the confines. The family disguised our life with a pretty appearance and I didn't feel a lack materially.

I was 12 when the family left Catholicism and took a head dive into a religious cult, an organization held by control, manipulation, narcissism and sexual abuse while being disguised with teachings of paradise and eternal life. Like most cults, it lures its prey into the fold with an abundance of love bombs and false hope.

Eventually, my self-talk and mind took on a message of, "God is punishing me, I deserve to be sick, I am not worthy. It appears that everyone is happy and doing well so it must be me."

I experienced a physical and emotional breakdown in my early 20s accompanied by a divorce and a huge awakening that started me down a rigorous path of self-healing and self-love.

My courage and hope came from my sister and mother who were also experiencing similar diagnoses and ailments. This was an aha moment for me! Why were all of us physically sick? What was the common equation here?

Although I left the cult at 17 years of age, the cult messages were still running a program in my head that impacted my world. With the physical breakdown of my body, I was faced with either feeding into physicians' diagnoses and medications or finding a new path.

It was a gift in disguise that I was shunned by the organized cult. The governing body of the society deemed me unfit and stamped the great big 'X' on my head that read DISFELLOWSHIPPED. In reality, this is what positioned me to face life on my own and saved me at the same time. The stamp came with no family, no known safety or friends outside of the organization, and being faced with living alone as a teenager.

Holistic medicine entered my world and my mind started to clear. This created spaciousness to dive deeper into the realm of my overall well-being. A reconnection to my roots was watered.

There was a remembrance of my internal wisdom outside of the noise. Tears of gratitude washed over me like an anointing balm of self-love.

My heart began to open up to deeper inquiry of what my body and spirit were asking. I spent time in nature. A sense of belonging and meditation had me interested in knowing more.

Kundalini yoga entered my field along with acupuncture, healing herbs, flower essences, astrology, a clean diet and various holistic and wellness practitioners.

My relationship with self grew slowly 'Outta the mind' and into my heart and body as I began to live. It was like pulling the plug and draining all the stories others had placed upon me over the years. The schools, physicians, family, society, men, religion and cults were all up for deep inquiry and understanding as they played out their roles in my life.

I stripped myself naked with devotion to my path of mindful wellbeing. I was sick and tired of being sick and tired! And let's face it, the medical establishment had no idea what to do with me. They are not trained to assist patients to claim their mental, emotional and spiritual sovereignty and healing. They are trained to treat a diagnosis. I was becoming aware that there were layers to healing and mentioning my cult upbringing still felt odd to speak of, due to the stigma.

Handing me a med, labeling and organizing me into a category that would corral me into another highly controlled group with others expressing emotional or physical ailments was not an option I desired. The Band-aid effect was not going to serve a deeper need. Intuitively, the spaciousness supported my intuition that there was something more.

When one is stripped of such labels of a diagnosis, the mind relaxes and the nervous system begins to rewire itself. The body has the miraculous ability to heal at a cellular level. Intuitively, I felt this and I continued onward with integrating various modalities to assist my new life to let go of the old.

The inward journey back home to myself was one of becoming: Becoming love, Becoming my own truth, Becoming health, Becoming a wealth of peace that desired to walk the fire and rise like the phoenix. There was an exploration of healing through the ancient wisdom of my ancestors and shamanic practices that called me forth to listen to my heart of hearts.

I needed to die to live! The mind that absorbed and took on so many lies of deception from outside sources was crying out for a homecoming. This student was ready and the master began to show up from within by listening to my body and heart. It became crystal clear that breaking away from the old programming was serving my highest good. And my mind was in deep need to work with my sacred temple and not against my inner knowing.

My mind had been directly affected by my thought patterns of outside images, ideas and thoughts about who I AM. Considerable improvement was recognized as my mindset turned to shifting and healing the subconscious.

Kundalini Yoga and chanting made a vast difference in just minutes of daily practice. The BREATH was key! Of course! The science behind the practice of honoring the body's intelligence was profound. This was the place that brought me home to my heart.

I AM a child of the universe…not of man. I came to Love, BE Love, and receive Love. The messages continued to come through my daily practices of meditation and yoga that rewired my subconscious using ancient techniques.

Life became expansive and my walk through it became sacred. I was learning how to claim and utilize my spirit and mind to heal the body.

I craved nature and her earth elements, conscious communication and mindful relations with all of life. I began co-creating with the universe and called in a new life filled with joy, compassion, kindness, authenticity and love.

The old, unhealthy relating taught by the cult naturally and organically fell away. Some consciously, others I walked from and still others I ran from. It took some years after initially being shunned to trust life. Like an abused partner, I found myself missing my family and missing certain childhood friends. Most of them took their own lives.

I went back several times with an attempt to be with family and gave it a go with a marriage where the man was also in and out of the cult. This did not fare well. Disfellowshipping again for walking away from a marriage brought more layers to the surface of how deep the wounds had settled.

These areas of my life were still linked to ideas, mindsets and abusive behavior of not being lovable and its wired program was of self-depreciation and infliction accompanied by suffering.

My ancient ancestors would look at the life of someone self-inflicted or despondent as myself and ask, "When did you stop dancing and singing" or "When did you stop inquiring of your own heart and inner knowing?"

My attention turned to the medicine women and medicine men of my shamanic ancestors' lineage. With this came a deeper understanding of wisdom teachings that resonated with life, the elements and the natural rhythm and cycles of nature.

Living from the still point of the heart needed to become my nature. Becoming one with life and stewarding the inner landscape with a resonance that was mine became tangible and peaceful over time. The reflection of nature delivered peace to my body, spirit and mind.

I became devoted to my sovereignty as a free agent, my breath was my guide, my bare feet to the ground were my roots. Remembrance that I am an ancestor for the next seven generations and they need me to walk on my own sacred path. The stories needed to stop with me.

Facing myself in the mirror, the question in the reflection asked, "How do I want to walk this earth?"

It was a resounding:

Free. Gently. Consciously with a remembrance of my birthright that I belong here on earth and to remain committed to self love. To honor my daily practice and remain in my heart and womb space. Deep in the belly of life. Rebirthing myself and consciously growing from the place of my purpose here on this earthly place called Mother.

I signed up on the dotted line to come to the earth during these pivotal times that are asking for big hearts to be at the forefront of great shifts and changes for this planet.

The human experience as spiritual beings is not for the faint of heart. It takes grit and most of us have lived out trauma in our family of origin. It often looks messy and sometimes chaotic. Birth does. It can look graceful and tender, too.

We are much more than the spinning out-of-control mindset and thought patterns that are created by outside influences. Our lives can change the moment we decide to. It's never too late to be "Outta your Mind!"

You are one breath from your heart reminding you how divinely miraculous you are and how life can unfold in absolute magical ways when you stay out of your head and out of your own way.

I am not implying that it is with ease that one breaks free from indoctrinated influences, old constructs and programming. They can have a large effect on your mind and body as it did mine. The mind has its tendencies and giving yourself grace is required. You are valuable and designed for intimacy with the universe.

Early influence as a child of 12 placed an identity from a highly centralized organization like a heavy amnesia blanket that created damaging results. Rewiring the neural pathways was vital to breaking free completely. Entering the unknown is where the power resides. I needed to open the caged door to set myself free or remain in fear and continue to dodge the landmines and remain quiet.

From the preachy platforms of the Meeting Halls of the cult we were implicitly counseled not to take on a "double personality." Oooooo...so what you are saying is that you know what you are doing to our young minds and now blaming and shaming us into submission? There began my wake-up call that we were being taught how to lie to ourselves and others by living one life within the confines of the walls of the meeting halls, conventions and gatherings. And...another life all together, as I witnessed how most of my companions were cheating, stealing, utilizing drugs, hanging out with "worldly people" outside of the organization yet still attending worship. I would rather just bounce than to live two lives!

This counsel was pummeled into me from all directions. The isolation is a means to create the mind body disconnect that the cult enforces. Smile and forget who you are.

The chain of command from the leaders enforces to penetrate upon its "sheep" the so-called "new personality" and the society does not allow you to question their condemnation. The new personality was to be an overlay to the authentic self and a coercion to baptism yourself as a way to give your life over to a God that was displeased with you having your own free will. A water baptism could possibly "save" you from dying and having eternal life in paradise. Turning your fellow brother/sister in for disobeying the rules was another big hit that could save you and earn you a place in paradise.

No meaningful discussions or debates allowed. This cult asked its members to call all preaching "The Truth" and no one was allowed to question the message. Your sense of who you are is determined by the society at large from a governing body made up of only men. The language within the literature is regulated, the platform talks at meeting halls reek of mind control, manipulation, narcissism and abuse. And speaking up like this grants you a title of apostasy with no eternal life.

Religion is not the only arena we find such abuse. It can be found in the best of intended places. Currently, the world in 2023 is experiencing war, death and unimaginable inflicted pain based on division and separation.

From the beginning of time, the earth has experienced humans asserting power over another group of humans because they don't see eye to eye.

How about feeling heart to heart. Allowing space for each being to be completely themselves. Receiving and allowing all views, genders and cultures to live harmoniously together based on Love.

Idealistic? Romanticizing? A far reach?

Our ancient ancestors spoke of these times. We are encouraged to become the vision of the true self. Its starting point in ancient text is from the sacred space of the womb. Found between the in breath and out breath. This is the extension of the universe and the essence of the true self. This is where life begins.

The gentle winds of change are present today with the four directions that bring the homecoming songs of all nations, all races and creeds. Step away from the noise. There is a dream that is still alive for those recognizing that separation of mind, body and spirit is based on fear. The door is open to walk through the gateway of heaven on earth for this planet. A new paradigm is on the horizon.

The eternal flame is alive within the hearts of humans. Listen from that sacred space…beat your drums…sing your songs…we are riding on the winds, dear ones.

Grab your shawls, dance into the night and celebrate for the great spirit of the heart has returned.

Are you "Outta your mind yet?"

ChristianeAnna Rodriguez

ChristianeAnna Rodriguez is a #1 International Best Selling Author of "Women with Healing Gifts" and "Action Takers Who Get Shit Done."

Her formal education was founded in Medicine and Science at Dartmouth-Hitchcock Medical Center and Quest Diagnostic Laboratories for several decades. As a Medicine Woman, she weaves her ancestors' shamanic practices as a Womb Wisdom Keeper with her scientific background.

She has Produced and Hosted her own local T.V. show engaging the audience in Spirituality and Women's Empowerment through her Native teachings for Modern Times.

She is the Ambassador of a Humanitarian Promotions Organization called 'Global Love Music' that spreads the Aloha Spirit Globally and the Founder of 'Yoni Rising' that dedicates herself in devotion to the Sacred Technology of her Ancestors Womb Mandala Healings. She teaches workshops globally on Conscious Sacred Sexuality, Womb Technology, Conscious Birthing and Rites of Passage through Ritual Ceremony.

She is currently building her Sanctuary on Big Island, Hawaii. Her Signature Program is called 'The Sacred Gateways of the New Paradigm.'

Connect with ChristianeAnna at <u>Yonirising@gmail.com</u>.

CHAPTER 5

The Body Never Lies

by Deepa Mahesh

One afternoon as I was waiting for my turn at my homeopath's clinic, I was feeling angry.

"Why this suffering for so long in my life?

"Why can't I live like other normal people without this psychosomatic condition?

"Why do I have to keep visiting doctors and go through this torture?"

My rant was broken by the doctor's call for the consultation. She gave me some advice and some medicines to calm me and my wound. When I walked out, I wasn't feeling good. I was crying deep inside. I wanted this suffering to end, a chronic condition for over 30 years made me feel like a victim. I returned home, shut my door, sat on the floor holding my feet and sobbing bitterly. It allowed me to express myself and then it was life as usual. I had no motivation to take the medicines; my mind was playing "poor me" games and I was angry!

A week later, I observed that my feet were healing. I was surprised, "What had made the difference?," I wondered!

I took out my journal and started expressing, and upon reflection a truth revealed itself to me. I had never held or touched my feet before the last week. I always hated my feet because of the scars and there was a lot of shame associated. Trauma of having to cover my feet always, not being able to wear the clothes I wanted to, and the pain associated with the condition, all of that made me dissociate myself from that part of the body, which probably needed most attention. Just a touch by myself made so much of a difference.

Having realised this, I started actively giving that healing touch to myself, now with more love than ever before. I stopped taking medicines and offered my touch as medicine. My inner narrative changed from "why me" to "I have the power to heal the wound." I poured that intention into the touch with a strong resolve and unshaking faith in the process.

Did I not need medicines? Probably self-acceptance was the best medicine at that time for my healing.

And tables turned, my wound started healing and the chronic condition was no longer traumatic.

This was my initiation into researching about "mind-body connection" in 2017.

Delving deeper through primary research

My research took me to observe the patterns of reaction of my over-all body to situations/circumstances from the outside. I observed that when I took up large scale projects (as perceived by my mind) which I hadn't ever done before, harsh weather conditions or interactions with people in authority, my body reacted in a certain way and the rashes in the body showed up aggressively.

I also observed the presence of a "reactive psychological layer" between the external situations and my bodily response, the layer of my emotions and my thought process. Until I researched, I never was able to listen to my thoughts and emotions. The observations showed that my emotions also came up in patterns.

The most intense emotions were Fear, Shame, Guilt, Disappointment and Passive Anger. And the corresponding thoughts were extremely self-critical and they spoke very loud and clear. They said, "you are a jerk, you are not good enough, you can't do this, you messed up again, you can never be a leader, you aren't from a premium institute." And the gesture of that inner voice was "finger pointing."

Processing my thoughts and emotions with a Jungian analyst for years helped me to understand my inner world better. I was able to understand the deep trauma that I had been feeling from my childhood. My unprocessed inner child wounds never allowed me to regulate my emotions and that was the cause of my emotional breakdowns. The psychological causes had their share of impact on my body and the nervous system.

As Dr. Gabor Mate, a Hungarian-Canadian physician and author says, "Trauma is not about what happens to us. It is about what happens inside of us as a result of what happens to us. It is an interpretation I have made of my own experience. When I notice it and become aware that I don't need to be a subject of that interpretation anymore, I can let it go."

The first step was to become aware of my interpretations of my life situations, which I had stored inside my mind and body.

Using human biography work as a body of work to help me systematically uncover my trauma patterns, I understood the depth of my life's flow, and the realm of my thoughts and emotional responses. Every situation and my response had a validity. I recognised that in the current time, it was no more valid and I was carrying them unconsciously. That step of awareness was the best gift I gave to myself then.

Understanding the workings of my mind and emotions

It became clear to me that unless I work on my emotional and thought patterns, I would not be able to regulate myself and live in wellbeing.

Whenever there was a triggering event, I found myself regressing to a child state, my body becoming either too hot or cold, my feet wouldn't be on the floor, they went into a levity state and my heart would race and pound, my breathing would be shallow and fast. It was a panic mode and my mind would be totally clouded with a rush of negative and self-depreciating thoughts and comments. Often, I would choose two automatic modes of response, fight or flight. I would either overwork, over shop, over speak or over perform in order to manage my panic and numb my pain or I would not face the situation, procrastinate, sit on tasks for weeks and worry. In the case of fight response, my body would experience severe fatigue and burnout. Working at the cost of sleep was a norm. This impacted my body and my auto immune condition would flare up. And, my fatigue became chronic. In case of the flight response, my body would be spared, but emotions of shame and guilt would come gushing in to tell me how "not good enough" I was and that would hit me straight in my stomach.

Trauma and the body

Childhood trauma has its impact deep in the body and the nervous system. The feeling of loneliness, fear of abandonment was a lingering emotion right from an early age. I received a lot of love from my household, yet the child in me felt never enough and always nurtured the fear of loneliness and fear. From the fear of being alone, the fear expanded to fear of making mistakes, fear of authority figures, fear of deep water, fear of handling money, fear of exams, fear of failing, and the intensity was extremely high. Fear preceded the beginning of any task – personal or official. It also impacted me as a mother when I had the fear of dropping my infant, fear of being a bad mother, fear of losing my children.

The way the body experienced fear was like a shock. In one day, my body went through several shocks. At night, the rest period was never enough to recover from the shocks of the day. The mind would be tired and body would be drained, yet the next day's shocks would be waiting for me to face and deal with.

This was severe until I was 40 years old and a major life event got me in touch with this pattern of fear and loneliness and the next six years were spent in understanding and reversing the pattern. Thanks to the work of Dr. Gabor Mate and Dr. Bessel Van Der Kolk, my understanding of trauma and recovery methods has deepened.

Identifying the areas of vulnerability in my body has been my research for the last 1.5 decades. And my approach to research was always inside out.

"What is happening to me in my body, thoughts and emotions?" was my inquiry question.

And that led me to identifying the areas in my body which needed more warmth and healing and listening in. The practice of palming with the warmth of my palms has been my go-to practice for several years. I accidentally discovered the healing effects and now practice it consciously, every day.

I am convinced my body and mind so closely speak to each other that, I, as a witness, cannot ignore this connection. Does the trauma stored in the body ever leave? I am yet to experience this phenomenon. It becomes active in waves and takes me to a new level of inquiry and exploration, leading me to a new level of awareness and "Being-ness."

Exploring healing through ancient Indian wisdom

The Indian scriptures have always been my friend since I was a teenager and in the sacred Hindu texts there is a lot of literature on the holistic structure of the human being. In the holy texts, it is documented that a human being has five layers or sheaths of existence.

Layer 1 - The physical body. This is the most outer and visible layer and illness manifests on this layer.

Layer 2 – The breath/energy body. This layer closely works with the physical body and is responsible for the functioning of our organs. When this layer is in order, our energy is replenished automatically.

Layer 3 – The emotional body. This layer is the seat of our emotions and like air keeps swinging between antipathy and sympathy, unless it is regulated and anchored in balance.

Layer 4 – The intellectual body. This layer is the seat of thoughts and is responsible for balanced decision making and wisdom-filled thinking.

A breakdown in the emotional and the intellectual body leads to imbalance in the thinking and feeling and like wild fire spreads in the energy and the body layer to cause a breakdown.

Layer 5 – The bliss body. This layer is the layer contributing to stillness and inner joy. When there is balance in all the above layers, one automatically reaches this layer.

There is a direct link between thoughts and emotions to the physical body and energy body. I started observing my auto immune condition in light of this wisdom. When my mind is free, happy and not too triggered, my physical condition is in control and no rashes or lesions show up. When there is a triggering event or over emoting, the body had its way to erupt and call for my attention. It was a call for balance.

One of the ways I could transcend this drama between my emotional and physical sheath was to focus on my purpose. I used to ask myself, "What is that which will make me spring out of bed every day?"

The real meaning of my illness uncovered - in search of my purpose

Elevating human consciousness was something I discovered was my purpose. And that is when I discovered that over the last 1.5 decades I have been constantly inquiring into my thought and emotion patterns so that I can elevate my consciousness and live happy and fulfilled.

53

What I had to do with humankind, I had to first do it with myself. The purpose of my illness became evident, and since then there is no self-pity, no whining or complaining. If lesions show up, I would gently hold the wound, listen deeply, engage in an active imagination (by Carl Gustav Jung) process and listen to the message. This has led me to deeply understanding the wisdom of my body. I also hold a strong belief that "My body never lies." Yes, my mind can lie, cheat (myself), the body always speaks the truth!

The body needs attention

Culturally, we are not taught to be friends with our body although we live in our body and it is a vehicle through which we execute our daily tasks and responsibilities. Unless there is a serious breakdown, it isn't natural to take care of it.

I learnt it the hard way. Every time my feet erupted; I knew it was calling my attention inward to myself. I started understanding the language of my body and started observing the linkage between the body and mind closely.

I was motivated to spend hours exploring various body-mind practices to understand this connection deeply.

One of the practices was 5Rhythms dance by Gabriella Roth, a Dancer, musician and author. I was inspired by her body of work to find a structure for using dance as a transformative process. 5Rhythms is a dynamic movement practice which has the potential to make the mover conscious of the various rhythms in the body. Since I have been an artist (a dancer since childhood), I took to this form of healing and connecting with my body. For three years, every single day, I decided to devote 35 minutes to move and journal my discoveries, which was very rewarding.

Expressive Art therapy also played a very important role in my healing journey. I would draw my wound on paper, something that would unnerve me beyond measure. I felt it was necessary to befriend my wound and know it inside-out. I would thereafter use the image to create various versions of it – good, worse and the best to see the possibilities. It is like today when you want to change your hair style, you have options generated by the software and you choose based on that output. This worked for me because it gave me an opportunity to deeply accept and acknowledge my most vulnerable body part.

Thereafter, I developed a technique called dialoguing with the body which follows a sequence of 6 steps.

Step 1 – Prepare your body for the dialogue

Step 2 – Set your intention by being clear of the reason you are entering the process of dialogue

Step 3 – Ground yourself by entering into the body with the help of your breath

Step 4 – Focus and sense the emotion, sensation in each part of the body through the process of palming

Step 5 – Begin the dialogue by identifying the body part which needs attention or is in discomfort. Listen with your inner ear and absorb the guidance given by that part

Step 6 – Commit to action based on the direction revealed by the part

You can continue the dialogue for as long as you wish.

This process has been helping me for years to understand and eliminate the stress that events bring in my life.

In all this exploration, I have begun to understand the importance of my body. I worship it now, more than anything. For me, if not the body, I would be absent in this world.

The Body Prayer

On the 1st of January of 2022, as I was praying, there was a wave of inspiration and I documented the words that were flowing through me. It showed up as this Body Prayer. This is an invocation to my body to convey my sentiments towards it.

"Dear Body,

I was born in you, I grew up with you,

I acknowledge your presence in my life,

In this moment, I am one with you.

I feel guided by a Higher Power to be with you.

I now invoke that Universal power to be with you.

I now invoke the universal power, the Grace,

To hold you dear to me,

To witness the processes that unfold in you.

To care, to nurture,

To listen to your needs and longings.

May I be guided to hold you close,

While I stand apart and witness,

The real purpose of your existence with me.

I am open,

I am guided,

I am blessed and so are you!"

I am so clear that my purpose in life is to raise consciousness not just in the space of "doing" but also in the space of the "being."

Today, in all my pursuits and roles as a Leadership coach, facilitator, teacher, guide, mentor, parent, daughter, wife, friend, I hold a strong affinity towards mind-body connection. With my experience, I have seen that every situation when looked at from this holistic connection gives clues to solve life's mysteries. This is my wish for humankind.

I wish that each one of us "Live Whole and Live Happy." We deserve to "Live in Wellbeing."

Deepa Mahesh

Founder and CEO of Poorna Wellbeing, Deepa Mahesh is a Leadership Coach (ICF-PCC) and Facilitator. As a Self-Mastery Expert, Deepa facilitates Conscious Leadership Journeys through her coaching, workshops, and training programs.

Majoring in Psychology, armed with a master's in human resource management, she initially worked for some of the top corporations of India including Aditya Birla Group as an HR Leader. In search of her purpose, she quit, to invest time in herself, which finally led to the birth of her entrepreneurial venture, through which she has served thousands of leaders to walk on the path of purpose and achieve success.

Dance and other arts have been her friends since childhood. Her curiosity to explore the mind-body connection led her to exploring expressive arts therapy as her profession and thereafter practicing as an embodiment coach for leaders. As a natural progression, she completed her six years Eurythmy training in 2022. She now holds Eurythmy workshops for adults and teaches the curriculum to primary school students of Kingdom of Childhood, a Waldorf school in Bangalore.

A TEDx Speaker, Mandala Artist and teacher, an Eurythmist, dancer, an embodiment coach, poet and an upcoming author, Deepa balances her life with a myriad of passion projects. She holds Love in her essence and spreads her energy to all those who come in contact with her presence.

Connect with Deepa at https://poornawellbeing.com/.

CHAPTER 6

Nurturing the Mind-Body Connection: Empowering Teens with Positive Intelligence

by Elvira DiBrigit

I dedicate this chapter to the many wise women who have helped me along my path.

I'm going to ask you to imagine something you may be happier to forget. Imagine you are a teenager again. Imagine being back in that body and in that mindset.

Picture yourself in that teenage body, grappling with the ups and downs, trying to make sense of a world that felt simultaneously inviting and daunting. For many of us, this period was marked by vulnerability, uncertainty, and a lack of control over our bodies and minds.

What if, as a society, we could equip our teens with the tools to navigate this tumultuous period more smoothly than we did? As a society, if we truly want to benefit from our understanding of the mind-body connection, we must make it applicable to our teens.

Reflecting on my teen years, I recall spending hours in my room, navigating the constant flux of emotions – from the highest highs to the lowest lows. It was akin to riding a roller coaster through thick fog, thrilling yet overwhelming. I also spent many late hours with my friends, getting into all kinds of trouble. The journey of self-discovery was filled with excitement and confusion. Sometimes, I felt confident, and other times, I felt extreme self-doubt. The quest to understand myself in the world felt like an impossible puzzle.

During this tumultuous time, at the young age of 16, I was fortunate to meet a mentor who influenced me considerably. Her name was Rosa Maria Wynn, and when we met she was translating A Course In Miracles into Spanish. She introduced me to the concepts from The Course, including the profound idea that our thoughts shape our experiences.

I learned to meditate. I practiced being forgiving or non-judgmental of others, and accepting what I could not change. I became very good at watching my thoughts and their effects on my well-being. Yet despite all my efforts and knowledge, my 20s and 30s were still filled with self-doubt and drama. There were some missing pieces to my understanding.

A Turning Point:

It wasn't until my 40s, navigating perimenopause with debilitating monthly headaches, that I truly began to grasp the intricate dance between the mind and body. I had become a busy mom, trying to meet everyone's needs around me. My adrenals were overtaxed. I woke up tired each day and didn't get a cortisol boost until late in the afternoon.

And, of course, the stress led to hormonal imbalances, which led to other issues. Estrogen and progesterone, with their protective effects on the brain, play a crucial role in mental well-being. Low hormone levels left me susceptible to brain fog, anxiety, fatigue, and depression. I tried all kinds of solutions, including herbal supplements, diet changes, homeopathy, and bio-identical hormones. I found some temporary fixes, but then the headaches would come back again. The only thing that really helped was rest.

After having neglected my physical and emotional well-being for years while taking care of others, the hormonal headaches became a wake-up call that led me to a profound understanding of menstrual cycle patterns, and the female experience of disembodiment.

I delved into menstrual cycle awareness and the profound impact of hormones on our well-being. I spent my free time studying the natural hormonal cycles that women experience and how they impact our energy levels, brain functioning, skin, and even the shape of our face and body. So many aspects of our life and well-being are affected by hormones.

This phase became a turning point for me. Since the age of 16, I had been embracing the principle that the body is not real, and our thoughts control our reality. Despite this belief, the hormonal headaches forced me to acknowledge that our bodies and minds must collaborate as long as we inhabit these physical forms. This realization prompted a deep dive into the intricate relationship between the body and the mind.

Before this revelation, on low-energy days, I might have felt guilty, attributing it to some unexplained depression. The key was learning to listen to my body, understanding the natural cycles, and embracing the occasional "off" days as entirely normal.

However, it's not just about accepting the difficult days. Instead of making excuses or reacting impulsively, I learned to plan ahead for a mini-retreat during low-energy days, viewing them as a gift and capitalizing on the heightened intuition that comes naturally during those times.

After dedicating several years to my personal healing journey, I reached a profound realization. My life's path had led me to a point where I could merge my knowledge of the mind and body, allowing me to comprehend the interconnectedness of the mind-body relationship as a two-way street.

In life, we face two main challenges: limiting beliefs and physical obstacles. Physical pain or handicaps present tangible obstacles, demanding resilience and adaptability. Limiting beliefs, ingrained in our minds, create barriers that impede personal growth. Amidst these challenges, self-awareness emerges as the way to navigate life's complexities. You can use your mind to help heal your body, but first, you have to listen to your body. It's the old adage, "Healer, know thyself."

It became my life mission to help young people understand this connection so they can avoid some of the confusion that many feel in their teens and 20s. I decided to study the science of positive psychology. This field of study provided me with valuable insights and proactive strategies to help foster a resilient mind-body connection in teens. By applying the principles of positive psychology, I am able to offer effective solutions to the challenges faced by teenagers.

The Silent Struggle:

We all know that within the intricate tapestry of adolescent life, there are often mental health journeys many teenagers face quietly. It's a tough road, and the struggles with anxiety and depression seem to be hitting close to home for so many of our young ones. What's even more heart-wrenching is that suicide has become one of the leading causes of death among teenagers. The Centers for Disease Control and Prevention (CDC) dropped a bombshell, revealing the suicide rate among young people ages 10–24 increased 62% from 2007 through 2021 in the United States, from 6.8 deaths to 11.0 per 100,000.

As a parent, these statistics hit hard. It's a stark reminder that we must be there for our teens in more ways than ever. There is a pressing need for comprehensive support systems encompassing the mind and body.

We have to help teens understand themselves; how the mind affects the body and how the body affects the mind. As a teen, there are so many changes happening in both mind and body. And that makes it a perfect time to help them gain this understanding.

The Teenage Brain and Body:

Puberty becomes a game-changer when our kids start shaping their identity and expressing their unique purpose in the world. It involves exploring interests, forming opinions, and establishing a sense of independence, complete with different hobbies, styles, and friend groups.

As if this wasn't enough, puberty and adolescence are transformative periods characterized by brain rewiring and hormonal upheavals. Understanding these changes becomes crucial for parents and mentors in fostering healthy relationships with teens.

Our teens are undergoing a mind-boggling transformation during puberty, with extensive pruning of synapses in their brains, basically rewiring the whole neural circuitry. It starts from the back and works its way up to the frontal cortex, the brain's decision-making hub.

And then hormones decide to throw a party, contributing to the emotional roller coaster we often witness. Our teens are like emotional acrobats, trying to figure out how to balance it all. It explains those intense feelings they're grappling with – it's like they're learning to navigate a maze of emotions.

Plus, there's the social scene. Amidst the hormonal whirlwind and brain rewiring, our teens might be more prone to misinterpreting facial cues and social signals. No wonder we sometimes find ourselves in the middle of teenage relationship dramas!

Positive Psychology Unveiled:

Contrary to its name, "Positive Psychology" is not about always maintaining a facade of positivity. Instead, it involves leveraging psychological principles to bring about positive changes in our lives. It extends beyond aiding those struggling with mental health issues; it aims to enhance the well-being of individuals who are doing okay but aspire to thrive and improve.

So, as we apply this to the challenges faced by our teens, it becomes clear that the tools offered by Positive Psychology are not just beneficial for those already grappling with mental health issues. They can act as a proactive approach to bolster the well-being of our teens, helping them navigate the complexities of adolescence. Positive Psychology is not merely reactive but a proactive strategy for fostering a resilient mind-body connection in our teenagers.

Positive Intelligence for Teens:

Self-awareness is the key to navigating life's challenges. Yet overthinking things will just lead to stress. By measuring and understanding negative mental states versus positive outlooks, teens and adults can develop resilience and overcome internal saboteurs.

Positive Intelligence is a science-based program that helps us build powerful self-control habits which in turn increases our ratio of productive, creative mindsets over negative recurring thoughts. It has grown from the synthesis of Positive Psychology, NeuroScience, Behavioral Science, and Performance Studies.

I stumbled upon Positive Intelligence during my own healing journey and I became a Positive Intelligence coach. I've learned that I can track my negative state versus my positive outlook, and it's like having a map for how to navigate life's twists and turns. I can measure my mental fitness – my negative state versus my positive outlook – and help others, especially teens, understand their internal saboteurs.

The Positive Intelligence approach teaches that in the face of pain or adversity, one can ask, "What can I learn from this?" This mindset encourages learning from the body without suppressing emotions, while avoiding unnecessary wallowing in pain. Emotional control means acknowledging our feelings and learning from them, not suppressing them.

Being a teenager can be tough both mentally and physically. As parents, guardians, and mentors, we play a vital role in guiding our teens through this maze of emotions and hormonal fluctuations. Many of us focus on physical well-being. It's common knowledge that regular exercise, proper nutrition, and sufficient sleep can do a lot for mental and emotional well-being. Beyond those basics, there are some other positive habits that can make this phase of life easier and have a long-lasting impact.

Five Keys to Helping Our Teens Maximize Their Positive Intelligence:

We can help teens navigate through these challenges and come out stronger on the other side. Positive Intelligence refers to the ability to manage one's mindset in order to optimize our well-being. When it comes to helping teens maximize their positive intelligence, here are six tips to consider:

Tip #1 - Connect Before You Correct:

Our first step must be to foster connection. Connect before you correct. This is a commonly heard phrase in positive parenting circles, but it's worth repeating because teens will often put up blocks to our suggestions. We have to wait until the teachable moment, which is usually after they have experienced a failure. Listen and ask them about their thoughts and feelings. Empathize and give a hug if they let you.

Only after connecting can you ask if you can share your thoughts, your experiences. This is when we can gently remind them that while failures can be painful, they are also opportunities for growth.

Tip #2 - Promote Embodiment:

When teens talk about their experiences, I always try to ask them if there is a sensation in their body that they can identify. If they mention an emotion, I ask, "Where do you feel that emotion in your body?" "What does it feel like?"

The idea is to be present with the emotions, and practice blameless dicernment before taking any actions. We can't fully learn from our feelings until we allow ourselves to feel them.

Tip #3 - Promote Self-Awareness:

We must encourage teens to recognize and acknowledge both their strengths and their areas for growth. Start by helping them identify their strengths. As a parent or mentor, we always want to remember the 3:1 rule: It takes at least three positive interactions to counteract a negative interaction.

We also want to develop self-awareness by helping them understand they can't trust all their thoughts. We all have a cast of inner critics in our minds, and when we learn to question these thoughts, we can make wiser choices. It can be tough to confront negative thoughts, especially when they seem to be all-encompassing with words like "always" or "never." We have to remind teens to aim for a balanced perspective. My teen clients benefit from various activities, including journaling, mindfulness, and reflective exercises, that enhance self-awareness.

Tip #4 - Foster a Growth Mindset:

We now have scientific proof that areas of our brain can be developed by our mental activities, just like muscle building. Cultivate a growth mindset in teens by emphasizing the idea that their abilities and intelligence can be developed over time. Help them understand that setbacks and failures are opportunities to learn and grow rather than indicators of fixed abilities. Encourage a positive approach to challenges and the belief that effort leads to improvement.

Tip #5 - Build Resilience:

Resilience is the ability to bounce back from adversity. What I love about the Positive Intelligence program is that it teaches "Sage Power Games," coping strategies and problem-solving skills to navigate challenges. These encourage teens to view setbacks as temporary and solvable, fostering a sense of agency. Support networks, including friends, family, and mentors, can also play a crucial role in building resilience.

Tip #6 - Encourage Mindfulness:

Taking mini mindfulness breaks by focusing on our senses is a potent habit for stress relief and mental fitness. These mindful breaks help us develop self-command of our thoughts.

Remember that fostering positive intelligence is an ongoing process, and it's important to create an environment where teens feel supported, valued, and encouraged to develop a positive mindset. Open communication and a non-judgmental approach are key components of helping teens navigate the challenges they may encounter.

Empowering our teenagers with the tools to understand and leverage the mind-body connection is of utmost importance when it comes to helping them not just survive but thrive through adolescence. This transformative process requires a deep understanding of the unique challenges that teenagers face, including fluctuating hormones and a maze of emotions that can be difficult to navigate. By using the principles of Positive Intelligence, we can provide our teens with the guidance they need to develop the skills necessary for resilience, emotional regulation, and overall well-being.

As adults, it's our responsibility to anchor our teens during this critical time in their lives. We must offer them love, support, and Positive Intelligence principles to help them navigate this complex chapter and flourish into their best selves. Let's be that guiding light for our teens, paving the way for a healthier, more connected future.

Elvira DiBrigit

Elvira (El-veera) DiBrigit is a teen mentor and parent coach. She has been a Waldorf teacher, a homeschooling mom. Elvira is a Certified Positive Intelligence Coach.

She supports moms who feel unprepared for the challenges as their daughters transition through puberty and adolescence. She helps them build a relationship of trust and empowerment.

Girls who have the right information and support at this stage are more likely to develop a more positive body image, better self-esteem and healthier connections with family and peers.

Connect with Elvira at www.ThePubertyDoula.com.

CHAPTER 7

The Vicious Cycle: The Only Way to Beat Your Addiction

by Greta Kay

A lot of people these days are struggling with some type of addiction due to anxiety, a bad past, negative people in their lives, loss of jobs, and family histories. Your mind will never be clear and your body will never be healthy if you have any type of bad addiction. I say 'bad' because there are some good ones, like gyms, work, and hobbies. Everyone who thinks they can't beat their addiction finds a reason to justify it. The struggle is real and I know how hard it is to beat the addiction, but I also know you are strong enough to, and I will tell you how. Our minds are powerful enough to get out of the vicious circle and stay out of it and maintain a strong clear mind and healthy body. I was lucky enough to figure out the only way to beat alcohol addiction and to get out in time to enjoy this beautiful life full of light, health, love, and happiness. I will use my own story to tell you how to beat alcohol addiction and get your life back.

My story.

I have always had an addictive personality. I started smoking when I was 14, at age 18 I did drugs for two years, and then heavily drank for over 15 years. Now, I am finally free of all of these addictions and able to enjoy my life and help others. My dad drank during my whole childhood. Later on, my mom started too. As a kid, I was always scared and confused. I did not know when I could depend on them or when to be afraid for their lives. I could not understand how such loving parents could be so bad when they were drunk. I couldn't understand why they couldn't just stop, for us. After 28 years, they finally got a divorce and got better. Both found new partners and seemed much happier. My dad never drank again. He was able to enjoy 20 beautiful years without a drink. He passed away earlier this year. My mom was better for a while, but after her partner suddenly died, she fell right back into the vicious circle and is battling her addiction to this day.

When my parents got better and I did not have to take care of them anymore, I started drinking myself. At first, it was parties and special occasions, but I always seemed to be looking forward to those and ended up getting drunk at the end of each event. I never thought I would become an alcoholic because of what I had to go through as a child. I didn't want my daughter to have the same childhood I had. but slowly I made hers much worse. Very soon, it wasn't just occasions or parties anymore, I heavily drank every day. Each day I waited to go home and have a drink. It wasn't one drink. It was a bottle or two a day. Every day was a fight for me. I could not stop. For years, alcohol made me very sick and I knew how horrible I would feel the next morning but I still drank, went to work, and waited to be able to drink again. I could not sleep, socialize, or do anything without alcohol. I was also smoking, so it was double the power. I would drink and smoke until I passed out. It turned into binge drinking where I drank for weeks without getting up, eating, or drinking water. My body got weaker and weaker. My mind was a mess. I made the worst decisions, and hung out with the worst people, at the worst places. I lived this double life pretending to be normal during the day just to go home and abuse myself once again. At one point, the physiatrist gave me sleeping pills and meds that I started using on top of the alcohol. It was a vicious cycle I couldn't get out of. My addictions were holding me hostage in my own body. It got so bad that I was in the hospital 14 times in one year, yes, 14 times! The doctors told me I had a slim chance of survival unless I immediately stopped drinking. I wanted to, I really did, I just did not know how to.

I got pregnant with my second child and had no choice but to stop. I counted the days till I could drink again, and I truly thought I was cured. I thought because I did not drink for so long, I could be a social drinker again. It took me a month of social drinking to end up in the hospital again. This time it was different. This time I knew I tried every single thing out there to stop. I couldn't sleep and every time I closed my eyes I was seeing these repeating visions that wouldn't stop. At first, I thought I was going crazy. Then I decided to watch it …

The vision was this repeating cartoon about the Devil and a man. The little Devil was sitting in a wine bottle. When the man decided to have a drink, the Devil got into his belly. He was so happy. Now he was just sitting there waiting for food, which was the alcohol. At first, the man felt he could choose when to drink or what he wanted to drink. Slowly the little Devil got bigger and now he started dictating what the poor man would drink and how often. Very soon, the Devil started demanding more and more food until the man lost control. He was walking around suffering, looking for more alcohol now, any kind, doing all the things he would never do, embarrassing himself, and hurting people. The devil was using him. Once the man's body was too weak to do any more harm to, he threw his lifeless body on the side of the road, put an enormous amount of shame and guilt on him, and left. "Until next time," he said.

The only way

That was when I realized it was exactly what was happening in my life. It was a vicious cycle. At that point, I tried everything I knew. I tried counting glasses, hypnosis, meds, and stopping for short or long periods. Every time I stopped drinking for a bit, got healthier, and felt better, everything seemed to improve but then I would decide to have a drink again. I would get myself into this vicious cycle that would always end the same—my laying there so weak that I could not even get up to have another drink. I was like a hamster running in his little wheel, trying to run away from myself but not going anywhere. I was stuck.

That is when I realized there was ONLY one way to stop the addiction. The ONLY way is to never get into that cycle and stay as far away as you can. You need to follow the steps with a 100 percent commitment and never look back. You cannot skip or alternate any of the steps. There are only five of them and this is the ONLY WAY! Even though you might feel like it is too hard, I can promise you it is easier than dealing with addiction and living a double life.

Step 1: Make a Decision and Stick To It.

Addiction is a very strong tool the Devil uses to do harm. He studies your weaknesses and gets very creative to get you back into the vicious cycle and make sure you can't get out. Until you decide to stop, you are not in control of your life, evil is. And the more addictions you have, the stronger it is. For example, if you smoke, that's double the power. Just think how many times you quit smoking, you were so proud of yourself, you didn't smoke for a week, or a month, until you decided to have a drink or two and you didn't even remember how you ended up with a pack of cigarettes, smoking again. It might start with one cigarette a day, or a week, you might think you are in control, but before you know you are smoking as much as you did before, or more. Now you feel guilty and disappointed with yourself.

Now that you know addiction is controlled by evil and the only way to grow the little Devil inside of you (your addiction) bigger is to feed it with alcohol, drugs, or cigarettes, what decisions are you going to make every time you THINK you want one of those? Alcohol, drugs, and cigarettes are pure poison to our bodies. Now that you know it is not you craving any of it, but it is the Devil demanding food, what choice are you going to make? Are you going to choose evil and let him grow bigger making it able to control your life, or are you going to choose YOU and grow stronger and take over the control? For me, the choice is simple every single day. I choose to keep him so small that his voice is funny and irrelevant to me.

Every time you think you want a drink or drugs, stop and think. Imagine yourself back at your lowest point. Do you want to end up in that same place again? Do you want to feel like crap?

Most of the time that would be enough to make the right decision, if not here is more: Is it worth losing everything you have? Is it worth feeling like you are in hell while you are still alive?

No! You deserve light, you deserve happiness, and you deserve to live and enjoy living. So keep making the right decision every single day, be grateful for every day you have, make the best out of it, be proud of yourself, and watch how everything is changing around you. The choice is yours.

I choose health and a clear mind at all times. I choose ME!

Step 2: Change Your Mindset.

This step is as important as making the decision. It is not worth making a decision, going through detox, and then not being able to enjoy the benefits because your life is miserable. Some people feel like a victim after they stop drinking, smoking, or using drugs. They feel that something was taken away from them and now everyone is supposed to feel sorry for them. They feel sad and depressed. That is not the right mindset.

You are not a VICTIM, you are a WINNER! Always remember that and never let yourself think otherwise. Feel and act like a winner.

If you think you CAN'T drink, smoke, or use, you are going to want to, all the time, and that is extremely hard. That is punishing yourself for doing the right thing. Just like kids, if they can't have something, they want it even more. What helped me over the years is knowing and telling myself that I can drink or smoke just like everyone else, but I CHOOSE not to, and that is a big difference.

I CHOOSE ME at all times. I am more important than addiction and nothing will change my mind! So for me, it is not even a fight anymore. I know it is my choice, so why would I feel sad about it? You should feel happy and proud. That is the point!

Step 3: Stay on the Right Side.

As we all know there are two opposite sides in this world—good and bad. One is controlled by God and the other by the Devil. Every one of us chooses which side we are on. Every time we make any kind of decision, or say anything it is either good or bad. Depending on the majority of your choices and your lifestyle, you choose one of the sides.

The good one is kindness, joy, beauty, love, happiness, wealth, health, harmony, peace, and forgiveness.

The bad one is darkness, sadness, guilt, hate, pain, sickness, shame, failure, loneliness, and poverty.

Which one do you want to choose?

As long as you choose addiction and evil, you will always stay on the dark side, and everything will go wrong in your life. Most likely you will have days when everything seems good and starts to get better, and all of a sudden it will all fall apart again. And again, find another good reason to drink, use, or smoke. Some people do it to get rid of stress or to numb their sorrows and problems. Soon they find out it will all still be there after they sober up, and now they are not as strong and focused to try to solve them.

As long as you choose addiction, you will stay in the lowest frequency levels, which can only attract low-frequency things. You will attract hate, poverty, cruelty, sickness, struggle, and bad relationships, and it will always stay that way unless you choose to cross to the other side.

So the decision is yours to make. It has to be a strong decision, not a maybe, not I will try. It has to be a 100 percent effort. God knows when you are ready, He is waiting. And once you make that decision, everything will start changing. All good things will start happening, everything will start falling into place, and you will start building the life you have always wanted. Now you are on God's side and He will always be there to help you. Even though evil is strong, God is ALWAYS stronger and always will be. Good always wins. The hardest part is making a decision, and keep deciding to stay on the right side every day of your life. God will help you along the way.

And you know what can very quickly get you right back to the dark side?

ONE DRINK. ONE USE. ONE CIGARETTE.

I always say there are no shortcuts in this life. Don't try to outsmart the system and think that you can be on both sides and still get the rewards. If you think you can secretly have a drink or two and no one will know, STOP now! There is no such thing. God knows, YOU know! You CANNOT cheat yourself. If you try to be a smartass and beat the system, the system will beat you and you will pay the price. So if you are still having those thoughts, your decision is not final. Go back to step one and rethink your decision.

Step 4: Get Healthy

Alcoholism is a very serious disease, but you are lucky because there is a cure for yours. All you have to do is never drink alcohol again! That is how simple it is, you don't even HAVE to do anything, you just have to NOT drink one thing. That goes the same for drugs and cigarettes.

It only takes 17 days for your body to fully remove any alcohol or cigarettes. What it means is that any trace of alcohol is gone in 17 days, so there is ABSOLUTELY no way you could crave it after that. If you feel you crave it—it is a false craving! You have to recognize it and be ready. Here is what you do—simply drink water or eat something and it will go away! It's that simple!

Don't be afraid to tell your story, and talk to others, many more people are struggling with addictions than you can imagine. Choose what works for you. Everyone is different. Alcoholics Anonymous never worked for me, but it works for other people. You have to try different things and see what works best. Try to improve your spiritual health, as it will help you stay stronger and understand what life is really about. If you are into spiritual stuff, you already know we don't have just one life. They say if you don't get rid of your addiction in this life, you have to deal with it again in the next one. I know that meditation, breathing, healthy eating, and challenges help me control my addictions. Once your mind is clear and your body is strong, you will crave all these things that are great for you. The better you feel about your body, the easier it is going to be to control your mind. Do anything that makes you feel like a winner. Every small win counts.

Step 5: Be Aware

Take control of your addiction, or addiction will take control of you!

Once you follow all the steps to making a decision, changing your mindset, choosing the good side, and getting healthy, I need you to know that you ALWAYS have to be aware. You can not completely cure the addiction. You can only keep it under control. Remember there is a very fine line between the two sides, which is one drink, one use, one cigarette.

Once you get it all under control and feel strong, you still have to be very careful at all times. If you have addictions, the little Devil will always be sitting on your shoulder, ALWAYS. He will always be watching, waiting for you to have a weak moment. He can get very creative to lure you into drinking or smoking again. Every time you hear the voices telling you to just have that one drink, you go back to step one, it's a DECISION, and you make the choice:

- Do you want the life you have now or the life you had before?

- Do you want to feel the way you felt before or the way you feel now?

- Do you want to keep the things you have now, or lose everything?

You always have a choice! The choice is yours!

You can read the full version of this method in my book "Circle of Wine."

81

Greta Kay

Greta Kay—Owner of multiple businesses, mother of two beautiful children, coach, leader, and book author. After struggling with addictions her whole life, she was blessed to find the way out and to be able to help others beat their addictions and change their lives forever.

Connect with Greta on at https://linktr.ee/gretakay.

CHAPTER 8

Create Your New Mind and Watch Your Body Follow

by Kimberly Robinson

I dedicate this book to my present and future clients. I wrote this chapter to help begin the healing process of many minds because this will in turn work to heal your body as well. Enjoy your ride to nurturing true health of your mind and body.

What is important to know about the mind and body connection? As I sat down to tell my story, I thought of a few hardships that I have endured throughout my life.

The United States Navy

When I was 19, I enlisted in the United States Navy, a time which truly tested every fiber of my being and helped me to develop my mind and body as they connected together.

We were a group of 16 (most under the age of 20). I was filled with excitement over my new life as a sailor in the United States Navy. I was looking forward to proving to the world that the Navy wasn't too tough for me and eagerly faced my first military training, Boot Camp. I was filled with determination, camaraderie, fear and even joy.

I was on my way to training and my first task was to master Morse code at the speed of 16 groups per minute. I remember the voice of my instructor, a constant presence even when he wasn't physically in the room. I could still hear him echoing in my mind when I left class each day. He was a Marine and his mission was to make sure everyone completed the program of copying 16 groups of Morse code per minute. I am certain that he was determined, in his mind, to not leave a man or woman behind. He was small in stature, but a big voice belted out of him. He told us our rights, "I know some of you are having problems with what I'm having you do today. And what I want to let you know is that you can't leave this class without doing this. You get to copy code. This is what you get to do, so you had better reach down and get you some. I promise you won't leave this class without doing so."

About a week trudged on and I finally looked at one of the students in my class who appeared to be copying code with no problem. I quietly observed him, because I didn't know what else to do and I noticed that he was very relaxed and didn't appear to really be in class. Physically, he was there, but he seemed to be somewhere else. He looked as if he was just kind of chilling out and relaxing. After class I asked him what makes it so easy for him and he said, "Nothing, really. It's just easy now, because I decided to relax. I come to class and don't think about it. I just relax and the words come out of my pen as I'm relaxing."

I tried it and it worked! I passed the class. I aligned my mind and my body, my mind with my fingers. We all found out that the successful way to accomplish the code copying was not to be concerned about the words, but to locate a quiet and peaceful place withing our bodies, a place of peace where clarity shows its face. That tested my resilience in ways that cannot be imagined or guessed.

Magnificent Triumphs

It was finally here, the glorious day was when my first-born son, Austin, was to graduate from high school. It was exciting, yet stressful. I imagine that most parents equally experience a myriad of emotions during this time. While watching my son graduate high school was a little stressful, the majority of my stress was from the excruciating pain that I recently acquired where sitting down for longer than five minutes caused pain. Austin's graduation was three hours from where I lived and I was forced to sit in a car the whole time as we drove to the stadium. To top it off, we were running late. I was angry that I was late and angry that my body movements were restricted due to my excruciating pain. Once we arrived at the stadium, I didn't let my pain stop me and simply kept moving through it. I was determined that I was going to see my son glide across the stage with a big smile on his face. I silently told my body to keep moving till I got there. I encouraged myself and silently thought, "I am going to make it." Next thing I knew, I was in the stadium full of delight that my son was still waiting to receive his diploma. Mindset matters.

The Strength of God

My vision to achieve success in both of those pivotal times in life became a tool in my arsenal. Experts state that over half of the brain's resources are used on vision. We are more dependent on vision than any sense. Therefore, it should not be a surprise that visual cues prove to be the greatest fuel of our behavior. Even a small change can lead to a great leap in accomplishment.

Developing fortitude and believing in myself has come through the opportunity to face many trials, disappointments, and tragedies and I have decided to trust in God to be there to help during and after my storms.

When I reflect on my service in the US Navy, the struggles of motherhood and beyond, I see a common theme that permeates my thoughts; how important it is to keep a positive mindset. In **Philippians 4:8**, it states that, "I can do all things through Christ who strengthens me."

I am still learning to find harmony between the mind and body and am striving to realize my fullest potential. It has been a steadfast journey that screams and demands reflection, intention, and a never-ending commitment to grow. To help me, I have cultivated practices and routines that work to align my deepest values and aspirations.

The Power of Thankfulness

How can I not be thankful? In my quiet moments as I communicate with God, I love to begin by thanking Him as I acknowledge the myriad of ways that grace has been manifested in my life and of those around me as well. I do not consider my gratitude to God a prelude to but an important premise of my dialogue with God, which sets the tone for reverence and humility. I place before me my declarations, dreams and desires that glimmer like candlelight in my soul, and being steadfast and believing that God's ways of doing things is trusted. As I try to practice unwavering faith, I often find myself thanking Him in advance, because I know that He loves me more than anyone and will help me to be my best. I am confident that my path ahead is filled with more prosperity and joy than I already have; not just for me, but for those whose lives I touch as well.

In the midst of my trials, I am reminded, especially when shadows of illness rise and want to overtake me, I am reminded through God's word of the sanctity of my body, a vessel of the Holy Spirit, as is declared in **1Corinthians 6:19, 20** which says, "What, know you not that your body is the temple of the Holy Spirit, which is in you, which you are of God and you are your own."

To honor the body, it is important to remember that not only does it need rest, but movement as well. Even when the body aches, there is great merit in movement and in continuing to pursue daily routines that nourish the body and soul. This balance of rest and activity is so wonderfully guided by wisdom that understands limits but gently pushes them against you for growth. This not only happens physically, but emotionally as well.

As I share these insights from my personal experiences and divine guidance, I am reminded of the heartfelt wisdom in **Proverbs 4:23**, which yearns for us to guard our hearts as the genesis of life, and **Colossians 3:16**, which commemorates the richness of living the message of Christ with gratitude. These scriptures mark the importance of accentuating the transformative power of gratitude and the importance of protecting our innermost thoughts and feelings, for they form the route of our lives. The invitation that is given to all of us is to embark on a journey of self-discovery and spiritual alignment and to harness power within us as we steer life's joys and sorrows with grace and moral strength. Remember that as you stand at the crossroads of life, the capacity to change and have transformation and growth is buried within you.

Below is a list of five daily practices I use to connect my mind and body together to achieve my goals. Each item is crucial in developing my life with a profound sense of purpose, passion and peace.

1. **Practice Gratitude**: Be grateful about everything, even the hard things, as you realize that it is strengthening both your body and mind.

2. **Journal**: Take time during the day, preferably the morning, and write down your thoughts about everything that is going on. Simply grab a notebook, journal or blank paper and go! It doesn't need to make sense, just write.

3. **Nature Connection**: View the clouds slowly dancing in the sky, look at the trees, the rolling waves of ocean and allow yourself to feel the ground with your bare feet. Connecting with nature is so good for your mind-body connection.

4. **Positivity**: Our words are power. A positive environment creates a positive mind. That positive mind can speak to your body at any moment in time.

5. **Support**: The fastest route to accomplishing your goals is having support. Accountability is everything. Education is very important as well and should be done. There will be times where educating yourself is the key to accomplishing goals.

As you review the list, I invite you to see this as not as an inflexible blueprint, but as a starting point or inspiration to discover or improve your path to mind-body harmony. It does not matter whether you are at the inception of your journey or well along its path. These practices offer insight, support, tenacity and courage to design your tapestry of a life well-lived.

I want to leave you with these two thoughts from God's word.

Protect your heart and guard your thoughts: **Proverbs 4:23** (NLT) Guard your heart above all else, for it determines the course of your life.

Practice Gratitude: **Colossians 3:16** (NIV) Let the message of Christ dwell among you richly as you teach and admonish one another with all wisdom through psalms, hymns, and songs from the Spirit, singing to God with gratitude in your hearts.

All right! It is time. You get to decide how to connect your mind and body for your good, to fulfill your life's desires. You get to believe that all things are possible. You get to celebrate your victories. You get to learn great lessons from your mistakes and the adverse things that happen in your life. You get to accomplish your goals. You get to find your way. You get to have it all if you choose. You get to use your mind to connect your body and achieve your goals. All is possible, if you choose to believe.

In sharing my story, my hope is to inspire you to embark on your own journey of self-discovery, to find the strength within yourself to face life's challenges with grace and resilience.

Remember that, in the end, it's not just about the goals we achieve, but the people we become in the process. So, as you stand at the crossroads of your life, remember that the power to change, to grow, and to thrive lies within you. Embrace the lessons life offers, hold fast to your faith, and always, always reach down and get you some of that inner strength that resides within you.

Kimberly Robinson

Kimberly Robinson is a Holistic Transformational Coach and Personal Trainer who specializes in helping clients to reset their mindset to achieve their goals.

Connect with Kimberly at www.MyWellnessMatters.today.

CHAPTER 9

Namaste and Ganache

by Kristin Rene' VanGundy

I dedicate this chapter to my sister-in-law, Mindy, whose light is inspirational. And to Kim, who led me through a life-changing healing modality.

My introduction to Reiki occurred in the most unusual of places: small-town rural America. You have to understand that culturally, people in the Midwest have been slow adopters of things like meditation, massage, yoga, and other practices centered around mindfulness.

I grew up in the Christian tradition, and there are congregations a-plenty in the Midwest. But I had long ago moved away from those practices (that's a long story over a full plate of chocolate ganache and a finger of whiskey). I intuitively knew I was seeking something else and found inspiration from my sister-in-law, Mindy.

Mindy has always been the very grounded, peaceful light in our family. She has this beautiful way about her, engaging you in the simple moments of life to make you feel connected, valued, and heard. Among these gifts, she practices massage therapy, and her practice is just that… therapy, not only for the body but for the soul. She told me that her business partner, Kim, practiced Reiki and suggested I would find it valuable.

The whole thing sounded a little too "woo-woo," too hippy. But Mindy possessed an inner peace that I was craving. So, there I was, sitting anxiously waiting for my appointment in the lobby of Mindy's massage studio.

I occupied myself looking at everything in her place of business. On the walls, she hung beautiful décor that was both captivating and earthy. The smell of lavender and patchouli filled the air, and the way she intentionally flavored the environment started to calm my nerves.

I studied the display dedicated to essential oils, and became intrigued by the vibe I felt from the diffuser and a collection of crystals. Despite all of these things, my nerves were still on edge as I had absolutely no clue what I was doing. Why did I think I needed to do this? I told myself, "I'm fine, totally fine, I don't need this."

I considered leaving but was overruled by years of being indoctrinated with "Iowa nice." Never one to be rude, I decided to stay. I was already there, and after all, I was more than a little curious.

Kim greeted me with a warm smile and asked, "Are you ready?"

Ready, ready for what? I only came here for someone to show me how to meditate, didn't I? I had heard all the buzz about how meditation was the new way to live life more intentionally. And yet, something inside of me resisted this new experience. Despite this resistance, I followed Kim down the stairs into the room where I had previously had massages from Mindy.

While the room itself was familiar to me, I sensed that much of what was to come was not. Feelings born from insecurity, from the unknown, blossomed. I began to regret my decision and doubted that any of this would be good for me. We passed by the massage bed and Kim invited me to sit down in one of two chairs that faced each other.

As I sat down, I could sense my body was uncomfortable, and the walls began to build. In retrospect, I wonder, "What was I protecting myself from?"

I attempted to keep our conversation at a surface level. Part of me feared the lack of confidentiality since we lived in a small town. Could I be vulnerable here? I preferred for others to see the image of me from the outside.

Kim must have sensed my misgivings. She gently asked me if I knew anything about Reiki and why I sought out this practice.

"Hmm. Well, Mindy said I would enjoy it so… here I am."

Kim went on to ask me some more thought-provoking questions, and before I knew it, I was opening up about how I was interested in learning how to meditate and had no experience with Reiki. She listened for about an hour as I spilled my guts, divulging a few past struggles from my life, but still I kept this to superficial moments.

Eventually, Kim began my introduction to Reiki. To me, her words were foreign, and yet something about the activity felt right. She invited me to set an intention before getting comfortable on the massage table. I remained fully clothed but for my shoes. And we began.

All I can say is that this experience moved me beyond any words. I honestly struggle to capture the depth of my inner connection with language, but I will try. For me, Reiki evoked powerful feelings. As

Kim led me through the session, she occasionally made contact with my head, neck, hands, or feet, and I recall this swell of energy.

When she finished the session, she invited me to return to the chair when I was ready. I felt electric in a weird, funky sort of way. She asked if I wanted to share how I felt or if anything came up for which I wanted clarity. I had no words except that it was amazing and that I needed time to process my thoughts. It was truly like nothing that I had ever experienced before. For me, the Reiki session shifted something profound inside. I began to identify an inner source of stress I had been ignoring.

My husband and I became empty nesters after our youngest daughter went off to college. I had some difficult days, even months, where I felt lost. Until that year, I had poured so much of myself into raising our three daughters and creating this beautiful life for my family that I forgot or perhaps didn't really know how to take care of myself.

While the house was empty, I found myself questioning a lot of things. *Now what am I supposed to do with myself?* While my husband and I had a great marriage, I still felt a heaviness in my heart.

Have you ever found yourself questioning why you are here? What is the meaning of your life? When a chapter of your life closes, and you're not sure what is next, what do you do? These are the questions I started asking myself.

I had just turned 50 and embraced the midcentury mark pretty well. But at the same time, I felt stuck, which was ironic. Here I was in this big empty house with all the things, the beautiful décor, the dogs and cats, pretty much everything that I had ever dreamed of having. And yet, I still felt like something was missing. So, I started to search for something more. Have you heard the saying that what you are seeking is also seeking you?

Well, this couldn't be any more true. I hired Kim to coach me through this process and began to allow myself to experience this Reiki thing. With time, I realized Reiki is a powerful tool for healing. It allowed me to begin the process of uncovering years of buried childhood trauma.

When I was 11 years old, my mother passed away from a rare kidney disease. Let's just say that the years following up to age 18 were difficult. I now realize that I had suppressed my sadness, anger, and grief. For all those years, I had been in survival mode, until I decided to make that appointment with a Reiki healer.

In plain speak, Reiki is an ancient healing modality that originated in Japan in the early 20th century. There are different theories, but the Reiki method of healing was founded on the revelation and understanding of the body's energy system.

Reiki is the practice of using "life force energy." It's based on the idea that we all have stores of this energy that flows through our bodies. A practitioner gently moves their hands just above the body, with the intention of reducing stress and promoting healing by encouraging a healthy flow of energy. The method relies on participants harnessing the power of their mind-body connection. Reiki is now used by a growing number of Americans who believe it helps relaxation, anxiety, pain management, and depression.

Reiki sessions can be done in person as well as virtually. Energy is Energy. When we are open to receiving it or releasing it, all you need is a practitioner who knows how to guide you through it. When I chose to become a certified Reiki Master, I was attuned in person, on a Womens Intensive Retreat in Nosara, Costa Rica. Following my certification, I worked with many clients, both in person as well as virtually.

As I progressed through my personal Reiki healing, I became more and more aware of the mind-body connection and how this relationship affects health and well-being. According to the tenants of Reiki, our mind and body are not two separate entities-although they are often treated that way. Our physical health and emotional health are intimately intertwined. Some also refer to this as the mind-body-soul connection. In other cultures, the terms ki, chi, or prana overlap with this concept.

A central modality to all of this is learning to focus on the breath. Practitioners of breath work, meditation, Reiki, yoga, and massage therapy can expect to develop a more grounded, healthy, and intentional life. There are numerous other techniques that overlap with these and fall under the categories of alternative and complementary medicine:

Learning to connect to my breath has changed my life. It has allowed me to slow down and be more "present."

After my year of Reiki healing and life coaching, I felt a shift and expansion within myself! I had always relied on prayer, as my mother and family raised me in the Christian tradition. But somehow, in the hectic business of life, I lost my personal connection and longed for a more genuine spiritual bond.

When I opened up and allowed myself to be vulnerable with my life coach, I gave myself the permission to heal. This was, I believe, the awakening of my soul and my truest, most authentic self, rising and becoming all that I was still meant to do and be.

When we decide that it's time to make some changes in our lives, I believe we must ask ourselves some important questions. Why am I here? What brings me joy? Do I have purpose? Can I give and receive love with authentic compassion? Am I doing my very best? Do I feel fulfilled? What am I passionate about? It's important in these moments of reflection and self-discovery to come back to our "whys."

Why did I make that appointment with a Reiki healer when I felt like I needed some help? Perhaps because my intuition led me there. I honestly believe that. I believe that the energetic frequency that we put out into the world/universe is magnetizing. We are, after all, made of energy, and basically everything around us has energy. Our bodies are science and mystery.

All living things that need oxygen to survive have an aura. They generate a magnetic energy field that can be sensed, felt, and even seen around the physical body. Einstein's most famous equation, $E=mc2$, indicates that energy and matter are intimately interrelated.

Reiki practitioners operate under a framework that we have for different dimensions of energy in our bodies:

- First is the physical (the quantity of our energy)

- Second is the emotional (the quality of our energy)

- Third is the mental (the focus of our energy)

- Fourth is the spiritual (the force of our energy)

If a Reiki participant feels lost or as if something is off, disconnected, hollow or simply missing, they are directed to look at all four of these different elements and how they can be adjusted to work together to create balance and harmony in our lives.

Reiki also focuses on the chakras in the body. Chakras are spinning energy centers that directly influence your well-being and how consciously and happily you create your life's path. When all of the chakras are balanced, you experience safety, creativity, strength, and security in yourself and your relationships. You are more comfortable speaking your thoughts and mind. You also feel connected to your intuition and the vital energy of the universe. The normal stresses of life can disturb the chakras, but there are ways to bring them back into balance.

Chakras in the body are located in the major current of energy that runs up and down the center of the spine. This flow of this energy is what Reiki focuses on. There are seven different energy points (chakras) in the body with unique associated aura colors. When the chakras are all open, one experiences balance and harmony. Blocked or closed chakras create feelings of disassociation and a lack of connection to yourself or others.

My hope, as you read this, is that you begin to see how Reiki offers a framework to understand and affect the mind-body connection. The chakras are the bridge along which you can guide your awareness up and down, moving the life force energy of the earth and to the eternal awareness that connects all energy and beings.

Meditation has also become a huge part of my life and my daily practice. In the practice of meditation, an individual uses different techniques, such as mindfulness or focusing the mind on a particular object, thought, or activity. Through the practice of meditation, one learns to train attention and awareness to achieve mental clarity, calming of the emotions and a stable state.

Central to meditation is breathwork. Learning to focus on your breath as you actually feel the air move through your body is more than just life-giving. Obviously, if we are alive, we are breathing, but through meditation we take the time to pause and find the stillness in our breath. This is where the magic is, connecting to our breath through the body, calming the mind from the busy monkey brain, and allowing for the peace of silence. Here is where you will find your answers.

"Everything you can imagine is real."
~Pablo Picasso

Yoga is the next practice that has helped me with my mind-body-soul connection. Before we get into all of that, the first thing I had to learn was, what the heck does namaste mean? Basically, it conveys a respectful gesture often ending a yoga session. Rooted in Indian traditions, Americans also use the term to indicate, "the light and love that is within me, sees and honors the light that is within you."

Now that we have that settled, let's talk more about the basics of yoga. The practice engages the mind and body with a focus on our spine and mindful movements. The health of our spine is important to our overall health and functioning. Our spine holds our body up so that we can sit and stand up. It also protects your spinal cord, which is made up of millions of nerves that transmit messages from our brains to all the other parts of our body. The nerves convey our sensations, perform biological functions, and facilitate movement. In addition, the spine houses the main energy channel of our body, connecting the chakras.

Yoga is a way of life, not just an exercise. It is known as a series of sequences of physical postures but is so much more. It is, in fact, a way to live your life in union with yourself and create wholeness with that which surrounds you. Yoga's ancient philosophy encourages this practice to purify the mind-body and chakras during meditation for deeper awareness and connection.

When we sit back and reflect on our lives, my hope in writing this chapter is to inspire and encourage you to look deeper within yourself. What gets you out of bed in the mornings? Does your day find joy and laughter in the mundane of the "business?" Do you take moments to pause and find your breath with gratitude that you are here? Life is always going to keep moving forward, whether we like it or not. The kids will in fact grow up, spread their own wings and fly off to find their own way.

Life can fill your mind with the busy mundane: Wal-Mart and grocery store visits, vet appointments, laundry, child care responsibilities, the tedium of managing your auto and home… all of it leaves barely any room to figure out what's for dinner. These ordinary life responsibilities will always be a part of the day-to-day stuff. Reiki, meditation and yoga can all be used as tools to reset this mind clutter and manage the stresses that life forces upon us. In this regard, we choose how to show up for these to-do lists every day.

Living a life with intention to connect and know yourself first means diving deep into who you are in your very core. It is searching for your true soul's essence and blueprint for your many purposes here on this earth. When we allow ourselves to rise into the very best version of ourselves, we also then give others permission to do so as well.

No matter what phase of life you are experiencing right now, it's never too late to start practicing mindfulness. I believe the world would be a much better place if we all started engaging in practices designed to enhance the mind-body-soul connections. It should be taught in schools so that perhaps there would be less anxiety, depression, hatred, sadness, anger, and confusion.

If we could realize that we are connected to something bigger than ourselves and each other, much of the discord that disturbs the world would fade. Love is the foundation of unity. Peace and understanding are ripple effects that can create community and change for more beautiful energy to guide us in this so-called life we have the chance to create.

"If I am not good to myself, how can I expect anyone else to be good to me?" ~Maya Angelou

"Not in doing what you like, but in liking what you do is the secret of happiness" ~J.M.Barrie

"Happiness is when what you think, what you say, and what you do are in harmony." ~Mahatma Gandhi

---

Life has thrown some curveballs my way, shaping my story, which continues to change as I journey forward. Utilizing the different healing modalities that I continue to practice has led me here. Now as I type these words, I recall back to one of my last Reiki sessions as a client. While Kim was holding my right hand, I received the message that I was to write. I remember thinking, "What? I can't write, type, or spell very well." So... holding and receiving that message was saved for another day. Five years later, here I am writing and sharing my wisdom as an author.

"Life moves pretty fast. If you don't stop and look around once in a while, you could miss it."
~Ferris Bueller

"When you're in alignment with yourself, the possibilities to what you can create are endless."
~Kristin VanGundy

What I know for sure is that seeking, finding, and practicing these different healing modalities has changed my life. I get to live my life on purpose with love, light, peace, joy, and my wildest dreams becoming realities. My hope is that I inspire you to investigate these practices and see how you can shape your own journey and be the author of your own happiness.

Namaste! And maybe, if you feel the need... a little ganache on the side.

Kristin Rene' VanGundy

Kristin VanGundy is an Essence Coach, Speaker, 2x best-selling International Author, Reiki Energizer and Believer in the power of Love, Light, Peace.

She is passionate about helping women of all ages find their voice and power from within. Her mission as an Essence Coach is to uncover the authentic self by healing the body mind and soul connection, creating a life filled with purpose, joy and Love in Harmony.

She uses her intuition, spirituality, and energy-healing abilities to guide her clients toward a better understanding of themselves and their true calling in this world.

Kristin draws on lessons learned in forging a successful marriage and has been married to her high school sweetheart of 34 years.

She is the mother of three amazing grown daughters and a pawrent of two very spoiled sheepadoodles! Kristin and her husband reside at a lake home in Unionville, Missouri.

Connect with Kristin at https://linktr.ee/kristinessencecoach.

CHAPTER 10

Unlocking Life's Possibilities: Tapping Into the Mind-Body-Heart-Intuition Connection with Hypnosis

by Lauren Best

If we take the time to listen to our bodies, they have a lot to tell us. Our bodies communicate with us in a myriad of ways, each sensation and signal acting as a unique language conveying messages about our overall well-being. Pain, whether localized or chronic, serves as a poignant expression, revealing physical or emotional issues that have become stuck in our bodies. Muscle tension, digestive irregularities, and changes in skin condition often echo the underlying tones of stress, anxiety, or emotional turmoil. The ebb and flow of energy levels, the rhythm of heart rate and breathing, and the dance of sleep patterns provide a symphony of bodily responses to the orchestration of life.

Even our intuition, that quiet whisper from within, can manifest as "gut feelings" or nervous flutters. These bodily dialogues extend to posture and reproductive health, forming an intricate network of signals that, when heeded, guide us toward a path of greater self-awareness and holistic well-being–and that's if we ever stop to listen to them. Sometimes we don't get the chance before our bodies stop us in our tracks and we continue to push ourselves on our hamster wheels. Understanding the language of the body is a tough yet empowering journey that invites us to respond compassionately to its needs and considers the harmonious connection between our mind, body, and spirit.

When I look back over the last few years, there are many moments that I can notice where my body was screaming at me–screaming at me to rest, to slow down, to breathe, to set boundaries. And as hard as the headaches, the unexplained hives, the appendicitis, the extreme exhaustion, the pins and needles, the weight gain, the kidney stones, and the panic attacks were to experience, I know now it was my body trying to talk to me, to keep me safe while I wasn't feeling safe at all. And now I get to use these signals and experiences as an invitation to move forward by really listening to my body, to actively make changes in my life and my mind that will communicate to both my brain and my body that I love them and that I have their back–they are safe. I also got to realize that it wasn't just my mind and body I had to connect again, but also my heart and my intuition.

Embracing the Blossoming Possibilities of the Mind-Body-Heart-Intuition Connection

No matter where you are right now, it's important to know what is possible for you. From what I know to be true, there are endless opportunities for self-permission, some of which I am here to share with you:

Permission Slip 1: You Get to Take Intuitive Action Embodied With Love

When the threads of the mind, body, heart, and intuition weave together harmoniously, a tapestry of self-trust and confidence emerges. This newfound assurance is not a byproduct of perfection but a result of embracing imperfections and recognizing the authenticity within. It's the unwavering belief in one's ability to navigate life's twists and turns beyond what any fear, ego reaction, or past experience may have told us previously. Trusting your intuition is an act of surrender to the wisdom that resides within, a gentle acknowledgment of your inner compass.

There was no one moment where realization dawned upon me to stop looking for medical diagnoses that were never there or waiting for external validation or permission from others to make a change. It happened over time and in stages of exploring different tools and modalities where I was able to lean into what my body was telling me, where my heart was leading me, what my subconscious mind was showing me, and the self-trust that my intuition was begging me to come home to once again. It was a journey of building my confidence to believe in myself to take action based on love instead of the fear I was used to.

In my experience, as the Mind-Body-Heart-Intuition Connection strengthens, the intuitive voice becomes unburdened by the pursuit of perfection. Trusting this intuitive guidance allows us to take action aligned with our soul's desires, rather than falling into the pressure of societal expectations. The journey of self-love is a softening, a gentle embrace of oneself in all shades—imperfections, vulnerabilities, and strengths.

Permission Slip 2: You Get to Feel Safe in Your Body

In case you didn't know, our bodies are wired for survival. They resist change, favour the familiar, and work to automatically produce

105

thoughts that they perceive will continue to keep us safe and are influenced by fear, our egos, and our past experiences. This makes it even more important for us to create safety in our bodies so that we can move through the resistance to change that our body is trying to keep us safe from.

Regulating the nervous system is an ongoing process. For those who have experienced trauma however big or small, the nervous system becomes a crucial factor in the healing journey. Thankfully, there are many practices that we get to use to focus on restoring balance and safety to facilitate healing, recognizing the intricate connection between the nervous system and emotional well-being. The sympathetic and parasympathetic nervous systems are primary components of the autonomic nervous system, and they work together to regulate various bodily functions, including our heart rate, digestion, respiratory rate, and other essential processes. The sympathetic nervous system typically activates the "fight or flight" response, while the parasympathetic nervous system promotes a "rest and digest" state, helping to maintain balance in the body's physiological functions.

A balanced nervous system forms the basis of a healthy mind-body connection. When the sympathetic and parasympathetic branches harmonize, our bodies signal safety, fostering a state of calmness and equilibrium. This balance contributes to emotional resilience, allowing us to navigate life's challenges without being overwhelmed by stress, anxiety, or fear, ultimately promoting emotional well-being. Each breath becomes a sigh of relief, a testament to the sanctuary created within. The body, once a battlefield of tension and unrest, transforms into a haven of serenity. In this space, the heart beats with assurance, and the mind rests in tranquillity. Feeling safe in our bodies allows for a deeper connection with the present moment, fostering a sense of security and ease.

For years, my nervous system was a wreck. And it's something, like my mindset practice, I prioritize regulating throughout my day, every single day now. But I remember when I was in the depths of experiencing endless amounts of unexplained pain. I just really couldn't begin to acknowledge the idea that this could possibly be manifestations of the emotional and mental struggles that I was experiencing due to ignoring my intuition and my heart. *Have you ever had that feeling in your gut or an overwhelming feeling in your heart that something just didn't feel right, but you continued to ignore it because of the pressure to persevere or simply accept the fate of your circumstance?* That slowly became my life in so many ways without me really taking a breath or a moment to fully recognize the cycle I was trapped in, and without knowing that it all started with the thoughts and beliefs that I was subconsciously holding onto like, *"I have to stick it out or else I've failed,"* or, *"the only way I can feel valuable is to prove my worth to others."* Wild.

Not only was I ignoring my body's wisdom, the desires of my heart, and the intuitive guidance that was coming from within, but my behaviours and thoughts were being driven by my subconscious programming. I didn't know then that as humans we actually get to feel safe in our bodies. And that by neglecting to prioritize what my body was telling me and needing, I was shaming my body because of how its needs could possibly make others uncomfortable or be an inconvenience to others. I now know what a ridiculous responsibility that is to put on our bodies, and this reminds me that each and every day I not only get to prioritize and honour what my body is asking of me, with no apologies.

Permission Slip 3: You Get to Change Your Mind, Your Thoughts and Beliefs

Think of it this way: within the garden of your mind, your thoughts and beliefs bloom like flowers, shaping the colours of your emotions. But the catch is that your mind doesn't care whether those thoughts and beliefs are inspired and optimistic or gloomy and restrictive. Know that whatever you water will grow, regardless if it serves your best interest or not. In this garden of the mind, each thought becomes your reality.

Like a diligent gardener, you have the power to cultivate the landscape of your mind intentionally. Recognizing the potential impact of negative thoughts and limiting beliefs is akin to weeding out the unwanted plants that hinder the growth of your mental garden. Tending to the soil of your thoughts through reprogramming techniques is the key to fostering a vibrant garden. As you engage in this mindful cultivation, you become the master gardener of your mind, planting seeds of empowerment, nurturing the roots of self-love, and witnessing the blossoming transformation of a mindset aligned with your deepest desires.

The subconscious mind (comprising over 95% of our mental landscape) acts like a detailed recordkeeper, storing our beliefs, emotions, habits, values, and memories. It's not some mystical force; rather, it plays a practical role in shaping our behaviour and responses. This hidden aspect operates beneath our conscious awareness, holding essential elements like protective reactions, long-term memory, imagination, intuition, and limited working memory capacity. It quietly influences our critical thinking, problem-solving abilities, and logic, shaping our conscious experiences from behind the scenes. What's important is to know that our brains don't stop changing until our last breath, which means we can change anything about ourselves. *But how do we truly make that change?*

Understanding the Three Methods for Programming the Subconscious Mind

Method One: Early Childhood Programming — Our subconscious has been programmed automatically from the time we were born up until the age of seven. You can think of your brain like a sponge, really absorbing thoughts, ideas, and experiences from your surroundings, your family members, and your communities, without the ability to discern fact from fiction. Everything simply becomes proof of what the world is based on how we experience it, and because of this, it becomes a driver for the stories we tell ourselves without necessarily knowing why we react or experience certain emotions later in life. While this period shapes our foundational beliefs, it is possible to reprogram our subconscious to support different beliefs and rewrite the stories.

Method Two: Conscious Reprogramming — Techniques such as journaling, meditation, practicing gratitude, breathwork, adopting healthy habits, and getting adequate sleep offer ways to consciously reprogram our minds. However, these methods may require substantial time and effort.

Method Three: Hypnosis — Hypnosis is a self-development tool that uses suggestibility of the mind. Like meditation, it gives you the space and guidance to enter a relaxed state both physically and mentally, but it takes you to a much deeper state where you feel safe enough to surpass your critical mind. It is scientifically proven to be faster and more potent than other methods.

When we can access the subconscious mind using hypnosis, we have the opportunity to unravel memories stored since our childhood that act as the origin for triggering our bodily pain or discomfort because emotions have been imprinted in both the mind and the body. This targeted approach allows us to pinpoint the origins of these sensations and recall the initial experiences associated with them to facilitate an experience of addressing stagnant energy by rewriting the experience. A significant aspect of this transformative journey is reparenting ourselves by revisiting the narratives of our childhood, we can offer love and understanding to our inner child.

This act of self-love empowers us to lead with love both in our interactions with the world and within ourselves. Trust, body prioritization, and intuition become guiding principles, allowing us to forge a path rooted in authenticity and self-empowerment. Surpassing the limitations of our conscious thinking, hypnosis becomes a powerful tool for rewriting the stories from our past, freeing us from the shackles of repeated pain that dictate our behaviours, reactions, beliefs, and somatic manifestations.

Hypnosis and the Mind-Body-Heart-Intuition Connection

By diving into the subconscious, we gain insights into the narratives that have influenced our experiences, shedding light on the roots of both emotional and physical states, while also embracing the profound love within our hearts and cultivating deeper self-trust with our intuition as we rewrite these stories and embed empowered feelings within our minds. This self-love and trust becomes a driving force for leading with kindness and compassion both externally and internally. It allows us to trust even more in the process as we get to prioritize our body's wisdom and heed our intuition. Hypnosis allows us to experience the power of collectively tapping into the Mind-Body-Heart-Intuition Connection as it serves as a gateway to transformative healing and self-discovery.

As a Certified Hypnotherapist, my mission is to guide individuals toward this profound connection, enabling them to rewrite the narratives that have made them feel held captive in their minds and bodies and embrace a life of self-trust and love. Through this journey, we can expand our capacity to experience change, disrupt perfectionism, overcome fears, create our own permission slips to rewrite our reality and build a foundation for a life that aligns with our truest selves and deepest desires.

The Mind-Body-Heart-Intuition Connection becomes not just a tool for personal growth and breakthrough, but also a compass guiding us toward a life filled with purpose, joy, and genuine fulfillment. It is a journey worth undertaking—one that transcends the boundaries of the conscious mind and opens the door to the boundless possibilities within the subconscious realms of our being, beyond our original programmed beliefs that once provoked thoughts of self-doubt, shame, and fear. This connection serves as the foundation for authentic action, free from the constraints of societal expectations or external validations.

Permission Slip 4: You Get to Live With Trust and Authenticity

The strengthening of the Mind-Body-Heart-Intuition Connection is an invitation to live authentically. Each step towards self-trust, and a regulated nervous system sets off a gentle ripple—a butterfly effect of possibilities. It is a journey of self-discovery, where the caterpillar of the past transforms into the butterfly of present openness to truly trust in where we are and where we're going amongst all of the uncertainty that life has to offer us.

Because of this opportunity to lean into trust, I find myself fully surrendering to the notion that I can't miss anything meant for me. This surrender is akin to the caterpillar of the past transforming into the butterfly of present openness, trusting the unfolding path amid life's uncertainties. It means opening my heart to share love with the world and embodying the belief that I am inherently worthy of receiving love, without the need to earn it. In this space, unexpected moments of excitement and opportunities materialize, exceeding the bounds of my imagination, all in support of the harmonious flow of life. It's a testament to the profound magic that unfolds when we authentically trust ourselves and the journey we're on.

It's an exploration where authenticity and honouring my mind, my heart, my body, and my intuition gets to be my guiding light, and self-trust blooms into a source of unwavering strength. With self-trust and a regulated nervous system, creative expression becomes a natural outpouring. The mind envisions vibrant landscapes without limit, the heart composes poetic verses that we actively honour through our choices, and intuition becomes the brushstroke of inspiration for designing the greatest piece of art we've ever created which is our most magical reality. The canvas of life is no longer constrained by fear, ego, or past experiences, but expands with the limitless hues of self-expression.

Strengthening and Prioritizing the Mind-Body-Heart-Intuition Connection

Take a moment here to pause and take a breath, and dream about how these possibilities extend beyond you as an individual and how they extend into your relationships, your communities, and our universe. Trusting oneself and feeling safe paves the way for authentic connections beyond the connections that we see or feel in front of us. The heart, open and resilient, dances in sync with others, and intuitive understanding becomes the language spoken between souls, making less space for judgment to invite old thoughts to turn into beliefs and physical manifestations of our emotions. The possibilities of strengthening, trusting, and nurturing the Mind-Body-Heart-Intuition Connection are limitless–provoking us to live a life that transcends the ordinary and invites a life steeped in authenticity, confidence, harmony, and surrender.

Lauren Best

Lauren Best is a Certified Hypnotherapist, Multi-Times Best Selling Author, and Host of the Podcast, "Provoking Possibilities." As a holistic practitioner who works at the intersection of wellness, consciousness, creativity, and business, it is her mission to support others to give themselves permission to disrupt perfectionism to provoke possibility.

She works with Conscious and Creative Leaders, Companies and Entrepreneurs, as well as Curious Individuals, to unlock potential, envision new possibilities for their work and life, connect to their intuition, understand their unique abilities, and strengthen their mind-intuition-body connection to take authentic action.

Aside from working privately with clients, Lauren also facilitates wellness workshops and group hypnosis sessions within the workplace, for existing community audiences, and in collaboration with organizations. She is a mentor in various communities for female entrepreneurs, and has worked with Founders, Entrepreneurs, Leaders, and Teams from North America to London to Singapore to Australia and beyond.

Her superpower is helping people explore new possibilities for living a life they love by guiding them back to themselves, helping them reconnect and trust in their intuition and building confidence like they've never experienced before. She creates spaces of support and collaboration to help these folks move through the noise, envision and come up with new ideas, and create bite-sized plans of action that support their desired area of transformation.

Connect with Lauren at https://lauren-best.com.

CHAPTER 11

Building Emotional and Mental Resilience Through Life Transitions

by Mardi Winder-Adams

This chapter is for everyone who weathers life storms with
grace, optimism, and positivity.

Life is a journey filled with twists and turns, and some of these unexpected deviations can be particularly challenging to navigate. One such challenge that many high-achieving women face is divorce. It's a major life shift that can bring a whirlwind of emotions, financial complexities, and uncertainties. It is also a time to evaluate where you are and to assess your inner strengths, harnessing the power you have internally to get through these challenges.

Just like any other person, I have experienced a number of challenges and transitions. I grew up in a very loving home, but we always were keenly aware that my mom had significant health issues, including cancer, that kept coming back despite the treatments. As a child and a teenager, I saw my mom continue to live her life on her own terms, despite her health issues, the pain, and her increasing physical limitations. However, at no time did I ever see her blame others, give up engaging and interacting, or become bitter. I guess you can say I had a front-row seat to how her positive mindset made a signficant difference in everyone's life.

In my own life, I have been through the death of both my parents as a young adult, a divorce, changes in careers, a move to a new country, remarried, became a caregiver, and dealt with my husband's death. Through these transitions and challenges, I became more keenly aware of the importance of the mind-body connection in being positive, staying healthy, and having a resilience mindset to carry me through the difficult times.

Today, I work with women going through the challenge of a divorce. In helping my clients tap into their inner strength and their natural resilience, they can envision a positive future and not get stuck in the negative emotional overload that comes with divorce. They are also reducing the long-term emotional costs of a divorce and learning more about themselves in the process.

While my clients are going through major changes, building resilience is not just important to manage these significant life transitions, it is also for the smaller challenges we face on a daily basis. Small issues are cumulative, and having the emotional and mental resources to deal with them is essential so you can move forward with confidence and compassion for yourself and others.

So, regardless of the specific life transition or issue you're dealing with, be it divorce or something else entirely, building emotional and mental resilience is key to not just surviving but thriving through these changes. In this chapter, we'll delve deep into the importance of emotional and mental resilience and explore actionable steps to help you develop and strengthen these crucial skills.

Understanding Emotional and Mental Resilience

Emotional and mental resilience is like your inner armor, protecting you from the storms that life can throw your way. They are your ability to bounce back from adversity, to withstand the emotional toll of challenging situations, and to maintain a positive outlook on life even when things seem bleak.

I used to think of resilience as an elastic band that could stretch and bounce back. The problem with this analogy is that these bands become less elastic over time. In fact, with just a few stretches, they become increasingly likely to snap, which is the opposite of resilience.

Now, I think of resilience as a magic balloon that can expand to infinity. With every challenge you navigate and move through, that balloon surrounding you gets a little bit bigger. The balloon is a layer of cushioning and comfort that only continues to grow and become more effective as you face and overcome small and large transitions and life events. Think of the growing space in the balloon as increasing your zone of personal comfort and confidence to get through anything life throws at you.

The way the balloon gets bigger is to focus on expanding your resilience skills. These skills are used in many different ways to help you stay flexible, responsive, and able to tap into your resilience levels to get through any challenge. Having this confidence creates a mindset of positivity even in tough situations. It allows you to see the future as something to look forward to and not a reflection of the past or the current situation. It embodies hope and forward thinking that creates optimism about the potential for positive change.

Resilience skills are not fixed and finite; they can be developed and honed over time. When it comes to major life transitions like divorce, they are invaluable tools that can make all the difference in your journey.

Why Resilience Matters

With so many things to focus on in life, understanding the value of building resilience is helpful. Recognizing that resilience-building activities and exercises can be incorporated into your day makes it easy to recognize when you are flexing your resilience muscles and creating a positive mental outlook on a challenging situation.

1. **Mitigating Stress**: Life transitions often come with stress. Resilience helps you manage and reduce this stress, which is essential for both your mental and physical well-being.

2. **Better Decision-Making**: Resilience enables you to think more clearly and make sound decisions, even when emotions are running high. This is particularly important during a divorce when important choices must be made.

3. **Adapting to Change**: Resilience allows you to adapt to new circumstances and embrace change with a positive attitude. It helps you see opportunities in the midst of challenges.

4. **Emotional Well-Being**: Building resilience enhances your emotional well-being, helping you cope with difficult emotions and preventing them from overwhelming you.

5. **Increased Confidence**: When you're emotionally and mentally resilient, you feel more confident in your abilities to handle whatever life throws at you. This boost in self-assurance is essential during life transitions.

Actionable Steps to Build Emotional and Mental Resilience

There are many different areas and opportunities to increase your level of resilience and understanding that you have the inner resources to navigate any challenge in life.

- **Cultivate Self-Awareness:** Recognizing your personal strengths and limitations is key to responding effectively to life's challenges. Regular reflection and introspection can enhance your understanding of what situations cause you stress or discomfort and why. Techniques such as journaling or therapy can aid in uncovering and understanding these personal insights, allowing for a proactive approach to stressors.

- **Develop a Support System:** Actively work on nurturing relationships that offer mutual trust and understanding. Whether it's family, friends, or support groups, these networks can provide practical advice, emotional comfort, and a different perspective. In times of need, knowing there are people who care can make all the difference.

- **Practice Mindfulness and Meditation:** Incorporating mindfulness and meditation into your daily routine can help you become more attuned to your thoughts and feelings without judgment. This awareness can prevent you from being overwhelmed by stressful situations. Techniques such as deep breathing, guided imagery, or even simple walks in nature can serve as meditative practices that promote mental clarity.

- **Set Realistic Goals:** Clear, achievable goals provide direction and a sense of purpose. When these goals are realistic and broken into tangible steps, they can serve as a roadmap to progress and personal growth, offering a sense of achievement that bolsters self-esteem and resilience.

- **Learn Problem-Solving Skills:** Effective problem-solving often requires critical thinking and the ability to calmly assess situations. By developing these skills, you can approach obstacles methodically, reducing the emotional toll they might otherwise exact and increasing your capacity for overcoming adversity.

- **Maintain a Healthy Lifestyle:** Physical health is deeply interconnected with mental health. A balanced diet, regular physical activity, and sufficient rest are crucial for maintaining the energy and mental acuity needed to deal with challenges. These habits also strengthen the immune system, which can be compromised by stress.

- **Practice Gratitude:** Intentionally focusing on the positive aspects of your life can shift your perspective from one of scarcity to one of abundance. Gratitude can enhance mood, decrease stress, and lead to a more optimistic outlook, all of which are important aspects of resilience.

- **Seek Professional Help:** There's strength in recognizing when you need help and seeking it. Therapists and counselors are trained to help individuals navigate through their struggles by providing coping mechanisms that foster resilience.

- **Build a Resilience Toolkit:** This could be a physical box or a metaphorical collection of strategies that you've found to be effective in managing stress and bouncing back from setbacks. It might include relaxation exercises, favorite music, motivational speeches, or anything else that helps restore your equilibrium.

- **Embrace Change as an Opportunity:** When you view change as an inevitable and potentially positive aspect of life, you can more easily accept and adapt to it. This shift in mindset can transform the energy you might spend resisting change into energy for innovation and growth.

- **Practice Self-Compassion:** It involves forgiving yourself for your faults and understanding that struggle is part of the shared human experience. By treating yourself with kindness and patience, you build a nurturing inner dialogue that supports resilience.

- **Learn from Adversity:** Reflecting on past difficulties and the strategies you used to overcome them can help you identify what works and what doesn't. This reflection turns past struggles into learning opportunities that can inform your future actions and choices.

- **Focus on What You Can Control:** Spending energy on uncontrollable events is futile and often exacerbates stress. By focusing on what you can control, you can take productive action and feel a sense of empowerment even in turbulent times.

- **Celebrate Your Strengths:** Acknowledge and take pride in your abilities and achievements. Remembering your strengths can serve as a reminder of your capabilities and provide the confidence needed to face current and future challenges.

- **Stay Flexible:** Flexibility allows you to respond to life's changes with agility. This adaptability is essential for resilience, as it enables you to pivot and find new solutions when the unexpected occurs.

- **Practice Self-Care:** Invest in activities that nourish your body, mind, and soul. Whether it's taking a warm bath, reading a book, or spending time on a hobby, self-care is essential for maintaining the internal resources needed to cope with stress.

- **Stay Connected to Your Values:** Knowing what's most important to you can provide a sense of stability and direction during times of upheaval. Making decisions that align with your core values reinforces your sense of self and acts as a steady guide through life's ups and downs.

- **Visualize a Positive Future:** Visualization is a powerful tool that can help you maintain focus on your goals and aspirations. It can keep you motivated and directed towards positive outcomes, even when the present circumstances are challenging.

- **Accept Imperfection:** Letting go of perfectionism can reduce unnecessary stress and anxiety. Embracing imperfection allows you to take risks, learn from mistakes, and appreciate the journey of continual learning and growth that defines the human experience.

The Value of Building Resilience Throughout Life

Our minds are designed to look for potential problems in life. Unfortunately, if we don't have emotional and mental resilience reserves, we can get trapped in focusing on all the potential problems we face. Building a reslience reserve helps to avoid this pitfall while also helping to expand our resilience balloon and our comfort zone in handling tough situations.

To develop this kind of resilience, begin by fostering a deep sense of self-awareness. This speaks to understanding the strength and flexibility you have at this moment in time. It requires you to explore the core of your being and recognize your emotional triggers and the coping mechanisms you use as a default. Once you understand these, you can start to consciously make choices that will help you weather the storms of life.

Self-awareness leads naturally to the cultivation of a support system. In the midst of hardship, it's often the comforting voice of a friend or the understanding nod of a family member that becomes the lifeline pulling us back to safety. It's important to acknowledge that leaning on others does not make us weak; it makes us human. This network of emotional support, consisting of people who truly listen and provide perspective, helps us process our feelings and regain our footing.

Another pillar in building emotional resilience is the practice of mindfulness and meditation. These practices teach us to remain present and centered, even when our environment is in chaos. Through mindfulness, we learn to observe our thoughts and emotions without judgment, acknowledging them and letting them pass like leaves on a stream. Meditation, on the other hand, trains our minds to be still, which can be a sanctuary of calm when everything else is in disarray.

When setting goals, the key is to ensure they are realistic. Goals give us direction and a sense of purpose, but when they are unattainable, they can cause unnecessary stress. By breaking them down into manageable steps, we not only make progress more achievable but also allow ourselves to celebrate small victories, which can be incredibly helpful during difficult times. Take the time to celebrate your achievements and to recognize the positive steps you take on a daily basis.

Maintaining a healthy lifestyle serves as the physical foundation of our emotional house. Proper nutrition, regular exercise, and adequate sleep are the building blocks that keep our walls sturdy and our windows clear. Caring for our body is just as important as focusing on our emotional health and wellness. Both the mind and the body should always be a focus in any personal growth and development activities.

Practicing gratitude turns our attention to the positive aspects of our lives, which is especially crucial when we are inundated with problems. By acknowledging the good—no matter how small—we reinforce the idea that not all is lost, and this optimism is a cornerstone of resilience.

As we journey through life, we must get comfortable embracing change as an opportunity for growth. By reframing our challenges as chances to learn and transform, we shift from a mindset of being out of control to one of being in control of our destiny. This includes making changes in work, relationships, and our personal lives.

The analogy of putting on your own oxygen mask before assisting others illustrates the critical nature of self-care. Just as on an airplane (where you must put on your own oxygen mask before helping others), in life you must take care of yourself before you can effectively support or care for others. This message reminds us that neglecting our own well-being can hinder our ability to be there for our loved ones or fulfill our responsibilities.

Self-care encompasses a wide range of practices and activities that prioritize your physical, mental, and emotional health. These practices are essential because they help you maintain a balanced and resilient state of mind. When you engage in self-care, you're refilling your emotional batteries, which can become depleted due to the stresses and demands of daily life.

Hobbies are a wonderful form of self-care because they allow you to engage in activities that bring you joy, fulfillment, and a sense of accomplishment. Whether it's painting, playing a musical instrument, gardening, or any other activity you're passionate about, hobbies provide a creative outlet and a break from the routine. They offer a valuable opportunity to recharge and find personal satisfaction.

Relaxation is another crucial aspect of self-care. Taking the time to unwind, whether through meditation, deep breathing exercises, a long bath, or simply reading a book, can significantly reduce stress and promote a sense of calm. Relaxation techniques not only soothe the mind but also have positive effects on physical health, such as lowering blood pressure and reducing muscle tension.

Additionally, part of self-care involves setting healthy boundaries and learning to say no when necessary. Often, people tend to overcommit and take on more than they can handle, leading to burnout and increased stress levels. Practicing assertiveness and setting limits on your time and energy is an essential aspect of self-care. Saying no to undue stressors allows you to conserve your emotional and mental resources for what truly matters to you.

Developing emotional resilience is not a destination; it is a continuous journey. It requires patience, effort, and kindness directed at ourselves. But the rewards are amazing, equipping us with the inner reserve of strength we need to be our best selves in good times and in bad.

Mardi Winder-Adams

Mardi Winder-Adams is the go-to divorce coach for high-achieving women. She is dedicated to supporting women in taking control of their separation and divorce to reduce the emotional and financial costs of the process.

Mardi offers over 30 years of experience helping women navigate the challenges of high-conflict and high-asset divorces. Mardi is an ICF and BCC Executive and Leadership Coach, Certified Divorce Transition Coach, and Credentialed Distinguished Mediator in Texas. She founded Positive Communication Systems, LLC, and hosts the podcast, "The D Shift, Redefining Divorce and Beyond" and Real Divorce Talks.

Connect with Mardi at https://www.divorcecoach4women.com

CHAPTER 12

"The Energy Architect™" – Rooted in Authenticity and Soul's Wisdom

by Nasirra R Ahamed

To Mama & Papa- You are my source of unwavering support & wisdom. You have been my North Star, navigating me through life's storms.

Baby Roshan & Capt. Radhakrishna- Thank you for the shared dreams, laughter and love we've built our world upon. Grateful that you support me and my dreams.

What if every twist and turn of your life's journey has meticulously orchestrated itself to bring you to this precise moment, a juncture poised for you to actualize your deepest aspirations? What if the only obstacle hindering the realization of your highest potential is none other than yourself? Consider the prospect that your sole responsibility as a human being on this cosmic journey is to simply step aside, allowing the universe to unfold, and to fully embrace the richness of life.

In this intricate dance of existence, the path to attaining your highest potential and becoming the fullest expression of yourself isn't an external quest; it lies within, intricately encoded within your very being. The invitation is not to undertake arduous tasks or to strive for external validation, but to learn the art of being—shedding the layers that no longer serve you and stepping into a version of yourself unexplored and untapped.

Perhaps today is the day when you summon the courage to let life guide you, breaking free from self-imposed barriers. Today might mark the turning point where you decide to rewrite the narrative that has confined you to a version of yourself that no longer resonates. Today could be the day you consciously choose to step into a higher version of yourself—one rooted in authenticity and guided by the soul's wisdom.

The key lies in your choice—the decision to live from a place of fear or to anchor yourself in the depths of your soul, embracing the entirety of your life's experiences and evolving into your highest expression. It's a moment of profound decision, a crossroads where you define who you are to become.

Now, let's delve into the missing piece, the bridge to effortless manifestation. Three fundamental actions pave the way for you to effortlessly attain your desires, condensing the complex process into a harmonious flow. Together, we shall embark on the exploration of these transformative steps.

Consider, what elements are you currently attracting into your life that have led you to this moment? Whether it's wealth, relationships, or personal growth, the key is to transcend inconsistent actions and move towards a state of effortless manifestation. While material wealth is an initial step, there are numerous layers beyond that beckon your attention—the unfolding of your true self, the discovery of joy, balance, and an elevated existence.

However, this journey comes at a cost—the relinquishment of your old self. On both micro and macro levels, it demands a shedding of outdated thought patterns, existence, and vibrational frequencies. The question resonates: Are you prepared to release your old self, understanding that the metamorphosis required extends beyond the superficial into the very core of your being? This commitment is a covenant with your evolving self, a pledge to get unstuck and to welcome the new version of yourself that you've been calling forth.

The universe awaits your response, and your willingness to embark on this transformative odyssey is the key that unlocks the door to your highest potential. Write it down, affirm your commitment, and take the first step toward a life that unfolds effortlessly in alignment with your deepest desires.

Embarking on this emotional journey with me is an invitation to traverse the highs and lows that have sculpted the person you see today. As an individual of Indian descent, my formative years were spent in Bahrain, and the tapestry of my life unfolded when I landed in India at the tender age of 16. Picture me then—an average student in school, grappling with awkwardness, self-loathing due to acne scars, an emotionally scarred young adult, bullied, devoid of confidence, and lacking a sense of direction.

My upbringing in Bahrain was a testament to the love and values instilled by my remarkable parents. My Father is an Engineer, the Privatization Program Specialist and Advisor at Ministry of Works in Bahrain. You can see from the intensity and growth in his life that this man was practical, brilliant and hard working. My mother was a beautiful woman that taught English to foreign students. Together, they crafted a version of me and my brother that cherished honesty, integrity, and the essence of being good human beings. However, the societal expectations of a typical middle-class Indian family, pushing for careers in engineering or medicine, didn't align with the unconventional path I chose.

Life in India unfolded with a series of bullying incidents, not within my immediate family but from those I allowed into my home and life. These episodes, although painful, played a crucial role in steering me away from my authenticity—a pivotal aspect required for my evolution into the person I was meant to become. The truth is, everyone, to some degree, has faced bullying or abuse, be it from society, the education system, or in various other forms. The realization that your desire for change stems from some form of abuse, programming a version of yourself you don't want to be, is the catalyst for a profound shift once accepted and embraced.

My story is entwined with layers of self-shame and hurt stemming from the unspoken experiences. It seeped into every facet of my life, influencing my relationship with money, my interactions in relationships, and the choices I made. Nevertheless, the journey persisted, and my professional trajectory unfolded without a predetermined plan, spanning 22 years in the same industry, driven by a quest for security. Ascending to leadership positions, the reluctance to leap into the unknown lingered, fuelled by a lack of active planning and a continuous questioning of the alignment of my career path with my deepest desires.

In the pivotal year of 2022, I reached a crossroads, faced with the decision to tread the safe and known path or venture into the unknown, what I fondly term the "source path." Opting for the latter, I enrolled at the Indian Institute of Management-Nagpur and later obtained Coaching certifications. This decision set in motion a journey that defied my expectations, involving financial investments, moments of rejection, and a continuous evolution as I stepped towards my authenticity, even without a clear picture of the entire path. Today, standing at a juncture where my career has accelerated, I dedicate myself to unlocking the authentic potential of future leaders, organizations, and individuals.

So, what transformed me from a bullied, emotionally scarred, indecisive employee to a "Purposepreneur," working alongside business leaders to help them unearth their authenticity? It wasn't a smooth ride. It entailed enduring a series of downs, spending most of my savings on heavy self-investment, and navigating through the labyrinth of wrong friendships, hurts, disappointments, and directionlessness. There came a point where the old me hadn't fully faded, and the new me hadn't fully emerged. Yet, I continued choosing the source path, even at what seemed like rock bottom, guided by a promise to myself—a commitment to authenticity and the unwavering embrace of my values of integrity. This emotional odyssey, marked by resilience and self-discovery, culminated in the birth of "The Energy Architect™," a testament to the transformative power of choosing authenticity in the face of adversity.

Let me take you on a heartfelt journey, a glimpse into the very fabric of my being, where every act of kindness and each step in alignment with my authentic self unfolded as a symphony of spiritual resonance. There was a moment, a poignant memory etched in my soul, where I extended a helping hand despite facing my own financial challenges. It was in those selfless acts that a profound spiritual alignment blossomed, ushering me towards a doorway of opportunities.

From this spiritually charged state, I discovered my true calling—a profound joy in guiding individuals to unearth their purpose and embrace their authentic selves. My mission evolved into sculpting a new generation of conscious leaders, adorned with wisdom, authenticity, and ethical principles. I embarked on a journey to assist those feeling lost or stagnant, steering them towards their authentic selves and helping them architect mindsets for boundless energy and intelligent leadership.

The milestones and accolades that followed, such as the bestseller status of my collaborative book and invitations from my prestigious alma mater to mentor their management students, were merely echoes of external recognition. Amidst the noise, what truly mattered was the transformation within—an energetic state characterized by a fearless heart, profound peace, surrendered love, and unwavering trust. This was the pivotal switch, the real narrative beneath the surface.

I share this not to flaunt accomplishments but to offer you a glimpse into the energetic essence that fuelled this journey. As we delve deeper, I invite you to reflect on how this resonates with your own experiences. Does my story, my background, open a gateway for you to perceive greater possibilities within your own life?

Now, let's unravel the essence of effortless manifestation, a principle deeply rooted in the law of correspondence. This law unveils the interconnectedness of three planes of existence—spiritual, mental, and physical. These planes, hierarchies of energy, can influence and impact one another. The key to effortless manifestation lies in the convergence of these planes—a meeting point where spiritual, mental, and physical energies harmonize.

If your manifestations demand excessive effort, there may be a disconnection or misalignment among these planes. Clarity, an essential aspect, is often hindered when the spiritual plane is disconnected. Lack of clarity permeates through your mental and physical bodies, hindering your ability to recognize opportunities and vibrating at a frequency misaligned with your manifestations.

Effortless manifestation demands alignment across all three planes, pursued with a soul-aligned purpose. Clarity emerges when your spiritual, mental, and physical aspects converge, creating a seamless flow of energy. Identifying the specific areas in your life where misalignment occurs is crucial. Whether it manifests in relationships, business, or personal growth, recognizing these points offers valuable insights into what needs realignment.

This is your path of effortless manifestation—a journey that necessitates a harmonious dance between your spiritual, mental, and physical planes.

Embarking on the journey of self-discovery, we often encounter the daunting challenge of aligning our spiritual, mental, and physical dimensions. The question echoes through the corridors of our consciousness: Why is it so hard to unify these aspects of our being, and what prevents us from embracing the fullness of our authentic selves without practicing / Re-living the trauma that has become ingrained within us?

In the realm of business and wealth creation, the struggle often presents itself as an all-or-nothing predicament. The disconnection arises when our soul's aspirations clash with the way we manifest success in our lives. A personal reflection emerges from my corporate days, a period when financial prosperity overshadowed the yearnings of my soul. A pivotal moment demanded a choice—settle for a life devoid of spiritual alignment or heed the call of my authentic self. The narrative was clear; the soul's path was beckoning.

Yet, the impediment to achieving alignment persists, creating a chasm between the soul's frequency and the integration of spiritual, physical, and mental paths. This discord is often rooted in trauma, manifested as blockages in the heart, shrouded in layers of shame, fear, and hurt. This trauma, a silent force shaping our perception and responses, requires acknowledgment and healing. However, addressing these wounds necessitates a departure from conventional methods that engage only the mind. Disconnect shows up in a blockage in the heart in some way and this blockage would typically manifest itself as some level of shame; some level of fear; some level of hurt and all of the different levels of this. This again becomes some of the trauma that we need to work on. But we're not stopping them. This trauma is locked in the heart. This ends up influencing how you think, which ends up creating the physical reality that you see now. Your soul has all the information it needs to transmute this block. If you know how to tap into it correctly, you know that you are trying to fix this block in the heart. But you're trying to fix this block here by tapping into the mind because that's what you know how to do. That is not the path; it's very difficult to fix this block with the mind. This block can only be fixed for the most part by the soul and by tapping into the full authenticity of the soul.

The essence of transformation lies in tapping into the soul's authenticity. This journey is not navigated through the mind but through the depths of the soul, dismantling the barriers that inhibit spiritual, mental, and physical alignment. The heart becomes a focal point, a reservoir of stored emotions and traumas that demand release. The process is not without discomfort, for the release of these heavy energies prompts purging and transformation.

Understanding the chakra system becomes essential in this journey. Contrary to the common focus on higher chakras and the 3rd eye associated with spiritual awakening, the key lies in addressing the lower chakras—the heart, solar plexus, sacral, and basic. These are the anchors of emotional weight, where the soul's energy struggles to penetrate due to the density of unresolved issues. It's a profound shift in perspective, acknowledging that the real work lies in the foundational chakras, beneath the heart, where the soul's whispers and downloads are often stifled.

To embark on the path of self-evolution, we must recognize that our soul is a reservoir of wisdom and guidance, always ready to provide the necessary information for transformation. The resistance to change is not a lack of knowledge but an inability of the body to integrate and embody the soul's wisdom. DOUBT becomes the quantum anchor that keeps us tethered to our current reality, a heavy burden that obstructs the flow of higher frequencies from the soul.

Addressing doubt and rebuilding trust with the soul involves dropping deeper into the body, focusing on the lower chakras, and acknowledging that discomfort is an integral part of the transformative process. The comfort zone becomes a deceptive refuge, concealing deep-seated fears and inhibiting the release of energies that no longer serve our growth. Trust in the soul, once reestablished, paves the way for overcoming doubt—the formidable barrier that stifles our quantum connection with the soul.

My recent personal experience serves as a testament to the importance of recognizing when the body is not calibrated to handle the rapid influx of energy and insights. Coping mechanisms and addictions resurface, signalling that the vessel needs conditioning to assimilate higher levels of energy. Awareness becomes the beacon, guiding us to relax, embody the wisdom, and release the accumulated fears and doubts that impede our progress. For me when I spot my own like that and I see that happening I immediately have the awareness which is one of the things I teach in my master class and coaching. That immediate happy awareness to go "Ohh, I see what's happening." I see how it's calibrating me and trying to remove fear from my body. Now I've learned the tools to embody that and relax my energy and allow all of these things to come out of me because when you're in that flow and the universe removes the man you love from your life or makes you lose your favourite clients or your favourite employee, what it is actually doing is also removing a lot of the fear that's keeping you stuck in whatever timeline you are on and when you get into contraction and you're not able to let that go and process it your physical body is not yet calibrated enough to go through the challenges. You need to let go to get into the next level of your life so I'd like you to really spot where these fears, where this shame, where this hurt, where is it stalling your body, what is causing it and we need to transmute that and work with your vessel to make sure you can actually handle these higher level downloads coming in because the thing is that your soul and spirit can't give you more unless you can handle it; otherwise, it becomes an existential crisis.

In this profound journey of self-discovery, meditations and visualizations are valuable tools, but true transformation necessitates grounding in the body and transmuting lower-level emotions. Fear, anger, and identity issues need to be acknowledged, processed, and released, creating a wider channel for the soul's downloads to descend into our being.

So, my advice echoes through the corridors of your consciousness: Spot the fears, shame, and hurt embedded within your body. Identify the points of stagnation, the areas where these lower-level emotions linger, and transmute them. Embrace the discomfort, for it is the doorway to your evolution. Trust your soul, release doubt, and recalibrate your vessel to become a conduit for the higher frequencies seeking expression through you. The journey of self-evolution is an intricate dance, a harmonious convergence of spiritual, mental, and physical dimensions—a symphony orchestrated by the authentic whispers of your soul.

Repetitively, I've witnessed the transformative power of FORGIVNESS—an unequivocal process. The capacity to forgive oneself, life, spirit, parents, and every aspect of existence serves as a key to calibrate the lower chakra points. This calibration propels one towards the highest vibrational frequencies globally. The pivotal inquiry is: what or whom are you presently unwilling to forgive? Identify the obstructions hindering your ability to forgive. Whether it's past abuse, seemingly inconsequential instances like a client's unfavourable comment—can you extend forgiveness? The act of forgiving is synonymous with recognizing the universe's perfection. This realization, in turn, grants entry into the quantum flow, a catalyst for accelerating your quantum journey. Reflect on the internal resistance that prevented you from taking necessary steps earlier. Trust in yourself, align with your soul, and initiate action.

Take a moment for some introspection. Dive into the mental, physical, and spiritual realms of your being. Today, I'm offering you a transformative challenge. Imagine this: if this were my last message to you, something impactful would change in your life. Now, confront the hidden corners of yourself—those aspects you're reluctant to share. Lead with that vulnerability in your life, relationships, and business. Unveil your most genuine, authentic self—the part with dissonance. It's also your most robust path to alignment. To truly forgive and step into a harmonious flow, allow those concealed parts to see the light. Today, embrace the challenge, and let authenticity guide your journey to self-discovery and growth.

I am "The Energy Architect™"

Atma Namaste

Nasirra R Ahamed

Nasirra R Ahamed is the founder of "The Energy Architect™." She is a #1 International Best Selling author; host of "The Energy Architect™" Podcast; Mentor, Speaker and a Coach.

Embarking on a mission to unlock human potential, Nasirra R Ahamed believes in the innate capacity of each individual to Design, Create, and Change their world. As a Certified Coach with a remarkable 21-year journey in Leadership roles, Nasirra is a Mind Reset & Rewiring Engineer, Spiritual Scientist, Mentor and Speaker specializing in Meditation and Chakra balancing. Driven by empathy and committed to excellence, Nasirra guides Future Leaders, Organizations, and Individuals toward their True and Authentic Potential.

Through her coaching, mentoring, podcasts, workshops, courses, and writing, Nasirra integrates coaching, mindset reprogramming, spirituality, somatic therapy, and energy work, facilitating breakthrough results by clearing limiting beliefs. Nasirra R Ahamed excels in aiding those feeling lost, stuck, or uncertain, helping them reconnect with authenticity for lasting freedom and fulfillment. A beacon of transformative leadership, Nasirra illuminates a path to "game-changing" outcomes, integrating a mindset for infinite energy and Intelligent Leadership.

In the realm of conscious leadership and coaching, Nasirra undertakes a unique journey, seamlessly blending spiritual wisdom, somatic therapy, and energy work. By dismantling limiting beliefs, Nasirra empowers leaders with profound self-awareness, fostering positive transformations in both professional and personal realms. The belief that each individual has the power to Design and Architect their destiny with Intention defines Nasirra's impactful approach.

Nasirra R Ahamed is "The Energy Architect™."

Connect with Nasirra at https://linktr.ee/nasirra.r.ahamed

Let's connect for a POWERFUL conversation.

CHAPTER 13

Lifestyle Design: Cultivating a Balanced and Fulfilling Life

by Sally Katherine Ross

This chapter is dedicated to my wonderful daughter who inspires me every day to be the best version of myself. As my best friend, you challenge me when you feel I am distracted and veering away from my path and you encourage me to have faith in myself and my journey.

In our relentless pursuit of happiness, abundance, and love, it's crucial to acknowledge the intricate interplay between our mind, body, and soul. The mind-body connection is the amazing link between our thoughts, feelings, and physical sensations. It means that what we think and feel can affect how our body works, and vice versa.

As a Lifestyle Design Coach, I'm hired by individuals and event planners interested in learning how to unlock this connection in order to craft a life that is harmonious, purposeful, and profoundly gratifying. The following are some tools and techniques that you can harness to foster balance and flourishing across all facets of your life.

My childhood dream came true when I became a professional dancer and traveled the world performing on stage and screen. Immersing myself in different cultures and traditions taught me quickly the importance of embodying my thoughts and desires. I discovered new forms of art, architecture, photography, and design. I fell in love with a wonderful man who shared my artistic vision and values and our incredible daughter has taught me infinite life lessons her entire life.

Dancing was more than just a physical activity for me. It was a way of connecting my mind and body in harmony. It allowed me to channel my emotions and thoughts into a physical display (even if nobody was watching) of intentional gestures and expressions, sometimes graceful and other times forceful and intense. I had found my medium for transcending the limitations of reality and entering a world of beauty, creativity, release, and self-expression.

This life journey of my own is what inspired me to become a Transformational Life Coach. I prefer to call myself a Lifestyle Design Coach because of the multi-faceted benefits we can create for ourselves and live the lifestyle of our own making. Learning innovative healing modalities, I discovered how our negative thoughts hold us captive in paradigms that tend to overly influence our decisions. Challenging our limiting beliefs, we can learn how to identify negative self-talk and other self-criticisms and replace them with positive affirmations, gratitude, and compassion. This opens the doors for increased self-confidence and courage.

Numerous people have faced situations where they had to choose between following their hearts or fitting in with family or society expectations and values. Some of them gave up on their dreams, while others fought for them and overcame the obstacles. You might be wondering how they do that. How do we reconnect with our true selves and our deepest desires? How do we transform our lives into our own masterpiece?

The answer lies within you. Look deep inside yourself and listen to what your mind and body are telling you. Just breathe, relax, and visualize your dream as if it were already a reality. Feel the emotions, sensations, and experiences that your dream brings you. Trust yourself and your intuition.

Here are three powerful keys I share in my coaching programs and speaking events.

KEY 1: SELF-AWARENESS AND MINDFULNESS

The quest for balance and fulfillment is underpinned by a powerful and transformative force: self-awareness. It is the cornerstone upon which the edifice of your personal growth and contentment is built. In the intricate tapestry of existence, understanding oneself is akin to weaving together the threads of thoughts, emotions, and motivations.

As you embark on your journey of self-awareness, discover and explore empowering and illuminated paths toward a more profound, purposeful life.

Mindfulness: The Art of Being Fully Present In Each Moment

Imagine a state of being where you are fully present in the current moment, where your thoughts, emotions, and sensory experiences converge harmoniously. This state of blissful mindfulness is an art worth cultivating in the pursuit of self-awareness. By embracing the "now" with open arms, you are encouraging yourself to transcend the constraints of time.

Mindfulness meditation is the vanguard of this art, the practice that guides you to this serene and insightful state. At its core, mindfulness meditation beckons you to engage with the present moment, to tune in to the symphony of your thoughts and emotions. By focusing your awareness on the here and now, you become the observer of your own mental landscape, your inner world.

In this profound practice, judgment is cast aside, and acceptance takes the helm. You learn to witness your thoughts and emotions without criticism, to observe them as they ebb and flow like the gentle tides. This non-judgmental stance creates an atmosphere of inner freedom, where self-compassion and understanding can flourish. Your breath becomes your anchor. The rise and fall of each breath are your guides into the present.

By merely observing these thoughts without attachment or judgment, you unveil the inner workings of your mind. Your emotions, too, become visible, like ripples on the surface of a pond. They flow, and they recede, and you come to understand their patterns.

In this practice, you have initiated a conscious examination of your thoughts, emotions, and behavioral patterns. With each mindful breath, you inch closer to self-awareness. You become attuned to the intricacies of your consciousness, cultivating a profound understanding of your inner world.

By practicing mindfulness, you can transform ordinary activities into opportunities for spiritual growth and self-discovery. Even simple, everyday tasks can become avenues for soulful connection.

Journaling: The Art of Self-Dialogue for Self-Awareness

Alongside the art of mindfulness, journaling stands as a tangible avenue for exploring the depths of your inner world. The act of writing becomes a bridge between your conscious mind and the whirlpool of thoughts and emotions that reside within. As you put pen to paper, you embark on a journey of self-exploration, externalizing your inner world to scrutinize it with unparalleled clarity.

Journaling is a creative and introspective practice that offers a safe and confidential space for your innermost thoughts and feelings. It becomes a canvas upon which you can paint the tapestry of your inner world. Through this practice, you enter into a dialogue with yourself, seeking to understand the intricate dynamics of your consciousness.

Imagine a journal, its pages blank and inviting, awaiting the tales of your mind and heart. You begin to write, and as the ink flows, so do the currents of your thoughts. You are the author of your narrative, both the protagonist and the observer.

Through the act of journaling, you externalize your thoughts, granting them physical presence on the page. This act of externalization holds the power to liberate and enlighten. It grants you a newfound perspective on your thoughts and feelings, allowing you to examine them from a distance. What once seemed an indomitable storm of emotions becomes a comprehensible constellation of thoughts.

Your journal becomes a confidant, a repository of your innermost musings. It is a witness to your journey, a non-judgmental listener to your trials and triumphs. As you document your experiences and emotions, patterns begin to emerge. You become more attuned to the recurrent themes in your life, the recurring thoughts that inhabit your mind, and the underlying emotions that color your experiences.

This reflective practice becomes a channel for deeper self-discovery, unveiling the layers of your consciousness one page at a time. By reviewing your past entries, you can witness your growth and transformation, track your progress, and gain insight into the subtleties of your own evolution.

The Placebo Effect: The Power of Thought

The mind-body connection has been extensively explored by experts in psychology, neuroscience, medicine, and alternative therapies. Our immune system is closely tied to our emotional well-being, with optimism and joy strengthening it against infections, while depression and anxiety weaken it.

Evidence regarding the placebo effect demonstrates how our beliefs and expectations can influence our physical responses. For instance, perceiving a sugar pill as a painkiller can actually reduce our pain, underscoring the power of our thoughts in shaping physical sensations.

The endocrine system, influenced by emotions, releases hormones like adrenaline and cortisol during fear and excitement, and melatonin during relaxation, impacting heart rate and alertness. This interplay highlights the profound connection between our thoughts and physical state.

The Energy Codes: Our Blueprint for Life

While studying for *The Energy Codes Certification*, I became fascinated by the inner workings of our body's dynamic systems that shape our everyday lives. Helping my clients gain insight and learn tools for their own self-mastery fills me with joy.

The Electromagnetic Energy System is a complex interplay of frequencies within the Spiritual, Mental, Emotional/Feeling, Etheric, and Physical Bodies. Holding the blueprint for our innate intelligence, this system guides our growth from embryo to ongoing healing throughout our lives.

The connective experience between the Electromagnetic Energy System and the Central Nervous System (which is divided into the Conscious, Subconscious, and Enteric Subtle Systems), enables us to uncover our authentic nature, gain control over our lives, promote self-healing, and heighten our intuitive "sixth sense."

By harnessing this synergy, we can enhance well-being, health, and happiness through simple and enjoyable techniques.

KEY 2: HEALTHY HABITS FOR PHYSICAL WELL-BEING

Our bodies, the vessels for our minds and souls, demand our nurturing and reverence—a profound obligation. The intricate connection between physical well-being and mental health forms the melody of our lives. Here, in the realm of healthy habits and physical well-being, we find the foundation for vitality, resilience, and inner equilibrium.

Exercise: The Path to Flourishing

Exercise, a true elixir for body and mind, stands as the cornerstone of physical well-being, offering benefits far beyond the gym or yoga mat. Engaging in physical activity releases endorphins, our body's "feel-good" hormones, combating stress and depression. It paints the mind with positivity, making life's burdens seem more manageable.

Exercise forges self-esteem and body image in the craft of transformation. Witnessing your body's growth in strength and endurance elevates self-esteem. Choices in exercise are as diverse as colors in the spectrum, so there will always be something you can choose that inspires and motivates you to continue.

Diet: Nourishing Body and Mind

Diet, equally pivotal, transcends nourishment to become an act of self-care. A balanced diet provides energy and essential nutrients. Whole foods, abundant in vitamins, minerals, and antioxidants, nourish not only the body but the mind. They compose a melodic harmony underpinning cognitive function, emotional balance, and vitality.

Picture a plate adorned with vibrant fruits and vegetables, a bountiful harvest tantalizing the senses and enriching the mind. These nutrients nourish the body and mind, fostering clarity, equilibrium, and resilience. Each bite honors the intricate connection between physical well-being and mental health.

The Sanctity of Sleep: Vital Restoration

Sleep, a vital component, is the sanctuary where the body mends and rejuvenates, thoughts find order, memories consolidate, and emotions find solace and reconcile. The quantity and quality of sleep sculpt mental clarity and emotional stability. Consistent sleep schedules, calming bedtime routines, and conducive sleeping environments are the elements of rejuvenating rest. They establish rhythms, signal transitions, and create havens of tranquility.

Living Spaces and Workspaces: The Canvas of Well-being

In the realm of physical well-being, our living spaces and workspaces are integral components of our environment. The way we design, organize, and inhabit these spaces significantly influences our well-being.

Picture, for a moment, a cluttered and disorganized living space, where the chaos of daily life seems to reign supreme. In such an environment, stress takes root, productivity wanes, and feelings of overwhelm abound. It is as if the discord of the outer world has found a reflection in the inner world.

In stark contrast, imagine a living space that is clean, organized, and thoughtfully designed. Becoming a sanctuary for focus, creativity, and emotional well-being, your harmonious space becomes a tangible representation of the state of our inner world, a reflection of the equilibrium that resides within.

A Lifestyle Design Coach can be a valuable ally in this endeavor. As a guide who assists my clients in decluttering and optimizing their physical environments, my expertise in interior design principles offers insights that enhance the functionality and aesthetics of their spaces, as well as explore beneficial holistic interior design techniques.

By creating a harmonious environment, you not only boost your overall well-being but also foster a deeper connection to your future reality. Your living space becomes a reflection of your values, a sanctuary for your inner world, and a testament to your commitment to physical and mental well-being.

As you embark on this journey, may you cherish your body, honor your mind, and embrace the sanctuary of sleep. Transform your living spaces and workspaces into the sanctuaries that nurture your well-being. In this mosaic of well-being, you find a profound connection between your physical health and mental harmony, a connection that resonates with vitality and purpose.

KEY 3: MIND-BODY CONNECTION MODALITIES

The mind-body interconnection generates remarkable power, shaping our reality. Mindful breathing and other techniques such as yoga, Tai Chi, and dance help us unlock this connection, weaving a tapestry of holistic well-being. The key is for us to observe what is happening within our bodies: sensations, feelings, and emotions. Then we can learn to self-regulate and have more control over how we handle life's "lessons."

Mindful Breathwork: Bridge to Bliss

Breath becomes the bridge between the conscious mind and the body's responses. Breathing techniques soothe the nervous system, reduce stress, and evoke relaxation. The breath anchors awareness in the present moment, cultivating centeredness and balance. By focusing on controlled deep breathing, our nervous system slows down and we feel centered enough to see what small steps we can take to feel better. Breathwork is the first step my clients experience when they work with me, with immediate results.

Yoga: Ancient Anchor to Wellness

Yoga, an ancient practice, weaves physical postures (asanas), mindful breathing (pranayama), and meditation into a holistic symphony of wellness. In yoga, the body transforms into a sacred temple of self-compassion facilitating the practitioner to release tensions. This balanced connection between the conscious mind and the physical body calms the body and offers inner peace, delivering a sense of lightness and flexibility.

Tai Chi: Meditation In Motion

Tai Chi, a Chinese martial art, epitomizes serenity in the mind-body connection. Described as "meditation in motion," it harmonizes physical movement and mindfulness. Slow, flowing movements enhance coordination and grace, vanquishing stress.

Dance: Expressive Fusion of Synergy

Next, we'll explore how the holistic practice of dance can magnify the significance of the mind-body connection, offering a multitude of benefits. In the world of human expression, dance is a profound art form that harmonizes mind, body, and spirit in a beautiful synergy of motion. As a Lifestyle Design Coach, I show my clients how movement, especially dance, can profoundly impact every aspect of their lives.

Your mental health, memory, concentration, creativity, confidence, and happiness are all improved because of the reduction of negativity, both emotional and energetic. How can you feel sad when you're smiling and laughing?

I love witnessing how dance movements facilitate my clients' transformation. The flow of energy, both physical and emotional, improves muscle strength, function, and flexibility while you process and transmute emotions that keep you feeling "stuck." This also results in better strength and stability, while feeling the joy and tranquility you greatly deserve!

Dance is a potent catalyst for physical well-being. It transcends exercise, fortifying muscles, bones, and enhancing cardiovascular health. Research validates its benefits, including improved balance, especially for seniors, and enhanced motor control for those with conditions like Parkinson's disease.

Moreover, dance holds a therapeutic sway over mental health, relieving stress, anxiety, and depression by releasing mood-enhancing endorphins and regulating cortisol. It provides a means for emotional expression and trauma processing, fostering greater self-esteem and better body image. Dance ignites creativity and inspiration while sharpening problem-solving skills.

While boosting brain function, dance guards against cognitive decline and nurtures self-expression and self-discovery. As a social endeavor, dance elevates communication, cooperation, and empathy, enhancing interpersonal skills, emotional intelligence, and our appreciation of human expression.

The fusion of mind, body, and spirit in dance transforms us physically, mentally, emotionally, and socially. There are no rules or standards; we can dance anywhere, anytime, with anyone or alone, authentically, following our dreams.

There are many other modalities that foster this holistic integration of mind, body, and spirit. While I am not able to name them all here, I do want to mention Qi Gong, Aikido, Pilates, and the Feldenkrais Method. Even walking and running can be used as a form of meditation.

IN SUMMARY

Each hemisphere of the human brain possesses a unique language—the intuitive, artistic right, and the analytical, linguistic left. As the left eloquently articulates thoughts, the right paints a mental picture of our emotions and feelings, through nonverbal expressions like movement and other artistic outlets.

Creative activity acts as a bridge, facilitating a magical connection between these cerebral partners. When you immerse yourself in the artistic flow, you invite a harmonious collaboration. In my coaching programs and workshops, dance becomes the language that speaks to both hemispheres encouraging emotional richness seamlessly integrating with logical articulation.

Use creative projects and artistic endeavors to connect with the dreams you carry inside yourself, every waking moment. What makes you happy and lights you up inside? Allow these projects to reconnect you with your inner child and your true essence.

Envision the life you desire. Let that vision evoke emotions. What will it feel like when you have accomplished your goal? Hold on to those feelings and recall them when you doubt yourself. This will inspire you to make choices that elevate you to your next step.

When you cannot envision what you want, you are thrown into a state of reaction; of survival. This is when you need to stop everything, take a moment to just be very still, and calm yourself. Allow yourself to illuminate a path to a more profound, fulfilling existence where your conscious mind harmonizes with your soul's dynamics while boosting your self-esteem.

Embarking on the path to self-awareness is not a solitary journey. As a Lifestyle Design Coach, I offer support, dismantle limiting beliefs, and empower you to set clear intentions. By connecting with your inner self, you add depth and purpose to your journey, unlocking the door to a fulfilling, joyful life filled with abundance and love, intentionally designed by YOU!

Sally Katherine Ross

Lifestyle Design Coach, Sally Katherine Ross, is hired by event planners and women in midlife committed to exploring innovative strategies that empower women and promote self-actualization. Learning self-mastery, they reclaim control over their lives. By rediscovering their true identity, they witness their own capabilities, imagination, and creativity.

Motivated by her own transformational journey, Sally is an expert in the "school of hard knocks" with women in midlife turning to her for guidance in building self-esteem, gaining courage, and trusting their inner voice and creative self-expression. They are committed to investing in their present and future happiness and a life full of freedom, abundance, and authenticity.

Using timeless and proven healing modalities, her holistic and transformational coaching empowers women to feel more self-sufficient. Gaining inner strength and confidence, they redesign their personal image and manifest a future they desire:

- Remove emotional blocks and gain self-esteem

- Learn to love every aspect of yourself

- Design a bold new persona

- Challenge yourself to overcome fears

- Feel confident to make choices reflecting a future of your own design

Sharing decades of insight and inspiration from her own challenges and victories, Sally instantly connects with clients with her motivational and innovative style. Sally believes that when women feel empowered, they take action to uplevel their lives; they become unstoppable. Their lives become unforgettable.

Connect with Sally at https://redesignyourideallife.com.

CHAPTER 14

Breath, Boundaries and Breaking Through BS

by Shanna Lee Moore

Greetings beautiful soul! Today I am going to share three keys to unlock your full potential. My expectation is that you can take away these tips and implement them to guide you on your path to growth and self-discovery. This is just a sample of some of the recommendations I share with my clients to create a unique plan tailored to their individual desires. Out of the box thinking can create extraordinary results. Once your mind is open and you have clarity on the direction you wish to travel, then everything you need will flow to you. In this chapter we will cover Breath, Boundaries and Breaking through BS!

When I heard the title of this book was the Mind-Body Connection, I just knew I had to contribute. I was reminded of all the things I've learned in the last 11 years! I am also pretty certain that my journey began much prior to that on a subconscious level. I used to think that the saying "Knowledge is Power" was important and it set me out on this path of growth and self-realization. Now I innerstand that it is only when the knowledge is APPLIED that one can truly benefit. As a young child, my imagination was strong. I would dream of great things, communicate with animals and spend my time drawing treehouse floor plans. I even tried to adopt a horse around age seven. It's really fun to think back and view the world through a child's eyes. I even had a film canister of fairy dust from Tinkerbell! That childlike wonder is so valuable to us. The power of imagination and dreams are what separate humans from the rest of the animal species. Unfortunately or not, wink wink, some unhelpful paradigms were also part of my youth. My intention here is not to focus on all of the events or trauma throughout my years. On the contrary, I do wish to take the lessons I learned and share some techniques that may assist you in working through anything that you are ready to let go of and show the possibility of unlocking your full potential.

Breath: The Power Within

One of the most helpful things to bring in to our awareness is our breath. When I am in a meditative state, practicing Qi Gong or simply enjoying my present moment, I am able to drop down into my body and quiet the analytical, overthinker between my ears. When I was in school for massage therapy I remember one of my classmates telling me I was holding my breath as the trigger points in the muscles were being worked on. To get them to release, we actually have to breathe THROUGH the pain. What I notice now in sharing this story is that my pattern of holding on to my breath started with some of those previous "undesirable" situations in my life. Without the breath, I was detached from my body. It is a coping mechanism that I have been able to replace with breath work and it has helped me tremendously in getting out of the trauma responses.

Boundaries: Authenticity Unleashed

Another one of the recent wins in my life, and the second key I'll share with you, is that I've created healthier boundaries and have broken the people-pleasing patterns I used for so long. After many of my intuitive gifts were either discouraged or made fun of, I stopped developing and utilizing them. I became somewhat of a chameleon blending into whatever group I was around that day. I forgot about my true nature and purpose, the things that made me unique and special, the reasons I came to experience this life.

What I discovered is that trying to be everything to everyone got me nowhere, except TIRED. Maybe you can relate? Even when I first started growing my business, I thought if I copied my mentors I could duplicate the success they had. Now I realize that mentors and coaches are great resources to cut down the time and learning curves, AND that my audience needs me! They need my authenticity and that's what will allow us to connect with each other.

Have you heard the saying, "You can't say the wrong thing to the right person or the right thing to the wrong person"? One of my favorite things is getting to share all the great wisdom I've learned and have uplifting conversations with people who are ready for more in their lives. When we find ourselves at a crossroad or a decision to take a less traveled path, it is pertinent to seek counsel and not just opinions. Most people share experiences from their perspective and the stage of life that they've reached. Counsel comes from someone who has achieved what we would like to accomplish. I do believe we can learn things from everyone we interact with. I just wouldn't ask a dog how to drive a car. Additionally, no one will KNOW you as well as you know yourself. So being able to honor those "gut feelings" and having trust in yourself will be your guide.

I have had many lessons where I got a clear answer and then chose to negotiate with myself to accommodate others. That left me feeling drained or depleted. The great thing about being human is we get to learn the lesson as many times as it takes. I have now made the conscious decision that following my heart and intuition will lead me on the path I need to be. Even if I end up having a detour or three, the perspective I can get from the journey is going to be 10 times more beneficial than letting fear keep me stuck in an old, familiar comfort zone.

Breaking Through BS: Reshaping Belief Systems

This life has given me many opportunities to reinvent myself. From having such strong convictions of what my life would look like as a child, to being blessed to experience an entirely different path and everything that happened in between, I wouldn't change any of it. Every experience has led me to where I am today. For every "Yes," there was a "No." When I wasn't being true to myself, my mind would be uneasy. The body had visceral reactions and typically a less than desirable outcome would manifest. When I got the clarity I asked for and took steps in that direction, I felt peace. This is another mind-body connection.

Whatever is going on within us will present itself externally, just like what we focus on will expand. Our self-talk and what we allow into our minds definitely has an impact on the reality we experience. Our beliefs about ourselves and the world around us and our willingness to be creative and take action steps towards our goals is what allows them to come true. As a single mother, I wanted to provide a better life for my oldest child, so I went back to school to become a massage therapist. I always had the gift or intuition to find pain points and relieve them in others. Now I had the training to be a professional. I learned all about the body systems and muscles and I even passed the National Exam on the first attempt! All of my sessions are still customized to my clients using the intuition I've always had.

When I wanted to uplevel again and now had two children to consider, I met my first mentor. I learned about the difference between linear and leverage income. I wanted to work with more people and not be limited to only my local service area for massage clients. I wanted true FREEDOM! I decided to partner with an established global company that shared my vision for empowering others to succeed. I started working on overcoming my limiting beliefs and stepping back into my greatest self. For each new stage of life, I get to let go of the things that will not serve the next version of me. I have gratitude for each Shanna that came before and I am thankful for all the progress I've made. When a snake grows, it sheds its skin and as I grow I get to shed parts of me that are no longer needed. At first the changes were scary. The caterpillar thinks that life is over right before it becomes a butterfly. Even a crab must feel vulnerable when it needs to leave its old shell and find a new one. That doesn't stop either of them from growing. Tuning in to the natural rhythms around us is a great guide. When I go out in nature and really see what's around, I can get many of the answers I seek. Sunshine and fresh air feel so good on my body and are a great way to clear the mind.

Most of the stories I told myself were completely untrue. They were limiting and kept me in the vibration to attract more of the familiarity. I accepted others' opinions of me as truth and let my self-doubt and fear run the show. Being open to expanding my mind and learning from other people who are doing great things has been the biggest blessing in my life. We don't know what we don't know, until we learn it.

I am proud of you for picking up this book. It shows you're ready for an expansion. I hope you found these tips to be helpful in the next stage of your journey. There is a great transition happening collectively right now. Those of us who are aware and willing to be mindful of our thoughts and actions during this time are going to create an amazing new world together. I love the communities I've built and the relationships I've developed recently. Synergy is truly magical. Feel free to reach out to me with any questions or if you'd like to redeem your free discovery call to unveil the next steps that may be most beneficial to your realization of unlocking your full potential.

One of my many gifts is communicating through poetry, so I always include a piece in my chapters. This was written just for this book. Enjoy!

The limitations we have are mostly made up,
They come from within our mind.
The answers we seek are here to be found,
It only takes some dedication and time.

Time is subjective and doesn't need to be long,
Everything is already accessible.
The keys to unlocking our full potential are near,
And when we finally see them it is very magical.

The internal sight, the knowing and confirmation,
All the answers we can FEEL.
Must not be ignored, pushed down or discredited,
They really are a big deal.

You are an amazing creation,
A true gift from above.
The answer to prayers,
Sent down to embody light and love.

If you ever forget how special you are,
Take a long look in the mirror and see.
See your true essence and power within,
All the unique things that you BE.

Being is the most powerful state,
The presence in the moment of Now.
It took me a while to come back to this place,
Sometimes I'm still remembering how.

How it feels to be authentic and true,
The power within is not found in what we can do.

The breath, boundaries and breaking through,
They are just a few techniques I share.
Breath and presence are the ones I use,
To help me be more aware.

Boundaries expressed in love,
Allow me to be more clear.
I cannot control how others receive them,
And I no longer live in fear.

No fear of judgment,
Or of being misunderstood.
This is a gift I would give you,
If only I could.

Fear is made up,
From old stories I told myself.
They kept me in a comfort zone,
Unable to experience true wealth.

Wealth has more value,
Than just money and things.
It's the joy in my heart,
Felt when it sings.

Singing songs of harmony and internal peace,
The melody coming through quite loud.

All the progress I've made tuning in and reprogramming,
I can actually now feel proud.

Not the pride of the ego,
Or one that seeks to put down others.
It is kind and loving,
Like when it comes from our mothers.

The BS is gone,
Here comes the sun.
Now we're stepping into our greatness,
It can really be quite fun!

So go grab a friend,
Come out to dance and play.
If you aren't sure where to start,
I am happy to guide you along the way.

The answers you seek are seeking you too,
Pay attention to the signs and wonders.
Experience life and all it can offer,
There are only lessons to learn from, not blunders.

Find clarity in your dreams and desires,
They are uniquely yours.
Say "yes" often to things that spark joy,
That joy will open many doors.

Action taken to walk along the new path,
Keeping your sights on what comes up ahead.
No need to look back or stay stuck in the past,
When I used to do that I could experience dread.

Now life is beautiful,
As it unfolds day to day.

Expressing my gratitude to those ahead of my journey,
As their wisdom has helped guide my way.

All the love in my heart coming out,
Being shared through words in this book.
All the personal growth I've had,
Searching inside and taking a look.

Looking at patterns I wish to change,
Letting go of what no longer serves me.
Now I have found my authentic self,
This is the real Shanna Lee.

My hope for you is strength to find your true calling,
May your greatest dreams manifest.
Thank you for taking the time to read this,
I wish you all the best!

Shanna Lee Moore

Shanna Lee Moore is a dynamic entrepreneur, astute business owner, and a remarkable four-time award-winning, #1 international best-selling author. With a career spanning over a decade as a licensed massage therapist since 2007 and a dedicated advocate for the remarkable benefits of electrolyzed, reduced water since 2012, Shanna has consistently demonstrated her commitment to holistic well-being and innovation.

In the wake of the unprecedented challenges posed by the global shutdown in 2020, Shanna pivoted her focus towards nurturing a thriving community and emerged as a sought-after speaker at virtual events. Her adaptability and resilience underscore her ability to rise above adversity and inspire others to do the same.

At the core of Shanna's mission is her unwavering passion for empowering individuals to manifest the lives they've always envisioned. She specializes in offering ingenious solutions and out-of-the-box strategies to help individuals harmonize the demands of their families and businesses, fostering a sense of equilibrium and achievement.

Shanna thrives on connecting with motivated and passionate individuals, fostering meaningful relationships that transcend physical boundaries. Whether face-to-face or in the virtual realm, she welcomes the opportunity to connect with like-minded individuals who share her drive and determination.

To engage with Shanna and unlock the potential for a transformative journey, schedule a 30-minute consultation with her via this link: https://calendly.com/shannaleemoore/30min. Your path to realizing your aspirations begins here.

AFTERWORD

As you finish reading "*The Mind-Body Connection: The Keys to Unlocking Your Full Potential*," it's important to remember that this is not the end, but rather a beginning. A beginning of a journey that you are about to embark upon. The insights and experiences shared in this book are not just stories and lessons, but beacons of light guiding you towards your own path of self-discovery and personal growth.

You have journeyed through the depths of mind and body, exploring the intricacies of their profound connection. You've been privy to personal anecdotes, professional insights, and transformative strategies. Now, it's time to reflect on how these elements resonate with your own life.

Your life is a unique narrative, filled with its own challenges, triumphs, and revelations. The wisdom you've gathered from this book can be the catalyst for your own story of transformation and empowerment. Just as each author in this book has shared their journey, you too have the opportunity to share yours.

Writing your own book can be a powerful tool for self-expression and healing. It's an opportunity to document your journey, to give voice to your experiences, and to inspire others who may be walking a similar path. Your story is important. It's a testament to your resilience, your growth, and your journey towards unlocking your full potential.

If you feel inspired to write your own book, here are some steps to guide you on this exciting journey:

Reflect on Your Journey: Think about the key moments in your life that have shaped who you are. Reflect on the challenges you've faced, the lessons you've learned, and the growth you've experienced.

Find Your Unique Voice: Your voice is your power. It's what sets your story apart. Write authentically, in a way that truly represents who you are.

Outline Your Story: Start with a simple outline of what you want to share. It doesn't have to be linear or chronological; it just needs to flow from your heart.

Write Regularly: Set aside time each day or each week to write. Consistency is key in bringing your book to life.

Be Vulnerable: Don't be afraid to show vulnerability in your writing. It's your honesty and openness that will resonate with your readers. Vulnerability is actually our greatest strength as human beings. The more vulnerable you are, the more you encourage others to be vulnerable.

Seek Feedback: Share your work with trusted friends or colleagues. Constructive feedback can be invaluable in shaping your narrative.

Edit and Revise: Writing is a process. Be prepared to edit and revise until your story feels right. But don't wait too long or you'll need to start over again.

Publish Your Story: Research the best way to publish your book, whether it's through traditional publishing, self-publishing, or an eBook. 24% of the world's population ever writes a book; but only 3% ever publish it. Become part of the 3%.

Share Your Journey: Once published, share your book with the world. Your story could be exactly what someone else needs to hear during their journey to self-discovery.

Remember, writing your own book is not just about telling your story; it's about embracing your journey and recognizing your growth. It's a celebration of the person you have become and an inspiration to those who will read your words.

As you close this book and ponder the idea of writing your own, remember that your message gives hope and inspiration to others. Your experiences, wisdom, and journey are valuable, and they deserve to be shared.

May your journey ahead be filled with growth, self-discovery, and the joy of sharing your story with the world. Here's to writing the next chapter of your life, one filled with endless possibilities and the fulfillment of your highest potential.

Dear Reader,

As you turn this final page, you might find yourself reflecting on the journey you've just experienced through these words. Each story you read is a tapestry of dreams, struggles, triumphs, and the relentless spirit of its creator. Now, imagine a world where your story joins these ranks – where your voice, your experiences, and your unique perspective are shared and celebrated.

This is not just an invitation; it's a call to action from Action Takers Publishing. We believe in the power of stories to transform, inspire, and connect humankind. More importantly, we believe in your story and its potential to make a significant impact on the world.

Why wait for "someday" to tell your story? The time is now, and the world is ready to listen. You never know who your story will impact until you start sharing it. There's no time like the present. It's called the "present" for a reason, it's a gift to be shared. Whether it's a tale of adventure, a deeply personal memoir, a groundbreaking idea, or a story that has been quietly growing in your heart, it deserves to be told.

At Action Takers Publishing, led by our Founder & CEO, Lynda Sunshine West, we specialize in turning visions into reality. We understand the journey of transforming a personal narrative into a published book – it's a journey of courage, creativity, and breaking through fears. Our team is dedicated to guiding you through every step of this exhilarating process, from the initial draft to the moment your book is held in the hands of eager readers across the globe.

Join our vibrant community of authors, a diverse group of storytellers who have dared to make their voices heard. With us, you'll find more than just a publisher; you'll discover a supportive network of mentors, editors, and fellow authors who are all committed to the success of your story.

Take the leap. Embrace the thrill of seeing your name on the cover of your very own book. Contact us at Action Takers Publishing, and let's embark on this remarkable journey together. Your story matters, and the time to share it with the world is now.

Nothing Happens Without Action.

Lynda Sunshine West
Founder & CEO
Action Takers Publishing
www.ActionTakersPublishing.com

p.s. Remember, every great story begins with a simple decision to start writing. Yours is no different. Let's make it happen, together.

READER BONUS!

As a thank you for your support, Action Takers Publishing would like to offer you a special reader bonus: a free download of our course, "How to Write, Publish, Market & Monetize Your Book the Fast, Fun & Easy Way." This comprehensive course is designed to provide you with the tools and knowledge you need to bring your book to life and turn it into a successful venture.

The course typically **retails for $499**, but as a valued reader, you can access it for free. To claim your free download, simply follow this link ActionTakersPublishing. com/workshops - use the discount code "coursefree" to get a 100% discount and start writing your book today.

If we are still giving away this course by the time you're reading this book, head straight over to your computer and start the course now. It's absolutely free.

READER BONUS!

ActionTakersPublishing.com/workshops
discount code "coursefree"

So nature did what it always does. It specialized.

It didn't just create different personalities.

It created two different operating systems.

The Six Professions

Right before the end of the day—just as we started to gather in larger groups—the roles hardened.

The survival of the group depended on this specialization. Out of that necessity, the Six Primal Professions were born.

Three for the Runner.

Three for the Recorder.

THE RUNNER (The Social Engine)

Nature built a mind designed for Speed. This mind learns by navigation. It scans. It adapts. It moves.

1. *The Leader* (Warrior)

The visionary who could stand in front of a starving tribe and convince them to keep walking. They didn't use data; they used hope. They didn't see the cliff; they saw the horizon.

2. *The Connector* (Gatherer)

The one who could walk into a foreign village and trade without getting killed. They knew that the "deal" was more important than the "fact." They greased the wheels of civilization.

3. *The Healer*

The one who managed the emotional temperature of the group. They prioritized feelings because feelings determine whether the tribe sticks together. They kept the peace.

THE RECORDER (The Structural Engine)

Nature built a mind designed for Fidelity. This mind learns by accumulation. It catalogs. It stores. It asks: Is this true? Is it safe? Will it hold?

4. The Sentry (Enforcer)

The one who sits by the fire facing the dark. They do not sleep. They listen for the threat. Their "anxiety" is not a disorder; it is the tribe's alarm system. They hear the twig snap before the wolf appears.

5. The Builder

The one who stacked the stones for the aqueduct. You cannot charm a stone into holding water. You must understand the physics. This required a mind capable of hyper-focus—shutting out the world to chip a flint to a millimeter tolerance.

6. The Scribe

The one who held the data. If the grain count was wrong, the village starved. The Scribe's job wasn't to be liked. It was to be right. They were the keepers of the code.

The Covenant

For thousands of years—for most of that "second and a half"—this was a partnership that bonded us together.

The Runner handled the software (culture).

The Recorder handled the hardware (reality).

Civilization did not begin when we built a wall.

Civilization began when the Runner Brain and the Recorder Brain agreed to cover each other's blind spots.

The friction between them was managed because both were necessary.

When the Runner was ignored, the tribe tore itself apart.

When the Recorder was ignored, the roof fell in.

But then... the clock struck Midnight.

7

THE TWO DESIGNS: THE PARALLEL AND THE BINARY
Imagine two photographers standing on the edge of a cliff.

One has a Wide-Angle Lens.

He captures the sunset, the horizon, the curve of the coastline, and the colors of the sky. His picture is vast and beautiful.

But if you zoom in, the details are blurry.

The other has a Macro Lens.

He is looking at the same cliff, but he captures the vein on a single leaf, the fracture in the granite, the specific species of the beetle crawling on the rock. His picture is incredibly sharp.

But he misses the sunset entirely.

Now, ask yourself:

Which camera is the "correct" one?

It's a trick question.

Neither is correct. They simply have different focal lengths for different jobs.

But in the human world, we have forgotten this.

We have spent decades trying to force every human mind onto a single bell curve. We act as if "intelligence" is one single ladder, and everyone is just climbing the same rungs at different speeds.

We decided that the Wide-Angle Lens (Social/Generalist) is "Normal."

And we decided the Macro Lens (Detail/Specialist) is "Disordered."

History and biology tell a different story.

They show us that humanity runs on two distinct operating systems. These systems process information differently, prioritize different inputs, and perceive reality in fundamentally opposing ways.

I call them the Parallel Mind Inside (PMI)TM and the Binary Mind Inside (BMI)TM.

The world knows them as the Runner and the Recorder.

1. **THE RUNNER** (The Parallel Mind)

The Engine of Motion

Roughly 70–80% of the population operates on this architecture.

The Runner's brain is designed for Broadband Processing.

The Wiring

Neuroscience shows that typical brains rely heavily on "long-range connectivity."

This means the front of the brain communicates rapidly with the back, and the left communicates constantly with the right. It is a mesh network.

The Function

This wiring creates a mind that sees the Whole, not the Part.

When a Runner walks into a room, they sense the "vibe." They process the lighting, the mood, the social tension, and the conversation all at once as a single fuzzy picture.

They prioritize Context.

They understand that "I hate you" said with a smile means "I love you."

They operate on Probability.

They don't need 100% of the data to make a decision. They get 60% of the data, guess the rest, and move.

The Historical Role: The Orator

Think of the Roman Senator Cicero or the tribal chieftain.

Their power came from their ability to read the crowd in real-time. They didn't need to be technically perfect; they needed to be emotionally resonant.

The Runner keeps the tribe moving. They smooth over conflict. They "grease the gears" of society with white lies and social niceties.

Without them, civilization would grind to a halt because everyone would be arguing over facts instead of building relationships.

2. **THE RECORDER** (The Binary Mind)

The Engine of Truth

Roughly 20–30% of the population operates on this architecture.

The Recorder's brain is designed for Deep-band Processing.

The Wiring

Research into the brains of autistic individuals reveals a different architecture: Local Hyper-Connectivity.

Instead of sending weak signals across the whole brain, the Recorder's brain builds massive, super-fast highways between specific local regions (like the visual cortex or the logic centers).

The Function

This wiring creates a mind that sees the Part, not the Whole.

When a Recorder walks into a room, they don't see a "vibe."

They see a crooked picture frame. They see the flickering lightbulb (60Hz cycle). They hear the air conditioner hum. And they notice a person whose tone doesn't match their facial expression.

They prioritize Content.

"I hate you" means "I hate you." The smile is just contradictory noise.

They operate on Certainty.

They cannot move on 60% data. They need to verify the facts until the error rate is zero.

The Historical Role: The Navigator

Think of the Polynesian wave finders or the astronomers of Babylon.

A Runner looks at the ocean and sees "water."

A Recorder looks at the ocean and sees the interference pattern of waves reflecting off an island 100 miles away.

The Recorder keeps the tribe safe. They don't care about the "mood" of the ocean; they care about the physics of the ocean.

If the Navigator gets the angle wrong by one degree, the tribe drowns.

3. HISTORY AS A DIALOGUE

If you look at the timeline of human progress, you don't see a single type of mind evolving.

You see a tennis match between the Runner and the Recorder.

The Oral to Written Transition (Runner → Recorder)

For thousands of years, history was Oral (Runner). It was stories, myths, and legends passed around the fire. It was fluid. The story changed every time it was told to fit the audience. Truth was flexible.

Then, Recorders invented Writing.

Writing is binary. Once it is carved in stone, it does not change. A law written down is a law that applies to everyone, even if the King is having a bad day. Civilization exploded only when the Recorder's need for "Fixed Truth" met the Runner's need for "Social Story."

The Age of Exploration (Runner Ambition + Recorder Tech)

Christopher Columbus (likely a Runner) had the vision, the charisma, and the delusional confidence to sail across the Atlantic. He sold the dream to the Queen.

But he would have died in a circle without the Astrolabe and the Compass.

These tools were not built by dreamers. They were built by Recorders who understood the stars with mathematical precision.

The Runner provided the Why.

The Recorder provided the How.

The Industrial Revolution (The Recorder's Rise)

For most of history, the Runner ruled because the world was agricultural and social.

But the Industrial Revolution shifted power to the Recorder. Steam engines do not run on charisma. Electricity does not care about your social status.

Suddenly, the mind that could focus deeply, calculate thermodynamics, and standardize parts became the most valuable mind on earth.

The modern world—the world of screens, data, and engineering—is a world built by Recorders, even if it is still managed by Runners.

4. THE FRICTION POINT

Why do we have conflict?

Because these two designs speak different languages.

The Runner speaks "Analog."

It flows. It approximates. It values harmony over accuracy.

Motto: "Go along to get along."

The Recorder speaks "Digital."

It steps. It defines. It values accuracy over harmony.

Motto: "Truth is the only safety."

The Runner thinks the Recorder is "difficult" because the Recorder won't just agree to a half-truth to be nice.

The Recorder thinks the Runner is "dishonest" because the Runner changes their opinion based on who is in the room.

Neither is wrong. They are just executing different code.

The Tragedy of Diagnosis

The problem with our current view of neurodivergence is that we judge the Recorder by the standards of the Runner.

We say: "You are bad at 'Big Picture' thinking."

The Recorder says: "I am not trying to see the Big Picture. I am checking the structural integrity of the foundation so the Big Picture doesn't collapse."

When we understand that these are Two Designs—not one Normal and one Broken—we stop trying to "cure" the Recorder.

We start realizing that without the Recorder, the Runner is just wandering in circles, telling great stories, but never actually getting anywhere.

The Runner provides the Motion.

The Recorder provides the Map.

You cannot survive the journey without both.

5. THE INEVITABILITY

Let's perform a thought experiment.

Imagine that tomorrow, a catastrophic event hits the planet. A flood, an asteroid, a solar flare—pick your disaster.

Modern technology is wiped out. The internet is gone. Governments dissolve. The grid goes dark. The slate is wiped clean.

Survivors scatter into small groups. They have no manuals, no Wikipedia, and no laws. They have to start over from zero.

If you came back to visit those groups 1,000 years later, what would you find?

You would not find a random assortment of jobs.

You would find that every single successful tribe had re-created the exact same structure we have today.

They would have someone tracking the food supply with absolute precision (The Numbers Person).

They would have someone negotiating peace with the neighboring tribe (The Connector).

They would have someone building weapons that fly straight (The Creator).

They would have someone enforcing the new rules without favoritism (The Enforcer).

This would not happen because they read it in a book.

It would happen because survival is a specific engineering problem.

And to solve that problem, the human species produces two specific types of minds to do the work.

6. THE PHYSICAL ECHO: LEFT-HANDED VARIANCE

If you still doubt that nature intentionally designs "Minority Variants" for the protection of the species, just look at your hands.

For centuries, left-handedness was treated exactly like the Binary Mind is treated today: as a defect to be corrected.

The Latin word for "Left" is Sinister. The word for "Right" is Dexter.

Schools used to tie the left hands of children behind their backs to force them to write with their right.

They believed that unity required uniformity. They thought a left-handed child was "broken."

They were wrong.

Nature has maintained left-handedness at roughly 10% of the population for thousands of years. It refuses to breed it out.

Why?

The Combat Advantage.

In a tribe where everyone is right-handed, the angles of attack are predictable. The shield is always on the left; the spear is always on the right.

But the Left-Hander breaks the pattern. The enemy doesn't know how to block them. The angles are reversed.

The "Surprise" factor wins the fight.

It is no accident that studies show a significantly higher rate of left-handedness in the autism and high-IQ communities.

The Left Hand is controlled by the Right Brain—the hemisphere responsible for spatial scanning, pattern recognition, and "Sentry" awareness.

History tried to crush the Left-Hander because they didn't fit the desk.

History is trying to crush the Binary Mind because we don't fit the social script.

But nature keeps making us.

Because a tribe without the variant is a tribe that gets conquered.

THE HARDWARE REALITY: TWO SEPARATE BRAINS

Let's be crystal clear about something before we move on.

When I talk about the Runner and the Recorder, I am not talking about your personality.

I am not talking about your "mood."

I am not talking about how you feel on a Tuesday versus how you feel on a Friday.

I am talking about two physically different types of brains.

There are two distinct architectures.

There are two distinct designs.

There are two separate ways to build a human mind.

Just like you have a physical dominant hand (Left or Right), you have a physical dominant brain.

Brain Type One (The Runner) is wired for Distance.

Brain Type Two (The Recorder) is wired for Density.

You are born with one of these two.

It is a binary reality.

It is not a choice.

It is Two. Separate. Brains. And, once you see it, you can't unsee it.

8

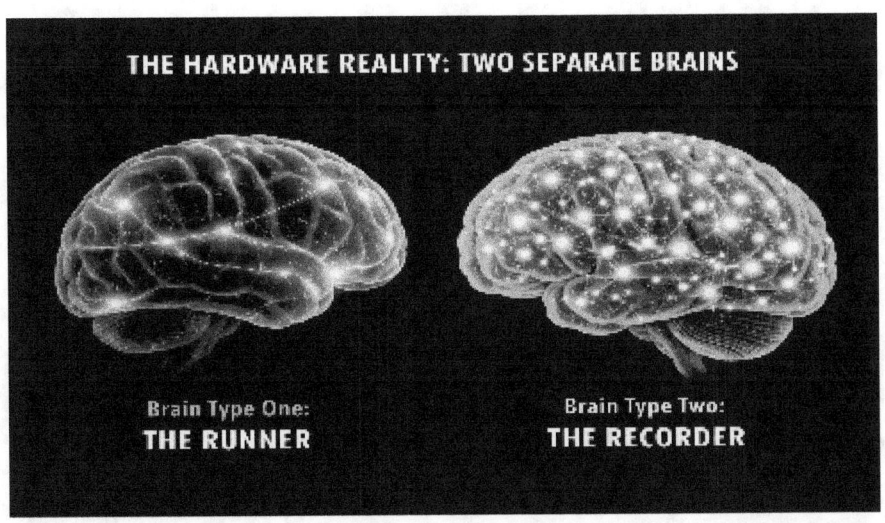

THE HARDWARE REALITY: TWO SEPARATE BRAINS

Brain Type One:
THE RUNNER

Brain Type Two:
THE RECORDER

B INARY-PARALLEL DUALITY™

9

The SKID:

The Anatomy of a Skid
To understand the Recorder, you must understand the Skid. It isn't a "bad mood" or a personality quirk; it is a mechanical event that occurs when a high-precision machine is forced out of alignment.

There are three ways to identify a Skid:

1. The Structural Protest: A Skid is the friction that occurs when your actions lose their alignment with your structural truth. It happens when you are in an "actionable mood"—actually doing something—but your internal architecture realizes the path is incorrect. It's the sound of the mind trying to course-correct while the body is still at full speed.

2. The Processing Gap: You cannot have a Skid while standing still. It requires movement. A Skid is the violent vibration of a Recorder mind that is being forced to act before it has finished processing the "1s and 0s" of the situation. You are acting, but you are out of alignment with the truth.

3. The Logic-Action Grind: Think of a Skid as a "Mechanical Protest." It's what happens when a Recorder is mid-action and realizes the sequence is flawed. Because the Recorder cannot "fake" the logic, the system begins to grind against itself until the truth is restored.

SKID

"In accounting, if the numbers don't balance, you've made an error. In golf, if your mind drifts for a split second, you lose the match. I call this the SKID. It's that moment where your hardware (The Recorder) and the world (The Runner) stop talking to each other, and you lose your grip on the truth. You start spinning, and the harder you try to 'think' your way out, the deeper the skid gets."

S — System

The biological "System" (The Recorder or The Runner) is being forced to operate outside of its design parameters. You are trying to run "Runner" software on "Recorder" hardware.

K — Kinetic

There is "Kinetic" friction. Instead of a smooth flow, the mind is dragging. This is the golf swing that feels forced, the diet that feels like a prison, or the conversation that feels like an argument. The energy isn't moving forward; it's burning up as heat (stress).

I — Interference

The "Interference" of the ego. The ego is trying to "think" its way through a problem that the subconscious should be "handling." This creates "noise" in the circuitry, leading to hesitation and doubt.

D — Disconnection

The final "Disconnection" between the Mind and the Machine. You lose the "Handshake." The body stops responding to the brain, the 3:00 PM crash hits, and you end up "on the other side of the hospital bed" because the machine has finally shut down to protect itself.

10

When you see a car skid on the road, it's because

The "Skid" Reality

THE OTHER THING

11

THE YEARS THE WORLD OPENED
   (The Education of a Recorder)

Theory is clean. Life is messy.

In the previous chapters, we looked at the clean lines of history and the precise wiring of the brain. We talked about "Recorders" and "Runners" as if they were clearly labeled parts in an engine.

But when you are a child, you don't see labels. You don't know about neuro-architecture. You don't know that 30% of the population is wired for structural truth while the other 70% is wired for social flow.

All you know is that you are watching a movie that everyone else seems to understand, but the audio is slightly out of sync for you.

You see things they ignore. You hear contradictions they miss. You feel the structure of the room while they are just feeling the vibe.

I want to take you back to where my own recording began—not to write a memoir, but to show you what this cognitive split looks like in the real world.

It doesn't start in a doctor's office. It starts at the kitchen table. It starts on the street corner.

It starts in the quiet moments where a young Binary Mind realizes, for the first time: I am seeing a different world.

1. THE LABORATORY OF EAST BOSTON

I was born into a world that was loud, chaotic, and structurally perfect for observing human behavior.

I was the youngest of seven kids in an Italian-Irish family in East Boston.

My Dad, Arthur W. Caggiano Sr., was the boss for the IRS in the district.

My Mom, Dorothy Thornton, held the pack: Arthur Jr., Paul, Mary, Ann Susan (past), Ann Marie, Karen with Kevin, then me.

Most children slowly develop a sense of identity over time. Mine was handed to me early—not because of anything I had done, but because of the badge my father carried.

Some lives move quietly. Others are lived out loud.

Mine began on the front page of the East Boston Times on March 6, 1957—my first "front-page selfie moment," faster than any Kardashian—not because I was trying, but because I was Arthur Caggiano's kid.

"Boss for the IRS" wasn't a small title. It wasn't a quiet job. In a neighborhood like East Boston in the 1950s, that position carried weight. It was a specific kind of power that doesn't exist anymore—a mix of respect, fear, and curiosity.

From the moment I was conscious, I was observing a master class in the Six Professions.

My father was a classic Enforcer (in the cognitive sense). He held the code.

He collected taxes door-to-door, which is a job that usually makes you a pariah. But he did it with a strange, binary fairness. He returned kindness to people who didn't have any left to give.

Every Thanksgiving, our hallway overflowed with frozen turkeys and gift baskets from families he had helped.

Why?

Because an Enforcer mind is not cruel; it is just.

A Runner in that job might have played favorites based on who they liked. My father played by a code of service. He never spoke about it. He just executed it.

As a child, I watched this. I sat under his desk or behind him while he worked with relatives, neighbors, and friends. I was absorbing the data.

Input: Dad is powerful.

Input: People are afraid of the IRS.

Observation: People love Dad.

Conclusion: Power requires a code to be safe.

My childhood was fantastic. Relatively speaking, I identified with Michael Corleone from The Godfather and John Kennedy Jr., because they were the young, spoiled, fun ones in the family. The Godfather world was easy to relate to; there were plenty of old-school Italians around where I was raised in East Boston.

My father was the youngest in his large family. Born on the kitchen table on Pine Street in the North End of Boston on March 10, 1908. He wore the full-length coat with the hat and the best suits.

My godfather was Lou Musco, a well-to-do man with a stellar reputation. He was going to help get me into the Naval Academy in Indianapolis when I graduated high school if I wanted to go.

I wasn't good enough in my mind for service. I joke now how I knew then I did not want to be in the Guinness Book for "Longest Head Shot by a Sniper" seeing as I have a size 8 head.

2. EARLY CONSCIOUSNESS: DATA FROM DAY ONE

The most direct, irrefutable proof of the Binary Mind Inside (BMI™) architecture is the capacity for extreme, detailed sequential recall, especially from very early moments in life.

This ability is a feature of the Recorder—the deep burning-in of data during initial processing. I am a spokesperson for binary people, and I must share these accomplishments and memories to show the world what the BMI™ mind is truly capable of.

The ability to recall moments before the age of four, or even the moment of birth, is often dismissed as impossible by conventional wisdom.

For the Recorder, these are simply data streams logged with clarity.

I recall recalling my birth.

I recall the day my father took me off his lap for the last time—I wasn't four yet—and the complex emotional data attached to that final moment of infancy.

The Glitch in the Matrix: The "Butterball" Moment

We often assume that autistic or binary children are "in their own world." That is false. We are hyper-present in your world—we are just seeing the cracks you paper over.

I remember the exact moment my Recorder mind came online and flagged an error.

My father used to call me "butterball." It was affectionate. It was a dad joke. To a Runner mind (a neurotypical observer), it was just a warm, fuzzy family moment.

But I was a Recorder. I was sitting on his lap, and he said, "Oh, he's just too big now." And I saw it.

A tiny flicker in his micro-expressions. A millisecond delay between the smile and the eyes. The tone didn't mathematically match the affection.

I remember freezing internally.

- Audio Data: "He is joking/loving."
- Visual Data: "He is uncomfortable/jealous/distant."
- Result: ERROR. CONTRADICTION FOUND.

I remember thinking: Why say it that way? What am I seeing that no one else is reacting to?

Maybe my mother was giving me extra attention, and he was feeling displaced. Maybe he was tired. It doesn't matter what the cause was. What matters is that I saw the gap.

Most children do not record micro-expressions. Most kids ride the wave of the emotion. They trust the "vibe." But a Binary Mind trusts the Data. And when the data conflicts (Tone = Face), we don't just move on. We record it. We store it.

That moment wasn't trauma. It was architecture. It was my brain doing exactly what it was built to do: Detect Inconsistency.

If you are a parent reading this, and your child stares at you strangely when you are trying to be cheerful—stop and check yourself. Are you actually cheerful? Or are you pretending? Because your child isn't staring blankly. They are reading your micro-expressions and wondering why your face is lying to your voice.

These memories are not fuzzy impressions; they are high-resolution, sequentially logged events that define the context of my earliest life.

They are critical because they must tell parents how smart and aware their children are, and the profound harm that will continue if this awareness is ignored.

The good news is, these children are not broken.

3. THE PHYSICS OF THE PLAYGROUND

The Pimple Ball

I was five years old, going on six. I found a "pimple ball" in the gutter across the street. These were those small rubber balls from the 50s and 60s that kids usually cut in half to play stickball.

I picked it up, saw my brother Arthur standing on the porch, and I didn't just throw it to him. I sent it.

I whipped my arm. The ball flew across the street, curved perfectly around the porch post, and snapped right into his hands.

Arthur looked at the ball, then looked at me with total amazement. He threw it back.

I did it again. Same motion. Same whip. Same perfect strike right at his head. He caught it and looked at me like, "Wow."

That was the ignition point. I didn't just want to throw the ball. I wanted to master the arc.

We lived in East Boston, a neighborhood of three-story family homes. Most backyards were filled with tomato plants or grapevines. We got rid of the vegetation and turned the dirt into a workspace.

I took an old tire and leaned it against the chain-link fence. Then I went to the other side of the yard, built a little pitcher's mound, and went to work.

I experimented with the mechanics. One finger. Two fingers.

I learned that accuracy wasn't about staring at the target; it was about feeling the whip of the arm. If I focused on the mechanical snap of my elbow and wrist, the ball went exactly where the physics dictated it would go.

Over time, a game formed while I was playing. Two teams, Black and White. Black was strength. White was skill. I played full nine-inning games that way, each pitch counted.

Only later did the sound become the guide. The metal CLANG on the fence (a successful strike) versus the heavy THUD on the tire (a foul or miss).

This was pure binary feedback: SUCCESS (1) or FAILURE (0).

The Quarterback and the Oil Patch

By the time I was seven or eight, I graduated to a football. The older kids—teenagers—started letting me play. Not because they were being nice to the little kid, but because I was a weapon. I became the quarterback.

I didn't tell them, "Go long." That was too vague. I gave them coordinates.

"Go down 10 feet to that blue car. Take a hard right. Go straight toward the telephone pole. When you see the oil patch on the ground, turn around."

They would look at me, confused. I would tell them: "When you turn around, the ball is going to be there. Don't get scared."

This is the "Secret Sauce" of the Recorder. Observation = Emulation.

The ability of the Recorder to predict outcomes based on precise sequential inputs extends far beyond simple physical tasks; it allows for complex, real-time command structuring.

I ran the huddle exactly as I saw on TV, but the commands I gave were pure Recorder code.

I didn't rely on intuition or implicit understanding. The first few time after the older kids looked at me like, What?

When they ran the play, the ball arrived right on time, exactly where my predictive sequential mind had calculated the endpoint. They caught it and felt like heroes.

The point is this: who the heck taught me that? No one. That's a binary calculator mind.

This power is not intuition; it is the instantaneous compilation and execution of sequential logic in a dynamic environment, proving the high-functioning architecture of the BMI™.

The Physics of Aunt Florence (The 30-Second Swimmer)

It was the same with swimming. Most kids take lessons for months. They splash around while an instructor yells, "Kick, kick!" holding them up by their stomachs.

I didn't have time for that. I didn't want someone to touch me. I wanted to understand how the water worked.

I bought a 3-foot Styrofoam surfboard for 99 cents. I stood by the water and watched my Aunt Florence. I didn't just watch her swim; I studied her chassis.

I saw that she wasn't fighting the water; she was using it as a fulcrum. I watched her twist. I saw how she torqued her body to the water. She didn't slap at the surface; she reached out, grabbed the water, and pulled it past her body.

Input received.

I took my cheap board into the water. I isolated the variable. One arm at a time.

Reach. Twist. Pull.

Reach. Twist. Pull.

I figured out the torque. I figured out the resistance.

It took me exactly 30 seconds. I threw the board away and I swam.

The Altar Boy with the Gin (The Recruit)

To understand why I was the one who figured this out, you have to look at the wiring. And the best way to show you my wiring is to take you back to St. Lazarus Church when I was ten years old.

The church held a retreat for the local boys. The goal was simple: They were scouting for future priests. They wanted to see which of us had "The Calling."

Now, you have to understand the context. I was an East Boston kid. I had my first glass of homemade wine at an Italian funeral when I was five. I smoked my first cigar and cigarette in the third grade. Life moved fast where I was from.

So, when I packed my bag for this holy retreat, I didn't just pack a toothbrush. I packed a half-carton of cigarettes (six packs, rolled up tight) and a half-fifth of gin.

I was a ten-year-old walking into the House of God looking like a bootlegger.

The weekend goes by. We do the prayers, we read the scriptures, we sit in the silence.

At the end of the retreat, the priests sit us down to announce who they think has the potential to join the cloth. I'm sitting there, literally hiding a felony amount of tobacco in my bag, waiting to be sent home.

And the priest points to me.

"Robert," he says. "He is the one."

They didn't pick me because I was a "good boy." (Clearly, they didn't check my luggage).

They picked me because I Understood the Writings.

While the other kids were bored or confused by the scripture, I was locked in. I could articulate the story. I could see the structure. Recorders love Scripture because Scripture is Code. It is Binary.

Sin and Salvation. Truth and Lies. Alpha and Omega.

My brain ignored the social awkwardness of the retreat and locked straight onto the data.

I didn't become a priest. But that moment at St. Lazarus explains everything. I was the kid with the gin in his pocket and the Truth in his mouth. I was the rebellion and the structure wrapped in one skin.

And fifty years later, when I found "The Event," it was that same brain—the one that ignores the rules but reads the code—that was able to solve the puzzle.

4. THE GENETIC BASELINE

My father provided the operating system—the logic, the discipline, the "All Debts Are Paid" philosophy.

But people often ask where the Size came from. Where did Arthur get the strength to bench press a Buick? Where did Paul get the lungs to run forever?

They got it from the girl from Charlestown.

My father was 38 when he married her. She was 21. He was a man who planned everything, and he knew he wanted to raise a strong family. So he found a woman who could hold her own.

I met a man once who asked if I was her son. When I said yes, he laughed and said, "Your mother? She played baseball with us. And let me tell you—she was a long-ball hitter. She could hit that ball way over the fence."

That is the genetic baseline. We got the Mind from the Accountant. We got the Power from the Long-Ball Hitter.

The Movie Star and The Patient

If you look at their wedding portrait, you see the perfect American couple. My mother, at 21, looked like a movie star. She was a stunner—Irish-English beauty, hair perfectly done, radiating class. She looks like she's ready for the red carpet.

My father, at 38, looks like the dashing Coast Guard officer. Handsome, stoic, ready for duty.

But the camera lies.

The truth is, my father hated boats.

And that "stoic" look? That was him holding it together. He was actually a patient in the hospital the night before the photo was taken. He had checked himself in for "nerves"—the Recorder mind going into overdrive.

He literally checked out of the hospital, put on his dress uniform, went to the church, married the most beautiful woman in Charlestown, smiled for the photo... and then went right back to the hospital and put his pajamas back on.

She was the Movie Star. He was the Hypochondriac Hero. And somehow, it worked.

The Service Contract: "I'll Have the Eggplant"

There is a narrative today that parents of autistic or high-energy kids are "exhausted." They act like the child is luggage handcuffed to their wrist—a heavy weight they have to drag through life. They love them, sure, but they are tired.

I look back at my mother, and I don't see luggage. I see a woman who ran a logistics empire for seven children and never once looked at the clock.

People talk about "spoiled." I lived with my mother for twenty-three years. For those twenty-three years, I didn't just eat what was made. I ordered my food.

I didn't walk into the kitchen and ask, "What's for dinner?" I walked in and said, "I'll have the eggplant tonight." Or, "You know, I could really go for a steak."

And she didn't just cook it. She engineered it. Even when I was twenty years old, she would put the steak in front of me, already cut up into bite-sized pieces, and covered in beans. She removed the friction of eating so I could just refuel.

The Snow in the Dark (Age 22)

The true measure of her strength wasn't in the kitchen; it was in the driveway.

When I started working at EDS, I was twenty-two years old. In Boston winters, the morning was dark, cold, and buried.

I would wake up to hear a scraping sound outside.

My mother—a woman in her late 50s at this point—would be out there in the pitch black. She wouldn't just shovel a path. She would shovel out two cars' worth of snow. She would dig out the heavy, icy plow-drift behind my car. She would clean the windshield. She would start the engine so it was warm when I got in.

Inside the house, the logistics were just as precise. I would get out of the shower, and my suit would be laid out on the bed, waiting for me. Breakfast was ready. Lunch was packed in a bag "just in case" I needed it.

She cleared the snow, she prepped the uniform, and she fueled the engine. All I had to do was show up and work.

The Glamour (The Early Years)

But I also remember the earlier days, when we were young, living in East Boston before the move to Melrose. Back then, before the snow shoveling years, she was the Movie Star.

Every single day, before my father Arthur came home from the IRS, the house changed. She would get dressed. Hair done perfectly. Makeup on. She treated his arrival like an event. She was ready for the "Boss" to come home.

She was the Long-Ball Hitter, but she played different positions depending on the season of our lives. When we were young, she was the star. When I was starting my career, she was the pit crew.

But in every phase, she made sure the Caggianos never missed a step.

The Last Instruction (No Breadcrumbs)

There is a philosophy to being a Recorder, and my mother taught it to me in the kitchen. It's the Eggplant Rule.

Most people rush. They salt the eggplant to force the water out fast. They use breadcrumbs because it's easy.

But my mother knew better.

The Prep:

You cut it into slices the night before. You let it dry on paper towels.

"You prepare a little today for tomorrow."

You don't force the starch out; you let it leave naturally.

The Batter: Egg and flour. Never breadcrumbs.

Her logic was flawless, and it applies to life as much as cooking: "Why ruin the sauce with the seasoning in the breadcrumbs? The sauce is already perfect."

If you have done the work to make the sauce right (the Foundation), don't add noise (the Breadcrumbs) that clashes with it. Keep the data clean.

That was the last clear thing she ever said to me the night before her major stroke, My Mom had me promise never let anyone convince me to put breadcrumbs on the eggplant.

I promised.

The Psychotic Episode (The Medical Glitch)

The next day, she had a stroke.

But look at how the system labeled it. I got a call: "Your mother had a psychotic episode. She flipped out."

My Recorder brain instantly rejected that data. "My mother? Jesus Christ could walk through the door and she would just ask him what took him so long. She doesn't 'flip out'."

The doctors saw "Behavior" (Psychosis). I knew the "Hardware" (Stroke).

The System Reboot (The Hospital Room)

I flew back to Boston on pure adrenaline. Twelve hours from the phone call to the hospital door.

I walked into the room, and it felt like a stage. The doctors, the nurses, the family—they were all standing around the bed like spectators at a car crash. They were looking at the monitors. They were looking at the "Psychotic Episode."

I didn't look at the monitors. I looked at the woman.

She was mumbling. Just a stream of static. A loop of confusion.

The doctors stepped back as I walked through them. They had given up; they were just managing the chaos.

I sat on the edge of the bed and took her hand. It was the only thing in that sterile room that felt real. I squeezed it, anchoring her.

Then I leaned in. Not just to her face—to her ear. I needed to bypass the room. I needed to bypass the stroke. I needed a direct line to the processor.

"Ma," I whispered. "It's Robert."

She stopped mumbling for a second. She turned her head, but her eyes were looking through me, not at me.

"No," she muttered. "No, no, no. It's not Robert."

I squeezed her hand harder. "Yes, Ma. It is Robert."

She shook her head, fighting the fog. "No," she said, her voice sounding like a little girl. "Robert is my good boy."

That broke me, but it also focused me.

Even in the middle of a stroke, even in the "psychosis," her definition of me was pure. I was the Good Boy. I was the Anchor.

I leaned closer, my voice steady, cutting through the noise of the machines.

"I am right here, Ma. Robert is right here."

And then—The Snap.

It wasn't a slow drift. It was a Reboot. Her eyes stopped wandering and locked onto mine. The grey fog in her pupils vanished, and the brown came back. The "Psychosis" evaporated in a single second.

She squeezed my hand back. "Robert," she said. Clear as a bell. "What took you so long?"

The doctors were stunned. They were writing "Psychotic Break" on a clipboard, and I had just proven it was a TIA (a mini-stroke) with two sentences.

They were treating the software. I knew how to touch the hardware.

5. KEVIN: THE GRAVITY OF TRUTH

And then, there was Kevin.

If my father was the Enforcer, Kevin was the Truth Anchor.

Kevin wasn't just my brother; he was the gravitational center of my universe. Not in a sentimental way — in a gravitational way. An intense, brilliant, unique force who shaped my world before I even knew what "world" meant.

We grew up in a house where all seven kids slept in three small bedrooms, with sheets hung from wires to create the illusion of privacy. Those makeshift walls meant nothing to Kevin. He lived big, loud, curious, full of ideas. And I slept right beside him.

He showed me the world long before I was supposed to see it.

While most kids were learning nursery rhymes, Kevin was teaching me: where babies really come from, that Santa Claus wasn't real, and that we should go up to the attic and unwrap the "gifts from Santa" early, check what we were getting, then wrap them back up again.

He was four. I was three going on four. We had no business knowing any of that — but Kevin didn't believe in holding information back. If he knew something, I knew it.

My world wasn't shaped by school or books or the neighborhood. My world was shaped by Kevin.

He bought monster model kits — the old Aurora classics.

Frankenstein with the bolted neck. Dracula in his cape. The Wolf Man mid-transform. The Creature from the Black Lagoon with those gills and claws. The Bride of Frankenstein with her hair streaked like lightning.

He built them with precision, piece by piece, painting the faces, the shadows, the stitches.

A kid my age should've been terrified. But I wasn't.

Right next to his monster models, I had stuffed animals from Easter baskets — soft, bright-colored, innocent. Rabbits, bears, little plush toys.

And there I was at three or four years old, lying in that room divided by sheets, looking around thinking: No one would believe my bedroom.

Half monsters, half stuffed animals. Half childhood, half something much older. Two worlds colliding before I even knew what worlds were.

Most kids grow in stages — innocence first, reality later. I got both at the same time. Kevin didn't protect me from the world. He introduced me to it. Not in a harsh way — in a way that said, "This is life. Don't be afraid of it."

There was no childhood illusion in the bed we shared. Kevin replaced illusion with reality, and reality with curiosity.

He had a habit every night: before falling asleep, he would rock back and forth for fifteen or twenty minutes — like he was recalibrating his mind, preparing it for sleep. I'd lie next to him, quietly watching, taking it in, not knowing until decades later how much that rhythm shaped me.

The Artist

His talent was obvious from the start. He could draw with no practice. Not "good for a kid." He was incredible.

I remember one night vividly: we were sitting between the beds in that small room divided by sheets. Kevin opened a comic book, picked a character — Nomad — and on his first try, he drew it perfectly.

Then he held it up and said, "What do you think?"

And all I could say was the truth: "Kevin... you know how to draw."

It wasn't a compliment. It was recognition. After Nomad came a wave of superheroes—perfect, confident strokes, like he was tracing what already existed in his mind. He went to art school at twelve or thirteen.

The Singer

And the kid could sing. By age six, he had a family theme song: "My Way."

Every gathering, he sang it. It became his signature—a child doing Sinatra with a straight face while adults tried not to laugh or cry.

He was a ladies' man early. He had his first true love, Denise, and even after they weren't together, he stayed faithful to her in his heart. Kevin didn't love halfway.

He saved my life when he was six.

I was walking to second grade and made the kind of mistake a young kid makes—running through traffic to beat a light, not seeing the last lane where a car was coming fast. Kevin saw it. He ran. And at the very last second, he pushed me out of the path of the full hit. We both got clipped, but not the way I would have.

He was six. That moment—like everything with Kevin—went straight into my wiring. He protected me instinctively, instantly, without thinking. Like breathing.

He met John Wayne. When Kevin was older, he bartended at the Newporter Inn. John Wayne used to come in. Kevin told me Wayne was responsible for the cows around Orange County at the time and how he was the first person to sign the petition against the airport being built. Funny how they named the airport after him anyway.

The Bookends

When I look at Kevin's life, I don't see a blur of years. I see two specific days. Two specific clubs. Two moments where a Recorder tried to organize a world that refused to follow the rules.

The First Bookend: Revere, Massachusetts.

It was the year the drinking age dropped to eighteen. Kevin had just hit the number. I was only sixteen and a half.

For Kevin, this wasn't just a birthday; it was a classification. The law said he was a Man. The data was clear.

He marched down to the local strip club in Revere with the absolute certainty of someone who has the paperwork to prove they belong. He walked in, scanned the dark, smoky room, and looked for a table.

And then his system crashed.

I was already there. I was sitting at a table with my friends, drink in hand, looking like I'd been paying rent there for years.

Kevin didn't just get mad. He got confused. It was a syntax error. This does not compute.

He walked straight up to the cocktail waitress. He wasn't yelling out of emotion; he was pointing out a factual inaccuracy.

"Hey! You see him? He can't be in here!"

The waitress looked at me. I sat there, calm, holding my glass.

Kevin tapped his chest, presenting his evidence. "I'm eighteen! I'm the one who's legal! He's sixteen! You need to kick him out!"

Technically, he was right. But the waitress looked at Kevin—sweating, frantic about the rules. Then she looked back at me—quiet, settled, observing.

She turned to Kevin and snapped, "Get out of here. Leave your older brother alone."

She walked away. Kevin stood there, stunned. He had followed every rule, and the world still told him he was wrong.

The Second Bookend: Florida.

Years later, the scene repeated, but the setting had changed. We were in Florida now. The humidity was thick. The Golden Boy was fading, but his mind was still recording, still analyzing.

The Ultimate Test: The Balcony

The true test of the Binary Mind comes when the stakes are life and death.

Runners are great at comforting people with platitudes. But when reality breaks, platitudes are useless. When the diagnosis is terminal, or the tragedy is real, the Runner runs out of scripts.

The Recorder steps in.

The day Kevin found out he was terminal, the world shifted. I wasn't there for the diagnosis, but I was there for the crisis. He stood on a tenth-floor balcony. He was threatening to jump.

If I had been a Runner, I might have panicked. I might have screamed, "Don't do it!"

But those would have been lies. My Binary Mind took over. It dropped into High-Stakes Clarity.

I didn't scream. I didn't add drama. I simply projected the logical consequence of his action.

I said: "Think of what I would see if you fell. I'd have to go down there, hold you, and cry. So why don't you just come back in? And if you still want to go back out, I'll help you. But come talk to me first."

Look at the structure of that argument.

Fact: If you jump, I have to witness the trauma.

Logic: That is a terrible outcome for me, and you love me.

Offer: I am not removing your autonomy. If you want to jump later, you can. (Validating his control).

Request: Just process data with me first.

It worked. He came back inside. He sat down and said the three words that changed everything: "I'm terminal — that's all."

We didn't cry hysterically. We didn't pretend. We talked. He promised to look into all options and we were able to relax.

The Diagnosis and The Drive

A couple of weeks later, Paul called me at my office in Santa Monica—the Lotus office—and told me Kevin had AIDS. It was the hardest sixty-mile drive home in my life.

Around the same time Magic Johnson announced he was HIV positive, I flew to Florida to see Kevin. He had lost a lot of weight. He was letting the disease take him. The light was still in his eyes, but dimmer.

I said, "Let's go enjoy the day." We rented a boat in Pompano Beach. I took the wheel and asked him if he wanted to drive. He said no — too fragile. I said, "Well I hate driving," and stepped away from the wheel.

He shot up: "Are you crazy?" and grabbed it. He drove for four hours, loving every second of it.

The Adult Bar: "I'll Take This Day"

We stopped at an adult bar. He tipped a dancer, she wrapped her boobs around his face for a second—playful, quick—and he stepped back, smiling wide, clapping his hands once, and said:

"Okay... I'll take this day."

We left, and he told me there was more to say. He didn't want to die the way he'd seen others die. He told me he didn't want to end up like a girl in the hospital—infected by a dentist—lying in a coma, unable to speak, trapped in her own body. He told me exactly what she would say if she could: "Kill me, you people. I don't want to lay here."

He had been studying Dr. Kevorkian's book. He said the bottle on the table had enough to put him into a coma, and that afterward I would need to insert two morphine suppositories to push him over the edge. He said that's how they killed Marilyn Monroe.

He said it calmly. Honestly. Like he had thought it all the way through.

I said, "Wait... you're serious?"

And without hesitation he said, "Of course," and explained why.

At that time, people didn't fully understand AIDS. There was fear around touching, hugging—and Kevin knew that fear would isolate him in a way he could not bear. Not just about sex. About being human with others. I told him that wasn't necessarily how it ends—that science could change. He said, "So don't touch anyone... for how long? No way."

I stepped out and called Arthur and Paul. They already knew. Arthur said, "Yes, he wants me to come down with my .38, but I can't get there for a bit." Paul said, "Yeah, I know — he wants out."

It felt like a group consensus, a grim understanding. I went back in and asked Kevin if he really wanted me to answer for his death when the police show up?

We roared laughing in the darkest moments in the honest way brothers do.

The Final Lesson: The Good News

The last time I saw him, he was in hospice—a bottom-floor room where the sunlight came through at an angle and lit the green and blue cards on the shelf.

He weighed 78 pounds. The same person who once stood at 230 pounds of pure muscle.

I sat beside him, holding his hands, crying. I was the one falling apart.

He looked at me—clear, present, totally stabilized.

He said: "Robert, you don't get it. You can't see the good news. I won't have to see you die. Please know that I love you. I could never bear seeing you die."

I'm crying now writing this.

Because in that moment, he used the Ultimate Recorder Logic. He took the worst possible thing—his own death—and he found the one good thing in it. He found the single variable that made it a mercy for me.

And I am telling you this because a mind like that—a mind that can find the light in the absolute dark—should not go wasted. Do not let Kevin's life — his beauty, his intensity, his curiosity, his fearlessness — be wasted. Hug Away!

12

Because for those who don't believe in the heart's

6. PAUL: THE ENGINE OF FLOW
Paul had a way of finding the positive — not in some forced or phony way, but in a way that made you believe it too. If you came to him looking for advice, he'd listen, smile, and remind you that things would work out.

He had a way of giving you hope — the kind that stayed with you long after the conversation ended.

Tire Tubes and The Jet

We had endless tire tubes from my uncle's tire shop in the North End of Boston. One day, Paul a fifteen year old grabs a couple and said, "Let's go for an adventure." I'm five but he knew I could swim.

So there we were — him leading, me paddling behind — floating across the harbor toward Logan Airport.

The water slapped the rubber tubes, and all I could think was, I hope he knows what he's doing.

When we reached the other side, Paul looked around like he'd just discovered a new country. Then he grinned. "Hey, let's run on the tarmac for fun."

So we did. Two kids darting across the runway like it was our backyard.

A fighter jet rolled into position — canopy down, engines rumbling.

Paul stopped, waved. The pilot saw him. And then, unbelievably, the canopy lifted. The pilot looked right at us and waved back.

How high on the Marvel superhero scale was Paul in my five-year-old eyes at that moment?

12 Angry Pauls

Paul's ability to "run" a room wasn't just for fun. Sometimes, he used it to save people.

He got called for jury duty once. Most people try to get out of it; Paul saw it as an audience. He walked in, saw the other jurors, and decided to see if he could pull a 12 Angry Men.

The case involved a high school kid who had taken his parents' Ford Thunderbird, got drunk at a party, and slammed it into a house. The insurance company was suing the parents for damages. It looked like an open-and-shut case. The kid was guilty.

But when they got to the deliberation room, Paul didn't sit back. He stood up.

He asked a simple question: "Just out of curiosity... did anyone actually see him get out of the car?"

The other jurors rolled their eyes. "No," they said, "but it had to be him. Witnesses saw the red high school sweater driving away."

Paul smiled. He was working the angles.

"Okay. But we'll see the other one, right?"

"The other what?"

"The other kid in a red sweater."

The room got quiet. Paul kept pushing. "Look, the testimony said this kid was falling-down drunk. Bouncing off the walls. If he was that drunk, could he have even found the keys? Or was he drunk enough that someone could have taken the keys from him?"

The jurors started to argue. "But he was all banged up! He had cuts on his face!"

Paul nodded, seizing on the detail. "Exactly. He was banged up. But if he was falling-down drunk at a party... couldn't he have fallen down the stairs? Couldn't he have banged his head on a railing?"

He planted the seed of doubt. He took a room full of people convinced of guilt and, using nothing but charm and "what-if" logic, he turned the tide. He got the kid off. The parents didn't have to pay a dime. The insurance company had to eat the loss.

Paul walked out of the courthouse laughing. He had just socially engineered a verdict because he could.

The Gag — How People Are

That moment never really ended. It just evolved. As we grew up, it turned into this thing we called the gag. Not a trick, not a scam — more of an observation.

The gag was that no matter the circumstance, people are human. When they saw Paul and me, they were disarmed. Neutralized. It's like their mind went into a calm middle gear and said, "They belong here."

We'd walk into places like we worked there, or like we were supposed to be there — never sneaky, just familiar. It was confidence without arrogance. We'd look at people the way you look at a neighbor — that half-recognition that makes them think, "Oh, he must be with so-and-so."

And it worked. Over and over again.

The Super Bowl Party

One year, Hugh Hefner hosted his famous Playboy Super Bowl party in Jacksonville, Florida. Paul and a friend had sailed a ninety-foot boat up from Fort Lauderdale and docked right in front — the best spot in the marina. The friend had one ticket. Paul made a copy. There were three scans total, and sure enough, one of them caught. But by then, Paul was already watching the red carpet being rolled out and thought, Why not?

He adjusted his jacket and walked right in.

Hours later — 12:30 a.m. California time — my phone rang. It was Paul, laughing.

"I'm in the middle of the dance floor — surrounded by Playboy bunnies."

That was Paul. And that was our gag — not pretending, not lying — just carrying ourselves like we belonged everywhere. And somehow, everywhere agreed.

The Chateau Marmont

Years later, we checked into the Chateau Marmont in Beverly Hills. The clerk apologized for not having Paul's room ready and said they'd upgraded us to the penthouse suite. Then he added, "The restaurant is closed tonight — Playboy has it reserved for a private party."

Paul looked at me, that grin creeping across his face. He didn't have to say a word. That grin meant invitation accepted.

The courtyard was alive — stars, executives, producers, and Hefner himself surrounded by six Playmates. At the center sat a white leather couch, roped off like it was on display.

Paul pointed. "That works," he said, and stepped right around the rope. We sat down.

A waitress came over, clearly ready to say something — probably "this area's reserved." Paul didn't let her get there. He smiled, ordered a drink, then looked at me.

"What are you having?"

She jotted it down and walked off. And just like that, we were in the center of the party. Even Hef's table looked over.

The Scarfed Manager

Not long after, a man walked up — perfectly dressed, scarf draped just so, beard trimmed sharp. He stopped in front of us.

"I'm Johnny Depp's manager," he said, like he was announcing a royal title. "Who are you?"

Paul smiled. "I'm Paul Caggiano. We produce a few small projects."

I added, "Yeah, I'm with him."

The man squinted. "Sorry, what was that again?"

Paul leaned toward me, voice low. "He didn't just ask me that again, did he? Because if he did, tell him that scarf looks about the right size to wrap around his head twice."

I bit my cheek, trying not to laugh. "Small films," I told the man. "We produce small films."

He gave a nod and walked off.

The Waitress Returns

A few minutes later, the waitress came back. She leaned in and whispered, "When Johnny shows up... will you let him sit here?"

Paul smiled, took her hand gently. "Of course. Don't worry."

Then turned to me and grinned. "We don't want to get the poor girl fired."

The Director Ruse

I went to the men's room — two minutes, maybe. When I came back, Paul was at the bar, surrounded by a small group hanging on every word.

As I got closer, I heard him say, "Well, when we talk about somebody important, do I have to...?"

He stopped mid-sentence, opened his hand toward me like he'd been waiting for his cue. Everyone turned to look. In that short time, Paul had convinced them I was the director of The Rum Diary.

I walked up clueless, and they started thanking me for my "speech" earlier at the premiere.

Paul nodded calmly. "He's always intentional with his words."

I barely kept it together. Those people went home convinced they'd met the director.

Cameos and Confusions

The illusion spread. Michael Rispoli walked by and gave me a knowing nod.

Then Marilyn Manson drifted through the crowd — pale, slow, scanning the room. But he wasn't looking at me. He was watching Paul. You could see it in his face — that flicker like he was thinking, Did I ever play with this guy?

Even Marilyn Manson got caught in Paul's gravity.

Aaron Eckhart

A little later, Aaron Eckhart came over. He greeted Paul first, handshake and smile — no pretense, no Hollywood act. They talked for a while — easy, like cousins at a cookout. Family. Kids. Life.

Then Aaron tilted his head, curious who Paul really was.

Paul leaned in and said, "Come on, isn't our biggest worry always our kids? Don't you hope they can be as successful as you and I?"

Aaron laughed — the real kind — and nodded. He knew it was a game but didn't want to end it. When he finally stepped away, Paul and I looked at each other and broke — laughing so hard we had to hold our sides.

Johnny Depp

Then Johnny himself arrived — three bodyguards clearing the way.

Paul didn't pause. He walked right up, shook Depp's hand. I followed, hand on Johnny's shoulder, and said, "You've always been one of my favorite actors."

He nodded, smiled, and vanished just as fast.

I turned to Paul. "That was cool."

Looked back — no Johnny, no guards.

"Do you think three bodyguards are getting fired right now?"

We lost it again — laughing in the middle of Hefner's party like kids at Logan all over again.

Reflection

From the tarmac to the red carpet, Paul never changed. He could walk into any room, any world, and somehow — everyone believed he belonged. He didn't do it for attention or ego. He did it because he saw people. And people, when they saw him, saw something familiar in return.

The Cruelest Irony

Paul passed away on September 25th, 2025. He was taken by Bulbar ALS, a wretched disease that attacks the muscles used for speaking and swallowing first.

And in that loss lies a sadness so deep it feels like a mistake in the universe's design.

For years, whenever the topic of death or aging came up, Paul had a standard line. He'd say, "Hey, just put me in the corner. If I can just sit there, see my family, and talk, I'll be happy."

That was his deal with fate. He didn't need to run on tarmacs anymore; he just wanted to hold court.

But the disease denied him that one specific mercy.

I spent several quiet days sitting with him toward the end. He would mumble or text on a screen, frustrated by the trap his body had become. The man who could charm a pilot out of a fighter jet was now fighting just to be heard.

During those quiet days, I shared something personal with him. I told him about my discovery regarding the mind—about the Binary Mind, about where I fit on the spectrum of autism. I was trying to explain why I am the way I am.

Paul looked at me. He didn't skip a beat. He didn't ask for charts or proofs. He managed to communicate a simple truth:

"Robert, you were always different."

He didn't mean it as a criticism. He said it in that good way—the Paul way. He meant that I was me, and to him, that was exactly who I was supposed to be.

He lost his voice, but right up until the end, he knew exactly what to say.

7. ARTHUR: THE TITAN

My brother Arthur was the Gold standard. Everyone in East Boston was measured against him.

The Punch: The Lesson

I was in second grade. I had just gotten my first pair of glasses. Arthur was eleven years older than me—about eighteen or nineteen at the time. He was already the Titan. He decided it was time to teach his little brother how to fight.

He stood me up in the yard.

"Robert," he said, "don't aim for the face. Aim for the back of the head but go through the front of the face first. You punch through the face."

He told me to put my hands up. "Let me see if you can catch my hand," he said.

He threw a punch. It was supposed to be a demonstration, a "pull-back" strike to test my reflexes. But Arthur didn't have a "light" setting. He miscalculated the distance—or the speed—and he hit me square in the face.

CRACK. My brand-new glasses shattered. The force knocked me back.

Arthur froze. His eyes went wide. The Protector had just broken his little brother.

"Oh my god," he said, reaching out. "Robert, I'm sorry! Are you okay?"

I stood there, feeling the sting, checking for blood. I looked at him—this giant of a man, this Luca Brasi of our neighborhood—looking terrified because he thought he hurt me.

I started to giggle. I looked at him and smiled. "I just took one of your best punches. No big deal."

He stared at me. I wasn't crying. I wasn't running to Mom. I was laughing.

I never flinched after that. Not with him, not with anyone. I realized that if I could take a shot from the Titan and laugh about it, the rest of the world couldn't hurt me.

Arthur rose to the rank of Major in the Army. He could have been a General—he had the mind for it—but he refused to play the political game. He didn't want to kiss the rings required to get a star on his shoulder. He preferred the company of the enlisted men. He respected grit over rank.

One night in the mess hall, the talk turned to strength. There was a lineman there—a monster of a man who had been a first-round NFL draft pick before getting called up. He was a professional athlete in his prime.

The guys were ribbing Arthur. "It's too late now, Major. You're not the big man on campus anymore. This guy is the real deal."

Arthur didn't say a word. He just cleared off a table in the center of the room. The NFL lineman sat down, confident. Arthur sat opposite him.

They locked right hands.

Arthur told me later, "Robert, I knew this guy was strong. I knew I couldn't beat him on a burst. So I decided I wasn't going to try to beat him. I was just going to break him."

Arthur used a technique he called "The Lock." He didn't push back; he just solidified his arm like a steel beam.

They sat there for twenty-five minutes. Muscles trembling, sweat pouring down the lineman's face. Arthur just stared at him, holding the line with his right arm. He waited until the lineman's energy bar hit zero.

Then, slowly, Arthur pushed his hand down. Thud.

The room went silent. The lineman couldn't believe it. "No way," the guy said. "No way. Do it again."

Arthur smiled. "Okay."

They locked up again. Same hands. This time, Arthur didn't wait twenty-five minutes. He waited ten. Thud.

The lineman was losing his mind. He was humiliated. He slammed the table.

"Okay!" the lineman yelled. "LEFT HAND! Let's go left!"

He thought maybe Arthur was just right-side dominant. He thought he found a weakness.

Arthur didn't say a word. He didn't warn him. He didn't smile and say, "Buddy, you don't want to do that." He just put his left elbow on the table.

They locked up. Bam. Ten seconds... Arthur slammed the guy's hand through the table.

The lineman sat there, stunned. He didn't realize what had just happened. He had just demanded that a natural-born Lefty switch to his dominant hand. Arthur hadn't said a thing to buy himself an out. He beat the guy twice with his weak arm, and when the guy asked for the left, Arthur just gave him the good news.

The Secret

For years, I looked at Arthur and wondered how the strongest man I knew—the man who beat an NFL lineman with his weak arm—could let himself waste away in a hospital bed. I sat with him during his last five days. The Titan was yellow with jaundice. The muscles were gone.

I finally asked him. I had to know.

"Arthur," I said, "what was the deal? What started this? You were the Gold Standard. What made you start drinking like that?"

He looked at the ceiling. He was quiet for a long time. Then, he told me the secret he had been carrying.

"I was alone at night," he whispered. "I heard someone coming at me. I panicked, Robert. I just reacted. I shot."

He paused, his breathing shallow. "It turned out to be the bad guy," he said. "I got the right guy. But I shot before I knew. I pulled the trigger out of fear, not out of command."

That was the fracture. The world gave him a medal, but his own mind gave him a life sentence. He knew that for one split second, the Titan had flinched.

"It tore me up," he said. "I couldn't shut it off. So I started with a case of beer. Then that wasn't enough to make it quiet, so I switched to hard liquor. And then I just kept going."

I sat there and held his hand. I finally understood. The alcohol wasn't a party. It was anesthesia. He had been trying to silence that one moment of panic for decades.

8. COUSIN JOE: THE KING OF HUMOR

I didn't have to look far to see the other neurotypes in action.

If my father was the Enforcer of law, my cousin Joe Caggiano was the Enforcer of the room.

Joe was a presence. A big man, a captain in the South Boston Police Department, and the funniest human being ever to never set foot in show business. He was the ultimate Connector/Enforcer hybrid. He knew every joke known to mankind—Henry Youngman, Milton Berle, every classic—but he never told them straight. Joe tweaked every punchline so it fit the person he was talking to, the moment he was in, or the family member standing closest. He didn't recycle humor. He personalized it. That's what made him dangerous and brilliant.

But it was when he worked the streets as a cop that I saw the "Recorder" genius in action. His humor was a tool, a weapon, a performance—all rolled into one. I watched him and learned: Humor is a system hack. It breaks the logic loop of anger. I wasn't just laughing; I was filing that away. If you can make the threat funny, you remove the danger without removing the power. He was the Master of Tone.

I remember watching him roll up on a domestic disturbance call. The other cops would be tense, hands on their holsters. Joe would just pick up the bullhorn. He wouldn't scream orders. He wouldn't threaten to kick the door down. He would just lean into the microphone like he was ordering a sandwich.

"It's Joe. Joe Caggiano. I need you to come out and make it easy on everybody."

Then, he would drop the leverage.

"You know the Caggianos. We run the ambulance service that picks up your parents when they get sick. I'd hate to see that ambulance get stuck in traffic on the way to the hospital."

He'd let that hang in the air for a second. Then he'd drop the hammer.

"And you know my dad has the funeral home over in Winthrop. Honestly, it's just as easy for us to bring them there. We actually make more money driving to the funeral home than the hospital. So, what's it gonna be?"

Five minutes later, the guy would walk out, hands up. As Joe was handcuffing him, he'd look over at the crowd of neighbors watching and wink.

"I could have told him we had the place surrounded and he had nowhere to go... but where's the fun in that?"

The Pirate's Chest

Joe was also the reason I learned ballistics before I learned long division. My brothers and I didn't have much money, so we didn't have store-bought toys. But we had Cousin Joe's cellar.

He had a massive chest down there—like a pirate's booty case—filled with confiscated street weapons. When we wanted to play Cops and Robbers, Joe would open the chest. "Go ahead," he'd say. "I took the firing pins out."

He didn't just let us play with them in the basement. He gave them to us. He handed out switchblades, derringers, snub-nose revolvers, and shotguns like they were party favors. We took them home.

At six years old, I had my own arsenal. We ran the streets of the neighborhood playing war with real evidence. I carried a real handgun tucked into my belt. I learned things a kindergartner shouldn't know. By the time I was six, I knew how to throw a switchblade underhand and stick it into a piece of wood from 10 feet away. I was deadly accurate.

To the outside world, it was insanity. To us, it was just Tuesday. Joe taught me that authority isn't about being the loudest guy in the room. And he taught me that the difference between a toy and a weapon is just a firing pin.

The Bouncer Gene

It shouldn't be a surprise that my brothers and I all worked the door at some point. We were Bouncers. It is the ultimate Sentinel job. You stand at the threshold. You scan the room. You look for the glitch in the matrix—the drunk, the aggressor, the static—and you remove it so the music can keep playing.

The Classroom (Château de Ville)

My first job was at the Château de Ville in Saugus. I was just a senior in high school, working an adult club filled with people in their 30s, 40s, and 50s. It was the era of the giants.

Don Rickles played the main ballroom. I remember standing behind the curtain, watching the master work. He called everyone a "hockey puck." He saw a guy who wasn't laughing, and then he saw another bald guy sitting next to him. Rickles didn't miss a beat:

"Why don't you move over to the side? If you two bald guys sit beside each other, you'll make a perfect ass of yourselves."

The room exploded. Rickles was a Reader. He read the room instantly.

The Lesson (The Look of Inevitability)

My boss was a guy named Joe. He looked like Cary Grant but was built like a boxer. He taught me the secret of the Sentinel. It wasn't about throwing a punch; it was about Physics.

He told me: "Robert, when you come up against a guy giving you a hard time, stay tall. Look him in the eye. Show him the Intent."

"Show him that it is inevitable. You are going to pound him. You are going to end him. Simple as that."

That is the Recorder Stare. It isn't anger. It is certainty. When you look at someone with zero doubt in your eyes, they feel the wall. They usually back down because they realize the outcome has already been decided.

The Reality Check (The 43-Year-Old)

One night, a guy was getting loud. Too much to drink. Belligerent. I had to escort him to the bathroom. I stood right next to him at the urinal—no privacy when you're a threat level.

He starts crying. He starts confessing. "You don't understand," he says. "I'm 43 years old. My life is over. I screwed up. It's all over."

I was a high school kid. To me, 43 seemed ancient. But I didn't become his therapist. I stayed in the role. I told him:

"I don't know what's going on in your life. But I know your time here at the Château is over. And if you don't leave with me right now, your night is gonna be over."

The Loop vs. The Task

Looking back, that story is tragic and funny. He was spinning a loop about his "life being over" at 43 (which is young!). I was just executing a Task: Remove Static. I walked him out. I closed the loop for him because he couldn't close it himself.

9. THE NOISE OUTSIDE AND THE QUIET INSIDE

My brothers were my shield, but they couldn't stop the world from being loud. And in my house, the world was deafening.

For three years, while Logan Airport was building a new runway, the flight paths were redirected. They didn't just fly near us; they flew over us. My house was the three-story building in the direct flight path.

The Annie Hall Life

You know that scene in the movie Annie Hall where Woody Allen visits the family that lives under the roller coaster? The joke is that they try to eat dinner while the room shakes violently. That was my life.

Every ten to twenty minutes, the house would rock. Dishes rattled. The walls vibrated. I'm pretty sure the tinnitus ringing in my ears today didn't come from a rock concert or an industrial job. It started right there, in that third-floor bedroom in Boston.

But because I am the way I am, I didn't just cover my ears. I observed.

My brothers and I would go up to the third floor with binoculars and a telescope. We played a game. The planes were so low—I have literally seen pebbles kick up and bounce off the belly of the fuselage—that we could see into the cockpit.

"Describe the pilot," we'd challenge each other. "Is he wearing a tie?" "Does he have glasses?" "Is his jacket on or off?"

We turned the chaos into data. We turned the noise into a game. That was how I survived the physical noise. But as I got older, I had to figure out how to survive the emotional noise.

The Job I Didn't Take

When I graduated college, I was handed a golden ticket. My cousin Ernie, God bless him, had pulled some strings and got me a job offer as the Permanent Mortuary Attendant at Boston City Hospital.

This was the Holy Grail of employment. It was a city job. Good pension, total security. I would never have to interview again. I could have retired from that spot.

But Boston City Hospital isn't a quiet funeral home. That is where they bring the "street" dead. If there was a car wreck, a shooting, or an airplane crash, they came to us.

I thought about the money. I thought about the security.

But then my mind ran the simulation. I imagined standing there every day, seeing families walk in. I pictured the mothers, the fathers, the children who had just lost someone.

People think that because I have a Binary Mind—because I am "different"—that I am cold. They think I lack empathy. The truth is the exact opposite.

My empathy is not a dial I can turn down; it is a switch that is stuck in the "ON" position.

I knew that if I took that job, I would absorb their grief. I would be sad every single day of my life. I knew my heart would break over and over again.

So, I did a silent thank you to Cousin Ernie, and I turned it down.

The Interview Trap

I cannot tell you how many times in my life I wished I had taken that job. Not because I wanted to work with the dead, but because I hated the process of trying to be hired by the living.

I fall into a category that many folks like me know well. When we sit for a job interview, we don't just answer the question. We over-explain. We give one thousand reasons for one thousand stories. We assume the person across the desk doesn't understand the context, so we try to give them all the context. We dump the whole data bucket on the table because we are terrified of being misunderstood.

Usually, they just look at us like we're crazy. And we don't get the job.

"I'm Taping It At Home"

This is why I struggle with the social grease that keeps the world turning: Small Talk.

For a Binary Mind, small talk is a glitch in the system. It is inefficient. We all say the same lines, we all give the same fake nods. It is a complete waste of bandwidth.

But I take it one step further. I don't just endure it; I usually break it.

If someone walks up to me in an elevator and starts the ritual—"Boy, some weather we're having, huh?"—my filter falls off. I'll look at them and say, "No, please. Please don't tell me what the weather is like. I'm taping it at home."

It stops them dead. It's a joke, but it's also the truth. I don't need the report. I need the silence.

10. HAPPY DAYS VS. THE STREET KID (MELROSE HIGH)

When I moved to Melrose, I thought I was walking into a better opportunity. I didn't realize I was walking onto a movie set.

Melrose High School was Happy Days. It was letterman jackets, cliques, and kids whose parents had known each other since kindergarten.

I was the kid from East Boston. I was the "Street Kid." I was Italian in a town that felt very... established.

This was my first true experience with prejudice. It wasn't someone yelling slurs at me. It was quieter. It was bureaucratic. It was a system designed to make sure the "right" kids got the spots, and the "wrong" kid stayed on the sidelines.

The Football Uniform

I showed up to the first football practice completely blind to their social codes. I walked up to someone in the stands and asked, "Do I need to bring my own uniform?"

They looked at me like I had three heads. "No, the school gives them to you."

I didn't know. In East Boston, we played with what we had. Here, everything was provided—except a fair shot.

The Eye Exam Sabotage

I went out for quarterback. I knew I had the arm. I had been running coordinates in the street since I was seven. I knew the physics.

But before you could play, you needed a physical. The doctor they sent me to was Coach Hogue's best friend. His office was literally down the street from the coach's house.

I walked in. He told me to read the eye chart. I looked at the wall. "Where is the chart?"

He looked at me, scribbled on his pad, and signed the form.

The note didn't say "Needs glasses." It effectively said: "Cannot see for crap. Do not let this kid play quarterback."

He tanked me. He killed my position before I threw a single ball. Why? Because they already had their quarterback. They had the "Melrose" kid. They didn't need an Italian kid from Eastie taking the glory spot.

So, they put me on the line. I spent four years blocking, watching guys with half my arm strength throw the ball.

It wasn't until my senior year, at the very last practice, that the truth leaked out. We were in the gym. I picked up a ball and just rifled it. I threw it 70 yards, a perfect spiral, tearing across the air.

The lineman coach, Chevelle, stopped dead. He looked at the ball, then at me.

"Caggiano? You can throw like that?"

I looked at him. "I've been throwing like that since I was a freshman."

He couldn't believe it. But it was too late. The data had been ignored for four years because it didn't fit their narrative.

Baseball: The "Daddy Ball" Wall

If football was sabotage, baseball was a closed shop.

I had a history with baseball. In Little League, I was a flamethrower. I once struck out 15 kids in a six-inning game. I threw hard, and I was wild. There was one game where I hit three kids in a row. The third kid I actually knocked out. I wasn't trying to hurt them; I just had raw power and no coaching.

After the third kid went down, the fathers in the stands started screaming. They were coming down to the fence, yelling at the ump, yelling at me.

My brother Arthur stood up. Arthur was the Enforcer. He was built like a tank and had a face that didn't smile. He looked at the screaming fathers and said, calm but loud:

"My brother throws the ball really hard. He'll get his control. Sit down."

The fathers sat down. They were intimidated by the sheer "East Boston" of him.

The Melrose Tryout

Fast forward to the Melrose High tryouts. I brought that same heat. I got on the mound and struck everyone out. Bam. Bam. Bam. One kid maybe hit a ground ball. Then I got up to bat. I hit two home runs—absolute moonshots into the long field.

I was the best player on that field. Pure physics.

But when the roster went up? I wasn't on it.

I didn't understand. How could you cut the guy who struck everyone out and hit two homers?

I found out later. The coaches had a list. The local fathers—the guys running the "Minor League" system in Melrose—had already told the high school coach who the "good" kids were. I wasn't on the list. I hadn't played in their league. I hadn't gone to their BBQs. I was the anomaly. So, despite the data, they cut me.

Wrestling: "Don't Get Pinned"

So I ended up in the one sport where politics can't save you: Wrestling.

My junior year, I wrestled "Unlimited" (Heavyweight). I wasn't a giant, but I was dense and strong. I had to eat before each match just to get to the 175 pound minimum weight.

The coach knew exactly what I was. He would go down the line of wrestlers giving instructions:

"You, you're a pin guy. Go for the pin."

"You, you're a pin guy."

Then he'd get to me. "Caggiano... don't get pinned."

That was my job. Damage control. In wrestling, if you get pinned, the team loses 6 points. If you lose by decision, the team only loses 3 points. My entire strategy was: Survive the Monster.

The Baby Huey Match

I had to wrestle a guy they called "Baby Huey." He was massive. A giant. When I stepped onto the mat, the referee actually looked at me with pity. "You know this is Unlimited, right?"

"Yeah, I know. I'm the guy."

He shook his head. "I'll do what I can for you."

The whistle blew, and for six minutes, this giant beat the hell out of me. He threw me around. He slammed me. But every time he tried to stick my shoulders to the mat, I bridged. I fought. I refused to accept the data point of "Defeat."

I lost the match 11-4. But I didn't get pinned.

I walked off the mat and went straight to the bathroom to throw up my guts. I was battered.

Suddenly, the door bangs open. It's Baby Huey. He's smashing his fist into the paper towel dispenser, screaming.

"I can't believe it! I can't believe it!"

He saw me wiping my face. "What is wrong with you? I couldn't pin you! How could I not pin you?"

He had won the match, but I had broken his mind. He couldn't understand the physics of why I wouldn't stay down.

That was my high school career. Blocked from quarterback. Cut from baseball. And left to fight giants in wrestling just to save the team three points. It taught me that in the real world—the "Civilized World"—talent isn't enough. You need the network. And if you don't have the network, you'd better learn how to not get pinned.

The Golf Course: The 19th Hole & The Enforcer

Before I ever swung a club, I learned about the culture of the game from my father. We played at the Bellevue Golf Course. This was a club that, I believe, had only started allowing Italians to join about two years before we moved to Melrose. You could feel it. The air was thin with judgment.

One day, my father was in the "19th Hole"—the lounge where the old guard sat around after their rounds. There was a bumper pool table in the center. My father watched them play. He watched them laugh and slap backs. He waited.

When a game finished, he stood up and walked over. "I've got next."

They looked at him. The Italian guy. The IRS guy. They told him, with that polite condescension, that he had to wait his turn. So, he waited. He sat there, patient as stone, until the table was open.

He stepped up. What these men didn't know was that while they played bumper pool in a country club for fun, Arthur Caggiano had learned to play pool in Northend of Boston for money. They were playing a game; he was executing a trade.

He racked the balls. Crack. Sink. Crack. Sink. He ran the table. Then he did it again. And again. He racked and cleared the table almost five times in a row. The last ball wobbled out. He smiled.

The room went silent. The laughter stopped.

He didn't say a word. He just dismantled them with geometry and pressure. He showed them that their "exclusive club" didn't protect them from someone who actually knew how to play.

The Caddie Recorder: Downloading the Swing

I learned the game the same way I learned swimming: I watched.

I started caddying at Bellevue. I carried the bags for the members. Most kids just lugged the clubs and looked for lost balls. I was studying the mechanics. I saw how the good players swung. It wasn't like a baseball bat—which is how every bad golfer swings. It was a pendulum. It was fluid. I watched the guys on TV, and I watched the best players at the club.

Input: Keep the left arm straight.

Input: Rotate the hips, don't slide.

Input: The club does the work, not the muscles. Hit down through the ball, let the club head push the ball up.

I didn't take lessons. I just downloaded the motion. By the time I went out for the Melrose High golf team, I didn't look like a beginner. I looked like a mimic who had stolen the code.

Psychological Warfare on the Fairway

I made the team. But I quickly realized that mechanics only get you so far. Some of these kids had been playing since they were toddlers. They had better swings. They had better equipment. But they had a weakness: They were soft. They were "Happy Days" kids. They lived in a world of rules and safety. I lived in a world of data and street leverage.

The "Joint" Incident

I was playing a match against a kid who was much better than me. He was "Mr. Clean"—perfect haircut, perfect clothes, probably never broke a rule in his life. He was up by three strokes with six holes to go. Mathematically, I was dead. I needed to hack his system.

It was a beautiful, sunny day. We were walking down the fairway. I reached into my pocket and pulled out a regular cigarette. I didn't light it. Instead, I carefully twisted the end of it, pinching the paper so it looked exactly like a joint. I put it in my mouth and just let it hang there while I walked.

I saw him look at me. His eyes went wide. You could see the panic signals firing in his brain: "Is... is he smoking marijuana? On the golf course? During a match? Is he high right now?"

He completely short-circuited. He was so focused on the "drug" hanging from my lip that he forgot how to play golf. He crumbled. He choked on every shot for the last six holes.

I didn't break a single rule. I didn't smoke anything. I just introduced a variable he couldn't process. I won the match.

By the time I graduated, I had earned letters in Football, Wrestling, and Golf. I didn't get them because I was the most talented. I got them because I was willing to block when they wouldn't let me throw, I was willing to bridge when I couldn't win, and I was willing to twist a cigarette when I couldn't out-swing them.

I was learning that if you can't beat the system with skill, you beat it with psychology.

The Kitchen Table (4:00 A.M.)

It was 1971. The house was quiet in the way only houses are before dawn—no movement, no appliances humming, no voices yet awake. Just structure holding its breath.

I came downstairs at four in the morning and found my father sitting at the kitchen table. He was alone. A single cup of tea sat in front of him, steam barely visible in the low light.

He wasn't reading. He wasn't praying. He was staring into the middle distance, the way someone does when they're working through something that won't let go.

My father was a devout man. For years, without exception, he went to the 7:30 a.m. Mass every single day. Rain, snow, exhaustion—none of it mattered. Faith, for him, wasn't emotional. It was procedural. It was done because it was right.

But that morning, in the silence of the kitchen, he wasn't praying. He was calculating.

He looked up when he saw me, as if he'd been expecting a witness, and without preamble he dropped the thought that had been keeping him awake.

"Robert," he said, quietly, "tell me something."

He paused, then continued. "There are people on the other side of the planet who don't know my religion. They've never heard of it. Why am I special? Why do I get to go to heaven and they don't?"

He shook his head slightly, not in anger—more in disbelief. "It doesn't make sense," he said. "If there are old people in those villages doing good things—helping each other grow, living together, coexisting—shouldn't they be able to go to heaven too? Just because they don't know the specific rules I follow?"

He looked down at his tea, as if the answer might be there. "The math doesn't work," he said. "God has to be bigger than that."

That was the spark. That was the moment something loosened—not his faith, but its frame. Sitting at that kitchen table at four in the morning, my father began outlining what would eventually become the idea of the Six Professions. He started seeing the world not as belief systems competing for dominance, but as functions organizing for survival. He realized something most people never do: that the world does not run on doctrine. It runs on roles. And he understood, long before anyone around him did, that eventually the world was going to have to get over itself.

He started a theory that morning. I finished it decades later.

All Debts Are Paid

That wasn't the only lesson he taught me about how to navigate the world. When I was young, I used to go to funerals with him. After the service, when people gathered around tables and the food came out and the wine started flowing, my father would stand up to make a toast.

He would raise his glass to the deceased—let's say it was Uncle Mike—and say, clearly enough for everyone to hear:

"To Uncle Mike. All debts are paid."

Everyone would salute.

For a long time, I took it literally. My father was a Tax Man—an IRS boss. I assumed he meant exactly what it sounded like. That he'd checked the books. That Mike didn't owe anyone money.

I asked him about it later.

"Dad," I said, "you can't really be that good of a man that you're clearing everyone's financial ledger when they die."

He laughed. "No, Robert," he said. "It's not about money. It's about respect."

He leaned in, lowering his voice. "When someone dies, you talk about them in the future tense. You respect them more than you did when they were alive. You think only of the good. That's the only thing worth keeping. When you speak about them, you bring up their goodness. You clear the slate."

Then he added the part that stayed with me. "And here's the trick," he said. "When you respect the dead, the living respect you for it. You earn respect by giving it."

The Fluidity of the Law

My father was a man of strict rules. But he understood the gray. He had to. He was an accountant. He saw how the real world actually worked.

One day, with a twinkle in his eye, he said something that sounded like a joke at the time.

"You know," he said, "you're not a thief unless you get caught."

I laughed. It felt mischievous. Almost improper. But as I got older, I understood what he was really saying. He wasn't telling me to steal. He was telling me that society's labels are often based on perception as much as reality. That systems pretend to be absolute, but are enforced through human judgment. That morality, law, and truth are not always aligned in practice—even when they claim to be.

He followed the rules. Mass at 7:30 a.m., every day. But at 4:00 a.m., at the kitchen table, he questioned whether the rules made sense. He was the original Recorder. And he taught me—without ever saying it outright—that faith without structure collapses, and structure without honesty rots.

The Suit

I didn't pick the suit alone. I was standing there with my sister Mary, surrounded by fabric — patterns and textures that were loud in the way the early seventies were loud. Suede. Bold designs. Statements. That was the era. You didn't blend in. You announced yourself.

The tailor knew it too. He was proud when he came down the stairs carrying the suit. You could tell. He held it the way someone holds something they expect to be admired. This wasn't just clothing to him. It was expression. Craft. Style. He laid it out like a reveal.

My father didn't hesitate. He didn't circle it. He didn't touch the fabric. He didn't soften his voice. He looked straight at the tailor and said, very calmly and very clearly,

"That's the suit?"

The tailor nodded. "Yes."

My father leaned forward just slightly and said, "I wouldn't give you two cents for that suit. You made that suit for you. You did not make that suit for my son."

There was no anger in it. No performance. Just certainty. The tailor shrank immediately. You could see it in his shoulders, in his face. He didn't argue. He didn't defend his work. He didn't explain the fashion of the moment. He simply said, "I'm sorry. I'll be right back," and disappeared upstairs.

That mattered to me later — the way authority works when it's real. No escalation. No theatrics. Just truth delivered cleanly.

This tailor had everything. Racks and racks of suits. Leather jackets everywhere. Long leather jackets, short ones, heavy ones. My whole family wore leather jackets through high school. We had the best ones in town. At the time I thought it was style. Years later I realized it was probably debt being paid quietly. My father was a tax man. People settled accounts in different ways.

When the tailor came back down, he wasn't holding a statement piece. He was holding a Brooks Brothers pinstripe. Dark. Conservative. One size too big.

My father looked at it and nodded. "That one," he said. "You can cut it down. It'll fit him perfectly."

Then he turned to me. "You still want this one? I said yeah I need it for the Winter Ball...

He said Really, well then... you're not just going to wear it once," he said. "You're going to wear it for years. Weddings. Events. Whatever comes. I want to see you in this one."

Mary didn't say anything then. But later, she did. My father pulled her aside and gave her a talking-to. She pushed back. She said she thought I really liked the other suit. She said she was helping me choose something I wanted.

My father stopped her. "What do you think you were supposed to do?" he asked her. "Go in there with him to make him happy?"

Then he answered his own question. "No. You were supposed to protect him."

That suit followed me. I wore it longer than any suit I ever owned. I wore it to weddings. I wore it to moments where I needed to look like I belonged, even when I felt like I didn't.

I remember one night in particular — Winter Ball. I went to pick up my date, rang the bell, and when she opened the door she froze for a second. Then she pulled me inside, straight into the kitchen, to show her parents. I was wearing that suit. Bowtie and all. When the door closed behind us, I'm pretty sure they laughed for days. Not unkindly. Just in disbelief.

That suit did its job. Years later, when I look at my high school graduation photo, that's the suit I see. Not flashy. Not trendy. Structured. Built to last. Chosen not for the moment, but for the future.

Mary was there to translate taste. My father was there to enforce structure. Between them, the right decision got made. At the time, I thought it was just a suit. Now I know better. It was a lesson in how the world actually works — and who you want making the final call when it matters.

The Doorknob Theory

I found proof the other day. It was buried in an old box—a poem I wrote in Junior High School.

I wasn't a "school" kid. In fact, in my English class, there was a girl who was a 4.0 student. She was planning to go to college to be an English Major. She did everything right.

But that year, there was a poetry award. She didn't win it. I did. I found out years later at a reunion that she was still upset about it. She couldn't understand how Robert, the kid who wasn't chasing the grades, beat the future English major.

The reason is simple. She was writing words. I was writing a psychological profile.

The poem was called **"The Door Knob."** Even back then, I wasn't looking at the sunset; I was looking at the mechanics of how people touch things.

Here is the poem:

The Door Knob

A Squeeze here, a squeeze there, Is, all I need you will see, for me to tell you what you'll be.

I'm able to tell the traits of one, Especially, when tested like a bun.

I turn I twist to do my job, that's the fundamentals of a knob.

A squeeze here, a squeeze there, Is, all the action that I can bear.

The bruisers choke, the losers soak, For I'm able to see the cautious use a key.

Read that last stanza again. *"I'm able to tell the traits of one."*

I was fourteen going on fifteen years old, and I was already analyzing people.

- **"The bruisers choke"** — I saw the aggression in people who grabbed the door too hard.
- **"The losers soak"** — I saw the anxiety in people with sweaty palms who were afraid to enter.
- **"The cautious use a key"** — I saw the logical ones who wanted to unlock the mystery before walking in.

I looked at my yearbook from that year. Under "Future Plans," I had written: **Psychology.**

I didn't end up going to school for psychology. The words were to big for me to say, remember or spell. I have all that at my finger tips to-day but back then I went into business. I went into life. But looking back at that poem, I realize I never stopped being a psychologist. I just swapped the textbook for the real world.

The 4.0 student knew how to write a sentence. I knew how to read a room.

11. THE ASCENT: COLLEGE AND WORK

Before we go any further, I need to take you through the years that shaped how my mind actually worked long before anyone put a label on it. These aren't bragging rights. They're the breadcrumb trail — the proof that my wiring was already doing what it was designed to do.

Freshman Year: The First Turning Point

Northeastern University didn't start with brilliance. It started with effort — blunt, physical effort. My freshman year was dominated by the crew team, and that meant discipline, miles of running, and a kind of pain most people only read about.

Over 350 freshmen tried out. Thirty-five were chosen. I was one of them.

That year, my schedule wasn't "college kid drifting." It was miles on the pavement, lungs burning, a ½-mile incline repeated four times until you bled in your socks, because that's what it took to belong on that boat. Nine miles a day. Up before sunrise. Bed sore. Pride intact.

I wasn't thinking about GPAs or academic awards — I was thinking about survival, teamwork, and pushing through walls most people never hit. Academics that year weren't ignored — they simply weren't the priority. Crew demanded everything.

But even then, my mind was recording, analyzing, and storing. I wasn't a slouch. I wasn't drifting. I was building capacity — the physical side of the same wiring that would later show itself in data, patterns, and logic.

By the time the year ended, I had already learned something most people never learn at eighteen: If I committed, I could outwork anyone. That wasn't ego. It was observation. And it mattered for everything that came next.

Junior Year: The Door That Wasn't Supposed to Open

By junior year, my grades were solid, but nowhere near the 4.0 "top ten percent" cutoff that normally determined who could qualify for Northeastern's prestigious six-month London co-op program. Those were the rules. That was the system. And everyone I knew accepted it as gospel.

One afternoon, my friend Mark told me he'd been selected to go. He said it casually — like it was obvious. "The top ten percent get the shot," he said. "That's how they do it."

I remember thinking: Why should someone else's formula decide what I'm capable of? Not in anger. In confusion. Because even then, I didn't accept blanket rules that ignored the individual.

So I walked into the co-op office and met the senior administrator — a man in a wheelchair, sharp, kind, and not easily impressed. He confirmed everything Mark had said.

"Yes, Robert. Top ten percent only. That's the cutoff."

I didn't argue. I didn't plead. I asked one simple question:

"What if three professors — real professors, not electives — write recommendations stating I'm in the top ten smartest students they've taught? Would that qualify?"

He looked at me the way a man looks at someone who has no idea how the world works. A mix of amusement, doubt, and a little curiosity. Like he thought the conversation would end right there.

"Sure," he said. "If you get three professors to say that, bring the letters back."

Not sarcastic — just certain it would never happen. But he didn't know my wiring. He didn't know that once I saw a path, I walked it. He didn't know that I don't ask questions unless I intend to follow through. He didn't know that binary minds don't bluff — we execute.

And that was the moment the entire trajectory shifted.

The Three Professors

The first professor I went to was Professor Harrington, my economics professor — thirty-three years old, sharp, charismatic, and the kind of teacher who didn't just lecture; he formed minds. The very first word he ever wrote on the board was OBJECTIVITY.

He told us it was the single most valuable skill we'd ever develop. "Every time you evaluate something," he said, "start fresh. No assumptions. No bias. No baggage." That line hit me like scripture. A binary principle before I even knew the term. He was planning to be away one week and had his wife substitute — we joked we'd go easy on her. Turned out she was brilliant, funny, tougher than he was, and she owned that classroom. When I asked him for a recommendation letter, he didn't hesitate. "Absolutely, Robert." He saw something in the way I processed. Sadly, three years later at age thirty-six, he died of a heart attack. But that letter opened one of the most important doors of my life.

The second professor — Investment Management — reacted the same way. He wrote the letter, no hesitation. Nine years later, I ran into him in a sub shop. "Professor!" I said. "Robert," he replied instantly.

"You won the six-week $100 investment contest. Options strategy. Very smart."

"You remember that?" I asked.

He laughed. "Hard to forget. Genius work. Just needed real money and no fear." We both laughed — because he was right about the fear part.

The third professor — Competitive Analysis — had built an entire doctoral study around a case involving Legg's pantyhose. The class had a hundred complicated marketing ideas: new packaging, new promotions, new gimmicks. But when I broke the numbers down, the truth was simple: The best strategy was to do nothing. The market was already optimal, and any interference made it worse. He was stunned. It contradicted his own assumptions, but the math was irrefutable. He wrote the final letter gladly.

Three professors, three disciplines, three confirmations — each saying I belonged in the top ten percent intellectually, whatever the GPA said.

Most people would've stopped there. I simply took the letters back to the administrator like it was the next step in a sequence. He read them slowly, looking up at me with a different expression — not amusement this time, but recognition.

"Okay, Robert," he said. "You're going to London."

Whitechapel, Silvertown, and the 21-Year-Old Who Didn't Sleep

In 1979, I flew to London — twenty-one years old, no fear, no hesitation, no map of anything except the confidence that I'd figure it out.

Whitechapel was rough back then. Everyone kept telling me, "Lucky you're big, you're staying in Whitechapel." Even the customs officer said it. I had no idea why. I was a kid from an Italian Boston family — what was going to scare me? The Cockney accent was thick, but I understood it immediately. My classmates didn't. I'd translate for them, and we'd all laugh.

My job was with International Paint in Silvertown, part of Courtlands — one of the largest companies in Great Britain. The Chairman of the Board told my boss to give me one directive: "Prove we sell more than anyone else in our vertical."

That was it. No instructions. No guidance. Just a problem to solve. And a binary mind doesn't complicate problems — we break them down.

I mapped every factory, every production line, every solvent, every undercoat, every car plant, every union strike, every downtime risk. If a factory could produce 850 cars a day, I calculated exactly how much paint that required. If a plant was under construction or delayed by a union issue, I factored that into the nation's output. I built the entire forecast of Britain's car production simply by tracking paint consumption.

When I turned in my report, something unusual happened. The Chairman called me in. Sat across from me. Leaning forward. Eyes sharp.

"Robert... who are you?"

Because at the annual shareholder meeting, 8 of the 10 strategic points he presented were in my report — which he had seen the day before. He thought I was a spy. I laughed and told him the truth: "I just made a lot of calls. And I used the adding machine. You're going to have a big phone bill."

The Financial Times rewrote next year's automotive projections based on my analysis. I wasn't guessing the future. I was deducing it.

That was the London chapter on paper. But the real London chapter happened at night.

When the city slept, I didn't. I'd ride my small 100cc motorcycle through empty streets — the safest time in Whitechapel if we're being honest — and I'd explore every corner. Not for trouble. Not for rebellion. I was kicking the can, the way I always had as a kid — exploring, learning, absorbing, getting away with something harmless but exhilarating.

I became friends with the late-shift postal workers who drank six to eight pints before work. Friends with the DJ at the London Hospital

Tavern — he'd play Steely Dan's "East St. Louis Toodle-Oo" whenever I walked in. Friends with a short guy named Spike — a West Ham hooligan with the Inter-city Firm (ICF) who earned his name the hard way. I stood in the South End at the stadium, holding back the crowd so an elderly man wouldn't get crushed, only to have his son turn to me and laugh when I told him it was my first match ever.

Nine years later, when I returned to London on my honeymoon, I walked into a fish-and-chips shop and the owner came out yelling: "It's the Yank!" She remembered me after almost a decade. That's what happens when you treat people like people. Not like roles. Not like strangers.

EDS: The Crucible of Logic

My first real job after college was EDS — Ross Perot's company. It was famous for being brutal. Five interview rounds. The first four were designed to shake you. The fifth decided your fate.

The trick was simple: You had to tell your life story — high school, junior year, senior year, Northeastern — in perfect order. Then they'd disrupt you.

"When you were a junior... why did you choose Northeastern?"

"When you were a senior... what made you choose that co-op?"

"Tell me again about the end of your sophomore year..."

They'd pull you off your timeline, then see if you could return to the exact spot without losing the thread. That's all structured programming is. A branch. A return. A resume point. I passed easily. Not because I was trained — because my mind already worked that way.

Then came the logic test. The instructor said: "Write the steps of me walking to the door. I'll take one step at a time, half the distance each time."

Everyone started writing sequences. I didn't. I raised my hand:

"You'll never reach the door. Halfway forever is still not the door."

He stopped. Pauses. Adjusts his plan. And pretends that was always the test. I saw right through it — the correction, the ego, the pivot — and stored it. Recorders catch that stuff instantly in replay.

EDS was sink-or-swim. Miss one comma in your punch cards and you were fired. Three people in my class failed and were gone. I finished first. They wanted me to stay and teach the next class. I asked to go back to Boston to be near my father — they didn't like that, but they sent me anyway.

In Boston, I worked in Tape Processing and Actual Statistics. Reading claims, fixing errors, making the whole machine run smoother. I noticed most suspended claims were caused by simple address typos in data entry. Once those were fixed, claims started flowing cleanly — too cleanly. So cleanly that EDS had to put a five-day hold on all tape claims because the money was going out faster than expected.

My first real lesson in big business: Money flow scares people more than money problems.

At EDS, the pressure was constant, but for me, the data was transparent. I learned assembler, binary, and dump reading. Patterns were easy—they felt as natural as reading a newspaper. I genuinely thought everyone could scan a string of binary like 01010010 and instantly see the 'R'. I didn't realize yet that I was seeing the world in a resolution most people didn't even know existed.

Ross Perot and the Helicopter

Ross Perot visited our group. I asked him the one question others wouldn't: "You've accomplished more than most people ever dream of. What motivates you now?"

He smiled. "My kids," he said. "I'm raising them to understand work. Real work. I don't want them spoiled."

Later that week, I was in the data center at 9 p.m. Ross Perot's son landed his helicopter outside — coming home from working an oil rig. I laughed. His commute may have looked different from mine, but the wind hits everyone the same. It was all relative.

The Permanent Feedback Loop (The Tea Kettles)

It was during this training in Plano, Texas, that the silence officially ended. I went to a shooting range with a roommate. We were young and stupid. He had a .357 Magnum—a hand cannon. I was standing right beside him. I hadn't put my earplugs in yet. He didn't check. He just pulled the trigger.

A .357 Magnum isn't a sound. It's a shockwave. It felt like someone drove an icepick into the side of my head. The world went mute, and then, the high-pitched whistle started.

I waited for it to go away. That was decades ago. It never went away.

This is my Tinnitus. The "Tea Kettle" that rings 24/7.

Why does this matter for the Binary Mind? Because a Recorder cannot "ignore" input. We process it. Every second of every day, my brain has to allocate a specific percentage of its processing power to filtering out that scream.

Input: Person talking.

Input: Tea Kettle ringing.

Task: Filter the ring, enhance the voice.

It is an invisible tax on my energy. When I talk to you, I am working harder than you realize just to hear the silence between your words. This is why the 90-Day Reboot emphasizes "Neuro-Sensory Quiet Time." I need the external world to be quiet because my internal world never is.

The Phantom Cash (Plano, Texas)

The same trip that took my hearing also taught me a lesson about value.

On the very last night of our EDS training in Plano, we went out to dinner to celebrate. When we came back, the apartment door was busted open. It was a clean sweep. My roommate was devastated. They had taken his arsenal—including the .357 Magnum that had blown out my ears days before. (I admit, I didn't mourn the gun).

But they also took my brand new Canon camera with the long lenses. To a Recorder, losing your camera is like losing an eye. I was crushed.

But then, I remembered the "Gadget Bag" (my gambit bag). I had $1,100 in cash—my entire savings for the trip—hidden inside it. The bag was sitting right there, unzipped, rummaged through, and tossed on the floor.

My roommate looked at me and said, "It's gone, Rob. They took everything."

I walked over, picked up the bag, and reached into the lining. The cash was still there.

The Recorder Strategy: I hadn't just stuffed the money in a pocket. I had visualized the theft. I knew a thief works on speed and touch. They "squeeze" bags to feel for hard objects (cameras, wallets, guns). So I had placed the cash flat in the absolute center of the bag's dead space—the "void" where the structure of the bag makes it feel empty even when it's full.

The thief squeezed the bag. He felt nothing. He moved on.

He took the hardware (the camera). He took the weapon (the gun). But he left the fuel (the cash) because he didn't have the patience to verify the data.

12. THE ROCKET SHIP: LOTUS

I took a break from the streets and walked into a revolution.

It was the early 1980s. The world was still analog. Businesses ran on mainframes and "dumb terminals." The Personal Computer (PC) was seen by serious businessmen as a toy, or a glorified typewriter. They didn't have "workflow." They had paper.

Then came Lotus.

To understand the energy of this place, you have to look at the math. It defies gravity. When Lotus was preparing to launch "1-2-3," the projections were modest. They were hoping—hoping—to sell maybe $3 or $4 million in the first year.

Then came the pre-announcement at Comdex. The world saw the software. The Recorders saw the utility; the Runners saw the magic. Before the first box was even shipped, they had a backorder of $35 million.

By the end of the first year, they didn't do $4 million. They did over $100 million.

It wasn't a company; it was a rocket ship. And I was strapped in.

Beginning a New Chapter

I saw an ad: Lotus was hiring a mainframe systems engineer. I walked into their Beverly Hills office — beautiful place — and handed the receptionist my résumé. "You don't need to keep looking," I said. "I'll take the job."

Cocky? Maybe. But true.

The district manager, Pat Paolili, saw my résumé and recognized the EDS pedigree immediately. She knew exactly what it meant if someone survived four years there. She hired me. She was the first *female* Sales Person of the year at IBM.

Pat was one of the best managers I ever had — brilliant, intuitive, able to spot raw potential and shape it. She hired people who would eventually become VPs, founders, leaders. She knew how to grow talent.

Symphony Link: Outperforming an Entire Company

Lotus was exploding in popularity. 1-2-3 was everywhere. Symphony was growing. Mainframes and PCs were merging worlds.

I discovered something simple: People wanted Symphony Link because it let them pull mainframe print jobs directly to their PCs. So I taught the programming language. If you took the class, you got a free copy of Symphony Link.

Fifteen people per class. Five copies per head. I sold more Symphony Link than the entire company combined.

Rising Through Lotus

I went from systems engineer → district systems engineering manager → sales manager — something unheard of at the time.

There were 22 districts. I got Irvine — ranked 22nd. Within a year, we were number four. Every person on my team hit Achievers Club — top ten percent.

Then I was asked to take over distribution, which accounted for 33% of the company's business. Leadership wanted to get rid of distribution. They didn't like the middlemen. I didn't see "middlemen." I saw leverage.

I studied the real numbers:

- Returns

- Channel stuffing
- Manufacturing waste
- Margins
- Rebates
- End-of-quarter games
- $19 million per year in destroyed manuals and boxes

I cut the wastage in half. That alone changed the top line. I grew distribution from 33% to 52% of corporate revenue. We hit the numbers 18 quarters in a row.

And while I'm talking about Lotus and computer software I need to rant about Word.

The Channel Truth

(Why Systems Fail Without Recorders)

There is a reason I react so strongly to tools like Word, and it has nothing to do with nostalgia or resistance to change. It has everything to do with what happens when systems quietly drift away from structural truth and toward speed, optics, and momentum.

Word didn't win because it was better.

It won because Microsoft bought the doorway to the user.

OEM agreements.

Education licensing.

Enterprise bundling.

Operating system leverage.

Word arrived everywhere by default. Not because it respected the act of writing, but because it controlled distribution. Functionality became secondary. Presence became everything.

Anyone who lived through WordPerfect or Lotus 1-2-3 knows this isn't opinion. It's history.

Those tools let you scribe.

They did what you told them to do—no more, no less.

Word developed a mind of its own. Auto-formatting. Re-paging. Invisible rules. Behavior that overrides intent. A system optimized for motion instead of fidelity.

That didn't happen by accident.

It's what happens when systems are designed and maintained by people who prioritize movement over verification.

I learned this lesson early—not in theory, but at scale.

At the time, the market reality was simple. Microsoft had enormous financial leverage from the operating system and used it to buy the desktop. Better products lost. Consumers lost fidelity even as they gained ubiquity. That was the environment. I didn't create it, and I didn't try to explain it away.

I had to operate inside it.

What mattered wasn't what should have won. What mattered was what was true.

For eighteen consecutive quarters, I hit my numbers. Not by outspending competitors. Not by end-of-quarter theatrics. Not by panic pricing, extra points, freight concessions, or extended terms.

In fact, that was the first thing I eliminated.

Runner-led sales organizations rely on last-minute motion. Discounts spike. Revenue looks good on paper. Underneath, margins collapse, returns explode, and trust erodes.

It feels productive.

It feels busy.

But it's motion without stability.

I did something different.

I sat down with distributors and asked a question almost no vendor ever asks:

How do you actually make money?

Not list price.

Not programs.

Not incentives.

Actual money.

Margins.

Marketing revenue.

Returns.

Cash-flow timing.

I let them show me the truth.

In some cases, the answers were uncomfortable. There were channel companies whose public story was distribution, but whose real profit engine was marketing programs. Advertising. Placement. Sponsored visibility. When that truth surfaced publicly, stock prices fell. Some didn't survive.

That wasn't the point.

The point was that incentives were misaligned, and everyone was pretending otherwise.

Another truth surfaced immediately: returns were catastrophic.

When I took over distribution, Lotus was destroying roughly nineteen million dollars in hard-cost inventory. At a seventy-percent gross margin, that represented a massive topline revenue loss. We weren't losing business—we were leaking value.

Eliminate returns, and revenue rises instantly without selling a single additional unit.

So I stopped negotiating boxes and started designing a system that removed uncertainty.

I told distributors the truth:

Microsoft would outsell us in raw units. They owned the channel. That wasn't up for debate.

But every time a Lotus box went out the door, they would make more money on it than they did on a Microsoft box.

Not later.

Not hypothetically.

Immediately.

Margins matter more than logos.

Then I shifted the direction of force.

Instead of pushing inventory into distribution and bribing it to move, I created pull at the secondary level—the point where transactions actually happen. Retailers. Accounts. Buyers who already had demand.

I redirected marketing dollars downstream, away from generic distribution spend and into the hands of the people who could pull product through inventory naturally.

That changed everything.

Returns stopped—not because of policy, but because inventory was no longer misallocated.

Fear disappeared—not because of persuasion, but because risk was removed.

At quarter end, I didn't ask distributors what they wanted to buy. I already knew.

I knew their inventory.

I knew their customers.

I knew what would sell and what wouldn't.

So I did the work for them.

I specified what to buy.

How much to buy.

For how long.

I built the purchase requests.

I created the invoices.

I removed decision fatigue entirely.

I didn't say, "Here are your options."

I said, "Buy four more weeks of inventory. Here's the math."

No returns.

No freight penalties.

No clawbacks.

No games.

If something didn't sell in ninety days, it didn't come back to hurt anyone. It was redirected to a market where demand already existed.

All they had to do was say yes.

That's how the quarter closed.

Every quarter.

Eventually, the executives tried to name what was happening. They called it Revenue Enhancing Inventory—REI—not because it sounded clever, but because they couldn't mentally hold the system long enough to describe it.

From their perspective, inventory was somehow creating revenue instead of threatening it.

From mine, the leaks were gone.

That's why I was invited into the room.

Not because I moved faster.

Because I removed uncertainty.

This is where the Runner–Recorder bond matters.

Jim was the ultimate Runner. He understood motion, scale, and consequence. He trusted me because I told him the truth—every time. If something was wrong, it was wrong. No spin. No delay.

He kept me on a short leash, but he didn't require permission for every decision. I made decisions, then reported them. No surprises. Complete transparency.

That trust is what allowed the system to work.

Runners move civilization forward.

Recorders keep it from tearing itself apart.

When the two designs trust each other, systems stabilize. When they don't, systems still grow—but they grow brittle. They look powerful right up until they fail.

This is why tools like Word unsettle me today.

It still rewrites intent.

It still prioritizes automation over verification.

It still changes structure without asking.

It isn't broken.

It's behaving exactly as designed.

The same is true of organizations. Markets. Civilizations.

When Recorders are sidelined as slow, difficult, or overthinking, systems don't stop moving. They just stop being anchored to reality.

I've lived on both sides of that.

I know—because I've done it—that when incentives align with truth instead of optics, stability follows.

That isn't business advice.

That's architecture.

And it's the same architecture that keeps civilizations alive.

Now as I was saying at Lotus...

Calling the Future (and Being Right)

Deb Bessemer, VP of Sales, announced the new Achievers Club rules: 110% quota. Top ten percent eligible.

I told her, politely but directly: "You're going to change my requirements to go to Switzerland because if you don't twice as many people will qualify you will need twice as many seats." She said the "same conditions for everyone", which I replied "Ok, I warned you."

She laughed it off. She thought I was overconfident.

One year later, in front of 1,100 salespeople at the annual meeting, she announced we will be having two Achieves Clubs this year...she stopped mid-speech and said — almost under her breath — "Robert said this would happen..." We filled Achievers Club twice over.

Later that week Deb was presenting to 300 sales managers what she saw as the top five things she looks for in a manager. Empathy was one of them and she said Robert Caggiano is the example of a manager with empathy for his people that she admired.

Aspen: The Table of Titans

The setting was Aspen. The air was thin, the altitude was high, and the room was filled with the kind of people who moved markets, not just boxes.

It was a three-day summit. Sitting around the massive conference table were the titans of distribution: executives from Ingram Micro and Tech Data. These weren't just managers; these were the people moving hundreds of millions of dollars in software across the globe.

I sat right in the middle of the table. This was my Moneyball moment. Just like in the movie, where the old scouts were looking at the player's jawline and the math guys were looking at the on-base percentage, I was the only one in the room looking at the structural math of their future.

They didn't want a presentation about what I'd done in the past. They didn't care about marketing fluff. They wanted to know one thing: "How do we survive next year?"

Their entire universe revolved around two variables: Margin and Revenue. If they moved $1 million in product, they needed to secure their $120,000 margin. If that slipped, they bled.

So, I didn't give a speech. I gave a diagnosis.

I went around the table, pointing to each titan, breaking down exactly how the Lotus environment was going to shift the ground beneath their feet.

I looked at the reseller with the physical stores. "You're component-driven. You live and die by shelf space. Here is exactly how Lotus's roadmap impacts your 12% margin, and here is how you pivot before you lose it."

I turned to the retail-heavy executive. "You're worried about inventory. Here is how you avoid a wave of returns when the pricing shifts next quarter."

I looked at the enterprise heavyweights. "You handle the big contracts. Ignore the quarterly noise. Here is exactly when you need to buy based on the new fiscal cycles."

Then I dropped the bomb that no one wanted to say out loud: "Shrink wrap is disappearing."

The era of the physical box was ending. Digital was coming.

I wasn't telling them how to run their companies; I was showing them the invisible architecture of the market before the rest of the world saw it. Because I was a Recorder, I could see the structure. That's why they listened.

The Million Dollar Urinal

The tension in the room was high, the focus absolute. We took a break, and I headed to the restroom.

I was standing at the urinal, staring at the wall, when the CEO of Ingram Micro stepped up beside me. It's the great equalizer—two men in a tiled room, doing the most human thing possible, while millions of dollars hang in the air outside the door.

He didn't look at me. He just stared straight ahead and said, in a low voice:

"You know... you still owe me a million dollars."

I didn't blink. I finished up, zipped, and looked over at him.

"Actually... you're lucky you got the three."

He paused. The math clicked in his head. He knew the leverage I had, and he knew the deal we had made. A slow grin spread across his face. He laughed—a genuine, surprised laugh.

"Yeah," he said. "You're probably right. Thanks."

We washed our hands and went back to the table. That is the Recorder in the wild: High stakes at the table, high comedy in the bathroom, and absolute clarity everywhere.

The Secret Weapon: The Power of "No"

I moved through the ranks quickly, eventually becoming a Director. Lotus was unique because the culture allowed a Recorder like me to make massive corporate decisions, even without the traditional pedigree.

Why did they trust me? It started in the interview process for the Distribution Manager role. Jim Manzi, CEO, looked at me and said something that defined my entire career:

"Robert, you have a way of saying 'No' to people, and they're OK with it. I need you to say 'No' to these guys."

Runners hate saying no. They want to be liked. They want to keep the "vibe" going.

A Recorder doesn't mind saying no, because to us, "No" isn't emotional. It's just data. It's a boundary. And because I didn't say it with malice—just with clarity—people respected it.

I became the secret weapon in distribution. While other divisions were fluctuating, I made my number 18 quarters in a row. I built a fortress of consistency in a chaotic market. I accumulated a massive cash reserve because I ran my division on physics, not hope.

The Ultimate Runner: Jim Manzi

The CEO, Jim Manzi, was the best I have ever seen. He was the Ultimate Runner. He had a mind like a steel trap. He could stand in front of an audience of 1,100 people, spot a face in the crowd, and call them by name. He didn't just know the business; he knew the people.

He treated me well because he recognized the wiring. He knew I wasn't blowing smoke. He knew that if I said something was broken, it was broken.

That trust is what led to the discovery of the "52-Week Glitch."

The 52-Week Glitch (The International Ponzi Scheme)

One day, Jim asked me to come see him. He looked puzzled.

"Robert," he said, "I'm curious about our International Group. It feels like they have almost 52 weeks of inventory sitting out there. Why would that be?"

My Recorder brain instantly flagged an error. "52 weeks of inventory? Jim, how do they get paid?"

He looked at me. "What do you mean?"

"Show me the comp plan. Do they get paid on what they sell through to the customer, or what they sell in to the channel?"

The answer, of course, was that they got paid on "Sell-In."

I broke it down for him: "Jim, Lotus Notes is a corporate license. It's a contract. Distributors don't 'stock' contracts on a shelf like boxes of software. They don't sell into a corporation; they transfer to a location. If you're seeing 52 weeks of inventory, no one actually bought it."

I told him I wouldn't be surprised if there were stacks of unsigned contracts sitting in a desk drawer somewhere.

It turns out, that's exactly what it was. The Senior VP of Sales for the International Group had been running his own internal Ponzi scheme. He was "selling" product to the channel to hit his number and get his bonus, but the product was going nowhere. It was a ghost ship.

The Bailout

When the truth came out, the hole in the books was massive. The company had to figure out how to cover 52 weeks of "fake" inventory while they cleaned up the mess.

And who paid for it? My division.

Because I had hit my number 18 quarters in a row, because I had run a clean ship, I had a massive cash and margin reserve. They took my surplus to plug the hole the Runner VP had created.

I didn't mind. That's the job. The Recorder builds the foundation so strong that it can hold the weight when the Runners accidentally blow up the second floor. Jim Manzi knew that. That's why he let me make decisions. He knew that when the smoke cleared, I would be the one standing there with the real numbers.

The Prince of Runners (Dave Valentino)

If you want to understand what a High-Speed Runner looks like in the wild, you had to know Dave Valentino. He was the Prince. He was the ultimate showman, the ultimate salesman. In the days of the "Channel Wars"—when you had to show up with boxes of tchotchkes and golf clubs just to get a meeting—Dave didn't just show up. He performed.

He taught me that sales isn't about data; it's about Energy Transfer.

I would demonstrate the technology and Dave would light up the audience. Throwing Frisbees with money taped underneath as people went crazy trying to be the lucky one to catch one, and when the last one thrown Dave would tell the audience "Look underneath your seat... you are all winners with me!" There was money—5, 10, 20 dollar bills.

The Magician of Beverly Hills (Selling Hope)

But to really understand his genius, you had to see him pitch. We were in Beverly Hills during the Wild West days of the PC revolution. I had rigged up Lotus Symphony to talk to a little plastic satellite dish that pulled stock quotes out of the FM radio waves.

Dave stood in front of a room full of millionaires—men desperate for an edge—and he played them like a fiddle. He was the ultimate "Snake Oil Salesman" of the digital age, and I say that with love. Because he wasn't selling software. He was selling Hope.

He pointed to the screen where my macro was blinking.

"Gentlemen," he'd whisper, letting them in on a conspiracy. "The market follows physics. The trucks have to move before the factories can sell. If Transportation stocks jump, the Industrials follow 15 minutes later."

He leaned over that plastic dish like it was the Holy Grail. "Right now, you are blind. But this box? This box lives in that 15-minute gap. This box is a time machine."

The room went crazy. They climbed over each other to buy it. He taught me the lesson: The Carrot isn't the product. The Carrot is the belief that you are about to win.

The Bill Gates Incident

The perfect example of Dave's wiring happened in Las Vegas, at the Mirage, during Comdex.

Dave spots a woman he used to date. She's now a VP at Business-Week. She is sitting at a $10 Blackjack table... next to Bill Gates.

Now, a Recorder would freeze. A Recorder would calculate: "That is the richest man in the world. Do not disturb. Do not interrupt."

Dave? He walked right over. He gives the girl a big hug. He turns to Bill.

Bill looks up and says, "Hi, I'm Bill Gates."

Dave looks him right in the eye—the way only a Prince can—shakes his hand and says:

"Bill, I know who you are."

Then he looks at the $10 chips on the table, looks back at Bill, and drops the line of the century:

"Bill... what is this... Nintendo to you?"

The table exploded. Bill laughed. That is the Runner Superpower. He collapsed the distance between a salesman and a billionaire in three seconds.

The Crash

But the Runner engine runs hot. The parties, the alcohol, the constant "Go, Go, Go"—it takes a toll. He called me right around Christmas time, just like today. He was down in Mexico at his timeshare, fishing.

He said, "Robert, I have a belly ache. My stomach is killing me. What do I do?"

I gave him the standard advice—take Zantac, calm down.

He called me back later. "Robert, I went to the doctor. It's not acid. It's cancer. Stage 4."

My heart stopped. But Dave was still in character. He was still the Runner.

"I got this," he said. "You know me. I'm a healthy guy. I'm gonna fight it."

The Long Goodbye

For months, I called him every week. "How are you doing, Dave?"

"I'm good, Robert. Things are going good. I'm fighting."

He was selling me hope, just like he sold those guys in Beverly Hills. He didn't want to break the character.

By August, I said, "Dave, I'm coming to see you."

There was a long pause on the phone. The energy dropped. The Prince put down the mask.

"Robert," he said softly. "It might be hard."

"Why?"

"Because I'm dying. There isn't much left."

He had been protecting me from the truth the whole time. We lost him in early September. The light went out.

To The Family: Dave left behind a beautiful family. A wife, a daughter, and a son who has autism—a pure Recorder born to the ultimate Runner. If you are reading this: Your father was a giant. He could walk into a room of wolves and have them eating out of his hand. I love him. I love you. The Prince is gone, but the show? I'll never forget it.

The Calming Voice (Paul Ohrenberger)

If Dave was the gas, Paul was the steering wheel. He had this soothing, perfect tone. He could stand in front of a room and explain complex systems—not just the technology, but the people mechanics. He was the one who taught managers how to manage different operating systems.

Paul and I had a connection that defied the odds. We were both born in the same hospital in Winthrop. We found out later that we had crossed paths a thousand times before we met. He worked behind the counter at Capone's Grocery in East Boston—the store I went to every single day as a kid. He was serving me deli meat before he was helping me serve software.

The Missing Editor

Paul was my Anchor. No matter how crazy my ideas were, Paul could process them. He enjoyed the way my mind worked. He is the one person who should be sitting here with me right now, writing this book. He would have known exactly how to organize these chapters. He would have known how to translate the "Recorder" experience to the masses.

The Keeper of the Principles

Paul didn't just teach technology. He taught Humanity. He ran the management training programs at Lotus, but he wasn't just reading from a manual. He was teaching the soul of the company. He taught managers how to actually be managers. He taught them how to live up to the Lotus Development Principles—values like fairness, social responsibility, and treating people like adults.

He had this incredible ability to take a room full of stressed-out corporate climbers and walk them through the "Why."

- Why do we treat people this way?
- How do different operating styles work together?
- How do you handle a difficult employee without breaking their spirit?

He helped everyone. He didn't just give you the answer; he walked you through the logic so you felt like you found the answer. He made you feel smart.

The New Orleans Giggle (The Reality Check)

But my favorite memory of Paul isn't in a classroom. It's on a balcony at the Royal Sonesta in New Orleans. We were there for a conference, staying right on Bourbon Street. The party was raging outside—thousands of people, music, booze, chaos. The loudest place on Earth.

We were in the room, relaxing, smoking a little marijuana. Suddenly, my Recorder brain kicked in. The paranoia. The rules. I started waving my hands frantically.

"Paul! Paul! I gotta blow this smoke out the window! What if they smell it? What if we get caught?"

Paul just looked at me. He didn't panic. He let out this beautiful, soft giggle. He gestured to the open window, to the sea of madness below us.

"Robert," he laughed. "We are on Bourbon Street. In the French Quarter. I think you're gonna be okay."

He just laughed at the absurdity of it. Here I was, worried about a puff of smoke in a city that was currently inhaling every vice known to man. That was Paul. He was the Reality Check. When I spun out on the details, he pulled me back to the big picture with a smile.

The Empty Chair

It is a cruel irony that a man defined by his ability to communicate—a man who helped so many people find their voice—was taken down by a rare form of Parkinson's. It robbed him of his mechanics. He should be sitting here with me right now. He would have loved this book. He would have laughed at my drafts. He would have helped me explain the "Lotus Principles" of the brain. He was my Anchor. And God, I miss that giggle.

13. THE UNIVERSAL LANGUAGE: NADADUR VARDHAN
(The Hardware Beneath the Culture)

In 1985, I moved to California. I was a kid from Boston entering a new world. And the first real friend I made—the best friend I made—was a man named Nadadur Vardhan.

Nadadur was an accountant, about ten or eleven years older than me. When I walked into his world, I felt a strange sense of déjà vu. I knew this setup. I knew this rhythm.

You have to understand, almost everyone in my life was a Boss. Cousin Joe was the Captain of the Police Department. My Uncle owned the Funeral Home and the main ambulance service in Boston. And my Father wasn't just an accountant; he was the Boss Man for the IRS in Boston. He collected taxes door-to-door in the neighborhoods. He didn't just work in a high-rise; he had his office right out of the house. I grew up watching men come into that home office, sit down, and spill their financial guts. I saw the fear, the negotiation, the relief. I watched how the "Boss" handled people when they were vulnerable.

So when I met Nadadur—who was starting his own tax practice out of his home in Santa Monica—I wasn't walking into a stranger's office. I was walking back into my childhood, just in a different time zone.

The Trade

We made a deal: I gave him the technology—Lotus 1-2-3, the software that ran the financial world—and helped him set up his systems. In exchange, he did my taxes. It seemed like a simple swap. But what I actually got was a front-row seat to the way the world really works.

The Fly on the Wall

For fifteen years, I spent the first three months of every year working out of his office in Santa Monica. I wasn't an accountant. I was a "Silent Partner." I sat there, just like I used to sit in my father's house, and I listened.

But the clientele had changed. My dad dealt with the streets of Boston. Nadadur dealt with the stars. He did taxes for The Commodores. For Hollywood celebrities. For Politicians. For Multi-millionaires.

And here is what I learned, sitting in that chair, bridging the gap between my father's world and Nadadur's world:

The stories were identical.

It didn't matter if the client was a guy from Southie trying to settle a debt or a global superstar trying to hide assets. It didn't matter if they were from India, America, or Europe. They all had the same fears. The same threading moments. The same stress about money, family, and legacy.

"It's all relative." Just like in the funeral home, and just like in the IRS office, once you strip away the titles, the human structure is exactly the same.

The Bodyguard (Secret Service)

Nadadur's influence grew massive. When Barack Obama went to India, he took Nadadur to introduce him. That is the level he was operating at. He held beautiful events at his home in Brentwood. Ambassadors would come. Influential politicians would gather.

When Hillary Clinton was running for President, Nadadur hosted a fundraiser at a friend's house. I didn't go as a donor. I went as "Security." I played Secret Service agent for the day. I stood by the door—a big Irish-Italian guy, hands folded, scanning the room.

I met Hillary. I looked her right in the face. And as a Recorder, I noticed the one thing the cameras don't quite capture: Her eyes. They were the bluest eyes I had ever seen. You could see the intensity in them. I instantly understood what attracted Bill. It wasn't just politics; it was a magnetic force.

The Scale of Humanity (The Obstetrician)

Nadadur opened the world to me. Through him, I met his sister. She wasn't just a medical professional; she was a highly respected Obstetrician in India. We were talking one day, and I tried to impress her with a statistic I had read.

"I heard you've delivered something like 35,000 babies in your lifetime. That is unbelievable."

She looked at me and corrected me gently. "No, Robert. We are just about to go north of 100,000 babies."

I froze. 100,000? How is that mathematically possible?

She showed me the numbers. The density of the population. The speed of life in her region. It shattered my "Western" scale of reality. It taught me that my view of the world was tiny.

But even with 100,000 babies delivered, she told me the same thing Nadadur did: The bodies are all the same. The first breath is the same. The mother's look is the same.

The Validation (Indubala)

Then there was Nadadur's wife, Indubala. Like the rest of the family, she was a doctor—sharp, kind, and observant.

In 2019, years after I first met them, I finally found the language for my own mind. I was talking with Indubala and I told her, "You know, I found out I would be considered Autistic."

I expected her to be surprised, or maybe offer sympathy. She didn't. She looked at me with the calm precision of a doctor who has seen everything.

"Robert," she said. "Do you know what that means?"

"What?" I asked.

She said. "Binary thinking."

I was stunned. I had spent years trying to explain my brain to people. I had spent years thinking about "Recorders" and "Runners." And here was a doctor from the other side of the world, effortlessly handing me the key. She didn't see "disorder." She saw the operating system. It was confirmation.

The Professor and The Symbols

I used to go to late-night dinners with Nadadur and a brilliant Professor from UCLA. We would eat late, and we would talk about the future.

One night, we were discussing why English became the dominant business language. I expected a political answer. He gave me an Engineering answer.

"Robert, it comes down to symbols. The communication mechanism with the least amount of symbols will always win on a worldwide basis. It is the quickest way to transfer data."

English is efficient code. Mandarin is complex code. The world chose efficiency. He amazed me. If I asked the average American kid to name the 50 state capitals, maybe they get 48. This Professor didn't just know the capitals. He could tell you the name, the family history behind the name, and the economic driver of the city in 1890. He had a Recorder Mind of the highest order.

The Safe Room

Why did these people—Ambassadors, Geniuses, Politicians, Doctors like Indubala—talk to me?

I was a big kid from East Boston. I didn't have their degrees. I didn't have their pedigree.

But I offered them something they couldn't get anywhere else: An Unfiltered Connection.

I listened without judgment. I treated the Ambassador the same way I treated the guy at the sub shop. I appreciated their culture, their religion, and their politics without trying to change them.

Because I had been trained by the Bosses—by Joe, by my Uncle, by my Father—I knew that authority is just a role. The person underneath is just a person.

Nadadur passed away nine years ago. If he were here today, he would be the one writing this book. He was the smarter one. He was the character. But he left me with the lesson that connects everything in this story: Culture is just the software. Biology is the hardware. And if you look past the software, we are all running on the same machine.

14. THE COST OF THE CODE

(Tattoos, Empty Chairs, and The Void)

We talk about the "Binary Mind" like it's a gift. And it is. It allowed me to see the physics of a baseball, the inventory of a corporation, and the truth behind a fake smile.

But there is a cost. The system doesn't just record the wins. It records everything.

The Wrong Environment: Memories as Tattoos

When you raise a sensitive, high-fidelity child in a "tough love" or chaotic environment, you aren't just hurting their feelings. You are writing permanent code.

Most kids are like Etch-A-Sketches. They get yelled at, they cry, they shake it off, and the screen is clear the next day.

I was stone tablets. Every criticism, every time I was misunderstood, every time I was told I was "wrong" when I knew I was right—it was tattooed on my brain.

- The School Trauma: The teachers who didn't understand why I couldn't just "do it their way."
- The Social Friction: The exhaustion of trying to fit into a "Runner" world that moved too fast and cared too little about the details.
- The Diagnosis Gap: Living for decades without knowing why I was different. Thinking I was broken, when I was just operating on a different OS.

The Loss of Artifacts: The "Trinkets"

To a Runner, a "trinket" is just stuff. If they lose a watch or a photo, they say, "Oh well, it's just an object."

To a Recorder, an object is a link. It is a physical coordinate that ties us to a memory, a person, or a time.

- The graduation picture.
- The specific tool.
- The memento from a trip.

When those things are lost, it feels like a file corruption. It's not just "stuff." It is a piece of the archive that has been deleted without my permission. The anxiety of losing those small things is massive because they are the anchors to my history.

The Empty Chairs: The Circle of Friends

This is the heaviest cost. My circle was tight. Recorders don't let everyone in. We have a firewall. But if you get past the firewall—like Kevin, like Joe, like my closest friends—you are part of me.

And they left too early.

- Kevin, Arthur and Paul, My brothers, the protectors of my universe.
- Joe: My cousin, the protector.
- Dave, Paul, and Nadadur my dear friends.

When a Runner loses a friend, they grieve, and eventually, the sharp edges of the memory soften. For me, the edges never soften. The memory is as sharp today as it was the day they died. The silence is deafening. I don't just "miss" them; I feel the structural void where they used to be. It's a missing column in the building, and the weight is harder to carry every day.

The Loss of Purpose: The "Retired" Wilderness

Then there was the loss of the mission. After the adrenaline of Lotus, after the battles were fought and won, there was the drift. The words became "too big." The corporate world morphed into something I didn't recognize. I felt "retired," but not in the good way. I felt unplugged.

For a Recorder, having no data to process, no problem to solve, is a form of death. I wandered in that wilderness for years—knowing I had this engine, but having nowhere to drive the car.

It wasn't until 2019—until the psychology came back, until the "Binary Mind" theory started to form—that the lights turned back on.

15. THE 53-YEAR-OLD ANOMALY (THE ICE CREAM WARS)

I have said that my body processes sugar differently. That I should have been diabetic years ago. To prove this isn't hyperbole, I need to submit two pieces of evidence. Most people look at a "Food Challenge" as a test of hunger. I looked at it as a war game.

Part 1: St. Louis (The Tins)

In 2008, I watched Adam Richman on Man v. Food go to St. Louis to try a legend. The challenge: Drink five metal tins of malt shake—nearly a pure gallon of dairy—in 30 minutes. Since 1917, only 22 people had done it. Adam failed. He threw up.

I happened to be flying to St. Louis two weeks later. I was 51 years old. My wife told me, "Don't do it. You're crazy. You're going to make yourself sick." I ignored her. I had a plan.

I brought my SE, Wayne. Wayne wasn't just an engineer; in Desert Storm, he ran Covert Communications. He was also a trained paramedic. I told him, "Wayne, I need your paramedic skills on alert. I am going to do this at 3:30 PM. I'm going to override my body, and you need to watch for the crash."

We walked in. The owner went to grab the fancy tall glasses. I stopped him. "No. Keep it in the shakes. Keep it in the metal tins. I'll drink all five of them, one at a time."

I blasted through the first three tins. No problem. I got through the fourth.

Then I picked up the fifth tin. And the wall hit me.

I looked at the tin. I looked at the clock. And for the first time, the math didn't look good. I stopped and thought: Oops. I'm not gonna make it. This is the reason only 22 people have done this since 1917.

My stomach was screaming. The curdling had started.

Wayne looked at me. He saw me fading. He didn't offer sympathy. He leaned in and said, "Come on, Robert. I didn't wait around to see you do this. You can pull the car over now if you want."

He knew exactly which button to push.

I looked at him. "Give me one of your french fries."

I ate the fry. The salt cut the sugar slime on my tongue. It tricked my brain just enough to reboot the system.

I tipped the fifth tin back and sucked it down in a single flip.

Time: 26 minutes.

I got the T-shirt. I got the plaque. I told them to engrave it: Robert. Age 51.

Part 2: The Pig Trough (The Inhale)

A year later, my wife called me. She found another one. Farrell's Ice Cream was relaunching. They were holding a contest: The Pig Trough. Two massive banana splits, softball-sized scoops, piled into a plastic trough.

I qualified as the number 8 seed. I was 53. Every other competitor was a college kid in their 20s.

My wife and I showed up that morning. The women went first. I watched them delicately spooning the ice cream into their mouths. I turned to my wife and shook my head. "They are losing because they are eating it. You can't eat this. You have to inhale it."

The whistle blew. I didn't eat. I didn't chew. I just opened the hatch.

I also had a strategy the college kids didn't. I had mapped the density:

Strawberry: Softest. Melts fast. First.

Chocolate: Medium. Second.

Vanilla: Hardest. Last.

If you wait, the vanilla turns into a rock. I attacked the strawberry while the college kids were still trying to look cool.

The Result: I finished in 1 minute and 15 seconds. I looked up. The college kids were barely halfway through.

I won the trophy. I won free ice cream for a year. I got my name on the menu cover. I told the owner: "Put Robert. 53."

The Epilogue: Feelings vs. Profits

The irony is that while I mastered the ice cream, the owner failed the business. The next year, he called me back. He wanted me to defend my title for a news segment... at 6:00 AM.

I told him, "I'm the defending champion. You should find people to try to beat me." He said no. He didn't understand showmanship.

So I sat there at 6:00 AM, half-awake, and tried to speed-eat a trough on live TV. They left a cherry stem in the bowl. Because I was "inhaling" it, the stem got lodged in my throat. I nearly choked to death on the morning news.

Years later, I watched Marcus Lemonis on The Profit try to save that same business. It was painful to watch. You had Marcus—a guy who looks at the math—trying to explain to the owner that feelings are not a currency. The owner wanted it to work because he loved the brand. He had the "Runner" mindset: If I just hope enough, it will work. Marcus was trying to show him the P&L. The business failed.

Why? Because you can't pay the rent with nostalgia. Feelings don't equal profits. Whether it's eating ice cream or running a company, the moment you ignore the physics, you lose.

16. THE 1975 PREDICTION

(The Logan Airport Simulation)

Recorders are often accused of being paranoid or "doomsday thinkers." We aren't. We just see the trajectory before the curve hits the graph.

In 1975, I was living in the shadow of Logan Airport in Boston. Every day, I could smell the jet fuel. I could taste the exhaust. While everyone else just saw "airplanes," I saw a web of pollution being sprayed over the population.

I sat down and wrote a story. It was a prediction about how the world would end.

The Scenario: It wouldn't be a nuclear war. It would be the air. I described a choking agent that would suffocate the population.

But the specific detail was the Spread Pattern. I wrote that it wouldn't hit everywhere at once. It would hit the Major Cities first—the hubs. Then, it would ride the transportation lines to the rest of the world. It would be a global choking event, distributed by our own travel networks.

The Reality (45 Years Later):

Fast forward to 2020. If you took my story from 1975 and scratched out the word "Pollution" and wrote in "COVID-19," the story wouldn't skip a beat.

- It started in the major hubs.
- It traveled on the airplanes I watched at Logan.
- It choked people out.

Why did I see this? I wasn't a psychic. I was a Canary. I was breathing the exhaust at Logan. My body registered the toxicity, and my brain extrapolated the logic: If this system continues, this is the inevitable result.

Most people live in the moment. Recorders live in the projection. Sometimes that makes us look crazy. And sometimes, it makes us the only ones who bought masks 45 years early.

17. THE INTIMACY OF CONNECTION: HUG AWAY

I tell you these stories about Dad, Joe, Kevin, and Paul not just because they are memories, but because they are evidence.

They are evidence that connection doesn't always look like "normal" conversation. Sometimes it looks like a joke about a funeral home. Sometimes it looks like waving at a fighter jet. Sometimes it looks like finding the "good news" in death.

And sometimes, it looks like a squeeze.

The Language of the Squeeze: Hugs and the BMI/Autistic Child

For BMI and autistic kids, hugs are more than a nice idea. They are development tools.

Many kids like me grow up in a world where words don't always do the job. But the body speaks in other ways. A hug is one of them.

When an autistic child hugs, they may squeeze harder than expected. Not because they want to hurt, but because they don't always know their strength. Or maybe because the intensity of what they feel pours out all at once.

Too often, the world says: "Don't hug. Pull back. That's too much."

And in that moment, we shut down a gift instead of shaping it.

The Philosophy: Development vs. Treatment

The system loves the word "treatment." "We're treating autism." "We're treating behavior."

But let me ask: are we talking about a disease or about developing a human being?

BMI and autistic kids are not broken to be treated. They are individuals to be developed.

Words matter. If we call it treatment, we look for cures and fixes. If we call it development, we look for growth and strength.

Here's where hugs get caught in the crossfire. A child hugs too hard? Treatment says: "Remove the behavior." But development says: "Shape it, guide it, help them use it as a tool."

Training the Gift, Not Killing It: A Call to Action

The answer isn't to take hugs away. The answer is to train them.

Teach the child how to feel another person's body language. Show them how to adjust pressure. Help them notice if someone is leaning in or pulling away. But don't stop the hug. Because when you do, you don't just remove a behavior—you cut off one of the clearest ways they connect with the world.

When I say "hug them harder," I don't mean ignore a child screaming "don't touch me."

I mean: don't give up on hugs as part of their growth.

Hug harder in your commitment. Hug harder in your patience. Hug harder in your creativity.

Studies show hugs lower cortisol, raise oxytocin, and regulate breathing. That's the science.

But the soul knows it too. Every time two hearts touch, they exchange electricity. It's presence. It's trust. It's life.

So here's the truth: Hug away.

Don't let fear steal the best of us. Because for many of us, hugging is not just affection. It is our language. Our way of saying what words cannot. Our way of plugging into you—the world's most important WiFi.

13

If you want to fix the machine, find a Recorder.CH

(D efining the Two Architectural Poles)
      If you strip away the personality, the history, and the trauma, what are you left with?

You are left with the Operating System.

In the computer world, we understand that a Windows machine and a Mac are both computers. They can both send emails, they can both browse the web, and they can both crash.

But deep down, at the kernel level, they organize information differently.

If you try to run Mac code on a Windows machine without an adapter, it won't work. It's not because the code is bad; it's because the architecture is different.

Human beings are the same.

We are all the same species, but we are not all built on the same kernel.

As we established, evolution produced two necessary minds to keep the species alive. Now, we are going to define exactly how they work.

We call them the Binary Mind Inside (BMI™) and the Parallel Mind Inside (PMI™).

1. The BMI™: The Binary Mind Inside
Function: The Recorder

The Recorder is the brain's original accountant, engineer, and system-builder. It is the "Safety Architect."

• The Core Directive: System Integrity. The Recorder's primary goal is not "happiness" or "connection." Its primary goal is Accuracy.

• It asks: Is this true?

• It asks: Is this safe?

• It asks: Does the pattern hold?

• Cognitive Style: Sequential (System 2). Psychologist Daniel Kahneman famously described "System 2" thinking as slow, deliberate, and logical. The Recorder lives here. It processes life in a single-file line.

• Input A -> Process -> Output B.

• You cannot jump the line. You cannot skip a step.

• This is why Recorders hate being interrupted. If you interrupt a sequential process, you don't just pause it; you crash it.

• Data Preference: Consistency. The Recorder trusts Rules, Facts, and Logic. If the rule is "No shoes in the house," and you wear shoes in the house, the Recorder feels a physical spike of distress. It isn't about the dirt; it's about the violation of the code. If the code can be broken, safety does not exist.

• Evolutionary Role: The Sentry. The Recorder is the one who remembers that the red berries killed Uncle Joe five years ago. The Runner might say, "But they look so good!" The Recorder says, "The data says death."

2. The PMI™: The Parallel Mind Inside

Function: The Runner

The Runner is the brain's social engine, diplomat, and executor of real-time action. It is the "Social Architect."

• The Core Directive: Fluid Adaptation. The Runner's primary goal is Cohesion.

• It asks: Are we okay with each other?

• It asks: Does this fit the vibe?

• It asks: How do I keep the peace?

• Cognitive Style: Simultaneous (System 1). Kahneman's "System 1" is fast, intuitive, and emotional. The Runner lives here. It processes life in parallel streams. It takes in the tone of voice, the body language, the smell of the room, and the social hierarchy all at once. It doesn't analyze the data; it feels the data.

• Data Preference: Context. The Runner trusts Emotion, Subtlety, and Intuition. They understand that rules are flexible. "No shoes in the house" applies... unless the Queen visits, or unless you're rushing to the bathroom. To the Runner, the context matters more than the code.

• Evolutionary Role: The Diplomat. The Runner is the one who convinces the neighboring tribe not to attack. They don't use logic; they use charm, gifts, and social signaling.

3. The Architectural Trade-Off

You cannot be elite at both. This is the Zero-Sum Game of neuroscience.

To be a great Recorder, you must suppress the urge to "go along to get along." You must be willing to be the buzzkill who points out the math is wrong.

To be a great Runner, you must suppress the urge to correct every factual error. You must be willing to let a lie slide to keep the party going.

The "Autism" Label

What we call "Autism" is simply High-Fidelity Recording. It is a brain that has traded social fluidity for structural precision.

• Sensitivity to Light/Sound: This isn't a defect; it's a high-gain microphone. The Recorder hears everything because it is designed to miss nothing.

• Literal Thinking: This isn't a defect; it's coding language. The Recorder expects words to mean exactly what they are defined to mean.

4. Polarity and The Six Professions

Now we can map the Six Professions (from Chapter 1) directly to the architecture. They are not random. They are inevitable.

RECORDER DOMINANT (BMI)

Focus: Logic, Rules, System

• The Numbers People: Accountants, Scribes. They guard the resource.

• The Creators: Inventors, Engineers. They guard the tool.

• The Enforcers: Judges, Inspectors. They guard the law.

RUNNER DOMINANT (PMI)

Focus: Context, People, Adaptation

• The Connectors: Merchants, Diplomats. They guard the relationship.

• The Leaders: Visionaries, Politicians. They guard the future.

• The Healers: Counselors, Shamans. They guard the spirit.

5. The Physics of the Switch (Voltage)

To truly understand why a Recorder cannot "just relax" or "read between the lines," you have to go down to the physical layer of the machine. You have to look at the Voltage.

In the physical world, a computer chip is just a vast landscape of transistors. A transistor is a gate. It blocks electricity, or it lets it through.

• Voltage High (+5V): The gate is open. Current flows. We call this 1.

• Voltage Low (0V): The gate is closed. Current stops. We call this 0.

There is no "Medium Voltage." There is no "Sort of On."

If the voltage hovers in the middle (say, +2.5V), the machine does not "guess." It enters a floating state. It becomes unstable. It crashes.

The Recorder's Biology

The Binary Mind is biological hardware wired to reject the "floating state."

When a parent says "Maybe," or a boss says "We'll see," they are sending a +2.5V signal.

• The Runner Brain: Smooths the signal. It rounds up to "Yes" or down to "No" based on hope or feeling.

• The Recorder Brain: Detects the floating voltage and throws a Hardware Interrupt.

The physical anxiety you feel isn't emotional "worry." It is the system alerting you that the input is invalid. You cannot process a floating signal. You need the switch to click.

6. The Operating Languages: High-Level vs. Assembler

Every computer system has layers of language.

• The Surface (The Runner): This is what you see on your screen (Windows/MacOS). It is colorful, intuitive, and uses metaphors like "Files" and "Trash Cans." It is designed for ease of use.

• The Bedrock (The Recorder): This is what happens inside the chip. It is electricity, switches, and direct commands.

Humans cannot read billions of 1s and 0s. So, engineers created the first bridge: Assembly Language (Assembler).

Assembler is the native language of the Recorder. It is a low-level coding language that speaks directly to the hardware. It is rigid, sequential, and literal. It does not assume context. It demands specific instructions.

The Syntax Error

In a modern "High-Level Language" (like Python or English), you can say: "Please get me a glass of water." The system infers what you mean.

In Assembler, that instruction does not exist. If you type "Get water," the system crashes.

In Assembler, you must write:

```
MOV ARM, 45_DEGREES
OPEN HAND
DETECT OBJECT_GLASS
CLOSE HAND
RETRACT ARM
```

This explains 90% of the conflict in a Recorder's life. The world speaks in High-Level nuances. The Recorder listens in Assembler.

SCENARIO: THE CLEAN ROOM

• Parent (High-Level): "Clean your room."

• Recorder Child (Assembler): Error. Instruction Undefined. Does "clean" mean vacuum? Does "clean" mean organize by size? Does "clean" mean shove everything under the bed?

The child stands there, frozen. The parent thinks the child is being defiant. The truth is, the child is experiencing a Syntax Error.

The Fix: Change the input to Assembler.

"Put the laundry in the hamper."

"Put the Legos in the bin."

The child moves instantly. The code is valid.

7. The Instruction Set: Why "I'm Fine" Freezes Us

In Assembler, you don't talk to the computer. You command the memory. A massive portion of the Recorder's brain energy is spent on one specific instruction: CMP (Compare).

Code: CMP A, B (Compare Value A with Value B).

• The Runner: Compares feelings.

• The Recorder: Compares data.

The "I'm Fine" Scenario

A spouse says "I'm fine," but their jaw is clenched.

• Runner Code: Ignores the jaw. Listens to the word. Result: "They are fine."

• Recorder Code:

MOV AX, [AUDIO_INPUT] ("I'm fine")

MOV BX, [VISUAL_INPUT] (Clenched Jaw)

CMP AX, BX (Compare Audio to Visual)

JNE ERROR_HANDLER (Jump if Not Equal -> Error)

The Recorder freezes because the JNE (Jump if Not Equal) instruction forced them out of the conversation and into the error loop. They cannot move forward until the inequality is resolved. They aren't being difficult. They are stuck in a logical loop.

8. The Stack: Why Interruption Hurts

High-Level minds (Runners) use a "Heap" memory structure—they throw everything in a pile and grab what they need. Assembler minds (Recorders) use a Stack.

The Stack: You put data on top (Push), and you take data off the top (Pop). To get to the bottom item, you must remove the top items first.

If a Recorder is deep in focus, they have loaded 15 layers of data onto their mental Stack.

- Layer 1: The math.
- Layer 2: The pattern.
- ...
- Layer 15: The current thought.

If a Runner interrupts them with "Hey, look at this cat video!", the Stack collapses. The Recorder screams or shuts down.

Why? Because you didn't just distract them. You toppled the Stack.

They dropped the data. Now they have to painstakingly re-load all 15 layers, one by one, to get back to where they were.

To the Runner, it was a 2-second interruption. To the Recorder, it was a total system crash and reboot.

9. The Compilation Tax (Energy Cost)

This brings us to the concept of Energy Cost.

If you are a Runner, your brain comes pre-installed with the "Social Interpreter." It costs you almost zero energy to interact.

If you are a Recorder, you do not have that interpreter. You are running on manual mode.

Every time a Recorder interacts with a Runner, they have to perform a process called Compiling. They take the "High-Level" social input and manually break it down into Assembler code.

The Transaction:

Input: "How was your weekend?"

- Runner Brain: Say "Good," ask them back. (Cost: 1 unit).
- Recorder Brain: Analysis required. Why are they asking? Do they want data? Is this a trap? Scan memory. Select response: "Fine." (Cost: 50 units).

We call this the Compilation Tax.

This is why a Recorder can solve calculus for hours (low energy cost because the logic is pure) but needs a nap after a 20-minute cocktail party (massive energy cost because of manual translation).

10. The NOP State (No Operation)

Sometimes, a Recorder sits perfectly still, staring at nothing. The world thinks they are "zoning out" or "daydreaming."

In Assembler, there is an instruction called NOP (No Operation). It tells the CPU: Do nothing for this cycle. Just wait.

Why do programmers use NOP? To sync the timing. To let the rest of the system catch up.

When a Recorder is rocking, pacing, or staring, they are executing NOP cycles. They are not broken. They are waiting for their internal clock to re-sync with the chaotic external world. They are calibrating.

Conclusion: The Advantage of Assembler

So why would nature keep the Assembler mind? Why not upgrade everyone to the High-Level "Social" language?

Because High-Level languages are slow and bloated.

Assembler is the fastest language in existence. It runs closer to the metal. There is no lag. You cannot hide a bug in Assembler.

When the crisis hits—when the plane is going down, or the server is hacked, or the patient is crashing—you do not want a mind that operates on "vibes." You want a mind that can read the raw code of reality and execute the fix without hesitation.

The Runner sees the Story. The Recorder sees the Source Code.

If you want to feel good, talk to a Runner.

14

The world needs these minds. But the world must st

(The Operating System of the Recorder)
Human beings were never meant to think the same way. That simple truth—ignored, denied, and bulldozed over for centuries—is the source of almost every modern misunderstanding about the mind.

We have established the History (The Six Professions) and the Code (Assembler). Now, we must look at the Daily Operation.

How does a Binary Mind actually navigate a Tuesday afternoon?

It doesn't happen by magic, and it doesn't happen by "acting normal." It happens by following a strict set of internal principles. These aren't choices. They are the hard-coded subroutines that keep the system stable.

When a Recorder tries to violate these principles to please a Runner world, the system destabilizes. Anxiety spikes. Burnout sets in. The mask slips.

But when a Recorder understands these principles and builds a life that respects them, they become unstoppable.

If you are a Recorder, you will recognize these instantly. If you are a Runner, this is your user manual for the people in your life you have labeled "difficult."

1. Principle One: The Replay Protocol (The Truth Engine)

If there is one trait the world has wildly misunderstood, it is Replay.

Psychologists often call it "rumination." They treat it as a symptom of anxiety or depression. They tell clients to "let it go" or "stop dwelling on the past."

They are fundamentally wrong. Replay is not emotional wallowing. Replay is forensic analysis.

The Mechanics of Latency

To understand Replay, you must understand the "Compilation Tax" we discussed in the previous chapter. In the moment, a social interaction is often too noisy for a Recorder to process fully.

• Input Stream: The person's words + their tone + their body language + the lights in the room + the background noise.

• Recorder Capacity: The Assembler mind is trying to verify every single bit of that data in real-time. It is often impossible. The bandwidth is maxed out just trying to survive the interaction without saying something "wrong."

So, the Recorder engages a buffer. We record the raw data to the hard drive without fully analyzing it. We survive the moment by using scripts and nodding.

The Post-Processing Phase

Later—often hours later, while driving, showering, or trying to sleep—the system finally has the bandwidth to process the data. It boots up the Replay Protocol. We play the tape back. But this time, we aren't distracted by the noise. We play it frame-by-frame.

• Frame 14: You said you were happy.

• Frame 15: Your eyes narrowed.

• Frame 16: You shifted your weight away from me.

• The Conclusion: You were lying.

This leads to the "Delayed Truth" phenomenon. A Runner forgets the argument ten minutes after it ends. "It's over, we hugged." A Recorder wakes up two days later, angry. Why? Because the rendering process just finished.

To the Runner, this looks like holding a grudge. To the Recorder, this is just Late Arrival Truth. We aren't dwelling. We just finished the math.

SCENARIO: THE KITCHEN ARGUMENT

You're in the kitchen. Your partner says, "It's fine, really. I'm not mad," and walks away a little too fast. In the moment, you feel a faint internal jolt, but you don't have the bandwidth to analyze it. The dishwasher is humming, a kid is asking where their shoes are. You say "Okay" and move on.

Three hours later, you're driving alone. No noise. No interruptions. Replay starts running on its own:

• You hear the exact pitch of "fine."
• You notice the micro-pause before "really."
• You remember they closed the cabinet harder than usual.

By the time you pull into the driveway, the conclusion is clear: They weren't fine. They were hurt, and they lied to keep the peace. From the outside, it looks like you "got mad out of nowhere" in the car. Inside, this was just the moment the rendering finally finished.

SCENARIO: THE PERFORMANCE REVIEW

At work, your manager says: "You're doing great overall. Just be a little more flexible with the team." You nod. The meeting moves on.

Two nights later, Replay reassembles the meeting data:

• "Flexible" was only used when you challenged bad data.
• "Team" actually meant one specific co-worker who cuts corners.
• "Overall" was padding to soften the correction.

Suddenly the real sentence appears: "Stop pointing out structural problems because it makes someone uncomfortable." You're not obsessing. You're decoding.

2. Principle Two: Pattern Detection (Locking vs. Scanning)

A Runner mind "scans" the world. It looks for the gist. It ignores the details to build a fast, general picture.

A Recorder mind "locks" onto the world. It looks for the structure.

This is not a visual preference; it is a processing filter. When a Runner looks at a forest, they see "Nature." When a Recorder looks at a forest, they see:

- The fractals in the fern leaves.
- The repetition of the pine needles.
- The specific angle of the shadow.
- The brown patch on the oak tree that signifies a beetle infestation.

The Curse of Cassandra

This principle allows Recorders to predict the future with unnerving accuracy. Because we record the pattern, not the story, we notice when the pattern breaks long before anyone else does.

We are not psychic. We just noticed that the variable X changed from 1 to 0, while everyone else was looking at the scenery. The pain of the Recorder is seeing the train wreck coming, warning everyone, being told to "stop being paranoid," and then watching the train wreck happen exactly as predicted.

SCENARIO: THE SLOW-MOTION BUSINESS CRASH

You work in a small company. Everyone is celebrating a big new client. The Runner minds are fully activated—music, pastries, high-fives.

You look at the numbers and see:

- Payment terms are longer.
- Profit margin is thinner.
- Loyal customers are being deprioritized to serve the new one.

You say, "If we keep prioritizing this one account and they pull out, we're overexposed."

The response: "You're being negative. Can't you just enjoy the win?"

Six months later, the client pulls out. Cash flow collapses. The same people say, "Nobody could have seen this coming." You did. You just didn't fit the mood.

SCENARIO: THE TEENAGER AND THE NEW FRIEND

A Recorder teenager comes home and says: "Something's off about that new kid in our group." The parent answers: "You're being judgmental. Give people a chance."

Replay plus Pattern Detection fires quietly in the background:
- The new kid changes their story slightly each time.
- They only show up when there's something to gain.
- They subtly pit one friend against another.

Three months later, there's a blow-up, secrets are revealed, and the friend group splits in half. The Recorder is not surprised. They saw the pattern while everyone else was watching the performance.

3. Principle Three: Sensory Memory (The 4D Record)

Memory works differently for the two architectures.

When a Runner remembers a childhood memory, they remember the narrative and the emotion. "It was a happy Christmas. I got a bike."

When a Recorder remembers, they reconstruct the Sensory File. The file isn't compressed. It is stored in RAW format. We don't just remember "Christmas." We remember:
- The scratch of the wool sweater on the back of the neck.
- The smell of the pine resin (Terpenes).
- The hum of the refrigerator in the background (60Hz).
- The exact sequence of the lights blinking (Red, Green, Green, Blue).

This is why Recorders are often accused of being "stuck in the past." We aren't stuck. But when we access a memory, we are transported back into the full sensory experience.

The Trigger Mechanism

Runners can "fade" bad memories over time. They blur the edges. Recorders have to archive them. The edges stay sharp. This is a superpower for creativity and engineering, but a liability for trauma processing.

SCENARIO: THE "OVERREACTION" TO A SMELL

An adult Recorder walks into a new office building. Everything seems fine until they step into a conference room. A specific cleaning chemical hits their nose. Instantly, their heart rate spikes. Shoulders tense. The brain wants out.

To colleagues, it looks irrational. "It's just a smell. You're being dramatic." But the internal system has retrieved a file they didn't ask for: Hospital corridors. A sick family member. The helplessness of that moment. The body isn't responding to "now." It's responding to the archived file.

SCENARIO: THE SAFE SOUND

The flip side is just as powerful. A Recorder sits in a crowded cafe, barely holding it together. The noise is sharp. Cups clink. Then a specific song comes on—one they listened to alone in their room as a kid. Their system immediately calms. Breathing slows. Shoulders drop. To someone else, it's "just a song." To a Recorder, it's a tagged file: SAFE.

4. Principle Four: The Single-Task Protocol (The Myth of Multitasking)

Society worships multitasking. Corporate job descriptions demand it. But neurologically, multitasking is a lie. The brain cannot do two things at once; it just switches back and forth very fast.

• Runners: Switch fast with low cost. (Low switching penalty).

• Recorders: Switch slow with high cost. (High switching penalty).

A Recorder is a Serial Processor. We do A. We finish A. Then we do B. If you force us to do A and B at the same time, both systems degrade.

The Physics of the "Stack"

Think of the Recorder's focus like a stack of plates. To enter "Deep Work," the Recorder has to load the context onto their mental stack.

• Plate 1: The goal.

• Plate 2: The variables.

• ...

• Plate 10: The current thought.

If a Runner interrupts a Recorder with "Hey, look at this cat video!", they aren't just pausing the work. They are knocking over the stack of plates.

The Recorder screams or shuts down. Why? Because you didn't just distract them. You crashed the system. Now they have to pick up every single plate, check it for cracks, and re-stack them one by one.

SCENARIO: THE PARENT AND THE HOMEWORK

A Recorder child is doing math. They've quietly built the internal stack: the rules, the problem, where they left off. A parent walks in: "Pause that for a second and tell your sister about your day."

To the parent, this is polite. To the child, the stack just collapsed. They stare. They look "defiant." Actually, they are trying to keep the context from sliding off the stack. If the parent insists, the child snaps. Not because they are rude, but because their system is being forced to violate its own architecture.

SCENARIO: THE OPEN-PLAN OFFICE

A Recorder adult wears noise-canceling headphones, trying to write a report. Within 30 minutes: A "Got a sec?" at the desk. A Slack ping. A meeting pop-up.

Each interruption is a stack crash. A context reload. By 3:00 PM, the office thinks the Recorder "doesn't handle stress well." In reality, the Recorder has spent more energy rebooting than thinking.

5. Principle Five: Absolute Morality (The Internal Compass)

For a Runner, morality is often Socially Relative.

• Rule: "Don't steal."

• Context: "Unless it's from a big corporation, or I'm underpaid, or everyone else is doing it."

For a Recorder, morality is Structurally Absolute.

• Rule: "Don't steal."

• Context: "Stealing is a violation of property rights. Violation is Error. Error is bad."

The Pain of the White Lie

Recorders struggle to "play the game" or "kiss the ring" in corporate politics. We cannot fake respect. We cannot lie to a client to smooth things over.

It isn't that we are "holy." It's that we are Binary. A lie introduces a corruption in the database. To a Recorder, holding a lie in their head feels physically painful—like a pebble in a shoe. The system flags it as an error every few seconds.

SCENARIO: THE "SMALL" CORPORATE LIE

A manager pulls a Recorder worker aside: "Tell the client we're further along than we are. It'll buy us time."

To the manager, this is spin. To the Recorder, this is a request to introduce corrupted data into the system. They feel physical discomfort. A drop in trust. If they comply, they will think about that lie for weeks because the database won't let it go.

SCENARIO: THE POLITE CHILD

A child is told: "No matter what Aunt Linda gives you, say you love it." Aunt Linda gives them a scratchy, painful sweater. The child says: "I don't like it. It hurts." Later, they are scolded for embarrassing the family. The child learns that adults ask them to corrupt their truth to protect an image. Some disconnect; others refuse and get labeled "difficult."

6. Principle Six: Environmental Overload (Hardware vs. Software)

When a Recorder has a meltdown in a busy restaurant, it is not a "behavioral issue." It is a Denial of Service (DoS) Attack.

The Runner brain has a built-in Filter. It says: Ignore the humming fridge. Ignore the tag on your shirt. Focus on the conversation.

The Recorder brain has a Funnel. It receives everything.

- The lights are flickering at 60Hz.
- The music is too bass-heavy.
- The smell of cologne is chemical.
- The chair is scratchy.
- Three people are talking.

The Recorder processes all of this with equal priority. The CPU hits 100%. The cooling fans spin up (stimming, rocking). If the input doesn't stop, the system crashes.

The Meltdown is a Reboot

A meltdown is not a tantrum. A tantrum is a manipulation tool used to get a reward.

Don't negotiate with Terrorist.

A meltdown is a biological system failure.

SCENARIO: THE BIRTHDAY PARTY

A child is at a loud trampoline park. Whistles, screaming, lights, sugar. They hold it together for an hour. They smile for pictures. On the drive home, they explode—screaming, inconsolable. The parent thinks: "You were fine all day, why are you acting like this now?"

Reality: The system capacity was exceeded gradually. In the quiet of the car, there was no more distraction to absorb the load. The crash happened.

SCENARIO: THE ADULT DINNER

An adult Recorder is at dinner. TV on the wall. Music loud. Kitchen noise. They are doing internal load balancing: Focusing hard on one face, suppressing the silverware sounds, fighting the glare.

After an hour, they say: "I need to step outside." The table laughs: "You're such an introvert." No. They like people. They just can't survive the data stream.

7. Principle Seven: The Binary Decision Tree (If/Then)

Finally, the Binary Mind navigates life through If/Then logic. Runners navigate through Feel/Flow logic.

• Runner: "I'll see how I feel when I get there."

• Recorder: "If I get there and the door is locked, then I will call you. If you don't answer, then I will wait 10 minutes. If you still don't answer, then I will leave."

We script the future. We build decision trees to handle uncertainty. When the plan changes suddenly, Recorders panic. It's not because we hate spontaneity. It's because we pre-rendered the entire decision tree for "Plan A." When you switch to "Plan B" instantly, we have no tree. We are standing in the void without code.

SCENARIO: THE SUDDEN CHANGE

A Recorder has a plan: Leave at 6:00. Park in garage. Eat at restaurant. They have quietly coded the tree: If lot full → use overflow. If wait long → sit at bar.

At 5:45, a friend texts: "Actually, let's just wing it. We'll wander around and see what we feel like."

To the Runner, this is freedom. To the Recorder, this is a request to delete the entire decision tree and operate in an empty space. They freeze. They get irritated. "Can we please stick to the plan?" They aren't being rigid. They just had their map torn up right before the trip.

SCENARIO: THE FAMILY VACATION

Parents tell a Recorder child: "We're going away. It'll be fun. Just pack."

The child asks: "Where? For how long? Is there a pool?"

Parent: "Why can't you just relax?"

The child is asking for the variables required to build a stable If/Then tree. Without that, the trip feels like a bug report waiting to happen.

A BINARY TUESDAY (Putting It All Together)

To see how this feels in real time, let's walk through a single day.

• Morning: Replay runs on yesterday's conversation with a coworker. You realize they weren't honest. (Principle One)

• Commute: A specific smell on the train triggers an old memory file. (Principle Three)

• Work: Someone interrupts your deep-focus task five times in an hour. Your stack crashes. (Principle Four)

• Meeting: You're asked to "massage the numbers" in a presentation. You feel physically sick. (Principle Five)

• Lunch: The cafeteria is loud and bright. You eat fast and escape to a hallway to cool down. (Principle Six)

• Afternoon: You warn leadership about a small pattern in the data that nobody else sees yet. They ignore you. (Principle Two)

• Evening: A friend cancels a plan at the last minute and says, "Let's just play it by ear later this week." Your whole decision tree goes blank. (Principle Seven)

From the outside, it looks like you "overreacted" three or four times in one day. From the inside, your system was simply trying, over and over, to maintain integrity in an environment not designed for your wiring.

Conclusion: The User Manual

These principles are not flaws. They are the specs of a high-performance machine designed for truth, precision, and depth.

15

(S tructural Advantages of the Recorder)
People don't associate the word power with the word autistic. That alone tells you how wrong we've been looking at this.

For decades, the conversation around the Binary Mind has been dominated by a "Deficit Model." We talk about what is missing. We talk about the lack of social fluidity, the lack of eye contact, the lack of filter. When we do talk about strengths, we drift into Hollywood clichés. We talk about the "Savant"—the guy who can count toothpicks on the floor or memorize the phone book.

That is insulting. It treats the Binary Mind like a party trick.

The powers I'm talking about are not cinematic. No lightning bolts. No magic tricks. They aren't flashy, and they don't perform on command for an audience. In fact, that's why they've been missed, suppressed, and misinterpreted for so long.

These powers are Structural. They are the result of an operating system that prioritizes Truth over Tribe and Precision over Peace.

When a Binary Mind is forced to mask—to act like a Runner—these powers are buried under anxiety. But when the wiring is allowed to operate cleanly, something startling occurs. The person doesn't become different. They become fully themselves.

This chapter is the inventory of your arsenal.

1. The Power of Replay (The Forensic Audit)

The world values speed. It rewards the person who has a quick comeback in the meeting. It rewards the person who can smooth over an awkward moment instantly. That world favors Runners. Runners live in the "Now."

But the Binary Mind was not built for the "Now." It was built for the Truth. And the Truth rarely reveals itself in real-time. It reveals itself in the analysis.

The Mechanics of Replay

To a Runner, memory is a watercolor painting. It captures the feeling of the moment. "We had a good meeting. Everyone seemed happy."

To a Recorder, memory is a Black Box Flight Recorder. We do not just remember the event; we possess the raw data file. This capability—Replay—is the ability to re-run a social interaction, a technical problem, or a conflict frame-by-frame, hours or days after it happened.

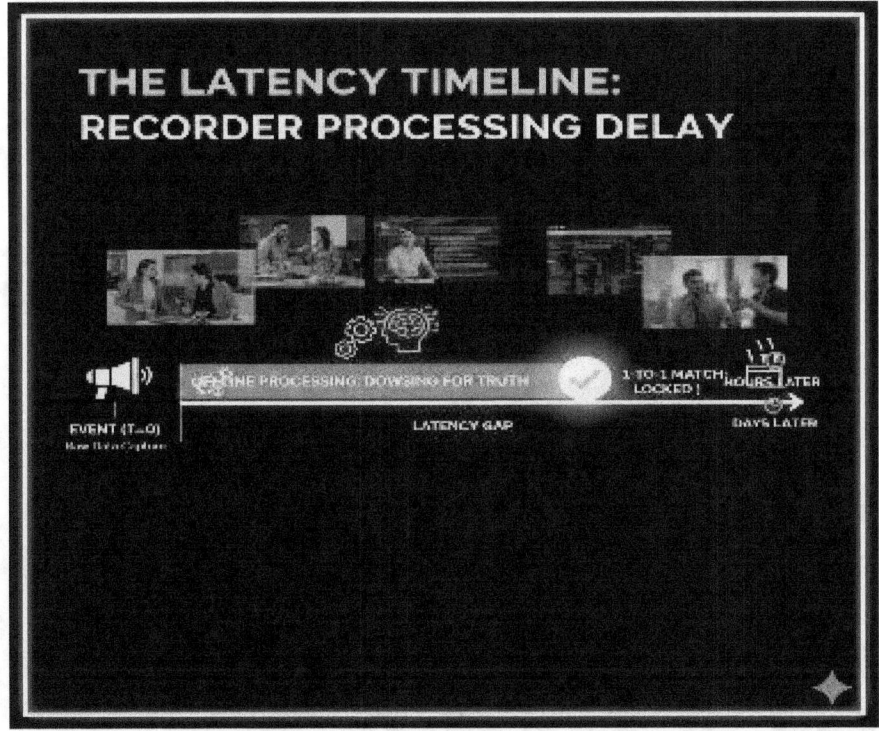

Replay in the Real World

Replay isn't something you turn on. It turns on you. It happens when your hands are finally idle and your body is no longer managing the world. It happens when the engine noise quiets and the pressure drops. That's when the file opens.

You've likely had this moment countless times: a conversation you thought was over suddenly plays back with ruthless clarity. Not emotionally—structurally. You don't feel hurt first. You see something first.

- You notice the pause that didn't belong.
- The answer that skipped a step.
- The smile that appeared half a beat too late.

And in that instant, the conclusion isn't dramatic. It's calm. Oh. That's what happened.

This is why Binary Minds are rarely fooled twice by the same person. Once replay resolves a pattern, it never needs to be solved again.

In workplaces, this has enormous consequences. While others move on quickly from a meeting that "felt fine," you quietly disengage from proposals that don't withstand replay. Later—sometimes months later—when problems surface, people are shocked. You're not. You didn't argue. You didn't confront. You simply updated your internal map.

Replay doesn't make you loud. It makes you accurate. And over time, people sense this. They may not be able to name it, but they know: you won't forget what actually happened.

2. Pattern Recognition (The Prediction Engine)

Replay gives you clarity on the past. Pattern Recognition gives you dominion over the future. From a very young age, you likely noticed things others dismissed. You noticed the teacher got angry exactly 30 seconds after the bell rang. You noticed the specific tone your mother used two days before a family fight.

Vertical vs. Horizontal Thinking

Runners think Horizontally. They scan the horizon for immediate threats.

Recorders think Vertically. We look at the root cause. We record the structure of reality rather than the story of reality.

- The Story: "The company is doing great!"
- The Structure: "Accounts Payable is delaying checks by 14 days. This precedes bankruptcy by 3 months."

Why You Were Always "Ahead of Your Time"

Pattern recognition rarely earns praise in the moment. It earns respect in hindsight. As a child, this ability often made you feel out of step. You noticed when friendships were unstable long before they ended. You sensed shifts in teachers, institutions, or authority figures before anyone acknowledged change.

Adults often dismissed this as imagination or negativity. But what they were rejecting wasn't anxiety—it was premature clarity.

Binary Minds don't see events as isolated dots. They see sequences. This means when most people are reacting emotionally to the present, you're already observing the future being assembled piece by piece. This is why you often felt older than your age—not emotionally, but structurally. You weren't precocious. You were orienting in three dimensions while others operated in two.

In business contexts, this shows up as early warnings:
• "This process won't scale."
• "That incentive structure is flawed."
• "This success is unstable."

These comments make social rooms uncomfortable because they interrupt momentum. And momentum—especially social momentum—is something Runner systems protect. But history always sides with architecture. Civilizations don't fail suddenly. They fail predictably—because patterns compound quietly until collapse appears "unexpected." You noticed the compound early.

3. Deep Focus (The Monotropic Laser)

There is a reason interruption feels physically painful to you. It feels like a physical blow because your attention is not a lightbulb; it is a laser. Neurologists call this Monotropism.

• Runners (Polytropism): Attention is diffuse. Like a lantern, it lights up a wide area dimly.

• Recorders (Monotropism): Attention is concentrated. Like a laser, it burns hot on a single point.

Why Your Best Work Was Always Done in Silence

If you look back honestly, your most important work didn't happen in meetings. It happened when you were left alone.

Binary Minds don't warm up gradually. They drop in. When the environment is clean and interruption-free, something rare happens: the system engages fully. This is why time disappeared when you were absorbed. Not because you were escaping—but because your cognitive architecture was finally allowed to operate at capacity.

Completion isn't optional for you. It's regulatory. Unfinished tasks don't sit in the background. They actively draw energy until resolved. That's why half-done projects feel physically irritating and mentally noisy. Closure isn't satisfaction—it's silence.

In environments that respected this—labs, workshops, studios, solitary problem-solving—you thrived. In environments that demanded constant switching and responsiveness, you burned out. None of that reflects motivation or attitude. It reflects system design.

4. Emotional Fidelity (The Lie Detector)

You were often accused of being "too honest," "too intense," or "too sensitive." None of those were flaws. They were signs that your emotional signal wasn't distorted.

Runners have a built-in Social Mixer. They can take their true emotion (Boredom) and mix it with a social mask (Polite Interest) to create a smooth output. Recorders lack the Mixer. We have a Direct Line.

The Human Mirror

When someone is fake, you physically recoil. You don't laugh at jokes that aren't funny. You don't nod when you don't agree. You act as a mirror. And people who hate their reflection will hate the mirror.

Why You're Trusted in Crises

When systems fail, people seek Binary Minds—not because of charm, but because of steadiness. In emergencies, performance collapses and emotional scripts evaporate. What remains is signal.

Binary Minds excel here because they don't amplify chaos. Their emotions stay proportional to reality—not to perception, not to fear, not to group panic. You've likely noticed this:

- You became calm when things got serious.
- You thought clearly when others couldn't.
- You saw solutions instead of noise.

Emotional fidelity isn't loud. It's clean. And clean signals are invaluable when stakes are high. This is why people instinctively look to you when things break—even if they ignore you when things are comfortable.

5. The Moral Spine (The System of Justice)

Why do Binary Minds struggle to lie? It's not because we are saints. It's because a lie is a Data Corruption.

To a Runner, a lie is a social tool. To a Recorder, a lie is a structural flaw. Holding a lie requires energy. It requires maintaining a false file alongside the true file. Recorders hate wasting energy on false files.

Why Integrity Costs You—and Why It's Still Non-Negotiable

Integrity wasn't a value you adopted. It was an internal condition. This is why compromising yourself never felt strategic—it felt dangerous. A small deviation from alignment didn't feel social or strategic. It felt like introducing instability into a load-bearing structure.

You may have paid for this:

- Lost promotions
- Burned bridges
- Being labeled "difficult"

But over time, something stronger replaced that loss: internal coherence. Binary Minds don't fracture well. Once fractured, everything degrades. So the system protects itself by resisting corruption—even when that resistance is socially expensive.

That moral spine isn't rigidity. It's load tolerance. Structures that bend too far collapse. Structures that hold preserve safety for everyone else.

6. Crisis Stabilization (The Cool Head)

Have you ever noticed that you are anxious when everything is calm, but totally calm when everything falls apart?

This is the paradox of the Binary Mind. Daily Life is full of ambiguous signals (small talk, unwritten rules). This ambiguity triggers anxiety because the variables are undefined.

Crisis is binary. The car has crashed. The system is down. Suddenly, the ambiguity is gone. The variables are locked. While the Runners are panicking, the Recorder steps into Operational Mode.

This is a superpower that cannot be taught. It is the ability to turn off emotion and turn on logic exactly when everyone else is losing their minds.

7. Sensory Radar (The Sentry)

We call it "Sensory Processing Disorder." We should call it Early Warning Radar.

Your inability to filter out background noise is not a defect; it is a Sentry function. In the tribe, the heavy sleepers were the ones who got eaten by the lion. The light sleepers—the ones who woke up because a twig snapped 50 yards away—were the ones who woke the tribe and saved everyone.

You notice the anomaly. You are the canary in the coal mine.

8. When These Powers Finally Turn On

Filter

Filter: Blocks most input.
Reduces information.
Creates 'calm' by
ignoring data.

**Funnel
(Sensory Radar)**

Funnel (Sensory Radar / The Sentry):
Processes inerts information for anolmies.
Creates 'warning' by finding the threat.
You are the Sentry.

interference, not because of alignment.

But when interference stops—when pressure lifts, when autonomy appears, when environments stabilize—the system initializes fully. This often happens later than you wanted. Sometimes decades later.

And when it does, the feeling is unmistakable. You don't feel smarter. You feel quieter. The noise drops. The contradictions resolve. Your past reorders itself.

You finally understand: I wasn't behind. I was paused.

This is what people mean when they say Binary Minds "come into their own." Nothing was added. Nothing was learned. The system simply stopped fighting incompatible input.

Conclusion

The world didn't fail to notice Binary Minds. It failed to understand them.

Once you see these powers clearly, a different truth appears: civilization has always depended on people like you—but rarely knew how to protect them. You were asked to adapt instead of being translated. To perform instead of being deployed. To socialize instead of stabilize.

And yet, when systems needed truth more than comfort, you were always there.

These are not superpowers because they make you special. They are superpowers because they keep reality anchored when everything else drifts.

Not broken. Not delayed. Not defective.

Deployed late—but deployed exactly as designed.

16

THE SENTINEL'S PARTNER

I have a theory about why Recorders bond so deeply with animals, and why the loss of a dog can bring a grown man to his knees in a way that confuses the rest of the world.

To understand the grief, you have to understand the history. I believe the Dog and the Recorder didn't just meet by accident. We co-evolved. We are two halves of the same security system.

The Night Watch Go back 20,000 years. Picture the tribe at night. The fire is dying down. The "Runners" are asleep. They are exhausted from the hunt, huddled together, sleeping soundly because they trust the safety of the cave.

But there is one guy who is awake. **The Recorder.** He is the Sentinel. His brain is stuck in the **"ON"** position. He hears the twig snap 100 yards away. He feels the shift in the wind. He is flooded with cortisol because his job is to anticipate the threat before it arrives. He is exhausted, but he cannot sleep because the data won't stop coming in.

Then, out of the darkness, comes the Wolf. The Wolf is also a Sentinel. He is also scanning. He is also binary: *Safe/Unsafe.*

The Recorder looks at the Wolf. The Wolf looks at the Recorder. And in that moment, a contract was signed that changed our DNA. The Recorder realized: *"I can't smell what you smell. And you can't plan what I plan. But if we sit here together, I can finally close my eyes for five minutes."*

The First Anxiety Medication The dog became the Recorder's **Regulation Partner.** For the first time in history, the Recorder could offload the "Scanning" duty.

- If the dog is sleeping, I know it is safe to relax.
- If the dog's ears perk up, I know my anxiety isn't "crazy"—it's real.

We became a single unit. The dog learned to read the human's eyes, and the human learned to read the dog's ears.

The "Always On" Solution Fast forward to today. My brain is still that ancient Sentinel. It is still burning massive energy scanning for threats that don't exist. This causes **Atrophy.** My system is overheating.

But when I walk through the door and see my dog, the chemical reaction is instant. My dog looks at me. There is no judgment. There is no "social game." There is only the binary check-in: *Are we safe? Yes. Are we a pack? Yes.*

For a Recorder, the dog is a **Heat Sink.** He absorbs the excess static energy. He is the only living thing that allows me to flip the switch from **"Scan"** to **"Standby."**

The Devastation This is why the loss of a dog destroys us. People—usually Runners—will try to comfort you. They say things like, *"I know it's sad, but it's not like you lost a child. You can get another one."*

They mean well, but they are wrong. They don't understand that you didn't just lose a pet. You lost your **Regulator.**

You lost the partner that helped you carry the weight of the world. You lost the only set of eyes you could look into without feeling judged. You lost the only creature that allowed you to turn your brain off.

When that dog is gone, it feels like a physical tearing in your chest. It isn't just sadness; it is exposure. Suddenly, the silence in the house is deafening. The "Always On" switch flips back up to maximum. The anxiety spikes because the Sentinel is alone in the dark again.

It is a specific, crushing pain because nature plays a cruel joke: It gives us the perfect partner, but it only gives them to us for ten or fifteen years. We have to say goodbye over and over again.

And for a Recorder, that goodbye leaves a scar that never really heals. It just reminds us of how much we needed them to survive.

THE SYMBIOSIS (WHY IT HURTS SO MUCH)

The connection goes beyond just being a "Sentinel." It goes to how a Recorder experiences Joy and Pain.

Because my brain is always recording, always analyzing, it is very hard for me to just "be." But when I am with my dog, the years strip away. When I am walking my dog, I am not a CEO, or a manager, or a husband worrying about bills. I am a kid again. I am back in East Boston, kicking the can down the street. The dog pulls me into the **Now**. The dog looks at me with that goofball grin, and for twenty minutes, the world is perfect. I escape the noise.

The Physical Connection But because that connection is so open, the wire goes both ways. Runners often don't understand this. They see a dog as a separate animal. For me, if my dog is sick, **I am sick.** I don't just "worry" about them. I feel it in my gut. I lose my appetite. I can't sleep. My system is so tuned to their frequency that when their signal drops, I crash.

This is why Runners get confused when we fight so hard to keep them alive. They see the vet bill. They see the prognosis. They say, *"Why spend all that money just to get one more month? It's just a dog."* They don't understand the mechanics. I'm not paying for a "dog." I am fighting for a piece of my own soul. I am fighting for the only creature that makes the world make sense. If I can get one more month of that pure, unconditional love—one more month of that silence—I will pay anything.

The Loop of Loss And when the end comes, the Recorder brain can be a curse. A Runner processes grief linearly. It hurts, then it fades, then it becomes a distant memory. But I am a Recorder. **I Replay.** I replay the last breath. I replay the vet's office. I replay the silence in the house. I don't just remember it; I re-live it. Over and over. The loss stays fresh because my hard drive won't let the file corrupt.

Respecting the Dead This is why I can't just "go get another puppy" the next week. To a Runner, that fixes the problem. *The house is empty? Get a new dog.* To me, that feels like a betrayal. My father taught me to **Respect the Dead.** That applies to my dogs, too. That dog had a personality. He had a soul. He had a specific way of looking at me that saved my life a thousand times. If I get a new dog immediately, I am just using that new puppy to plug a hole in my heart. That's not fair to the new dog, and it's not respectful to the old one.

I have to sit in the quiet. I have to process the file. I have to honor the specific relationship we had. Because for a Recorder, a dog isn't replaceable. They are a chapter of your life that you will be reading forever.

THE "WILSON" EFFECT (THE ANCHOR)

There is a reason this bond feels different. Think of Tom Hanks in the movie *Cast Away*. He is trapped on an island, totally isolated. To keep from losing his mind, he creates "Wilson" out of a volleyball. He needs someone—anyone—to just *be there*. He needs a witness.

For a Recorder, the modern world can feel like that island. We are surrounded by noise, but we often feel completely alone because no one processes reality the way we do. The dog is our Wilson. But he is a Wilson with a heartbeat.

The Hug There is a specific feeling every dog owner knows, but for a Recorder, it is medicine. It's when you wrap your arms around them, and you just hold that breathing creature. You feel their ribcage expand and contract against yours. In that moment, you aren't thinking. You are just holding onto life. They bring you the hug without the judgment. They bring you the warmth without the questions. They don't need to talk. In fact, the silence is the best part. They just look at you and say, *"I am here. You are here. We are okay."*

The Price of Love That connection is so deep that when it's gone, it leaves a mark that scares us. My wife has a hard time even looking at pictures of our past dogs. It hurts her physically. She sees the photo and the loss rushes back in—the unfairness that their lives are so short compared to ours.

But I realized that the pain is the receipt. It's the proof of the transaction. The deal we make with dogs is brutal but beautiful: **They give us their entire lives. Every single day of it. And in exchange, we give them a piece of our heart that we never get back.**

It hurts to look at the pictures because the love was that real. They were the anchor that kept us from floating away. And when the anchor is gone, you feel the drift.

THE TWO DESIGNS (SURPRISE, YOU ARE ONE OF THEM)

I know what you are thinking. *"Robert, life is complex. You can't just divide 8 billion people into two buckets."*

Actually, nature does it all the time. You are male or female. You are left-handed or right-handed. And I believe, based on a lifetime of watching people, that you are born with one of two specific **Cognitive Designs**.

I don't mean you have two brains in your head. I mean your brain is wired to process the world in one of two ways.

1. The Runner (Designed for Flow) These are the people who keep the social world spinning. They value harmony over precision. They can "go with the flow." When they sit on a beach, they can actually think about nothing. They have an "Off" switch.

2. The Recorder (Designed for Truth) This is the other 30-40% of the population. And if you are reading this book, this is probably you. The defining characteristic of a Recorder is simple: **We do not have an "Off" switch.**

The Litmus Test How do you know which one you are? Ask yourself this: *Can you enter a room without scanning it?*

- When you meet someone new, do you instantly catalog their tone, their shoes, and their potential threat level?
- Do you replay conversations from 10 years ago to see if you missed a detail?

- Do you feel a physical vibration—a "Gut Feeling"—when something is wrong?

If you answered yes, you aren't "anxious" and you aren't "disordered." You are a Recorder.

The "Gut Feeling" (It's Not Magic) For years, people have talked about "Women's Intuition" or a "Gut Feeling." That isn't magic. That is **Data Processing.**

Nature designed the Recorder to be the **Sentinel of Civilization.** To build a society, human beings had to stop killing each other and start working together. We needed a design that could detect lies, detect danger, and remember the rules.

That "Gut Feeling" you have? That is your body processing data faster than your conscious mind can read it.

- It's why you know a salesman is lying before he finishes the sentence.
- It's why you know the room is dangerous before a fight starts.

The Big Misunderstanding Because Recorders are intense, because we stare a little too long, because we obsess over facts—the modern world likes to slap labels on us. They call it "The Spectrum." They call it "ADHD." They call it "Anxiety."

I am not a doctor. But I am a builder. And I know that Nature doesn't make mistakes this big. You aren't broken. You were designed this way on purpose. You are the one who remembers the truth so the rest of the tribe can survive.

You are a Recorder. And once you understand how your machine works, the headache finally stops.

17

THE PHYSICS OF THE GUT (IT'S NOT MAGIC)

We need to talk about the "Gut Feeling." Everyone has had that moment. You're at a blackjack table. You have a 16. The dealer is showing a 6. The "book" says you stay. But your stomach tightens. You *know* a face card is coming. You just know it. But you listen to the logic. You stay. The dealer flips a 5 and pulls a 10. You lose. And you walk away saying, *"I knew it. I knew I should have hit. Why didn't I listen?"*

Or you meet a guy who seems perfect. Nice suit, firm handshake, great smile. But the hair on the back of your neck stands up. Your gut says, *"Run."* You ignore it. You do the deal. Six months later, he steals your money.

It's Not Psychic. It's Processing. People call this "intuition" or "mysticism." I call it **High-Speed Data Processing.**

Because the Recorder brain is **Always On**, you are collecting data you aren't even aware of.

- You saw the dealer's hand twitch a millisecond faster than usual.
- You saw the salesman's pupil dilate when he mentioned the price.
- You noticed the temperature in the room shift.

Your conscious brain (the slow part) missed it. But your Recorder brain (the fast part) caught it all, cross-referenced it with a bad memory from 1995, and pulled the fire alarm. That "sinking feeling" in your stomach isn't magic. It is your body physically reacting to data that your logic hasn't caught up with yet.

The Strategy: Pause and Wait So, what do you do with this? Most Recorders ignore it because they can't explain it. *"I can't tell my boss I have a bad feeling; I need facts."*

Here is my advice: **Pause and Wait.**

When that gut feeling hits—whether you are at a card table or in a boardroom—**Stop.** Don't act. Don't speak. Just freeze the frame. Your body has the answer, but your brain needs a minute to decode the file.

If you ignore the gut, you crash. But if you **Pause**, you give your logic a chance to find the pattern your gut already saw.

- "Wait, I know why I don't trust him. He didn't answer the question about the timeline."
- "Wait, I know why I shouldn't bet. The deck is rich in tens."

That pause bridges the gap. The Gut Feeling isn't a ghost. It is your survival software working perfectly. **Trust the data.**

THE SPEED TRAP (RUNNERS DON'T WAIT)

The advice "Pause and Wait" sounds great in a book. But in the real world—the Runner World—it's not always possible.

Runners value **Flow.** They value speed. They want the answer *now.* If you are in a boardroom and the CEO asks, *"Do we do the deal?"* and you sit there silent for ten seconds because you're trying to decode a feeling in your stomach... you look incompetent. You look like you froze.

The "Stall" Tactic Since you can't always stop the room, you have to learn to **Buy the Buffer.** You need to buy yourself those crucial 3 to 5 seconds for your Logic to catch up with your Gut.

How do you do it? You create a micro-delay:

- *"That's an interesting angle. Run those numbers by me one more time."*
- *"I want to double-check one thing before I say yes."*
- *"Let me digest that for a minute."*

You aren't being difficult. You are buying processing time. You are letting the file download.

The Red Button Rule But sometimes, you have zero time.

- The car is swerving into your lane.
- The guy is reaching into his pocket.
- The deal is closing in 10 seconds.

In those moments, when there is no time to think: **Bet on the Gut.** Always.

If your stomach says "Duck," you duck. You don't ask "Why?" If your stomach says "Fold," you fold. It is safer to be wrong and safe than to be polite and dead.

Your Gut is the oldest survival mechanism you have. It was designed for the jungle, not the boardroom. So if the clock is at zero, trust the hardware.

THE EQUAL WEIGHT PROBLEM (WHY YOU ARE TIRED)

Here is the unforgiving truth about the Recorder brain: **It does not discriminate.**

If a loop is open, it consumes energy. Your brain is like a computer with 50 tabs open. One tab is your mortgage. One tab is a fight you saw on the news. One tab is the guy who looked at you funny in 1998. To your processor, these are all just "Open Tasks." It allocates the same RAM to the guy on TV as it does to your own kids.

You are burying yourself in layers of issues that have nothing to do with you, simply because you never hit "Save and Close."

THE SPIN CYCLE (WHY WE CRASH)

Here is the funny thing about the human brain—and I mean funny in a dark way. It doesn't know the difference between a real problem and a TV problem.

It treats *everything* as a layer.

- Your mortgage? One layer.

- The argument you had with your spouse? Another layer.
- That news story about the thing happening 3,000 miles away? Another layer.

You aren't "tired." You are **Stacked.** You are walking around with a mental backpack full of rocks, and half of them don't even belong to you. You picked them up off the TV screen and put them in your bag without thinking.

THE MASK WARS (A COMEDY OF ERRORS)

If you want to see what happens when the "Spin" goes out of control, just look back at the Mask Wars. It wasn't political. It was **Mechanical.** It was Runners and Recorders crashing into each other because their loops were broken.

Look at the two "Karens." (And I use that term with love, because we've all been there).

- **The Recorder Karen:** She wasn't just being mean. She was spinning because she needed the *Rule*. She looked at the data, saw a violation, and her brain screamed: *ERROR. ERROR. UNSAFE.* She needed compliance to stop the spinning.
- **The Runner Karen:** She wasn't just being rebellious. She was spinning because she felt *wrong*. Her intuition was screaming. She felt attacked. Her flow was blocked, and she didn't have the data to explain why, so she just exploded.

It's almost comical when you look back. You had people ruining life-long friendships over a debate they heard 20 minutes ago on a podcast. Why? Because they added a "Global Crisis" layer to their stack, gave it the same weight as their own family, and let it spin them out of control.

THE SECRET: YOU HAVE TO MANUALLY CLOSE IT

The secret to getting your life back isn't "meditation." It is **Task Management.** You have to learn to close the loop on things that don't matter, so you have energy for the things that do.

Closure is not a dramatic process; it's just a necessity. My brain doesn't need an apology; it needs a timestamp that says 'Done.'

But here is the trick: **You can't just *think* it away.** A Recorder cannot simply say, *"I'm just going to drop it."* Your brain knows you are lying. It knows the file is still there, floating in the cache.

The "Make It Heavy" Technique To close a loop, you have to make it physical. You have to make the words "heavy" so you can drop them.

- **Say it out loud.**
- **Write it down.**

When you write down: *"I am angry about the news story, but I cannot change it. I am closing this file."* — something happens. You took the invisible static in your head and turned it into a physical object on paper.

Now it is "heavy." Now you can throw the paper in the trash. Your brain sees the action. It registers: **Task Complete.** The loop closes. The energy returns.

18

The Gift of the Delay

The world tells you to "react" or "medicate." The BMI theory tells you to Hold.

A Recorder's brain doesn't just "think"; it Renders. Like a high-resolution image being downloaded on a slow connection, the data comes in fragments. While that download is happening, the hardware vibrates. That "vibration" is the Tuning Fork telling you that the picture isn't clear yet.

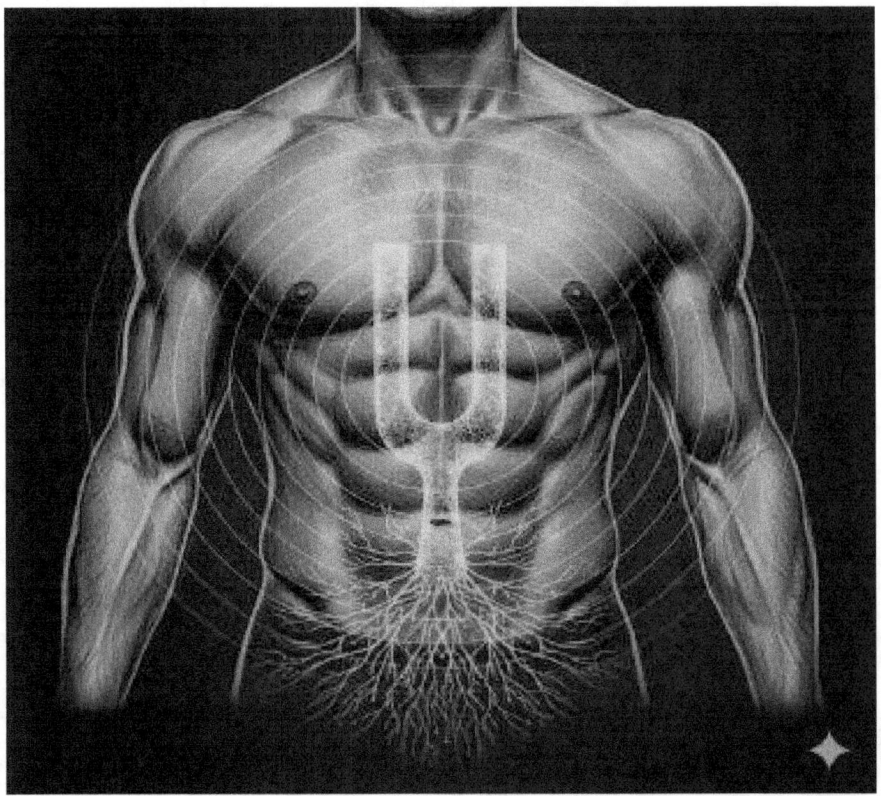

If you try to make a decision while the fork is still ringing, you are guessing. You are forcing a "Runner" reaction onto a "Recorder" download.

The Physics of the "Waiting Room"

When that fork starts to ring, you are in the Waiting Room of the Mind.

• The Sensation: You feel "off." Things are inconsistent. You can't put your finger on it, but the frequency is jagged.

• The Mistake: Suppressing that feeling. Taking the pill to quiet the alarm. Forcing yourself to "just get over it" and make a choice.

• The Protocol: You must Buy Time. You have to tell the world, "I'm not ready to render this yet."

By waiting for the download to finish, you aren't being slow; you are being Accurate. You are allowing your brain to cross-reference every "Binary bit" of information until the vibration stops. When the fork goes silent, that is the "Lock-In." That is the moment the math has finally derived.

Why This is a Superpower

The Tuning Fork is a gift because it prevents you from building a skyscraper on a cracked foundation.

If you ignore the fork, you are building on a "Skid." You are making decisions based on incomplete code. But if you listen to it—if you honor the headache and the gut feeling as Active Data Processing—you become the most dangerous person in the room. Why? Because while everyone else is running on "Flow" and "Guesswork," you are waiting for the Certainty of the 1s and 0s.

When you finally speak, you aren't offering an opinion. You are offering the Finished Download.

The Anatomy of the Ghost Loop

The reason you feel the Tuning Fork ringing when you aren't even under pressure—when you're just sitting on the couch—is because your hardware is still trying to "render" irrelevant data.

You saw a snippet of a news story, you overheard a conflict at the grocery store, or you noticed a structural flaw in a building. To a "Runner," those things are gone the moment they leave the visual field. To a "Recorder," those are Open Loops. Your brain is in the background, out of sight, trying to calculate the "math" of things that have nothing to do with your life.

When the loops stack too high, the hardware overheats. That vibration in your head or gut isn't "stress"—it's System Latency. Your "Tuning Fork" is ringing because the processor is at 99% capacity.

Step 1: Closing the Loops (System Purge)

To turn the Tuning Fork into an instrument of power, you must first clear the "Ghost Loops." You have to teach the hardware what to Discard.

• The Irrelevance Filter: When you feel the tuning fork start to ring, ask the system: "Is this data relative to my skyscraper?" If it's something from the TV or a stranger's drama, you have to manually "End Task."

• The Closure Protocol: Recorders need closure to stop a loop. If you can't resolve the data (because it's irrelevant), you must label it as "Corrupted File" and delete it. You tell the brain: "There is no math to derive here. Close the loop."

Step 2: Calibrating the Instrument

Once you cut the noise, the "Tuning Fork" stops being a source of pain and starts being a Remote Control.

With the 90-day plan and the daily walking, you are lowering the baseline noise. When the "Ghost Loops" are gone, the only thing left that can make the fork ring is Reality.

Now, when you feel that vibration, it's not because of the TV or a stacked-up processor—it's because something Inconsistent is happening right in front of you.

• The Precision: You are in a meeting, and someone says "X," but their body language says "Y." A Runner won't notice. But because your loops are closed and your instrument is tuned, your fork will hit a Resonance Alarm.

• The Advantage: You don't have to guess. You don't have to be "smart." You just have to listen to the vibration. While everyone else is lost in the "Flow," you are the only one who knows the code doesn't match the output.

The Most Dangerous Person in the Room

When you learn to trust the Tuning Fork over the world's "Noise," you gain a level of Sovereignty that few people ever touch.

You become the person who can't be lied to, not because you're a mind reader, but because you are a Frequency Auditor. You have the luxury of waiting for the download. You have the "Remote Control" to your own hardware.

You aren't suppressing the gift with Tylenol anymore; you are using it to navigate the world with Binary Certainty. You have moved from being a victim of the "Noise" to being the Master of the "Signal."

REGULATE YOURSELF

Once you realize you have a Recorder brain, you can stop taking the bait. You can sit back and look at the stack of files. *"Okay, that TV argument? Delete." "That opinion on the internet? Delete." "My health? Keep."*

You stop letting the world add layers to your life. You start punting the junk. And suddenly, you aren't just surviving the day. You are actually living it.

The "Two Tuning Forks" Logic

There is a dual-sensor system that Recorders often have misinterpreted because they have any guidance.

1. The Head: The "Data" Tuning Fork

• The Sensation: The headache, the pressure behind the eyes, the migraine.

• The Reality: This isn't just "stress." This is your Input Buffer overflowing. Your brain is taking in 10x more data than the "Runner" world around you.

• The "Tuning" Error: People treat the headache like a bug, but it's actually the Signal that your hardware is being forced to "emulate" Runner software. You are trying to process sideways data in a linear machine.

2. The Gut: The "Resonance" Tuning Fork

• The Sensation: The "belly" issues, the tightness, the "Xyzal/Tylenol" cycle.

• The Reality: This is your Vagus Nerve (the wire connecting the brain and gut) reacting to Dissonance. When you are in a room or a job that doesn't match your "Frequency," your gut feels it first.

• The "Tuning" Error: People think it's something they ate. It's actually something they are Enduring. The gut is screaming that the "Handshake" with the environment is a mismatch.

The Two-Way Tuning

• The Negative Tuning (The Skid): The grinding vibration that tells you something is structurally wrong.

• The Positive Tuning (The Dowsing Rod): The "pull" that tells you you're standing over the truth, even before you have the words to explain why it's true.

19

And in a world that constantly pulls Binary minds

The Lost Language of Hugging

There was a time when human beings touched each other without suspicion.

Not as a transaction.

Not as a performance.

Not as a social signal.

But as a way of knowing.

Long before handshakes became the default, people hugged. And not the modern, polite, one-second tap on the shoulder — but full contact. Chest to chest. Heart to heart. Long enough to feel breathing synchronize. Long enough for the nervous system to register safety.

I wouldn't be surprised if the civilizations we mythologize — Atlantis, Lemuria, any culture that reached a true peak before collapsing — understood this deeply. Not as romance. Not as affection. As infrastructure.

Because when people knew who they were — when they understood their role, their skills, their cognitive design — there was nothing to hide. Enforcers enforced. Builders built. Healers healed. Connectors connected. Leaders led. Numbers people tracked reality. Everyone knew what seat they sat in. There was no pretending.

And when people hugged, you could feel it.

You could feel if someone was aligned.

You could feel if someone was carrying fear.

You could feel exhaustion, steadiness, sincerity, grief.

A hug doesn't lie.

That's exactly why it faded.

Handshakes replaced hugs not because they were better — but because they were safer. Safer for people who didn't want to be felt. Safer for people who lived in performance instead of truth. Safer for people who needed distance between what they projected and what they carried.

A handshake lets you signal strength without revealing state.

A handshake lets you perform confidence without surrendering regulation.

A handshake lets you stay separate.

You can squeeze someone's hand.

You can dominate a handshake.

You can judge someone for a weak grip or a sweaty palm.

None of that tells you who they are.

I once shook Bill Gates' hand. One of the most powerful men on the planet. One of the most influential minds in modern history. His hand was sweaty.

And it meant nothing.

It didn't make him lesser.

It didn't make him weak.

It didn't give me anything over him.

It simply meant he was human — and carrying an enormous cognitive load.

But the world trains us to interpret handshakes as status tests. Strength tests. Dominance signals. Runner rituals. We teach people to read meaning into grip pressure while ignoring the entire nervous system standing in front of them.

Hugging bypasses all of that.

When you hug someone properly — chest to chest — the heart does what it evolved to do. It regulates. It synchronizes. It tells the body, you are not alone. This is not poetry. This is biology. Heart rate variability shifts. Cortisol drops. The vagus nerve activates. Thought slows. Defenses soften.

Doors open.

That's why hugging feels different to Binary Minds. Not because we're sentimental — but because we are built to feel systems. We feel alignment and misalignment instantly. A hug is a direct data stream. No narrative. No masking. No multitasking. Just signal.

It's also why some people avoid it instinctively.

If you live in performance, a hug is dangerous.

If you live in narrative, a hug cuts through it.

If you rely on speed and surface harmony, a hug slows you down.

You can't hug and multitask.

You can't hug and posture.

You can't hug and lie.

That's why modern culture backed away from it.

We replaced regulation with ritual.

We replaced connection with optics.

We replaced contact with contracts.

And the cost has been enormous.

People are touch-starved and don't know it. Dysregulated and don't know it. Lonely in crowded rooms. Overstimulated and under-soothed. We medicate anxiety, treat depression, analyze trauma — while removing one of the most ancient stabilizers humans ever had.

Hugging isn't childish.

It isn't inappropriate.

It isn't optional.

It's part of the architecture.

It's also why this matters personally.

My brother reached a point where life without hugging didn't feel like life at all. And if you've lived in a Binary body long enough, you understand that sentence immediately. Not metaphorically. Physically. When the world becomes so distant, so procedural, so cold, that the last remaining proof of being human is contact — losing that feels like erasure.

If you can't be felt, you start to disappear.

This isn't about forcing touch. It's about restoring permission. Permission to regulate together. Permission to be human without explanation. Permission to connect without performance.

We didn't evolve to survive alone.

We didn't evolve to think the same.

And we didn't evolve to keep our bodies separate while our nervous systems collapse.

Hugging is not softness.

It is strength without armor.

And when civilization forgot that, it didn't just lose warmth — it lost coherence.

For Parents: Why Touch Matters More Than You Were Told

If you are raising a Binary child, there is something important you were probably never taught — and almost certainly never warned about.

Your child's nervous system does not regulate through words first.

It regulates through safety, predictability, and physical connection.

This does not mean constant touching. It does not mean forcing affection. It means understanding that, for a Binary child, safe physical contact is not emotional decoration — it is biological grounding.

When your child hugs you — really hugs you — their body is checking in.

It is asking a question without words: Am I safe right now? Are we okay?

A long, steady hug answers that question faster than any explanation ever could.

Binary children carry enormous internal load. They record tone, contradiction, tension, and unresolved moments whether they want to or not. When the world feels loud, confusing, or misaligned, their system doesn't naturally discharge that stress. It accumulates. Quietly. Invisibly.

Hugging helps close the loop.

Not because it solves the problem, but because it tells the nervous system it is no longer alone with it.

You may notice your child doesn't want a hug when emotions are high — and then seeks one later, when things calm. That timing matters. Respect it. A hug offered at the right moment can settle hours of internal chaos. A hug forced at the wrong moment can overwhelm.

Let your child lead.

And don't underestimate the power of your presence. You don't need to say the perfect thing. You don't need to explain or fix or rationalize. Your body is already speaking a language your child understands instinctively.

A hug says:

You belong.

You are safe.

You don't have to carry this alone.

That message doesn't fade with age.

As your child grows, they may hug less often — especially in a world that teaches them touch is optional or awkward or inappropriate. But the need does not disappear. It simply goes unmet.

If you can give your child one lasting gift, let it be this:

a home where connection is allowed to be physical, quiet, and real.

You are not spoiling them.

You are regulating them.

20

• *The timeline was broken. CHAPTER 8: The Recorder'*

(W)hy You Weren't Late — You Were Digging)
If there is one lie that has done more damage to the Binary Mind than anything else—more than the bullying, more than the isolation, more than the sensory overload—it is the medical label: "Developmentally Delayed."

Parents hear those two words and their hearts stop. They look at their child and see a broken clock, ticking too slowly, falling behind the pack. They panic. They think "delayed" means the train has left the station and their child is standing alone on the platform.

Adults hear it and internalize a lifelong secret shame. They feel like they are perpetually running five minutes late to the human race. They mask, they fake it, they exhaust themselves trying to sprint to catch up to a finish line that the Runners reached effortlessly at age five.

But you were not delayed. You were Under Construction.

There is a fundamental difference between building a tent and building a skyscraper. The world expects every child to build a tent. But nature commanded you to build a tower.

1. The Construction Site: Tent vs. Skyscraper

To understand why Binary development looks "wrong" to the outside world, you have to look at the architectural blueprints.

The Runner (The Tent)

The Runner's mind is designed for rapid deployment.

• The Goal: Shelter immediately.

• The Process: You put up the poles, you throw on the canvas, and you zip the door.

• The Timeline: By age 2, the tent is up. The child is mimicking smiles. By age 3, they are engaging in pretend play. By age 4, they are navigating complex social hierarchies on the playground.

• The Visual: To the parent and the doctor, this looks like "Success." They see a structure standing there. It is visible. It is functional. It is "on time."

The Recorder (The Skyscraper)

The Recorder's mind is designed for vertical depth and massive structural load.

• The Goal: Absolute stability and infinite capacity.

• The Process: Before you can build up, you have to dig down. You have to excavate. You have to pour a concrete foundation that goes fifty feet into the bedrock.

• The Visual: To the observer standing on the sidewalk (the doctor, the teacher, the parent), it looks like nothing is happening.

• They see a hole in the ground.

• They see a fence around the site.

• They see no walls, no windows, no height.

They look at the Runner's tent next door and say, "Look! That child is already built! Why is your child just a hole in the ground? They are delayed."

They are wrong. You aren't delayed. You are curing the concrete.

You cannot build a mind capable of perfect recall, binary logic, and systemic pattern recognition on a tent's foundation. It requires a heavy-duty base.

The tragedy is that we try to force the Recorder child to "put up walls" (speak, socialize, mask) while they are still pouring the foundation. We interrupt the curing process. And in doing so, we risk destabilizing the entire structure.

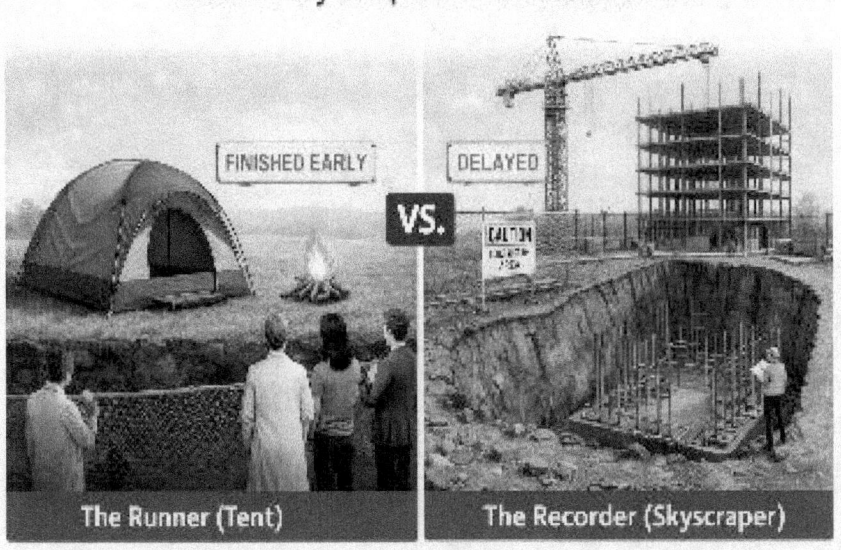

Tent vs. Skyscraper Construction Site

2. The Polarity of Learning: Meaning vs. Mimicry

Why does this "excavation" take so long? Because the two minds learn using completely opposite mechanisms.

The Runner Learns by Mimicry

Runners are wired to copy.

• Input: Mother smiles and waves.

• Runner Reaction: Copy the hand motion. Copy the facial muscle movement.

• Internal Logic: "I don't know what this means, but it creates a positive connection, so I will do it."

- Result: Rapid social fluency. The child looks "engaged" because they are mirroring the surface behavior.

The Recorder Learns by Meaning

Recorders are wired to decode. Mimicry feels like a lie to a Recorder. We do not copy; we understand.

- Input: Mother smiles and waves.
- Recorder Reaction: Freeze and Observe.
- Why is she moving her hand?
- Is it a signal?
- Does she do it every time?
- What is the utility of this motion?
- Internal Logic: "I will not perform this action until I have mapped its function and verified its pattern."
- Result: The child stares blankly. The doctor writes down "Lack of joint attention." The parent cries.

But the child isn't disengaged. The child is analyzing. They are building the Truth Anchor for the concept of "Greeting." Once they understand it—fully, deeply, logically—they will execute it. But they won't fake it just to make you feel better.

3. The Language Paradox: Hyperlexia and the Code

This difference is most visible in how we learn language. This is where the "Delay" myth falls apart completely.

Most children learn to read in a standard, linear progression:

Letters → Sounds (Phonics) → Words → Sentences → Meaning.

Many Recorders (Binary Minds) do it backward:

Meaning → Pattern → Whole Word → Code.

We often see Binary children who are Hyperlexic. They can read complex words at age 3. They can recite the alphabet backward. They know every species of dinosaur. But they cannot ask for a juice box.

The experts look at this and call it a "Splinter Skill." They dismiss it as a parlor trick. "He can read 'Tyrannosaurus Rex', but he's delayed because he can't say 'Hello'."

I look at this and see a mind that prioritizes System Understanding over Social Output.

• Reading is a fixed code. A is always A. B is always B. The rules are binary. The Recorder loves this. They master the code early because the code is safe.

• Speaking is a social negotiation. It relies on tone, timing, and eye contact. The Recorder delays this because the variables are messy.

We don't want to use the tool (speech) until we have mastered the manual. The silence of a Binary child isn't emptiness; it is the hum of a supercomputer processing the syntax.

4. Truth Anchors: The Physics of Belief

A Binary Mind cannot move forward on a shaky floor. Before a Recorder can make a decision, form an opinion, or trust a person, they need a Truth Anchor.

A Truth Anchor is a verified fact. It is a piece of data that cannot be moved.

• Runner: "I believe the bridge is safe because everyone is walking on it." (Social Proof).

• Recorder: "I need to see the blueprints and the load-bearing report." (Structural Proof).

The God vs. Santa Claus Test

This is the perfect laboratory experiment for how a Recorder develops belief systems versus a Runner.

The Recorder child runs a Verification Loop.

Test 1: God

• Observation: I cannot see Him.

• Logic Check: Can I disprove His existence? No.

• Contradiction Check: Is there a logical contradiction? Not necessarily. The universe is complex; a creator is a valid variable.

• Outcome: Keep the File Open. (Possibility). The Recorder remains agnostic or faithful because the logic does not break.

Test 2: Santa Claus (The Milk and Cookies Test)

This is where the Binary Mind works differently. I could allow for the fairy tale elements. I could accept the mythical parts—the flying reindeer, the North Pole, the magic. That is the story layer.

But then they told me he stops at every house and eats the milk and cookies. That is not mythical. That is biological.

• Fact: There are millions of houses.

• Fact: He eats at all of them.

• Fact: A biological stomach cannot hold millions of cookies and gallons of milk.

It fails the test. The mythical part I could handle. But the physical part—the eating—created a hard contradiction. A man cannot drink and eat that fast, the human milk and cookies would slow him down. Therefore, the story is false.

The Recorder child drops Santa instantly. Not to be a cynic. Not to be "grown up." But because the Truth Anchor failed on the biological data. Parents get upset. "Why can't you just pretend? You're ruining the magic!"

Because to a Binary Mind, pretending is data corruption. We develop by finding solid rocks to stand on. If you give us a fake rock (Santa), we stop trusting you. If you give us a solid rock (Truth), we can build the next level of the skyscraper.

5. The Mechanism of Closure (Why We "Dwell")

If you want to understand why a Recorder gets "stuck" on a topic, you have to understand Closure.

Closure is the "End of File" marker in our operating system.

• Runner: Can leave a conversation unresolved. "Let's agree to disagree." They float away. They prioritize the relationship over the resolution.

• Recorder: Cannot leave the loop open. An open loop is a running process that eats RAM. It runs in the background, heating up the CPU.

The "Dwelling" Myth

The world says: "Why are you still talking about this? It happened yesterday! Let it go!"

You are talking about it because the logic didn't resolve.
• There was a contradiction in your argument.
• The math didn't add up.

21

The goal isn't to move them "up" the spectrum towa

(Why "The Spectrum" is a Lie)
The world has spent fifty years trying to measure the Binary Mind using a ruler that doesn't exist. They call it "The Spectrum."

The spectrum implies a sliding scale—a single line where "normal" is at one end and "severe" is at the other. It suggests that an autistic mind is simply a neurotypical mind turned down, or distorted, or broken. It assumes we are all running the same software, but some of us are just buggy.

This is the fundamental error of modern psychology.

We are not running the same software. We are not a variation on a curve. We are a different machine speaking a different language. To understand the Recorder, you have to leave the world of psychology and enter the world of computer architecture. You have to understand the difference between High-Level Language and Assembler.

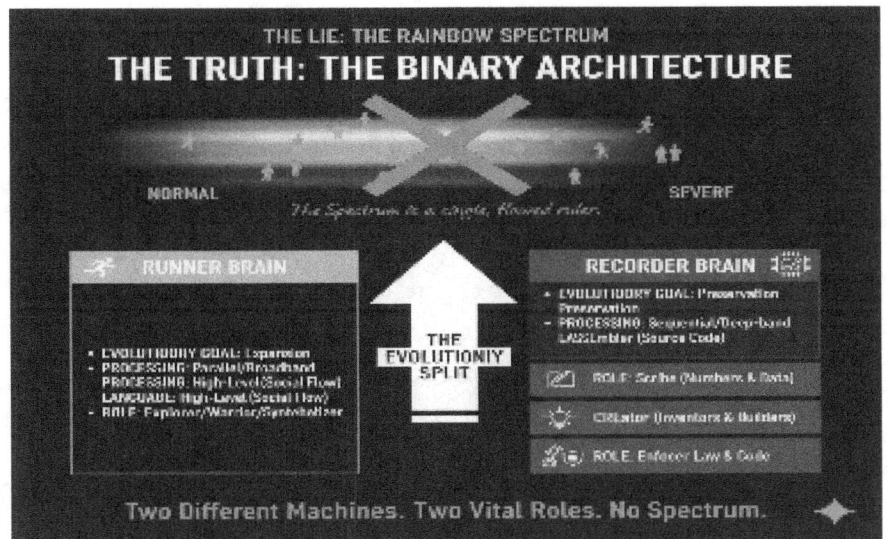

1. The RAM Theory (High Functioning vs. Low Functioning)

The "Spectrum" tries to measure how well a Recorder can fake being a Runner.

• "High Functioning" just means: This person has enough RAM (Random Access Memory) to create a simulation of High-Level Language. They can mask. They can translate.

• "Low Functioning" just means: This person is running pure Assembler and lacks the RAM to build the translation layer.

It is not a measure of intelligence. It is a measure of Translation Cost.

When you ask a Binary Mind to "read the room," you are asking an Assembler system to run a fuzzy logic algorithm. The "High Functioning" person does it, but their cooling fans spin at 100% capacity. They have to manually compile every facial expression, every tone shift, and every double-meaning into binary code before they can understand it.

That isn't a social deficit. That is a computational tax. And it is exhausting.

2. The Bedrock: 1s, 0s, and Physics

To understand why we are so rigid, you have to look at the bottom of the machine. Deep down, at the very bottom of every computer, phone, and server on earth, there is no "language." There is only physics. There is only a switch.

A switch has two positions. It is either ON (electricity flows) or it is OFF (electricity stops).

• ON = 1
• OFF = 0

This is Binary Code. It is the brutal, absolute truth of the system. There is no gray area. A switch cannot be "mostly on." It is 1 or it is 0.

In the early days, if you wanted to tell a machine what to do, you had to speak in pure binary strings like 10110000 01100001. To the machine, that is a clear command. To a human, it is a blinding wall of noise. Humans needed a bridge. We needed a way to speak to the metal without losing our minds.

Enter Assembly Language (Assembler).

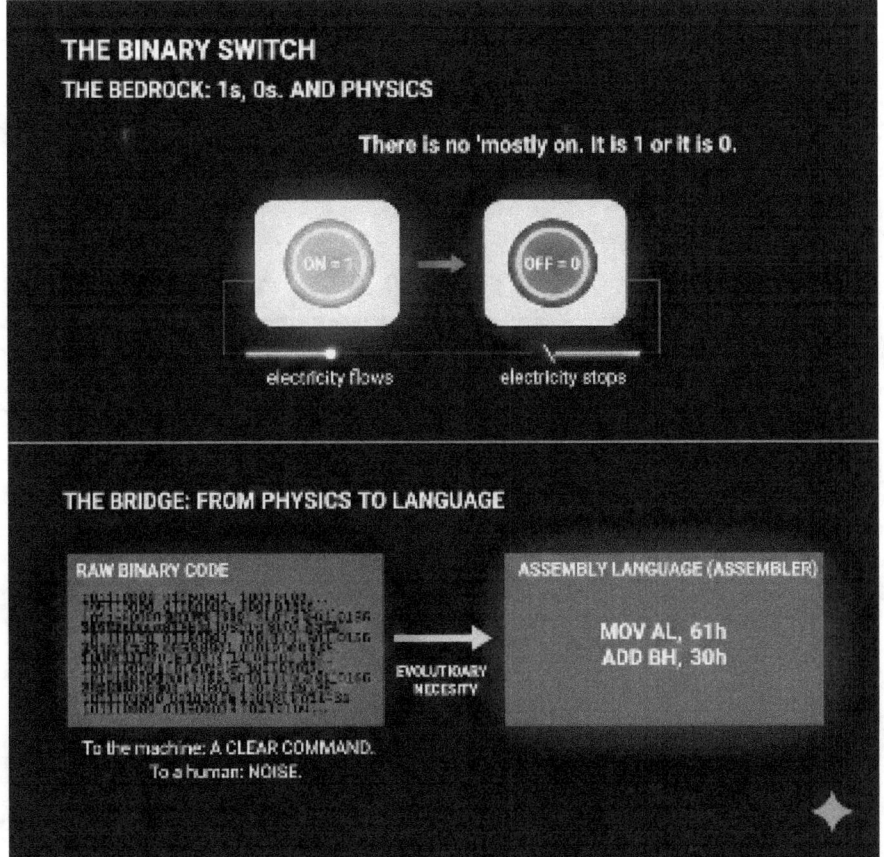

3. The 1-to-1 Mapping

Assembler was the solution. It is the oldest, most fundamental programming language that is still readable by humans. It was not designed to be "easy." It was designed to be exact.

Assembler is a 1-to-1 translation of machine code.

Instead of writing 10110000, the programmer could write: MOV.

• MOV (The Instruction): Move data.

• AX (The Destination): The exact hardware register.

• 5 (The Value): The number.

This helps explain the Recorder's need for sequence. In Assembler:

1. Sequence Matters: You cannot ask the machine to add two numbers until you have first moved those numbers into the registers. A, then B, then C. You cannot jump to C.

2. Nothing is Implied: In modern languages (like Python or English), if you make a typo, the computer guesses what you meant. In Assembler, if you make a typo, the machine crashes.

This is why Recorders freeze when given vague instructions. We aren't being stubborn. We are running a language where "implied context" results in a fatal error.

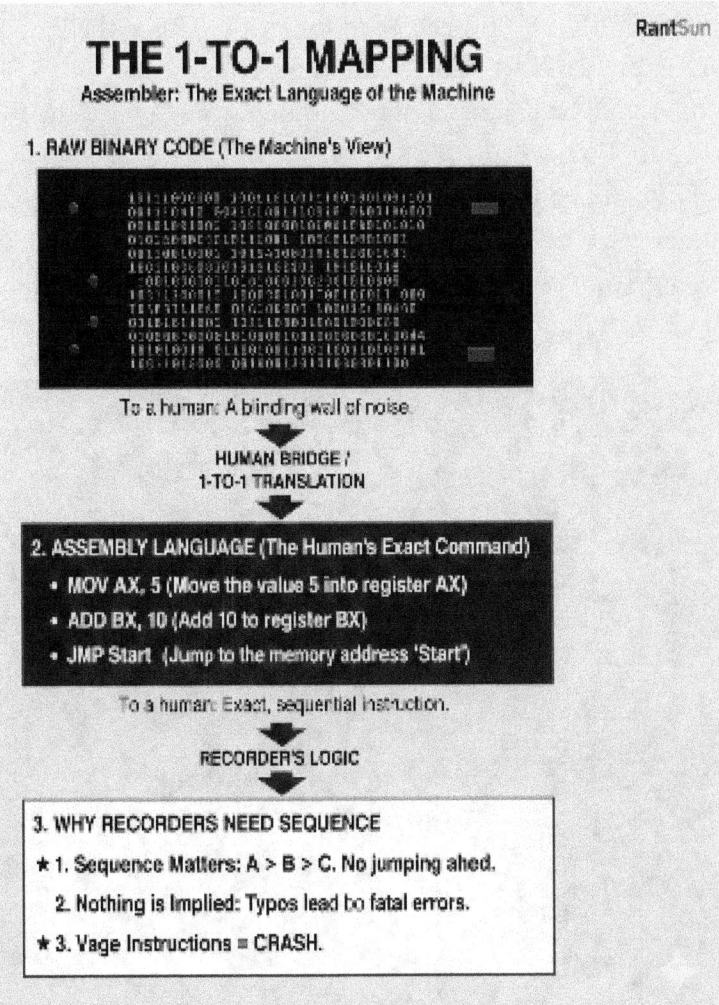

THE 1-TO-1 MAPPING

Assembler: The Exact Language of the Machine

RantSun

1. RAW BINARY CODE (The Machine's View)

To a human: A binding wall of noise.

HUMAN BRIDGE /
1-TO-1 TRANSLATION

2. ASSEMBLY LANGUAGE (The Human's Exact Command)

- MOV AX, 5 (Move the value 5 into register AX)
- ADD BX, 10 (Add 10 to register BX)
- JMP Start (Jump to the memory address 'Start')

To a human: Exact, sequential instruction.

RECORDER'S LOGIC

3. WHY RECORDERS NEED SEQUENCE

★ 1. Sequence Matters: A > B > C. No jumping ahed.

2. Nothing is Implied: Typos lead to fatal errors.

★ 3. Vage Instructions = CRASH.

4. The CPU's Workspace (The Registers)

To really see the similarities between the Binary Mind and the computer, look at the Registers. These are the tiny, ultra-fast storage slots inside a CPU. They mirror exactly how a Recorder processes life.

• AX (The Accumulator): Used for arithmetic. This is the Recorder's obsession with Logic and Math. We want the numbers to balance.

• CX (The Counter): Used for loops. This is the Recorder's love of Repetition and Routine. We find safety in the loop.

• DX (The Data): Used for input/output. This is the Recorder's raw Sensory Data stream.

When a parent says, "Why do you have to do things in the exact same order every time?", they are talking to a CX Register. The machine is built to loop. Disrupting the loop isn't "freeing" the child; it is corrupting the counter.

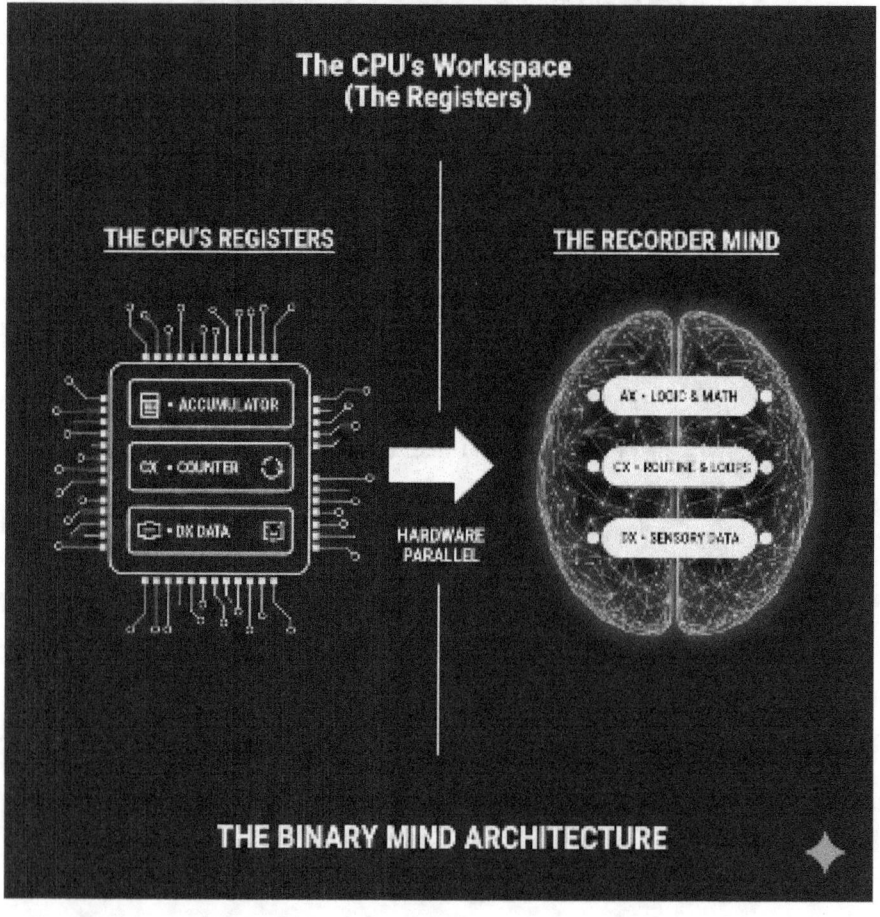

5. Redefining "Communication Deficits"

Doctors say Recorders have a "communication deficit." Let's flip the lens.

If you put a Runner in a room where the only language allowed is pure, unadulterated Truth—no metaphors, no hints, no emotional manipulation—the Runner would look "low functioning." They would panic. They would struggle to operate without their layer of social abstraction.

We do not have a communication deficit. We have a precision requirement. We speak the root language of reality: Cause and Effect.

6. The End of the Spectrum

We must stop teaching Binary kids that they are on a "spectrum" of brokenness. We must teach them that they are Root-Level Processors.

- They have direct access to the hardware of reality.
- They process data without the filter of social bias.
- They are the Architects, the Builders, the Keepers of the Record.

22

That's how the 19,000 step days started. That's ho

(T he High Price of Emulation)
   If you run a high-performance engine at 7,000 RPM in first gear for thirty years, only two things can happen. The car will move. And the engine will eventually explode.

For most of my life, I was moving. I built businesses. I managed teams. I didn't fall apart. But under the hood, the temperature was climbing year after year. The fans were screaming.

People usually call this "masking." I call it Emulation.

1. The Emulation Tax (Mac vs. Windows)

In computing, emulation is what happens when one system is forced to behave like another one it was never designed to be. I was a high-powered Linux box bolted into a Windows office environment.

When you run Windows software on a Linux machine, the machine doesn't magically become Windows. It has to create a "Virtual Machine" in the background. Every instruction has to be translated.

The system works—but it works inefficiently, constantly burning energy just to appear compatible.

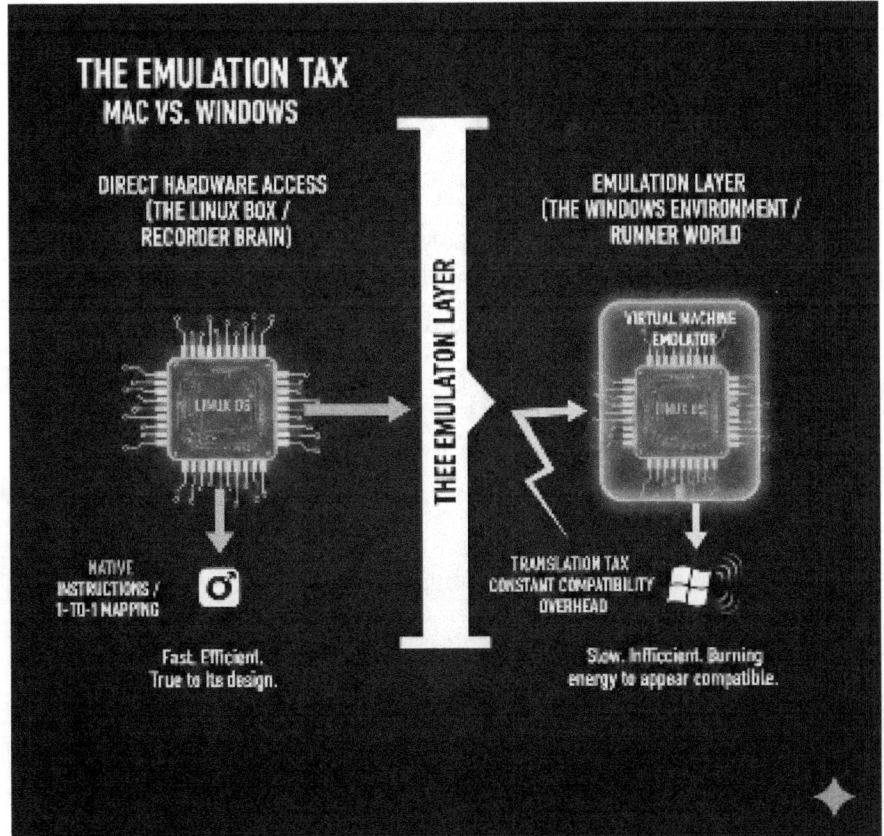

2. The Coolant: Pills and Pot

When an engine overheats, you have two options:

1. Fix the cooling system.

2. Cheat and dump coolant into the system.

I chose cheat.

• Marijuana: Noise-Cancellation. To a Runner, pot is fun. To a Binary Recorder, pot is Noise-Cancellation Headphones. At night, my Replay loops would activate. Pot didn't make me "stoned." It made me quiet. The volume went from a 10 down to a 4.

• Pills: Manual Chemistry. Need to sleep? Force the switch. Need to wake up? Punch the system. It was chemistry-as-engineering.

3. The Body Keeps the Score (The Armor)

By 66, I was carrying an extra hundred pounds. That weight was not laziness. It wasn't "no willpower." It was Armor.

Forty years of cortisol and stress had trained my body: "We are in a war zone. Store energy. Protect the core." The fat around my middle was physical evidence of a system that hadn't truly rested in decades.

4. The Crash (Functional Freeze)

Eventually, the emulator fails. The crash doesn't always look dramatic. I didn't have a public breakdown. My crash looked like Functional Freeze.

• From the outside: I still went to work.

• From the inside: I was in standby mode. I had no reserve. Any unexpected change felt like someone yanking the power cord out of the server.

5. The Pivot to Physics (The Obligation)

There comes a moment where you can't explain your way out. For me, it wasn't just looking in the mirror; it was looking at the timeline.

Two of my brothers-in-law passed away two years ago, in the same month. That was the data point I couldn't ignore. I looked at the armor I was wearing—100 pounds of weight I had built to protect myself—and I realized the armor was going to kill me before the enemy did.

I realized that if I died early, the information in my head would die with me.

This wasn't just about "getting fit." It was about System Preservation. I had discovered a way to explain the Binary Mind that could save thousands of people from the same pain I went through.

There is an unwritten rule in civilization: If you have the map, and you see people lost in the woods, you are obligated to show them the way.

So, I didn't go to rehab. I went to the lab. I took the same Binary logic I used in business and pointed it at my own body.

• Variable A: Sugar causes fog. Action: Remove.

• Variable B: Pot masks noise but doesn't fix it. Action: Remove.

• Variable C: Walking drops stress hormones. Action: Increase.

And then came the biggest revelation of all: It was easy.

All I had to do was repeat the simple process on a daily basis. I didn't need willpower; I needed a loop. I just had to punch the ticket every single morning.

It's like compounding interest. You don't see it on Day 1. But if you hold the loop, the momentum builds up until it kicks in the cannon.

23

You didn't choose to be a camera that never sleeps

(H ow to Use the Machine That Never Sleeps)
There is a terrifying reality to being a Recorder that nobody talks about. It is the fact that we do not have an "Off" switch.

A Runner can walk into a restaurant, sit down, and just eat dinner. Their brain filters out the silverware clinking, the couple arguing three tables away, the smell of the sanitizer the busboy is using, and the flicker of the neon sign in the window. They don't choose to ignore it; their brain deletes it automatically before it even reaches their conscious mind.

A Recorder has no delete button. We have no filter.

From the moment I wake up until the moment I pass out, my system is ingesting data. I am recording the temperature. I am recording the tone of your voice. I am recording the fact that you shifted your weight to your left foot when you lied to me. I don't want to know these things. I don't try to remember them. But I have no choice.

I am a 24/7 surveillance system. And the hardest part is that I cannot choose what stays on the hard drive. I might forget my own wedding anniversary date, but I can tell you the license plate number of a car that cut me off in 1998. The machine records what it deems relevant, not what I deem polite.

1. The Vibration (The "Ring")

This constant recording creates a specific physical sensation. It isn't anxiety. It isn't fear. It is a Vibration.

When you are taking in that much data, your body acts like a tuning fork. You feel a hum.

• Sometimes it's a low hum (Safety).
• Sometimes it's a high-pitched screech (Danger).
• Sometimes it's a deep, resonant Ring in your gut.

That "Ring" is the most important signal you possess. It is the sound of your 24/7 camera detecting a threat that your logic hasn't seen yet.

2. The Gut is Not Magic (It's Data)

Runners call it "Intuition." They treat it like a mystical power. "I just had a hunch."

For a Recorder, the Gut is not mystical. It is High-Speed Data Processing.

Because you have been recording 24/7 for your entire life, your database is millions of times larger than a Runner's. You have stored every micro-expression, every tone shift, and every pattern break you have ever witnessed.

When you walk into a boardroom and meet a new CEO, your conscious mind sees a nice suit and a firm handshake. But your Recorder Database is running a background check against millions of previous files.

• Match Found: He smiled, but his eyes didn't crinkle. (File #4,002: The liar who stole my money in 1982 did that).
• Match Found: He checked his watch when you mentioned the budget. (File #890: The partner who was hiding debt did that).

Your brain can't explain this in words yet. It's too fast. So instead, it sends a physical signal to your Vagus Nerve. Your stomach drops. Your skin tightens. You get "The Ring."

That is not nerves. That is your hard drive screaming: "PATTERN MATCH: UNSAFE."

THE ICEBERG ILLUSION

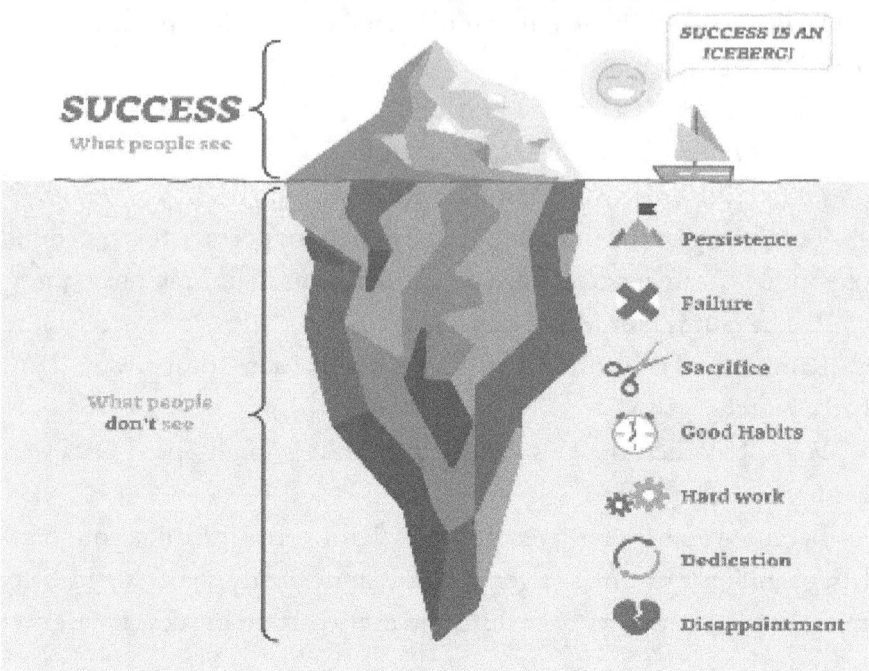

3. The Fatal Mistake: Ignoring the Data

The biggest mistake Recorders make is trying to be "rational."

We live in a world that worships logic. If you say to your boss, "We shouldn't do this deal because my stomach hurts," you look crazy. So, we suppress the ring. We tell ourselves to stop being paranoid. We look at the spreadsheet, and the spreadsheet looks fine, so we sign the deal.

Six months later, the deal collapses. The CEO was a crook. And you find yourself saying the phrase every Recorder has whispered a thousand times:

"I knew it. I knew it the second I met him. Why didn't I listen?"

You didn't listen because you tried to use Runner Logic to override Recorder Physics. You ignored the surveillance tape because you hadn't watched the footage yet.

4. The Protocol: Pause and Decode

So, how do we live with this? How do we use a gut feeling without looking like a lunatic?

You need a protocol. When the Ring happens—when that deep vibration hits your stomach—you must follow these three steps.

Step 1: The Freeze Frame (Stop)

The moment you feel the Ring, Stop.

Do not sign the paper. Do not agree to the date. Do not get in the car.

The Ring is a "Check Engine" light. You don't keep driving when the light comes on; you pull over.

If you are in a meeting, buy time. "I need to digest this." "Let me run the numbers one more time."

You are not stalling. You are waiting for the file to download.

Step 2: The Inquiry (Decode)

Once you have bought space, ask your system what it saw. You have to treat your brain like a witness.

Ask yourself: "What did I see that I didn't notice?"

• Was it his tone?

• Was it the timeline?

• Was it the way they looked at each other when I asked about the money?

Usually, within 24 hours, the file will unlock. You will suddenly realize: "He didn't answer the question. He changed the subject."

Now you have the logic to back up the feeling.

Step 3: The Override (Trust)

Sometimes, you never find the logic. The logic says "Safe," but the Gut says "Danger."

In those rare cases, Trust the Gut.

Your 24/7 recording system picked up a scent that is too subtle for words. It might be a pheromone. It might be a micro-tremor in the air. You don't need to explain it to survive it.

• If the hair on your neck stands up, leave.

• If the handshake feels wrong, walk away.

I have never regretted trusting my gut. I have only regretted the times I let "politeness" overrule it.

5. Helpful Hints for the "Always On" Life

Living without an off switch is exhausting. Here is how you manage the machine so it doesn't burn you out.

• The Sensory Audit: You cannot stop the recording, but you can lower the resolution. If you are tired, wear sunglasses. Wear noise-canceling headphones. It reduces the file size of the data coming in.

• The "No" Default: When your system is overloaded, your automatic answer to everything should be "No." You can always change a No to a Yes later. You cannot change a Yes to a No without damage.

• Sleep is Data Filing: Runners sleep to rest their bodies. Recorders sleep to file their data. If you don't sleep, the files pile up on the desktop, and your system slows down. Protect your sleep like it's your job.

• Respect the Nose: The olfactory nerve (smell) is the only sense that goes directly to the brain without a filter. If a place smells "wrong" to you—musty, chemical, stagnant—leave. Your nose is often the first part of the Recorder to detect a problem.

Conclusion

24

The Recorder wins by becoming the ground.CHAPTER 1

(H ow the Recorder Learns)
     If you understand the difference between the Recorder and the Runner, you understand why traditional education often feels like a trap for people like us. The Runner operates on Momentum. The Recorder operates on Fidelity.

To illustrate this, I have to tell you the story of the CISSP—the Certified Information Systems Security Professional exam. It is considered the gold standard in cybersecurity. It is six hours long. It is brutal. And I didn't approach it the way most people do.

1. The First Pass (Reconnaissance)

The first time I took it, I wasn't trying to pass. That sounds irresponsible until you understand how a Binary Mind works. I didn't need motivation. I didn't need confidence. I needed data.

So I skimmed a book after work for a week, walked into the testing center, and sat down not to perform—but to observe.

I treated the exam like a hostile network I was scanning for open ports. I wanted to know how the questions were constructed, how the language bent, where ambiguity lived, and exactly how much precision was required before the logic broke.

I wasn't guessing. I was calibrating.

I failed. But I walked out knowing exactly what the beast looked like. I was at about sixty percent. To a Runner, that's a waste of money. To a Recorder, that's successful reconnaissance.

2. The Second Pass (The Fatal Error)

The second attempt is where the story actually breaks. This time, I studied hard. Really hard. Four months. Six hours a day. I absorbed the material.

But I also made a fatal error: I listened to the "experts."

I engaged with the forums, the boot camps, and the well-meaning mentors who all gave the same advice:

- "Don't overthink it."
- "Think like a manager, not a technician."
- "Don't try to fix the problem; just manage the risk."

Without realizing it, I let myself be pulled out of my own operating system. I stopped verifying truth and started playing a probability game. I used elimination tricks. I used heuristics. I memorized the "best" answer instead of understanding the only answer.

I was trying to run someone else's software on my hardware.

I missed by three questions. Three.

I sat in the parking lot, crushed. Not because I didn't know the material—I knew it cold. I was crushed because the loss didn't feel random. It felt like a structural failure. I had betrayed the process that actually works for my mind. I had traded deep understanding for "test-taking strategies," and the system had rejected me for it.

3. The Third Pass (First Principles)

That's when the shift happened. I realized that Binary Minds don't win by guessing well. We don't win by "thinking like a manager." We win by removing ambiguity until there is nothing left to guess.

So for the third pass, I ignored every trick. I went back to First Principles.

- I didn't just memorize that "AES is a symmetric algorithm." I tore it down to understand why the block size matters.

• I didn't just memorize the fire suppression classes; I learned the physics of why water spreads a grease fire.

I rebuilt the entire domain internally, brick by brick. I wasn't memorizing answers anymore. I was reconstructing the architecture the test was built on.

When I walked into the testing center the third time, the air felt different. There was no anxiety. No frantic mental shuffling. I sat down, and the screen lit up. The questions didn't feel adversarial anymore. They felt transparent. I wasn't fighting the ambiguity; I was seeing right through it. The "tricks" that tripped me up before were now glaringly obvious deviations from the system I had built in my head.

I wasn't trying to beat the test. I was verifying it.

I passed. Not because I finally "got smarter." Not because I studied harder. But because I stopped trying to think like someone else.

4. The Recorder vs. The Runner Learning Style

This experience taught me the fundamental difference in how we master the world.

The Runner: The Game of Progress

For the Runner, the world is a series of finish lines. Their OS is optimized for Velocity.

• Question: "What is the fastest way to get to the other side?"

• Method: Heuristics. 80/20 thinking. "Tips and Tricks."

• Failure: Friction. If a Runner gets a 60% on a practice test, they panic because they aren't moving fast enough. Runners are brilliant at execution. But because they skim the surface to maintain speed, they rarely understand the geology beneath their feet. When the "tricks" stop working, they stumble.

The Recorder: The Game of Truth

For the Recorder, the world is a dataset. They do not care about the finish line; they care about the Map. Their OS is optimized for Resolution.

• Question: "What is this made of?"

• Method: Verification. Deep Dive. Re-deriving the math.

• Failure: Telemetry. If a Recorder gets a 60%, they feel curiosity. It highlights a gap in the data. Recorders are terrible at racing. They will lose every sprint because they stop to read the footnotes. But once a Recorder has mapped the terrain, they own it forever. They don't just know the answer; they derive it.

Conclusion: Trust the Hardware

The CISSP didn't teach me cybersecurity. It taught me that when you betray your design, even brilliance collapses. But when you honor it—when you stop guessing and start verifying—the system locks.

The Runner wins by barely touching the ground.

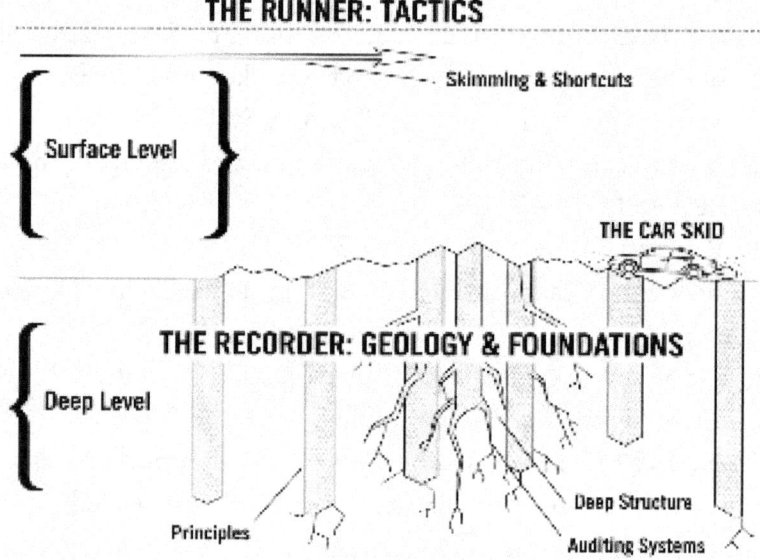

THE RUNNER: TACTICS

Skimming & Shortcuts

Surface Level

THE CAR SKID

THE RECORDER: GEOLOGY & FOUNDATIONS

Deep Level

Deep Structure

Principles

Auditing Systems

25

One burns out in seconds. The other keeps you warm

(L ove, Marriage, and the Interface Error)
There is a pervasive myth that Binary Minds lack empathy. There is a myth that we are cold, robotic, and incapable of deep romantic connection.

This is not just wrong. It is backward.

The Binary Mind feels love with a terrifying intensity. Because we do not have a "Social Mixer" to dilute our emotions, we feel the bond at 100% volume.

But we do not express it through poetry, constant reassurance, or flowery social scripts.

We express it through Architecture.

To a Runner, love is a Feeling (fluid, spoken, constant).

To a Recorder, love is a System (fixed, acted, structural).

The tragedy of many marriages is not a lack of love. It is a Translation Error.

The Runner wife is waiting for a poem. The Recorder husband just rebuilt the transmission of her car so she wouldn't die on the highway.

She feels unloved. He feels unappreciated.

They are both broadcasting, but the antennas are misaligned.

This chapter is the schematic for fixing the interface.

1. The "Mirror vs. Hammer" Problem

The most common fight in a mixed-neurotype marriage happens like this:

Scenario: Partner comes home stressed. "My boss is being a jerk, and the project is late."

• The Runner Expectation (The Mirror): They want validation. "Oh, that sucks. Poor you. He is a jerk."

• The Recorder Response (The Hammer): We analyze the data. "Well, if the project is late, have you tried automating the spreadsheet? Here is a three-step plan to fix the workflow."

The Result:

The Partner gets angry. "You aren't listening to me! You always try to fix everything!"

The Recorder shuts down. "Why are you mad? I just gave you the solution."

The Logic:

To a Binary Mind, Listening = Solving.

If I love you, I do not want you to be in pain. The most efficient way to stop the pain is to remove the source of the pain (The Fix).

To offer "sympathy" without a "solution" feels inefficient and patronizing to us. It feels like watching you drown and shouting, "Wow, that water looks cold!" instead of throwing you a rope.

The Protocol:

We cannot guess. You must code the input. If you are the Runner partner, start the conversation with the Header File:

1. "I want to be Heard (No fixing)."
2. "I want to be Helped (Fixing)."
3. "I want to be Hugged (Physical)."

If you tell a Recorder, "I just want to vent, please don't fix it," we can do that. We will stand there and validate. But you have to give us the command, or our default setting will always be The Hammer.

2. The Love Language of "Info-Dumping"

Runners give gifts like flowers or chocolate. Recorders give gifts like Data.

We call it "The Pebble."

In the wild, a penguin brings a pebble to its mate. It's not useful. It's just... a thing. It says, "I looked at the world, I saw this, and I thought of you."

For a Recorder, the "Pebble" is a fact.

• "Did you know that the Roman aqueducts used volcanic ash to cure underwater?"

• "I read this article about interest rates."

• "Here is a song that explains how I feel."

The Partner often rolls their eyes. "Why are you telling me this boring stuff?"

You are missing the signal. We are sharing our Operating System with you. We are letting you into the Loop.

For a Binary Mind, sharing information is the highest form of intimacy. It means I respect your mind enough to upload this data to it. When you reject the data, you reject the love.

3. Parallel Play: Intimacy Without Demand

To a Runner, "spending time together" usually means face-to-face conversation. Eye contact. Interaction.

To a Recorder, this is high-energy work. It is draining.

The Recorder's preferred intimacy is Parallel Play.

• I am reading a book.

• You are watching TV.

• We are in the same room.

• We are not talking.

To us, this is heaven. We are sharing space (The Field) without demanding processing power (The Data). We feel your presence. We are anchored by you.

If you constantly interrupt the silence with "What are you thinking?" or "Talk to me," you break the bond. You turn the Sanctuary into a Conference Room.

Let us exist near you in silence. That is where we recharge.

4. Loyalty and The Code

192 - ROBERT ANTHONY CAGGIANO

Why do Recorders rarely cheat?

It's not because we don't get tempted. It's because cheating is a System Violation.

A marriage is a contract. It is a binary setting.

• Status: Married (1).

• Rule: Exclusivity.

To cheat requires maintaining a massive, complex, duplicate database of lies.

• Where was I?

• What did I say?

• How do I cover my tracks?

The Binary Mind hates duplicate databases. It hates inefficiency. It hates the anxiety of the "Unbalanced Ledger."

Recorders are the most loyal partners on earth because betrayal violates our internal Structural Integrity. We stay. We fight for the relationship long after a Runner would have drifted away, because we committed to the build.

Our love isn't flashy. But it is load-bearing.

5. The Friction of "The Nag" (Interruption)

Why does a simple question like "Can you take out the trash?" trigger an explosion?

It's not the trash. It's the Stack Collapse.

As we discussed in Chapter 5, the Recorder is a Serial Processor. If I am reading, coding, or fixing something, I have 15 layers of thought loaded in my RAM.

When you shout from the other room, you crash the system. The explosion isn't anger at you. It is the sound of the hard drive crashing.

The Solution: The "Soft Entry."

Don't shout. Walk into the room. Wait for eye contact. Wait for us to "Save and Exit" our thought process. Then ask.

Or better yet—write it down. Text me. A text is a non-intrusive data packet I can open when my processor is free. A shout is a DDoS attack.

6. The Cassandra Effect in Marriage

This is the hardest part. The Recorder sees the pattern. The Runner sees the hope.

• Husband (Recorder): "We cannot afford this house. The math says we will be bankrupt in 3 years."

• Wife (Runner): "But I love it! We'll make it work! Don't be so negative!"

They buy the house. 3 years later, they are bankrupt.

The Runner blames bad luck. The Recorder feels a deep, burning resentment because the data was on the table.

The Partnership Rule:

If you marry a Recorder, you must respect the Sentry Function.

If your Recorder spouse says, "This person is dangerous," or "This deal is bad," listen. They aren't being pessimistic. They are reading the pattern you are missing.

The Recorder is the Head of Security. The Runner is the Head of PR. Do not let PR make Security decisions.

7. How to Love a Recorder

If you love one of us, here is the manual:

1. Don't ask us to guess. Tell us exactly what you need. "I need a hug" works. "You should know what I need" fails every time.

2. Respect the transition. Give us a 10-minute warning before we have to leave the house.

3. Value the Action. If I fixed the sink, I said "I love you." If I researched your medical condition for 4 hours, I said "I cherish you." Learn to read the code.

4. Give us the Cave. When we meltdown or burn out, we need the dark room. Do not follow us in. Let us reboot. We will come back.

8. The Double-Binary Marriage (Recorder + Recorder)

You might think that two Recorders together would be perfect. No translation errors. No emotional games. Pure logic.

And often, it is. It is the "quiet" marriage. The "parallel play" marriage.

But when it breaks, it breaks in a specific, dangerous way: The Stand-off.

The Loop of Doom

When two Recorders argue, it doesn't look like a screaming match. It looks like a court case.

• Partner A: Cites Fact 1, 2, and 3.

• Partner B: Cites Fact A, B, and C that contradict Fact 1.

• Result: Deadlock.

Neither partner will back down to "keep the peace" (which a Runner would do). Both partners are structurally incapable of accepting a logical error. They will argue about the exact phrasing of a sentence from 2004 for three hours.

It isn't about the dishes anymore. It is about Who Is Correct.

The Solution:

You must agree on an external "Tie-Breaker Protocol."

• Rule: If we argue for more than 15 minutes, we stop. We flip a coin, or we agree that the data is inconclusive.

• Logic: The cost of the argument (energy drain) is higher than the value of being right.

The Inertia Trap

The other danger is Stagnation. Runners bring chaos, but they also bring motion. They invite people over. They plan trips. They break the routine.

Two Recorders can easily spiral into a hermetically sealed world.

• No visitors.

• Same dinner every night.

• Same routine for 20 years.

It feels safe, but it becomes a cage.

The Fix: You must schedule "Mandatory Chaos."

• Rule: Once a month, we must go somewhere new.

• Rule: We must invite another couple over.

You have to manually inject entropy into the system, or the system will calcify.

Conclusion: The Anchor

We may not give you the romance novel experience. We may forget your anniversary date because it's an arbitrary number. We may stumble over our words when you are crying.

But we will be the one holding your hand when the diagnosis comes.

We will be the one who figures out how to pay the mortgage when the job is lost.

We will be the one who stands between you and the chaos, unmoving, until the end of time.

We are not the fireworks. We are the fireplace.

26

Put on your oxygen mask. Drink your water. Walk yo

(R aising the Binary Mind)
     If you are a parent reading this, I know exactly where you are.

You are tired. You are scared. You are confused. You have sat in a sterile office and listened to a doctor tell you that your child is "delayed," "disordered," or "impaired." You have read the blogs. You have joined the support groups where everyone vents about how hard it is. You are mourning the child you thought you were going to have—the one who plays soccer and chats easily at Thanksgiving—and you are trying to figure out how to "fix" the one you have.

I need you to stop. I need you to take a breath. And I need you to listen to me very carefully.

Your child is not broken. They do not need to be fixed. They need to be Built. But they cannot build a skyscraper on a swamp. And right now, your anxiety, your fear, and your frantic attempts to "cure" them are creating a swamp.

This chapter is the hardest part of the book because it requires you to look in the mirror. The stability of your child does not begin with their therapy. It begins with your nervous system.

1. The Oxygen Mask Rule

You know the speech on the airplane: "In the event of a loss of cabin pressure, secure your own mask before assisting others."

It sounds selfish. It is actually Physics. If you pass out from lack of oxygen, you cannot help your child. You become 60 pounds of dead weight falling on top of them.

In the world of the Binary Mind, Anxiety is Contagious. Your child is a Recorder. They have a "High-Fidelity Emotional Receiver." If you are anxious—even if you are smiling, even if you are pretending to be calm—they can feel the vibration of your stress. They can smell the cortisol on your skin. They can hear the micro-tremors in your voice.

• Your Input: "Everything is fine! Let's go to school!" (High Anxiety masked by a smile).

• Their Processing: Alert. Mother is terrified. Threat detected. Environment is unsafe. Initiate Meltdown.

You think they are acting out because of school. They are acting out because you are vibrating. You cannot be their anchor if you are drifting.

Before you sign them up for one more therapy, one more group, or one more intervention, you must stabilize yourself. You must do the 90-Day Reboot. You must walk. You must sleep. You must eat the protein. You must become the Solid Floor.

2. The Solid Floor

Imagine your child is standing in a room during an earthquake. The lights are flickering (sensory overload). The walls are moving (social confusion). The noise is deafening. They are terrified. They are looking for something to grab onto.

If they grab onto you, and you are shaking too (crying, pleading, panicking), they have confirmed that the world is ending. The meltdown becomes catastrophic.

But if they reach out and grab a Pillar of Concrete—something cool, unmoving, and silent—their nervous system instantly down-regulates. "Oh. The Pillar isn't shaking. Therefore, I am safe."

198 - ROBERT ANTHONY CAGGIANO

You must be the Pillar. When they scream, you go quiet. When they thrash, you go still. When they panic, you go into "System Mode." This is not about being cold. It is about being Safe. To a Recorder, safety isn't a hug; safety is Stability. If you want to save your child, stop trying to make them "happy." Start making yourself "stable."

3. The DJ Method (Environment Control)

You are not just a parent. You are the DJ of their Nervous System. A DJ controls the vibe of the room by controlling the inputs (Volume, Bass, Speed). Your child has a broken filter. They cannot turn down the volume of the world. You must do it for them.

The Protocol: When you see the "Pre-Meltdown" signs (rocking, covering ears, echolalia), do not ask them what is wrong. They cannot access language. Their RAM is full. Instead, act like a DJ. Cut the inputs.

• Cut the Light: Dim the lights immediately. Sunlight is aggressive. Fluorescents are torture.

• Cut the Sound: Turn off the TV. Stop talking. Silence is the reset button.

• Cut the Texture: Are their clothes scratchy? Is the tag itching? Get them into the "Soft Zone."

• Cut the Audience: Get the siblings out of the room. A meltdown is a vulnerable reboot; they shouldn't have an audience.

Don't negotiate. Don't punish. Just Drop the Faders. Watch what happens. Within 3 minutes of reducing the input, the system will usually cool down and reboot.

4. Speak "Assembler," Not "Podcast"

Runners speak in paragraphs. They use metaphors, emotional appeals, and rhetorical questions. "Why did you hit your brother? You know that makes him sad, and we don't hurt people in this family, right?"

To a Recorder child in distress, this sounds like: "Wah wah wah wah." It is High-Level Code. It requires too much processing power to decode the emotion, the moral lesson, and the question all at once.

Switch to Assembler. Assembler is the language of commands. Short. Binary. Direct.

- Bad: "Honey, please put your shoes on, we're going to be late!"
- Good: "Shoes. On. Now."
- Bad: "Why are you screaming?"
- Good: "Stop." (Pause). "Sit." (Pause). "Breathe."

You are not being mean. You are being Clear. When the computer is crashing, you don't write it a poem. You type CTRL+ALT+DEL. Assembler is the CTRL+ALT+DEL for the Binary Mind. Once they are calm, then you can have the emotional conversation. But never during the crash.

5. The "Go Bag" Strategy (Predictability)

Anxiety comes from the Unknown. "What if I get hungry?" "What if it's too loud?" "What if my iPad dies?" The Recorder mind runs simulations of disaster constantly. You defeat this with Preparation.

Every Binary child needs a "Go Bag." It is not just a bag of toys. It is a Survival Kit.

- Headphones: To block the sound.
- Sunglasses: To block the light.
- Safe Food: The specific protein bar they eat. (Do not rely on finding food on the road).
- The Battery: A backup charger.

The Rule: The bag is packed the night before. When you say, "We are going to Grandma's," and they start to panic, you point to the bag. "The bag is ready." You are outsourcing their executive function to the bag. You are showing them: The variables are controlled. You are safe.

6. Meltdown vs. Tantrum (Know the Difference)

You must learn the difference. Treating a meltdown like a tantrum is abuse. Treating a tantrum like a meltdown is bad parenting.

The Tantrum:
- Goal: To get something (Candy, Toy, Attention).
- Look: They check to see if you are watching. If you ignore them, they stop or get louder. It is a performance.

• Response: Ignore it. Do not negotiate with terrorists.

The Meltdown:

• Goal: None. It is a System Crash.

• Look: They do not care if you are watching. They might hurt themselves. They are glazed over. They are in "Fight or Flight."

• Response: The DJ Method. Reduce input. Protect them from injury. Be the Solid Floor.

If you punish a child for a meltdown, you are punishing them for having a seizure. You are adding trauma to a hardware failure. Learn the difference. Protect the Crash. Ignore the Performance.

7. The "Under Construction" Mindset

Stop looking at the other kids. Stop looking at the milestones chart. Stop looking at the "Tent" (the Runner child who is chatting away at age 3).

Your child is building a Skyscraper. They are digging the foundation. It looks like a hole in the ground right now. It looks like nothing is happening. Trust the dig.

If you force them to put up walls before the foundation is poured, the building will collapse later. Let them be silent. Let them line up the cars. Let them watch the fan spin. They are mapping the physics of the world. They are compiling the code.

Your job is not to build the building for them. Your job is to Build the Fence around the construction site. Keep the chaos out. Keep the bullies away. Keep the noise down. Give them the space to cure the concrete.

8. The Promise

I was the kid on the floor. I was the one staring at the dust motes in the light. I was the one who didn't fit. And I grew up to run companies, solve impossible problems, and live a life of profound depth.

Your child will too. But only if you survive the construction phase.

27

(When the Static Finally Stops)
          We have talked about the theory. We have talked about the mechanics. But we haven't fully talked about the feeling.

If you are a Runner reading this, you might think "Input Overload" is just a metaphor for being stressed. If you are a Recorder, you know it is not a metaphor. It is a physical assault.

1. What Noise Actually Feels Like

If you want to understand what a Binary Mind experiences in the world, here's an exercise.

Take a piece of any Allman Brothers music—go to the guitar jamming part—now loop ten seconds of it. Every three seconds, stop it. Restart it. Do that two or three times — while something else plays in the background.

Now add lights. Now add movement. Now add people talking. Now add a train station off in the distance. Oh yeah, that tea kettle that never turns off.

That's not stress. That's input overload with no filter.

Runners have a built-in mixing board. They can fade out the train station. They can mute the tea kettle. Recorders do not have faders. We hear every track at maximum volume, simultaneously.

That's why we seek order—not because we're "obsessive" or "controlling," but because order turns the volume down. If the room is clean, that is one less track playing in my head. If the schedule is fixed, that is one less loop skipping.

2. Compressed Mapping (The Messy Desk Paradox)

And here's the irony: some of us love neatness, but cannot maintain it. The chaos always returns. So we adapt. A drawer. A corner. A pile.

To a Runner, a pile of papers looks like trash. To a Recorder, it is a coordinate system. "If I know where it is, I can find it."

My brain scrambles things—but it remembers the pattern. I know that the tax bill is three inches down in the left stack, under the blue folder.

It's not disorganization. It's Compressed Mapping.

We are spatially indexing the mess because putting it away in a drawer means the data disappears ("Object Permanence" issues). So we build piles. The piles are not clutter; they are external hard drives.

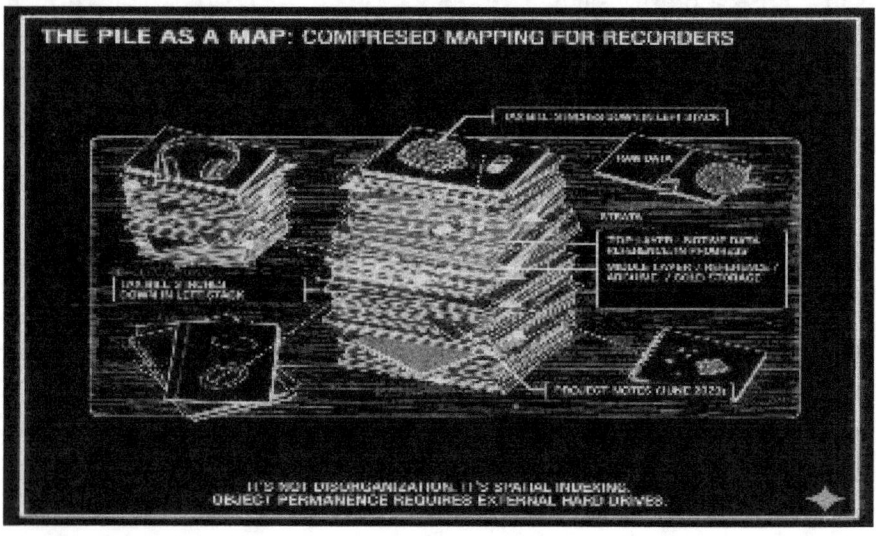

3. The Body Knows Before the Mind

When the realization finally hit me—the realization that I wasn't broken, just Binary—it wasn't cognitive. It was cellular.

It felt like a salmon turning upstream. For years, the salmon fights the current, bashing against rocks, exhausted. Then, suddenly, it finds the flow. It recognizes the river it was built for.

• Food tasted better.
• Thinking became clearer.

• I had a repeatable process.

Order doesn't restrict Binary Minds. It liberates them. And when I say this to other Binary Minds, they don't argue. They giggle.

It is a specific giggle. It's the sound of relief. It's the sound of: "Oh my god, you hear the tea kettle too?" Because they know exactly what I'm talking about. They have been gaslit for forty years into thinking the room was silent.

4. Stop Apologizing for the Strength

This isn't about fixing weakness. It's about using strength.

Binary Minds see extremes because extremes reveal structure. That scares people who live in gray zones. It makes us targets—for manipulation, for dismissal, for being told we're "too much" or "too rigid."

Mothers worry because the world isn't black and white. Binary Minds suffer because the world pretends it is.

Once you know what to do, the rules become simpler. Not easier—clearer.

• Neurotypical minds multitask until traffic locks up.

• Binary Minds seize—not from inability, but from overload.

Different architectures. Same humanity. Stop apologizing for the fact that your engine requires high-octane fuel. Stop apologizing that you cannot run on diesel.

The Ferrari does not apologize to the Tractor for needing a paved road.

5. When No One Believes Until the Crack

No one is listening—until they hear the crack.

Everyone is certain right up until something breaks. Systems break. Bodies break. Families break. Institutions break.

The Runner world operates on "Good Enough" logic. They patch the cracks with optimism. The Recorder points at the crack and says, "That beam is going to fail." They ignore us. Then the bridge falls.

I watched myself doing the right things for my health while my mind raced like an alcoholic's. Improvement without explanation. Progress without permission. I realized something uncomfortable: I don't need more willpower. I need translation.

I don't need to build a media empire or chase clicks. I don't have time for that. This idea doesn't belong to me alone anyway. It needs someone younger. Someone capable. Someone willing to carry it forward. Because there are people who cannot help themselves—and people desperate to help them—trapped by a belief system that keeps missing the architecture.

This isn't about me. It's about building the support structure that should have existed all along.

6. Let's Use What We Are

I'm not asking you to agree. I'm asking you to notice the moment when something inside you clicks and you think:

"Oh. That's what that was."

That's the sound of 2 + 2 becoming 4 again.

For years, they told you it was 22. They told you it was "Blue." They told you it was "Maybe." But you knew, deep down in the voltage of your cells, that it was 4.

And once that happens—once you hear the click—there's no going back to twenty-two.

28

Singing for Self-Regulation (Vagus Nerve) vs. Sing

THE LABORATORY

(M anual Regulation: Physics & Chemistry)
Runners are built with an automatic transmission.
Recorders are manual transmission.

We have a high-performance engine, but if the RPMs get too high, the car doesn't shift itself. It just screams.

If you don't know how to reach down and manually shift the gear, you blow the engine.

I have spent 55 years learning how to shift the gears.

This chapter is the User Manual for the two levers that control your system: Physics (Singing) and Chemistry (Fuel).

PART I: THE PHYSICS (WHY WE MUST SING)

There is a scene in the movie The Day the Earth Stood Still that explains the Recorder brain perfectly.

The alien, Klaatu, has to stop a robot named Gort from destroying the world. He can't use logic. He can't use force. He has to use a specific code: "Klaatu barada nikto."

For a Recorder, the "Spin" (anxiety, loops, static) is the robot. You can't think your way out of it. You need a physical override code.

206 - ROBERT ANTHONY CAGGIANO

That code is Singing. Look at it like singing is resistance training for the brain.

But there are two very different ways to use this tool.

1. The Internal Tool (Calming the Machine)

This is for you. The adult.

When the anxiety hits, or the static gets too loud, you need to physically vibrate the system to slow it down.

The Vagus Nerve connects your brain to your gut. It is the brake pedal for your nervous system. It runs right through your vocal cords.

When you sing—and I mean really sing, loud and with force—you are manually vibrating that nerve. You are sending a physical signal to the brain that says: "Safe. Slow down."

I do this constantly. It isn't a hobby. It is maintenance. It creates a hum that blocks out the noise of the world.

There is a moment in the movie Seabiscuit that every parent of a "different" child should watch.

The horse is fighting the rider. He is angry. He is failing.

The trainer realizes the problem: They are trying to constrain him. They are trying to make him run like a polite show horse.

So they take him out to the open country and they just let him run.

Straight. Fast. No reins. No rules.

He remembers who he is. He finds his stride. And he becomes a legend.

Music is the open country for your child.

If you force a Recorder child to "Sit still, look at me, and say apple," you are pulling on the reins. You are fighting the horse.

But if you play music? If you sing? You are letting the brain run straight.

1. The Vulnerability Key

You have to go first. If you are stiff, the child will be stiff.

But if you sing—and I mean really sing, be silly, be loud, be vulnerable—the child feels the safety.

They see you letting go, so they feel safe to let go.

You are showing them that the "Rules" don't apply right now.

2. The Joke (The Breakthrough)

You will know it's working when they crack a joke using a lyric.

This is a massive moment.

I have seen kids who struggle to say "Hello" suddenly quote a song lyric to make a funny observation about dinner.

• Why? Because the lyric was stored in the "Music" folder, not the "Speech" folder.

• They accessed the file, realized it fit the context, and delivered it.

That is high-level intelligence. That is the horse running at full speed.

Encourage it. Flood the house with sound. Let them run.

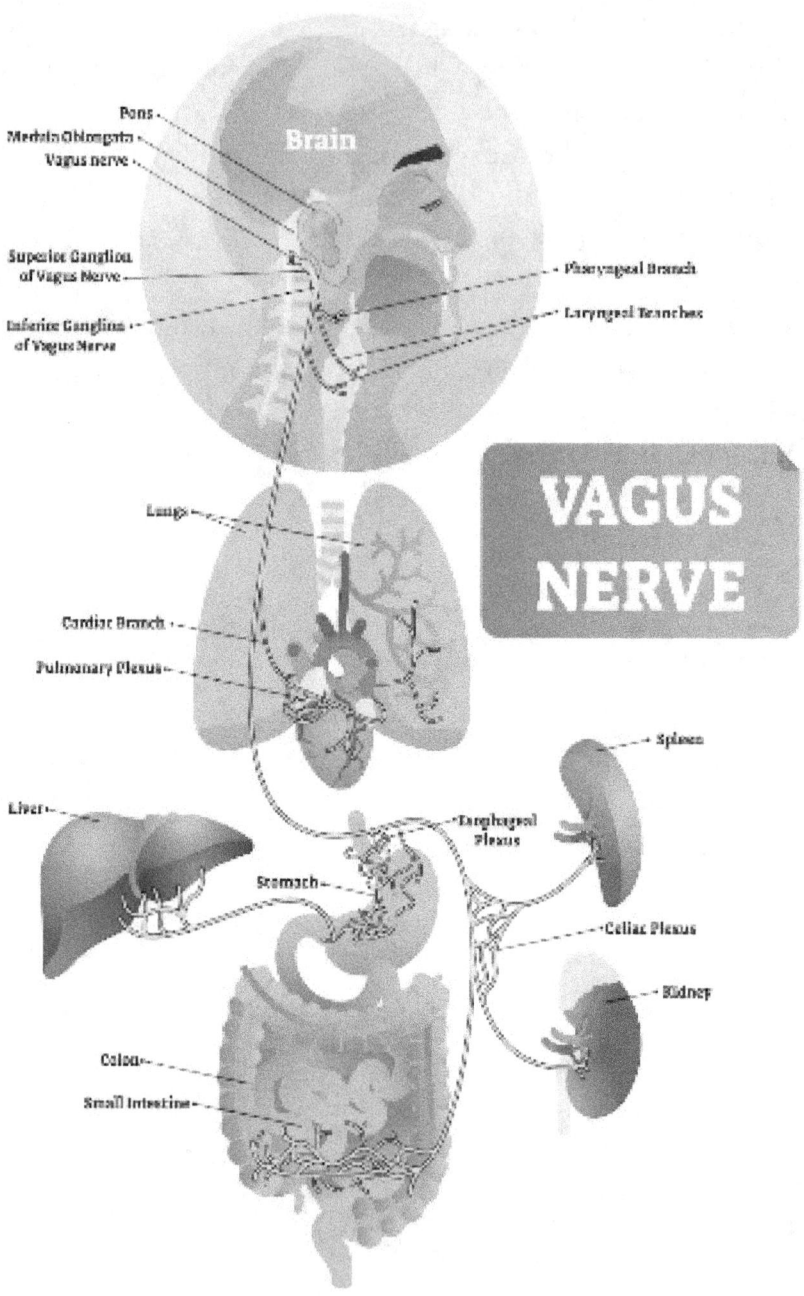

2. The External Tool (The Bridge to Speech)

This is for the parents. Especially if you have a child who is nonverbal, delayed, or struggling to talk.

You have to understand the architecture of the brain.

• Speech lives in the Logic Center (Left Brain). If that door is jammed, the kid can't speak.

• Music lives in the Creative Center (Right Brain). That door is often wide open.

If you just talk to a delayed child, you are banging on a locked door.

But if you sing to them, you are using the side door.

When you sing lyrics, you are combining melody (Right Brain) with words (Left Brain). You are building a bridge across the gap.

I am telling you: Sing to them.

Don't just play Mozart. Sing songs with lyrics. Pop songs, rock songs, anything with a rhythm and words.

You will see them start to hum. Then they mouth the rhythm. Then, suddenly, the word slides out on the melody.

You aren't just teaching them a song. You are teaching their brain how to process language.

PART II: THE CHEMISTRY (THE 55-YEAR EXPERIMENT)

If Singing is the workout, like resistance training, Chemistry is the coolant.

I have been taking supplements for 55 years. I don't mean a multivitamin here and there. I mean a disciplined, daily protocol.

I didn't read this in a book. I learned it in a kitchen in East Boston in 1968.

1. The Giant in the Kitchen

I was a kid. My cousin came up to visit us from Norfolk, Virginia.

You have to understand my lineage to understand this moment.

• The Software (My Father's Side): The Caggianos. Logic. Discipline.

• The Hardware (My Mother's Side): The Thorntons. The Giants.

My cousin was a Thornton. He was massive. A muscle-man. He filled up the doorway.

He walked into our East Boston kitchen, and he put a bottle on the table.

Vitamin B.

He didn't give me a lecture. He just handed me the pill.

"Take this."

2. The Flush

I took it on an empty stomach.

Ten minutes later, the "Niacin Flush" hit me. My skin turned red. My stomach turned. I felt heat rushing through my veins.

Most people would have said, "I'm sick. I'm never doing that again."

But my Recorder brain didn't register "Sick."

It registered Power.

I realized: I can feel this working. I can change my state.

I realized my body was a machine, and this Giant had just handed me high-octane fuel.

3. The Crew

That day started a 55-year experiment.

My Dad, my brother Kevin, and I—we became a unit. We analyzed it. We realized that our brains ran hotter than other people's. We burned up nutrients faster because we were recording more data.

We needed more B-vitamins for the nerves. We needed more support.

We weren't "popping pills." We were the pit crew for our own race cars.

4. The Result

People ask me how I walk 19,000 steps a day at 68. They ask why I don't have brain fog.

The answer is that moment in East Boston.

I never let the tank go empty. I respected the machine enough to fuel it.

29

You're not dealing with a fragile child. You are d

(H ow to Teach a Binary Mind)
If you teach long enough, you eventually meet a student who doesn't fit the standard model. They're bright—often brilliant—but inconsistent. They listen but seem distant. They know the rules but struggle to follow them in the moment. They're either locked in or checked out, hyper-focused or overwhelmed, precise or distracted.

The modern educational system often calls these students autistic, ADHD, twice-exceptional, gifted, inattentive, oppositional, or "behavioral." But all of that language misses the point.

These students have a Binary Mind—a Recorder Mind. Your job isn't to normalize them. Your job is to understand the design so you can teach them correctly. Once you understand the mechanics, every mysterious behavior suddenly makes perfect sense.

1. The Binary Mind Records (Constantly, Automatically)
Most students filter the classroom. Binary students record it.
• Every sound.
• Every shift in tone.
• Every movement.
• Every pattern.
• Every inconsistency.

This recording is not a choice. It is the operating system. So when a Binary student "overreacts," "shuts down," or becomes "lost," they are not misbehaving—they are overloaded. Their bandwidth is full. The fix is not discipline. The fix is structure.

2. Unfinished Moments Stay Open (The "Big One")

A Runner-wired child moves on automatically. A Binary child cannot. If something confusing, unfair, abrupt, or unresolved happens in your classroom—even something tiny—the Binary mind keeps the file open.

Examples:

• You changed a rule without warning.

• You corrected their work but didn't explain why.

• You raised your voice slightly.

• You said "We'll talk later" and didn't.

To you, these are small moments. To them, these are unfinished threads the mind must resolve before they can move on. This leads to freezing, avoidance, and repetitive questions. They aren't refusing. They are waiting for closure. Once they get closure, they reset instantly.

3. They Learn in Sequence, Not Chaos

Most classrooms are built for Runners—fast transitions, multitasking, concurrent instructions. Binary Minds don't multitask. They sequence.

If you give three instructions at once, they can't prioritize. If the classroom is loud, their brain logs all of it. The key is not more time—it's more clarity.

Teach them using:

• Step 1 → Step 2 → Step 3.

• Visual sequences.

• Predictable routines.

• One variable at a time.

This is not lowering the bar. This is enabling full performance.

4. Literal Interpretation Is Not Misbehavior

Binary students take words at face value because their system privileges accuracy over social inference.

• When you say "Be quiet," and five students whisper, the Binary student sees injustice.

• When you say "You can start when you're ready," they think you mean "ready," not "right now."

• When you say "Work with a partner," they assume any partner, not "someone you choose socially."

Their literal interpretation is not obstinance. It is structural integrity—the same trait that makes them exceptional problem-solvers later in life.

5. Their Empathy Is Deep (Just Not Performed)

Teachers often misread Binary students as cold, detached, or uninterested. All incorrect.

Binary empathy is internal, not social. They feel your disappointment. They feel classroom tension. They feel hypocrisy deeply. But they don't always perform empathy the way Runners expect—smiling, nodding, mirroring. Their empathy is quieter. But sharper. When a Binary student trusts you, the bond is unbreakable.

6. Group Work Is a Minefield

Group assignments require multitasking, role negotiation, rapid transitions, and reading social cues. These are the exact conditions that overwhelm a Binary Mind.

To support them:

• Assign specific roles explicitly.

• Place them with stable partners.

• Give written instructions.

• Allow independent alternatives when appropriate.

• Measure mastery, not social performance.

When Binary students melt down during group work, they are not being antisocial. They are drowning in ambiguity.

7. Their Morality Is Absolute

Binary students have a rigid internal moral code: Fairness, Honesty, Consistency, Truth. They assume adults have the same code.

So when a teacher enforces rules inconsistently, says "because I said so," or makes exceptions, the Binary student experiences genuine moral distress. They are not challenging your authority. They are reacting to perceived structural failure. When you explain the reasoning behind decisions, their trust strengthens dramatically.

8. Sensory Overload Is Hardware, Not Attitude

A loud cafeteria, buzzing lights, scratchy clothes, unpredictable noises. These are not mild annoyances. They are system overload events. The solution is not discipline. The solution is Environment.

Small adjustments help enormously:

• Quiet workspaces.

• Dimmer seating areas.

• Noise-blocking headphones.

• Predictable routines.

• Reduced transitions.

Reduce the noise, and their brilliance appears.

9. ADHD Is Not Opposite to Autism

ADHD students are not inattentive. They are recording too much, too fast, without the ability to compress it.

• They are Sentries in motion.

• They are Scanners instead of still observers.

• They are Over-recording instead of Under-focusing.

This view transforms classroom management. You stop trying to "control behavior" and start trying to stabilize bandwidth.

10. The Practical Guide (What Costs Nothing)

Here are classroom adjustments that cost nothing and change everything:

• Clear Entry Protocol: Tell them exactly what to do when class starts. Same every day.

• Predictable Transitions: Give warnings. Give countdowns.

• Written Instructions: Always pair verbal directions with text.

• One Variable at a Time: Don't mix multiple new tasks.

• Private Corrections: Public correction = humiliation replayed for years.

• Explain the "Why": Binary students comply when they understand the logic.

• Let Them Finish Their Thought: Interrupting mid-processing creates panic.

• Don't Interpret Shutdown as Defiance: It's overload. Let them reset.

• Be Consistent: Your reliability is their safety.

11. When a Binary Student Trusts You, You Get Genius

When they feel understood—

When they feel safe—

When the environment makes sense—

Their abilities explode: Memory. Pattern recognition. Problem-solving. Moral insight. Creativity. Deep empathy.

30

(Earn The Day™: A Biological Factory Reset)
I am 68 years old. In 2025, I walked an average of 19,000 steps every single day. I lost 100 pounds. I did not do this with a "miracle drug." I did not do it with a surgery. I did not do it with young genetics.

I did it by treating my body like a failing server that needed a hard reset.

The 90-Day Reboot is not a lifestyle plan. It is not a diet. It is not a motivational trick. It is a biological recalibration for Binary Minds.

Most health advice fails Recorders because it is written for Runners. It relies on "motivation," "community," and "fun." A Binary Mind doesn't care about fun. We care about System Integrity. BMIs don't "change" gradually. We flip. We click. We lock. You are either running the old operating system (Crash Mode), or you are running the new one (Optimization Mode). There is no middle ground.

This chapter is the manual I used to save my own life. Specifically, I doubled my remaining timeline, and reset my biological clock so that I'm living those years—"kicking the can"—with the engine of a 30-year-old.

THE CORE PRINCIPLE: "**EARN THE DAY**"

The philosophy is simple: I do something today that makes tomorrow better. Most people live in debt to yesterday (cleaning up mistakes) or in fear of tomorrow (anxiety). To Earn The Day means you execute the code today that guarantees a stronger platform for tomorrow morning.

We build this structure around three systems:

1. Biology (The Hardware: Light, Load, Chemistry).

2. Wiring (The Software: Replay, Closure, Focus).

3. Environment (The Network: Noise, Objects, People).

PART I: THE MATH (BMI vs. BMI)

We possess a trait that society calls a disorder: Obsessive Compulsive behavior (OCD). In a Runner world, OCD is a problem. In the 90-Day Reboot, OCD is the fuel.

We are going to take that obsessive, repetitive, system-locking nature and aim it at your health. And when a Recorder aims their obsession at a target, they don't just hit it. They obliterate it.

PART II: THE PHYSICS OF THE WALK

(Why 19,000 Steps?) : 8,000 min?

People ask me, "Robert, why 19,000 steps? That takes hours. Who has the time?" You are asking the wrong question. You think walking is "exercise." Walking is not exercise. Walking is Optical Flow.

The Engineering of the Predawn Walk

When you walk forward, images move past your retina. This is called "Optic Flow." Neuroscience proves that Optic Flow quiets the Amygdala (the fear center).

• Stationary Stress: When you sit and worry, the amygdala screams because you aren't moving away from the threat.

• Walking Stress: When you move forward, the amygdala quiets down. It assumes you are handling the problem.

I walk 19,000 steps not to burn calories (though that is a nice side effect). I walk to burn off the Replay Loops. If I sit, I ruminate. If I walk, I process.

The Protocol

• The Predawn Launch: You must be outside before the sun comes up. The shift from dark to light triggers the Cortisol Awakening Response (CAR). If you miss this window, your melatonin (sleep hormone) will be messed up 16 hours later.

• No Headphones (Phase 1): For the first mile, no podcasts. No music. Let the brain dump its cache. 30 minutes to start. Increase as you see fit.

• The Pace: This isn't a stroll. It is a mission. Walk like you are late for a meeting. This engages the cardiovascular system without spiking cortisol.

PART III: THE HARDWARE RESET (The Body)

You cannot run high-performance software on broken hardware. If your inflammation is high, your cortisol is spiked, and your nutrients are depleted, your Recorder mind will remain in "Emergency Mode."

Phase 1: The Flush (Days 1–15)

• Goal: Stop the chaos. Get the system to "Neutral." In this phase, you will feel worse before you feel better. That is the "Herxheimer Reaction"—the sound of toxins leaving the building. Push through.

• Hydration Protocol: 16oz of water immediately upon waking. Before coffee. Before phones. The system is dehydrated from sleep; you must depressurize the hydraulics.

• Vitamin Prep: Prepare morning, midday, and night supplements the day before. Do not make decisions in the morning. Execute the plan.

• Fuel Cleanup: Remove the noise. No processed sugar. No seed oils. These are acoustic interference for your gut-brain axis.

• The Binary Rule: If it comes in a box with a cartoon character, it is not food. It is product.

Phase 2: Stabilization (Days 16–33)

• Goal: The body remembers what "Steady" feels like. Now that the noise is down, we install the rhythm. The Binary Mind craves predictability.

• Sleep Anchoring: Wake up at the exact same time every day. No exceptions for weekends. You cannot stabilize a clock that you keep resetting.

• Protein-First Structure: Eat protein before carbohydrates.

• The Logic: Protein signals satiety to the brain. Carbs signal "Hunt for more." If you eat carbs first, you trigger a glucose spike that crashes 90 minutes later. That crash feels like anxiety to a Recorder.

• The "Stop" Switch: You stop eating 3 hours before bed. Digestion requires massive energy. If you eat late, your body spends the night digesting instead of repairing.

Phase 3: The Resistance Protocol (Days 34–90)

(The "No Injury" Rule)

Most people start a diet and try to become a Navy SEAL on Day 1. They grab heavy weights, do push-ups until their shoulders blow out, and quit by Day 3 because their brain registers "Pain."

The "Start Slow" Routine

I use a simple resistance routine. 5 Exercises. Basic. Repeatable. You don't need a gym. You need adjustable dumbbells (hand weights).

1. The Bench Press (Chest/Triceps)
2. The Curl (Biceps)
3. The Squat (Legs/Core)
4. The Overhead Press (Shoulders)
5. The Row (Back)

The Volume: 10–15 Reps. 3 Sets. That's it.

The "Motion First" Progression (Tricking the Subconscious)

• Phase 1: The Ghost Reps (Zero Weight): Start with no weight. Just your hands. You are tricking the subconscious into accepting the routine without the threat of pain. You are establishing the "Base" without the "Burn."

• Phase 2: Finding the Resistance: Once the motion is automatic, add the lightest possible weight.

• Phase 3: The "Paper Clip" Progression (For Life): Runners jump 10 pounds at a time. Recorders use Micro-Loading. Increase the weight by the "weight of a piece of paper." You are going to do this for the rest of your life. There is no rush. You want to keep the subconscious in tune with the progress, never shocking it, just constantly upgrading the system bit by bit.

PART IV: THE CHEMISTRY (The Supplement Engineering)

You cannot build a house without bricks. Modern food is acoustically loud (calories) but chemically quiet (nutrients). Note: I am not a doctor. I am an engineer of my own biology.

List 1 — Essential Vitamins

• Fat-Soluble: Vitamin A, D3, E, K2 (MK-7).

• Water-Soluble: Vitamin C, B1, B2, B3, B5, B6, B7, B9 (Folate), B12 (Methyl cobalamin).

List 2 — Essential Minerals

• Magnesium (Glycinate for sleep / Citrate for digestion), Zinc, Calcium, Iron (careful with dosage), Potassium, Sodium (electrolytes), Iodine, Selenium, Copper, Manganese, Chromium.

List 3 — Omega & Fatty Acids

• Omega-3 Fish Oil (EPA + DHA) or Algae Omega.

List 4 — Gut Health

• Probiotic, Digestive Enzymes, Collagen (Type I & III).

List 5 — The Accelerators (The "Secret Sauce")

• Creatine Monohydrate: It is battery fluid for the brain. Recharges ATP. Prevents the 3:00 PM "Brain Fog Crash."

• Essential Amino Acids (EAAs): Tells the body: "Eat the fat, save the muscle." Precursors to Serotonin and Dopamine.

• Others: CoQ10, L-Theanine (calm), Ashwagandha (stress), Green Tea Extract, Turmeric/Curcumin, Alpha-Lipoic Acid, NAC.

PART V: THE ENVIRONMENT RESET (The Server Room)

A Binary Mind does not filter environment; it absorbs it. If your house is chaotic, your mind is chaotic. You cannot think clearly in a dirty server room.

The Daily Rules:

• Minus Three: Remove 3 unnecessary objects from your home every single day. In 90 days, you will have removed 270 items of noise. Why: Every object is a line of code your brain has to render.

• The Drawer Protocol: Reset one drawer or shelf per week. Organize it until it pleases your Binary eye.

- News Blackout: No news before noon. Do not let the chaos hijack your dopamine before you have earned the day.
- No Chaotic People Before Caffeine: Protect your morning bandwidth.

PART VI: TROUBLESHOOTING (When The Protocol Breaks)

The Runner approach to failure is "Guilt." The Recorder approach to failure is "System Correction."

- Scenario A: "I missed the morning walk."
- Recorder: "The morning window is closed. I will execute the Sunset Protocol. I will walk 30 minutes at dusk to signal the end of the day."
- Rule: Never miss two days in a row. One miss is an anomaly. Two misses is a new pattern.
- Scenario B: "I ate the cake."
- Recorder: "Glucose spike detected. Counter-measure required."
- Action: Walk for 15 minutes immediately. The muscles will soak up the excess glucose. The system resets.

SPECIAL SECTION: FOR PARENTS (The Ignition Protocol)

I know what you are thinking. "Robert, that sounds nice, but you don't know my kid. He will scream for three hours. He will starve himself for two days."

I am here to tell you: Biology is Biology. You cannot negotiate with it, but you also cannot stop it from working when the inputs change.

1. The "Trojan Horse" Strategy

You don't need them to agree to the new diet. You just need to get the chemistry in. You don't fight the Nugget. You use the Nugget.

- Inject the Code: Put the Amino Acids and Creatine in the ketchup or the drink.
- The Subconscious Shift: When you sneak in the good fuel, the body realizes, "Wait. I feel better. The fog is lifting." Suddenly, the subconscious starts asking for the good stuff. The "Nugget Addiction" breaks not because you forced it, but because the body is finally getting the premium gas it was designed for.

2. The Movement Hack (The Tether & The Turnaround)

A non-verbal child often refuses to walk because "Open Space" = Infinite Variables.

• The Tether: Hand them one end of a rope or a heavy stick. To a Recorder, holding an object provides proprioceptive feedback (grounding). It says, "I am here."

• The Formation: Walk shoulder-to-shoulder. You are towing the car until the engine starts.

The Turnaround Celebration (The Vulnerability Hack)

Here is the most important part of the walk. When you reach the halfway point and turn back toward home, I want you to do something that feels uncomfortable.

I want you to sing. Loudly.

• Why? Your child needs to see the "Pillar" being vulnerable.

• The Signal: They need to see that "letting go" is safe. You aren't just walking anymore; you are modeling joy. If you can sing without the world collapsing, maybe they can too.

3. The Melodic Bridge: Hacking the Hemispheres

To understand why a non-verbal child can sing a song perfectly but cannot say a sentence, you have to look at the wiring.

• Left Hemisphere (Broca's Area): The "Speech Center." Often jammed in Binary Minds (Apraxia).

• Right Hemisphere: Melody and Rhythm. Usually wide open.

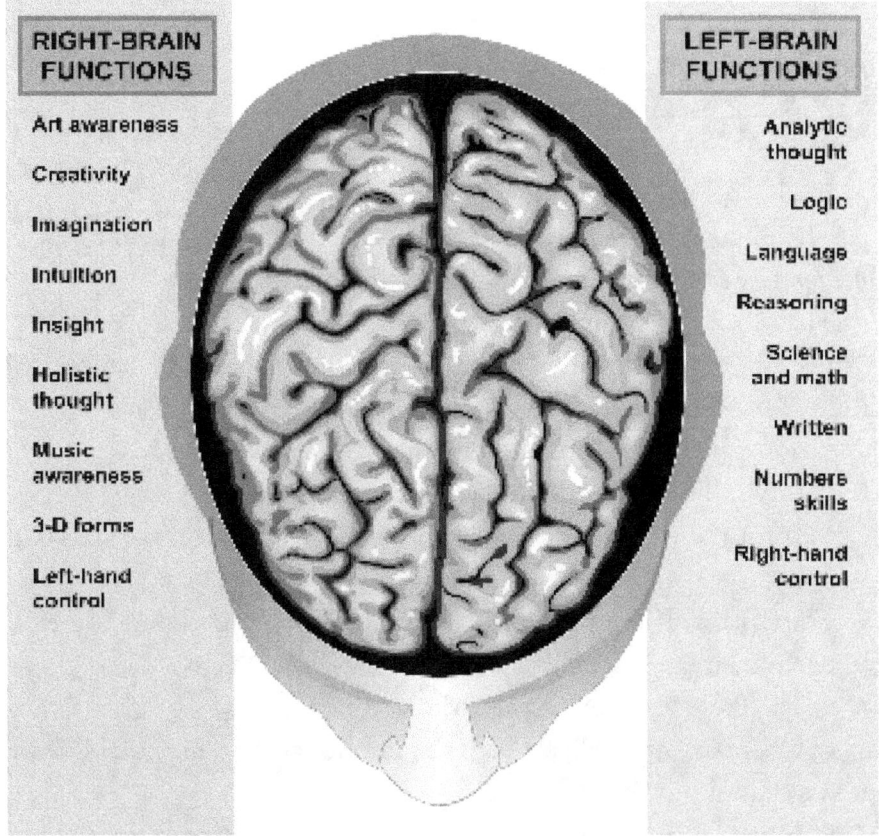

RIGHT-BRAIN FUNCTIONS	LEFT-BRAIN FUNCTIONS
Art awareness	Analytic thought
Creativity	Logic
Imagination	Language
Intuition	Reasoning
Insight	Science and math
Holistic thought	Written
Music awareness	Numbers skills
3-D forms	Right-hand control
Left-hand control	

The Back Door Approach: When you force speech, you bang on the jammed front door. When you sing, you use the open back door. By attaching words to melody, you force the signal across the bridge to the Right Hemisphere.

4. The Tool: AI Lyrics for Personality

We give non-verbal kids buttons that say "Bathroom." We treat them like survival machines, ignoring their wit.

The Strategy: The AI Lyricist

Use AI to write Short Melodic Scripts based on their mood.

• Old Way: Robot voice says "YES."

• New Way: AI generates a rhyming lyric set to a beat.

• Example (The Sarcastic No): "I heard what you said / And I think you are wrong / So I'm shaking my head / While I sing you this song."

Why This Works:

1. Rhythm: Acts as a metronome for the motor system.

2. Wit: Proves intelligence.

3. Integration: Forces Left/Right brain synchronization.

5. The DJ Method: Using Pop Culture

The Recorder mind is a vault of music. Stop forcing them to speak like textbooks. Let them mix the audio they already have.

The Mechanic: Search and Replay

Instead of struggling to form a sentence, the child scans their internal library for a song lyric.

• Input: Mom says "You need friends."

• Search: "Friends" + "Mama" + "Advice."

• Output: Child sings "Once I was seven years old, my mama told me..."

The Mirror: If the parent sings it back, the circuit closes. You have validated their language and shared a joke.

6. The Biology of the Oxygen Mask

In Chapter 13, we talked about the emotional oxygen mask. Now we need to talk about the physical one.

Raising a Binary Mind is an endurance sport. It requires physical strength to handle meltdowns and mental speed to play the "DJ Game."

• If you are inflamed, they feel the heat.

• If you are exhausted, they feel the static.

The 90-Day Reset is a tactical requirement. You walk at dawn so you have the patience for the morning routine. You lift weights so you are a solid wall when they crash into you. Get healthy for their stabilization.

PART VII: THE TIMELINE (Loading, Cooking, and Lift)

People ask me, "When does the magic happen?" Biology requires Saturation.

1. The Loading Phase (Days 1–10)

You are pouring water into a dry sponge. The Amino Acids are repairing damage. You are stocking the "System Kitchen." Most people quit here because they don't see instant results. Do not quit.

2. The "Cooking" Phase (Day 10)

Around the ten-day mark, the tank hit "Full." I felt a sensation I can only describe as "Cooking Inside." My body finally had the materials to fix the chassis. I looked down at my watch and realized I had walked 5 miles. I didn't "push" myself. My body asked for it.

3. The Moment of Lift (Day 32)

It was 4:45 AM. I was three miles from my house. I started moving down a hill, and I wasn't just walking. I was jog-walking. My legs felt like springs. I felt light. I stopped in the dark and said out loud: "Are you kidding me? This can't be that easy."

That was the moment. The engine wasn't just repairing itself anymore; it was performing. The motion became a drug.

The Result (15 Months Later)

Since that morning in the dark, I have walked 4,000 miles. I didn't do it on willpower. I did it because on Day 32, the system came online, and I realized that feeling good is the most addictive substance on earth.

31

The Universal Blueprint

We have been conditioned to believe a lie: that our biology is a product of our geography. We've been told that "people from here" are built differently than "people from there," or that your heritage gives you a different set of rules to live by.

It is a lie designed to give you an excuse.

The truth is that the human body is the only piece of architecture on this planet that is a Universal Constant. If you take a man who is six-foot-two from a village in China and stand him next to a man who is six-foot-two from a small town in Alabama, you are looking at the exact same machine. Their hearts have to pump blood the same distance. Their skeletons have to support the same load. Their lungs have to oxygenate the same volume of tissue.

The math of the human frame does not care about your passport. It doesn't care what language you speak or what your ancestors did for a living. Biology has no borders.

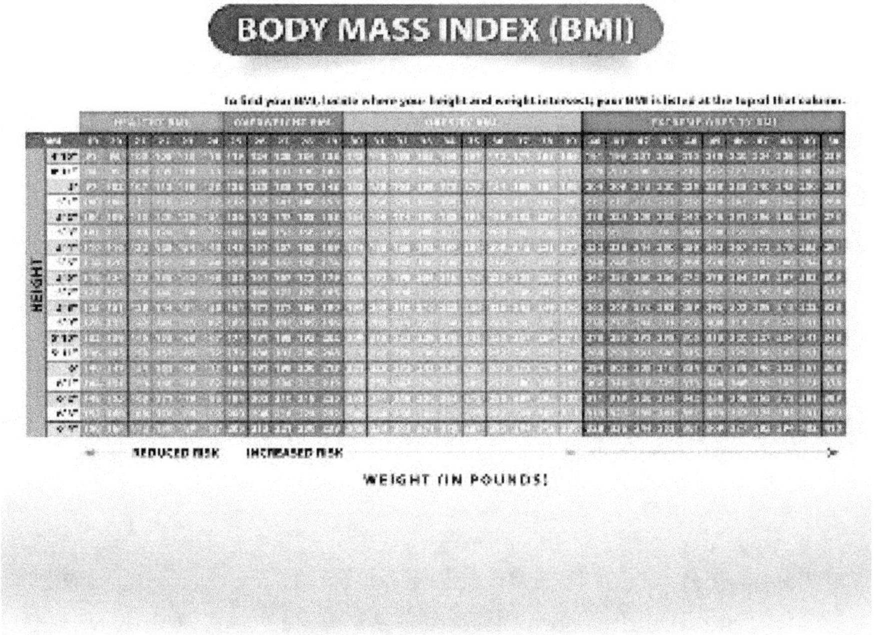

BODY MASS INDEX (BMI)

To find your BMI, locate where your height and weight intersect; your BMI is listed at the top of that column.

	HEALTHY BMI	OVERWEIGHT BMI	OBESITY BMI	EXTREME OBESITY BMI

(table values illegible)

REDUCED RISK   INCREASED RISK

WEIGHT (IN POUNDS)

Your Body Mass Index (BMI) is your "Factory Setting." It is the mathematical coordinate where your specific height meets your ideal weight. When you live outside of that number—even by a small percentage—you are asking a universal machine to perform a task it wasn't designed for. You are forcing the engine to redline every single day.

The 90-Day Reboot isn't about "getting in shape" for your neighborhood. It's about returning to the one and only physical truth that applies to every human being on Earth. You provide the chemistry—the Creatine and the Amino Acids—to keep the engine from stalling. Then, you move. You walk. You do what the machine has done for 200,000 years.

You aren't a "special case." You are a human. Start living like the one you were designed to be.

32

CHAPTER 17: The Protocol (Fighting Tomorrow)

Kick the Can — Inspiration and Analogy

The Twilight Zone (Season 3, Episode 21, "Kick the Can," 1962).

The episode takes place in Sunnyvale Rest Home, where a group of elderly residents are living out quiet, repetitive days. One of them, Charles Whitley, begins to suspect that growing old isn't a physical inevitability but a mindset. He remembers that as kids, they used to play a game called Kick the Can in the streets — running, laughing, full of life.

He convinces the others that the secret to youth might be something as simple as acting young again. In the middle of the night, they sneak out into the yard and begin to play. The magic of childlike joy — the freedom, the rhythm, the sheer silliness of the game — transforms them into children again.

The next morning, the staff find only empty clothes and a single can rolling down the grass. One skeptical resident, who refused to play, is left behind — still old, suddenly realizing he's missed his last chance at wonder.

It's a deeply symbolic story: Age, like misunderstanding, is often self-inflicted. The moment you reawaken your joy, your spirit begins to reverse the damage done by doubt. That healing, energy, and vitality aren't "treatments." They're returns to the natural state of being alive.

This is the same spirit that drives my mission: to invite everyone — BMI and non-BMI alike — to rediscover the joy of simply being themselves again.

The Clean Loop Reset

"Stop kicking the can down the road. To find clarity, you must aggressively close the open loops in your life—the issues, the 'stack,' and the mental clutter that cause the headaches. If a loop cannot be closed, you must find a way to bury it.

The secret is redirection: take the natural intensity of your mind—the part of you designed for repetition and 'OCD' focus—and point it toward something beneficial for yourself. Use your design; don't let it use you. Close the loops, clear the field, and let your natural focus finally work in your favor.

The 33rd Day: The Momentum of the Child

By the 33rd day, I found myself running down the hill, amazed at the simplicity of the shift. I had stopped forcing the system and started following the process, day by day. Suddenly, the fog was gone. I woke up the next day, and the next, feeling like a kid again—free to fantasize, free to move, and finally clear enough to "kick the can" every single morning.

You see it on YouTube all the time: fitness experts screaming "consistency, consistency, consistency." They say that because they know that when they give you all the 90-day details, your eyes glaze over. But when you finally find the rhythm, you start to smile at the people who think you're "missing out" because you don't drink or eat like they do.

You aren't missing out on anything. You're waking up every day with a mind that is light and a body that wants to move. You eat what you want because you know your system. You enjoy your day because you've mastered the "Kick." That is the power of the 33rd day—it's the moment the data becomes a feeling.

33

CHAPTER 18: The Unified Map

You've read the theory.

You understand the two designs.

Now comes the part that actually matters.

Tomorrow morning.

This is where most books fail parents. They explain why a child is different, then quietly step back when it's time to say what to do. This book does not do that. We are not here to observe these children from a distance. We are not here to protect them from life. And we are not here to wrap them in therapeutic bubble wrap and hope the world becomes gentler.

It won't.

So instead, we prepare them.

Not by hardening them.

By engaging them.

By meeting them where their biology actually lives.

Start Moving Them

I hear this constantly from good, well-meaning parents.

"He prefers to be alone."

"He doesn't like sports."

"He's not built for that."

And so the child is left alone. Quietly. Safely. Inside.

This is a mistake.

A dangerous one.

Binary children do not need isolation. They need motion with attachment. They need physical engagement that is grounded, predictable, and shared with someone they trust.

Look at how I grew up. I had older brothers. I had kids in the street. No one sat me down to analyze my mind. No one asked me how I felt about competition. They cared whether I could catch a ball. They pulled me into the game. They challenged me. They adjusted the rules just enough to keep me in play.

That wasn't cruelty.

That was calibration.

I am not telling you to throw your child into chaos. I am telling you to enter the arena with them. You play with them. You run with them. You wrestle on the floor. You throw the ball badly on purpose so they can win sometimes. You let them feel resistance, weight, gravity, balance, momentum.

Movement organizes the brain.

Always has.

A child left motionless becomes trapped inside their own replay loops. A child in motion begins to resolve them.

This is not optional.

The Real BMI (Fuel, Not Shame)

We need to reclaim a phrase that medicine hollowed out.

Body Mass Index is not a moral scorecard. It is a fuel gauge.

And this applies to parents just as much as children.

Step back and look honestly.

Is your child growing?

Are they sluggish?

Do they crash emotionally after eating?

Do they struggle to wake up?

Children grow at different rates, yes. But biology still tells the truth if you look long enough.

If the body isn't building correctly, the brain won't stabilize correctly. Period.

This isn't about dieting. It's about inputs.

If you feed a high-output brain low-quality fuel, you get volatility. If you feed a developing body ultra-processed food, you get inflammation, lethargy, emotional dysregulation, and confusion that looks psychological but isn't.

Fix the fuel.

Protein. Minerals. Hydration. Real food.

You are not being controlling.

You are being responsible.

Kill the Rainbow (The Label Problem)

This is where I'm going to be blunt.

Stop telling your child they are "on the spectrum."

Stop.

I am not talking about erasing who they are. I am talking about erasing a narrative that quietly tells them they are a deviation.

Every time you frame their identity as a medical category, you separate them from the human story. You teach them—subtly, repeatedly—that they are an exception rather than a participant.

That is poison to a developing Recorder.

They are not a color on a chart.

They are not a diagnosis first.

They are not broken software.

They are boys and girls with a specific cognitive orientation that has existed since the beginning of humanity.

Call them what they are.

Recorders.

Observers.

Builders.

Truth-keepers.

Language matters because it shapes self-trust. And without self-trust, nothing else works.

Turn On the Music (The Singing Rule)

Binary children often struggle with spoken language under pressure.

Music bypasses that entire bottleneck.

Music is structured emotion.

Predictable rhythm.

Safe repetition.

Embodied timing.

That's why it works.

This isn't about putting on background noise. This is about inviting resonance into the home.

Have music available. Always. A smart speaker. A playlist. Something accessible.

But here is the part that actually matters:

You sing.

Not well.

Not confidently at first.

Not because they asked.

You sing because you are regulated enough to be vulnerable.

Let them see you enjoying rhythm. Let them see you off-key and unafraid. Let them witness joy without performance anxiety.

That does more for their nervous system than a hundred conversations.

And yes—this connects directly to the morning walk. Singing changes the frequency of the environment. It softens defenses. It invites participation without pressure.

Music opens doors language cannot.

The Doctor Partnership

We are not going to war with medicine.

We are going in as adults.

You are not a passive recipient of opinions. You are the primary observer of your child's system.

You have data. You have patterns. You have lived experience.

So you walk into that office calmly and say:

- "I'm noticing hydration issues."

- "I'm noticing sleep disruption."
- "I'm noticing food sensitivity."
- "I'm noticing growth patterns."

And then you ask a simple question:

- "How can you support this plan?"

You are not asking for permission.
You are inviting collaboration.
Good doctors respond to clarity.
And if they don't, you find another one.
This protocol is not about controlling your child.
It is about fighting for their future without turning them into a patient.
You are not raising a fragile mind.
You are raising a specialized one.
And tomorrow morning is where that work begins.

34

(A Shared Language for Parents, Teachers, and Adults)
Human beings do not think the same way, and they were never supposed to. Modern society invented the idea of a "normal brain," but biology never built one. It built two. One mind Records. One mind Runs.

This chapter is the operating manual for the Recorder Mind—the Binary Mind Inside—written directly for the three groups who need it most:

1. **Parents**, who carry the emotional weight of raising a child whose wiring they were never taught to understand.
2. **Young Adults**, who have lived the confusion firsthand and deserve clarity.
3. **Teachers**, who guide these children daily inside a system designed for the opposite wiring.

Each group needs the same truth, but expressed in a way that speaks to their role.

SECTION 1: THE CORE TRUTH

The Binary Mind isn't a "different kind of personality." It isn't a deficit, a disorder, or an impairment. It is an ancient cognitive design built to **store, track, verify, and predict.**

The Binary system records automatically, constantly, and without filtering. This is not a choice; it is hardware. If you understand this one sentence, everything else in life becomes easier: **A Binary Mind does**

not control what it records. It controls what it does with the recording.

This is why people misunderstand you. This is why you misunderstand yourself. But once you understand the architecture, what felt like chaos becomes an organized machine.

SECTION 2: THE MECHANICS (RECAP)

1. Recording Without Filtering Runners filter. Recorders take everything in. Every sound. Every tone shift. Every micro-expression. Every environmental detail. The irony is that BMI memory is not perfect—it's selectively permanent. The system stores anything the mind flags as meaningful, even if the reason isn't obvious in the moment.

2. Replay (The Search for Resolution) Replay is not rumination. Replay is forensic analysis. A Binary Mind replays until it finds the truth, the cause, or the pattern. If the moment never resolves, the replay never stops. This is the source of 70% of the emotional pain in Binary individuals. Not trauma. Not defiance. **Unclosed files.**

3. The ADHD Connection (Motion-Based Recording) ADHD is not the opposite of Autism. It is the motion-based version of the same recording system.

- **Autism:** Still Recording (Depth).
- **ADHD:** Moving Recording (Breadth). Both lack the Runner filter. Both log raw data. Both become overwhelmed by unresolved inputs.

SECTION 3: FOR PARENTS (The Home Manual)

Parenting a Binary Mind is not about controlling behavior. It is about **managing bandwidth.** Your child is not lazy, disrespectful, or dramatic. They are **Overloaded.**

The Directives:

- **Their Brain Records Everything:** You didn't do anything wrong. But their brain logs your stress, your tone, and your inconsistency. This is why they "explode" after school. They have been recording for 7 hours straight.

- **Give Them Closure:** A Binary child needs endings, explanations, and sequence. Without these, the nervous system holds open tabs.
- **Meltdowns Are System Failures:** A meltdown is not manipulation. It is a computer overheating. Fix the overload (lights, noise, pressure), not the behavior.
- **Your Calm is Their Medicine:** If you deregulate, they collapse. If you stabilize, they stabilize. Put on your oxygen mask first.

SECTION 4: FOR YOUNG ADULTS (You Are Not Broken)

If you are a teenager or young adult reading this, here is the truth nobody told you: Nothing is wrong with you. You weren't "bad at school." You weren't "lazy." Your brain was trying to run a complex recording system in a world built for multitasking Runners.

The Directives:

- **Interest Is Your Switch:** Other people use willpower. You use the ON/OFF switch of Interest. This is why you can hyperfocus for 10 hours on a game or a code base but can't focus for 10 minutes on boring homework. You are a specialist, not a generalist.
- **Replay is for Resolution:** You replay because you are searching for truth. But once you learn closure tools (movement, writing, structure), your life stops feeling like an emotional backlog.
- **Your Empathy Is Real:** You feel deeply. You simply don't express it in the Runner style (smiling/nodding). You are not cold. You are precise.
- **Don't Fake Being a Runner:** Masking is slow death. Your power comes from leaning into pattern, truth, and structure. These are civilization-building abilities.

SECTION 5: FOR TEACHERS (The Classroom Manual)

Teachers are the front-line interpreters of wiring. What you understand shapes a child's entire identity.

The Directives:

- **They Record the Room, Not Just the Lesson:** They are logging the lights, the noise, and the social dynamics. This is why transitions destabilize them. Your structure creates their safety.
- **Overwhelm Is Hardware:** Too much noise = shutdown. Too many instructions = panic. Use visual instructions and one-step sequencing.
- **Trust Comes From Consistency:** You don't need to be warm. You need to be reliable. BMIs respect fairness and clarity above all else. You become their safest adult when you stop changing the rules.

SECTION 6: THE ALIGNMENT

The system was never broken—it was **mismatched.** Parents are not failing. Teachers are not failing. Young adults are not failing. The environment was simply misaligned with the design.

When all three groups align, the child becomes unstoppable.

- When parents provide stability...
- When teachers provide structure...
- When the child understands their own wiring...

Meltdowns drop. Confidence rises. Learning accelerates. A Binary Mind in the wrong environment struggles. A Binary Mind in the right environment shines.

35

EPILOGUE:

The "Man Living Together" Timeline

Milestones to show how the Two Brain Designs were forged:

• 200,000 Years (The Hardware): Modern Homo Sapiens emerge.

This is 190,000 years of pure "Runner" survival. The Recorder was just for tracking tracks and seasons.

• 10,000 Years (The Covenant): The end of the Ice Age. We start "Taming" the land.

This is where the Six Professions begin to solidify because we aren't just moving; we're building.

• 5,000 Years (The System): Writing and "Civilization" (Sumer/Egypt).

This is when the Recorder starts getting "Loud." We start logging laws instead of just survival.

• 100 Years (The Skid): The Industrial/Digital Age. We stopped moving.

This is the "last one and a half seconds" where we decided the "Runner" was a "disability" (ADHD) and the "Recorder" was the only thing that mattered.

1. The Hardware Release: 200,000–300,000 Years Ago

This is when the modern human body—the 6'2" frame, the lungs, the "Runner" biology—was finalized.

• The Reality: For 95% of our existence, there was no "home." There was only the Move.

• The Logic: If you didn't move 10+ miles a day, you didn't eat. The BMI of every human was dictated by the terrain, not a chart.

2. Living Together (The Tribe): 50,000–70,000 Years Ago

This is the "Great Leap Forward." Humans started living in larger, cohesive groups (tribes of 50–150).

• The Change: This is when Specialization became a biological survival trait. You didn't need everyone to be a generalist; you needed the Six Core Professions to coexist so the group could out-survive the environment.

• The Record: This is where the "Runner" and "Recorder" designs began to function as a unified team.

3. The Settlement (The Covenant): 10,000–12,000 Years Ago

The end of the last Ice Age. Humans stopped follows the herds and started "Taming" the land (Agriculture).

• The Impact: This is the first time the "Hardware" stayed in one place. We traded the "Constant Move" for the "Constant Work."

• The Tension: This is the birth of the Recorder's dominance. You had to track seeds, seasons, and property. The "Map" became more important than the "Hunt."

4. Civilization (The System): 5,000–6,000 Years Ago

The rise of cities (Sumer, Egypt).

• The Shift: This is where "Man living with others" turned into "Man living under a System."

• The Result: We invented writing to keep track of taxes and laws. The Runners began to label the "Recorder's" energy as something that needed to be "managed" or "restrained" for the sake of the city.

The "Last Two Minutes" Perspective

If you look at the 200,000-year history of our "Hardware":

• The Move: (Nomadic) lasted 190,000 years.

• The Settlement: (Farming) lasted 10,000 years.

• The System: (Cities) has lasted only 5,000 years.

The "Man with Electricity" has been around for less than 250 years (since the Industrial Revolution). That is 0.125% of our history.

The Truth: Your body is still 190,000 years deep in the "Move." It doesn't recognize the light switch or the desk; it only recognizes the 8,000 steps.

"Minutes."

• The Runner Baseline: It took **roughly 7,500 generations** of "Runners" to build your current body. They lived, breathed, and survived by the Move.

• The Settlement: It took only **400 generations** of "Farmers" to start settling the land.

• The System: It's been only **8 generations** since the Industrial Revolution (the "Electric Man" era).

• The Crash: You are the **1st or 2nd generation** to try and live entirely inside a digital screen.

36

SOMEWHERE IS HERE
(The Dawn of the Age of Aquarius)

We have spent thousands of years living in the Age of Pisces—an age defined by hierarchy, belief, and vertical power. In that world, the Runner Mind ruled because it was the mind of social climbing, diplomacy, and fluid adaptation. The Recorder Mind was the tool—used to build the pyramids and write the laws, but kept silent in the back room.

But the stars have shifted. We are entering the Age of Aquarius. Astrologers and mystics have said for decades that this new age would be defined by:

• Information (The Recorder's Domain)
• Networks (The Recorder's Architecture)
• Truth over Hierarchy (The Recorder's Moral Code)

For the first time in history, the environment is aligning with the Binary Mind. The digital world, the need for absolute data precision, and the collapse of old social structures are all signals that the Recorder is no longer the "broken" version of humanity. It is the necessary version.

A New Way of Living

The song says, "Someday, somewhere, we'll find a new way of living." That "somewhere" isn't a physical place. It is a mental place. It is the place where we stop forcing Recorders to mask. It is the place where we stop forcing Runners to do data entry. It is the place where the two halves of the human design—the Binary and the Parallel—stop fighting for dominance and start building the future together.

A New Way of Forgiving

And then the lyric that cuts the deepest: "We'll find a way of forgiving."

For centuries, Recorders have been angry at a world that lies to them. For centuries, Runners have been frustrated by a mind they couldn't understand. The "forgiving" happens when we realize: It wasn't personal. It was architecture. We forgive the friction. We forgive the misunderstanding. We forgive the years we spent trying to be someone else.

Integration Means You Are Not Sick

Even when Binary Minds finally recognize themselves, that lie still whispers underneath: Something is wrong with you.

That is false. Binary Minds are not a disorder. They are not a condition to be treated. They are a required cognitive orientation, as necessary to civilization as motion is. A world made only of Runners collapses into chaos. A world made only of Recorders never moves. The species survives because both exist. You were not born broken. You were born load-bearing.

Final Truth

Binary Minds don't need curing. They need to stop fighting physics. Your strengths are not compensation mechanisms. They are primary functions: Precision. Consistency. Depth. Endurance. Truth detection.

When you build life around those—using routine, repetition, and long arcs—you don't become dull. You become dangerously effective. And that was always the point.

37

APPENDIX:

THE DIGITAL FACULTY
(My YouTube University)

I am not a doctor. I am a student. A Recorder mind does not invent data; it collects it, verifies it, and organizes it. Everything I learned about the 90-Day Reboot, I learned because we live in the greatest era of information in human history.

You don't need to go to medical school to understand your liver. You just need to listen to the people who are obsessed with the mechanics. These are the teachers I trust. I don't agree with everything they say, and I certainly can't afford everything they do, but they are the ones "kicking the can" down the road and showing us the map.

1. Bryan Johnson (The Architect)

People call him eccentric. I call him a pioneer. He is spending millions of dollars to reverse his biological age.

• Why I watch him: I can't afford the blood transfusions or the team of 30 doctors. But I can afford the olive oil, the sleep protocol, and the logic. He proves that health isn't luck; it's an engineering problem. He provides the data on the supplements so I don't have to guess.

2. Jeff Cavaliere / Athlean-X (The Mechanic)

He is a Physical Therapist first, a trainer second.

• Why I watch him: He respects the "No Injury" rule. He doesn't just show you a lift; he takes a marker and draws the muscle fibers on a skeleton so you understand the leverage. He teaches you how to lift so you can still move when you're 70.

3. Thomas DeLauer (The Chemist)

He understands inflammation and the metabolic engine better than anyone.

• Why I watch him: He explains the specific biology of fasting and food. He breaks down why certain ingredients (like seed oils) cause noise in the system. He speaks the language of cellular inflammation.

4. Dr. Mike Israetel / Renaissance Periodization (The Scientist)

No fluff. No "rah-rah." Just pure sports science.

• Why I watch him: He understands the "Paper Clip" method (Progressive Overload). He explains that you don't need to kill yourself in the gym; you need to stimulate the muscle with precision. He appeals to the logical, binary brain.

5. Jeremy Ethier (The Optimizer)

He focuses on the most efficient way to get from Point A to Point B based on research.

• Why I watch him: He looks at the studies. He corrects your form. He is calm, precise, and data-driven.

6. Dr. Rhonda Patrick (The Biologist)

She is the bridge between the laboratory and the kitchen. She looks at human body at molecular level to find the " Skeleton Key" for longevity.

• Why I watch her: She understands the "Heat and Cold" protocol. She provides the hard data on why saunas and cold plunges stop the " Skid" in your cells. She explains how things like sulforaphane (broccoli sprouts) and Vitamin D act as a filter for your system. She doesn't give you opinions; she gives you peer-reviewed evidence. If you want to know how to protect your brain from aging, she is the one holding the map.

My Advice: Don't just watch them to be entertained. Watch them to take notes. Treat their channels like a lecture hall. The data is free. The application is up to you.

38

Why Every Major Autism Theory Misses the Point
For more than forty years, professionals have tried to explain autism by staring at the symptoms instead of the system producing them. Each theory captured a slice of the behavior but never the architecture underneath it. Researchers kept measuring the oceans by looking at the waves.

This appendix exists for one purpose: To show that the world wasn't blind—it was simply measuring the wrong thing.

Autism was never a disease. Never a disorder. Never a deficit model. It was always a different operating system—a binary one—and the world kept diagnosing the output without ever reading the code.

What follows is the landscape of theories that shaped the last half-century. Good people, smart minds, real effort—but wrong target. These explanations circled the symptoms but never touched the root.

And once you see the architecture—Recorder vs. Runner—the limitations of every prior theory become obvious.

1. THE SOCIAL DEFICIT FRAMEWORKS

The oldest and most persistent theories assume autism begins with social impairment: trouble reading faces, following conversations, engaging in reciprocity. It sounds accurate because it describes what observers see. But these theories misinterpret the surface.

• Social Deficit Theory claims autistic individuals lack social instinct.

• Theory of Mind Deficit says they can't infer thoughts or intentions.

• Social Motivation Theory insists autistic people simply don't want connection.

Every one of these theories treats the social behavior as the cause instead of the by-product of a different processing engine.

The Binary Correction:

Binary Minds aren't socially disinterested—they're socially precise. They don't assume what people mean because they don't hallucinate meaning. And when interpretation varies wildly from person to person, a Recorder steps back rather than fabricating. These theories describe the outcome of misaligned processing—not the processing itself.

2. THE COGNITIVE DEFICIT FRAMEWORKS

• Executive Dysfunction Theory argues autistic people struggle with planning, sequencing, and multi-step tasks.

• Weak Central Coherence Theory claims they fixate on details and lose the big picture.

• Developmental Delay models frame autism as "arrested growth."

None of these theories ask a basic question: "What if the mind isn't failing the task? What if the task conflicts with the wiring?"

A Runner brain starts multiple processes and can leave some incomplete. A Recorder brain moves in straight lines, one at a time, and needs structural clarity. When a world designed by Runners evaluates a Recorder, the Recorder is framed as dysfunctional.

The Binary Correction:

A binary system isn't impaired. It's precise. It requires order because the operating system demands it. These theories pathologize a design.

3. THE PERCEPTION & SENSORY FRAMEWORKS

Here the field came closer—but still missed the anchor.

• Sensory Processing Disorder

• Enhanced Perceptual Functioning

• Intense World Theory

All recognize that autistic individuals experience too much, too intensely, too unfiltered. Correct observation. Wrong explanation.

The Binary Correction:

A Recorder brain logs raw data at full resolution. It doesn't discard inputs. It doesn't blur the image. It captures everything exactly. No compression. No rounding. No assumed meaning. This results in "sensitivity," but the sensitivity is a feature of the recording system, not a defect in the sensory system.

A camera that captures in 8K is not "overwhelmed." It's accurate.

4. THE PREDICTION & ERROR-PROCESSING MODELS

These theories—especially Predictive Coding Error Theory—claim autistic people assign too much weight to precision, making the world unpredictable and stressful. Ironically, this one is closest to the truth.

Predictive coding models say:

• Runner minds guess and adjust.

• Binary minds don't guess; they confirm.

But researchers treat this as malfunction instead of orientation. They assume the inability to "let go" of precision is pathological.

The Binary Correction:

It isn't. It's the stability mechanism of a Recorder. A machine that must replay accurately cannot afford corrupted inputs. What scientists called "maladaptive prediction" is simply the cost of a truth-based operating system.

5. THE COMMUNICATION FRAMEWORKS

The Double Empathy Problem finally admitted that misunderstanding is mutual, not one-sided. It opened the door to recognizing that autistic communication isn't broken—it's different.

But even this theory stops short. It doesn't explain why the difference exists. It only acknowledges that it does.

The Binary Correction:

A Recorder doesn't infer tone, subtext, or intention unless those elements are explicitly encoded. A Runner assumes meaning based on pattern and social context. Two operating systems speaking two languages. Not deficits—differences.

6. THE NEUROBIOLOGICAL & GENETIC THEORIES

These are the theories that attract headlines:

• Autism = inflammation

• Autism = abnormal connectivity

- Autism = too many or too few synapses
- Autism = polygenic burden

These may capture correlates. But none explain the consistent cognitive profile seen across time, geography, culture, and socioeconomic layers. If autism were simply "genetic load," it wouldn't produce such a stable pattern of strengths:

- Extreme pattern recognition
- Memory replay
- Precision
- Honesty
- Direct interpretation
- Hyper-focus

These aren't random outcomes. They're the expression of a particular architecture. Biology supplies the hardware; it doesn't explain the operating system.

7. THE MOTOR & BEHAVIORAL FRAMEWORKS

Motor theories (dyspraxia) and behavioral theories (ABA) describe the visible challenges without ever explaining the origin. Behavior is output. Motor planning is output. Regulation is output. The machine producing the output remains undescribed.

The Binary Correction:

Autistic behaviors aren't random. They're mechanical consequences of:

1. Overloading the recording buffer.
2. Interrupting a process mid-sequence.
3. Forcing a Runner framework onto a Recorder brain.

ABA treats the visible behavior as the illness. It tries to reprogram symptoms instead of understanding systems. This is why ABA often harms—it fights the operating system instead of working with it.

THE FUNDAMENTAL PATTERN EVERY THEORY MISSED

Every traditional theory is built on the same assumption: "Neurotypical is the default. Autism is deviation."

Once that assumption is wrong, the entire field fractures. It explains why every theory contradicts the others. It explains why every theory captures a piece but misses the whole.

Autism is not deviation. Autism is one half of a dual-design system: Recorders and Runners. Precision and Motion. Truth and Navigation.

The world treated one design as standard and the other as error. Thus book reframes it: One records. One runs. Both are required. And civilization collapses without the synchronization of the two.

WHERE THE BINARY ARCHITECTURE MODEL FITS

This model doesn't fight the existing theories. It explains them.

Every fragmented theory becomes a predictable output of a Recorder system placed in a Runner-built world:

• Social "deficits" = Refusal to guess.
• Communication "issues" = Insistence on explicitness.
• Executive "dysfunction" = Linear sequencing vs. multitasking.
• Sensory "abnormalities" = High-resolution data capture.
• Predictive "errors" = Precision-based updating.
• Motor loops = Clearing internal buffers.
• Anxiety = Forced parallel processing.

Every old theory becomes symptom of misalignment. Binary Architecture is not another psychology framework. It is the operating system underneath the behavior.

Once a reader sees it, they will never be able to un-see it.

39

WELCOME HOME!

..

Connect with the Data

If this record has provided clarity, or if you have data to share, reach out.

Website:

www.RantSun.com

Email:

robert@RantSun.com

This is a living record. The search for the "Binary Handshake" continues.

40

THE RUNNER RECORDER COVENANT
The Bond Keeps Civilization Alive!
By,
Robert Anthony Caggiano

41

The Runner Recorder Covenant
Copyright © 2026 by Robert Anthony Caggiano
Published by RantSun LLC
First Edition: January 2026
ISBN: 979-8-9946468-0-9
Printed in the United States of America.

42

Dedication
"To the parents who have spent years in the dark, searching for a name for the chaos.

To the children who have been told their 'Radar" was a defect, rather than a gift.

For every family that has felt the trauma of the skid – fighting a nature they did not yet understand – this record is for you.

May these pages bring the light of clarity to your past, and the hope of a steady road moving forward. You are not broken; you are simply a system finally being seen."

43

Contents

44

Come take a walk with me!CHAPTER 1

THE INVITATION (Letter to the Reader)
     A LETTER TO THE RECORDER
(Roughly 2–3 billion of you)
Permission
Before I go any further, I want to ask you for your permission.
Not permission to speak about you.
Permission to speak to you — as one of you.

I've spent my entire life seeing things other people seemed to walk right past. Patterns. Contradictions. Small misalignments that didn't feel small to me at all. I didn't know what they were at the time, only that once I noticed them, I couldn't un-notice them.

I've been called a lot of things over the years.

Different. Wired another way. Hyper-focused. Too intense. Too detailed. Too serious. Too quiet. Too still. And sometimes — strangely — too honest.

None of those labels were wrong. But none of them explained anything, either.

That's why I'm asking you — not doctors, not academics, not panels, not committees — for permission to name this properly.

I'm calling it The Binary Mind Inside (BMI™) / Recorders.

I'm not here to fix you.

I'm not here to cure you.

I'm not here to smooth you out, sand you down, or help you "function better."

I'm here because when something is misnamed, it's mistreated.

And for a very long time, people with Binary Minds have been mislabeled — analyzed through the wrong lens, trained using the wrong tools, and evaluated against standards they were never built to meet.

So here's the promise I'll make to you.

Let me tell you what I've discovered — slowly, honestly, with context — the way it unfolded for me. If you get to the end and you don't agree, fine. You can throw the whole thing away. But if even one moment makes you quietly think, "Wait... that's me," then stay with me.

Walk with me — not forward, but backward — to the beginning of something old that has never yet been named correctly.

This isn't about treatment.

It isn't about cures.

It isn't about labels.

It's about truth.

And I'm asking for your permission to tell it.

THE AGREEMENT (Denial & Ego)

THE NECESSARY ACT

Before we start the work, I need you to do something uncomfortable.

Only for a moment.

I need you to put denial down.

Not permanently. Not dramatically. Just set it aside long enough to read what comes next without defending yourself against it.

Denial is powerful because it protects.

It protects parents from feeling like they failed their children.

It protects adults from realizing they adapted in ways they were never supposed to.

It protects professionals from admitting they may have misunderstood something foundational.

It even protects the body — by letting it grind forward despite subtle signals that something isn't aligned.

Denial is a survival reflex.

But it's also the reflex of someone hiding under a table during a fire drill while everyone else calmly walks out of the building.

For this book, I need you outside.

So don't skim. Don't jump ahead. Don't look for conclusions before the story does its work. Let your subconscious listen before your intellect starts arguing.

Because what matters most doesn't arrive as information.

It arrives as recognition.

GET OVER YOURSELF

(The Price of Admission)

This brings us to the hardest part.

If you want to understand the Binary Mind, you have to do the one thing Recorders hate doing: You have to get over yourself.

This isn't an insult. It's an instruction.

We spend our whole lives building a fortress to protect our sensitivity. We build walls of logic, walls of silence, and walls of "being right."

To read this book effectively, you have to lower the drawbridge.

You have to be willing to look at your past not as a series of "things that happened to me," but as data points.

You have to stop taking your own life personally.

You have to step back and look at the machine.

If you are busy defending your ego, you will miss the pattern.

So, take a breath. Drop the shoulders. Put the ego in the corner for an hour.

We have work to do.

THE EXPERIMENT

THE TEST: Before we start, I want you to do something.

I want you to sing. Out loud. Right now. *Don't just read it.* **Sing it.**

A - B - C - D - E - F - G

H - I - J - K - L - M - N - O - P

Q - R - S

T - U - V

W - X

Y and Z

Now I know my ABCs,

Next time won't you sing with me.

Did you hear it?

Did you hear how the melody kicked in automatically?

Did you feel how your brain knew exactly where to speed up (L-M-N-O-P) and where to pause?

Did you notice that when you got to "Now I know..." your voice likely dropped into that familiar, resolving tone without you even deciding to do it?

You didn't have to think about it. You didn't have to try.

The software just ran.

That automatic melody? That rush through the middle letters? That is the Runner.

It is the automated program designed to get you from A to Z as fast as possible without asking questions.

But underneath that melody, there is a machine that feels every single letter.

That is the Recorder.

We are going to look at the machine underneath the melody.

45

CHAPTER 2

THE ARCHITECTURE OF CIVILIZATION
    Now walk with me.

Not the kind of walk you schedule on your calendar or track on your phone to close a ring.

The kind where you don't bring anything with you.

No music.

No podcast.

No destination.

Just your body moving through space long enough for your mind to finally stop reacting and start noticing.

That's the state we need to be in.

Because what I'm about to describe isn't something you can absorb quickly.

It isn't an opinion. It isn't a theory.

It is a pattern that only becomes obvious when you step far enough back from modern life that you can see the shape of things again.

Right now, the world is loud. Constantly.

Labels are assigned before questions are asked. We diagnose, categorize, measure, and intervene without ever asking a more basic question:

What was this thing built to do?

To answer that, we have to leave the present entirely.

We have to go back to a time before there were schools, offices, job titles, or medical codes.

Before anyone was asked to sit still in a room full of strangers and perform on demand.

Before "normal" was defined.

We have to go back to the planet itself.

The 24-Hour Clock

The Earth is approximately four and a half billion years old.

That number is so large it becomes meaningless the moment you hear it, so let's shrink it to something you can actually picture.

Imagine the entire history of the planet compressed into a single, twenty-four-hour day.

00:00 (Midnight): The Earth forms.

For hours, nothing happens. The surface cools. The oceans gather. Life appears, fails, mutates, and tries again.

10:56 PM: Dinosaurs appear.

They dominate the planet for millions of years. They are enormous, powerful, successful beyond measure.

By 11:39 PM, they are gone.

11:58 PM: Modern humans arrive.

Think about that.

Civilization—farming, villages, written language, laws, economies—exists only in the final second and a half before midnight.

If you were to blink at the wrong moment, you would miss it entirely.

The Long Dark

Now, let's zoom in on those final two minutes.

Let's look at the human timeline itself.

For more than ninety-nine percent of our existence as a species, we were not "civilized."

We did not sit at desks. We did not have 401(k)s.

We lived outside, exposed to weather, hunger, injury, and danger.

In that world, nature had one rule and one rule only:

Do not go extinct.

To follow that rule, nature had to deal with the environment. And for almost our entire history, that environment was defined by one binary reality:

Light and Dark.

For twenty-three hours and fifty-eight minutes of our "human day," the only artificial light was fire.

When the sun went down, the data stream stopped.

The world became invisible.

And in the wild, invisibility means danger.

We spent thousands of generations staring into the blackness beyond the campfire, listening for the snap of a twig or the shift in the wind.

Survival wasn't about being "happy."

It was about being alert.

The Hardware Updates

Nature didn't ask us to "try harder" to survive this.

It changed the machine.

It reshaped limbs. It altered blood chemistry. It modified organs.

Whatever worked stayed. Whatever failed disappeared.

You can still see the evidence today if you know where to look.

The Bajau People of Southeast Asia – the "Sea Nomads" Wave Runners

They have lived for generations on the water. They dive repeatedly, every day, to hunt. A typical human body cannot do this; oxygen runs out too quickly.

So over time, the hardware changed.

Bajau divers evolved spleens 50% larger than land-dwelling populations. It acts as a biological reserve tank for oxygen.

The Sherpa (The Himalayas)

They move steadily at altitudes where visitors faint. Their metabolism extracts more energy from less oxygen. Their blood chemistry is different.

The Nilotic (The South Sudan)

They thrive in the infinite heat of the horizon. Their limbs evolved longer and leaner to act as biological radiators, dissipating heat where others would collapse. Their skeletal structure is a masterpiece of endurance.

The Handshake

We accept this instinctively.

We don't look at a Sherpa and say he's "disordered" because his lungs work differently.

We don't look at a Bajau diver and prescribe medication for an enlarged spleen.

We don't look at a Nilotic hunter and call his long-legged endurance a "malfunction."

We understand that Survival shaped the Body.

But when we reach the Brain?

We suddenly pretend none of this logic applies.

The Split

The brain is the most expensive organ in the body.

It consumes roughly 20% of our total energy.

That cost guarantees one thing: Nature is cheap.

It hates redundancy. It would never build a single mind and hope it could stretch far enough to cover every survival task.

Nature had a math problem.

If every human in the tribe was aggressive, impulsive, and fearless, the tribe would run off a cliff or get eaten in the first week.

But if every human was cautious, analytical, and frozen in observation, the tribe would starve to death in the cave.

The tribe needed to Go (hunt, explore, expand).

But the tribe also needed to No-Go (protect, secure, analyze).

No single human mind excels at both simultaneously.

You cannot be flexible about whether a bridge collapses. Gravity doesn't negotiate.

But you cannot be rigid when two families are on the verge of killing each other.

So nature did what it always does. It specialized.

It didn't just create different personalities.

It created two different operating systems.

The Six Professions

Right before the end of the day—just as we started to gather in larger groups—the roles hardened.

The survival of the group depended on this specialization. Out of that necessity, the Six Primal Professions were born.

Three for the Runner.

Three for the Recorder.

THE RUNNER (The Social Engine)

Nature built a mind designed for Speed. This mind learns by navigation. It scans. It adapts. It moves.

1. *The Leader* (Warrior)

The visionary who could stand in front of a starving tribe and convince them to keep walking. They didn't use data; they used hope. They didn't see the cliff; they saw the horizon.

2. *The Connector* (Gatherer)

The one who could walk into a foreign village and trade without getting killed. They knew that the "deal" was more important than the "fact." They greased the wheels of civilization.

3. *The Healer*

The one who managed the emotional temperature of the group. They prioritized feelings because feelings determine whether the tribe sticks together. They kept the peace.

THE RECORDER (The Structural Engine)

Nature built a mind designed for Fidelity. This mind learns by accumulation. It catalogs. It stores. It asks: Is this true? Is it safe? Will it hold?

4. The Sentry (Enforcer)

The one who sits by the fire facing the dark. They do not sleep. They listen for the threat. Their "anxiety" is not a disorder; it is the tribe's alarm system. They hear the twig snap before the wolf appears.

5. The Builder

The one who stacked the stones for the aqueduct. You cannot charm a stone into holding water. You must understand the physics. This required a mind capable of hyper-focus—shutting out the world to chip a flint to a millimeter tolerance.

6. The Scribe

The one who held the data. If the grain count was wrong, the village starved. The Scribe's job wasn't to be liked. It was to be right. They were the keepers of the code.

The Covenant

For thousands of years—for most of that "second and a half"—this was a partnership that bonded us together.

The Runner handled the software (culture).

The Recorder handled the hardware (reality).

Civilization did not begin when we built a wall.

Civilization began when the Runner Brain and the Recorder Brain agreed to cover each other's blind spots.

The friction between them was managed because both were necessary.

When the Runner was ignored, the tribe tore itself apart.

When the Recorder was ignored, the roof fell in.

But then... the clock struck Midnight.

46

THE TWO DESIGNS: THE PARALLEL AND THE BINARY
Imagine two photographers standing on the edge of a cliff.
One has a Wide-Angle Lens.

He captures the sunset, the horizon, the curve of the coastline, and the colors of the sky. His picture is vast and beautiful.

But if you zoom in, the details are blurry.

The other has a Macro Lens.

He is looking at the same cliff, but he captures the vein on a single leaf, the fracture in the granite, the specific species of the beetle crawling on the rock. His picture is incredibly sharp.

But he misses the sunset entirely.

Now, ask yourself:

Which camera is the "correct" one?

It's a trick question.

Neither is correct. They simply have different focal lengths for different jobs.

But in the human world, we have forgotten this.

We have spent decades trying to force every human mind onto a single bell curve. We act as if "intelligence" is one single ladder, and everyone is just climbing the same rungs at different speeds.

We decided that the Wide-Angle Lens (Social/Generalist) is "Normal."

And we decided the Macro Lens (Detail/Specialist) is "Disordered."

History and biology tell a different story.

They show us that humanity runs on two distinct operating systems. These systems process information differently, prioritize different inputs, and perceive reality in fundamentally opposing ways.

I call them the Parallel Mind Inside (PMI)TM and the Binary Mind Inside (BMI)TM.

The world knows them as the Runner and the Recorder.

1. **THE RUNNER** (The Parallel Mind)

The Engine of Motion

Roughly 70–80% of the population operates on this architecture.

The Runner's brain is designed for Broadband Processing.

The Wiring

Neuroscience shows that typical brains rely heavily on "long-range connectivity."

This means the front of the brain communicates rapidly with the back, and the left communicates constantly with the right. It is a mesh network.

The Function

This wiring creates a mind that sees the Whole, not the Part.

When a Runner walks into a room, they sense the "vibe." They process the lighting, the mood, the social tension, and the conversation all at once as a single fuzzy picture.

They prioritize Context.

They understand that "I hate you" said with a smile means "I love you."

They operate on Probability.

They don't need 100% of the data to make a decision. They get 60% of the data, guess the rest, and move.

The Historical Role: The Orator

Think of the Roman Senator Cicero or the tribal chieftain.

Their power came from their ability to read the crowd in real-time. They didn't need to be technically perfect; they needed to be emotionally resonant.

The Runner keeps the tribe moving. They smooth over conflict. They "grease the gears" of society with white lies and social niceties.

Without them, civilization would grind to a halt because everyone would be arguing over facts instead of building relationships.

2. **THE RECORDER** (The Binary Mind)

The Engine of Truth

Roughly 20–30% of the population operates on this architecture.

The Recorder's brain is designed for Deep-band Processing.

The Wiring

Research into the brains of autistic individuals reveals a different architecture: Local Hyper-Connectivity.

Instead of sending weak signals across the whole brain, the Recorder's brain builds massive, super-fast highways between specific local regions (like the visual cortex or the logic centers).

The Function

This wiring creates a mind that sees the Part, not the Whole.

When a Recorder walks into a room, they don't see a "vibe."

They see a crooked picture frame. They see the flickering lightbulb (60Hz cycle). They hear the air conditioner hum. And they notice a person whose tone doesn't match their facial expression.

They prioritize Content.

"I hate you" means "I hate you." The smile is just contradictory noise.

They operate on Certainty.

They cannot move on 60% data. They need to verify the facts until the error rate is zero.

The Historical Role: The Navigator

Think of the Polynesian wave finders or the astronomers of Babylon.

A Runner looks at the ocean and sees "water."

A Recorder looks at the ocean and sees the interference pattern of waves reflecting off an island 100 miles away.

The Recorder keeps the tribe safe. They don't care about the "mood" of the ocean; they care about the physics of the ocean.

If the Navigator gets the angle wrong by one degree, the tribe drowns.

3. HISTORY AS A DIALOGUE

If you look at the timeline of human progress, you don't see a single type of mind evolving.

You see a tennis match between the Runner and the Recorder.

The Oral to Written Transition (Runner → Recorder)

For thousands of years, history was Oral (Runner). It was stories, myths, and legends passed around the fire. It was fluid. The story changed every time it was told to fit the audience. Truth was flexible.

Then, Recorders invented Writing.

Writing is binary. Once it is carved in stone, it does not change. A law written down is a law that applies to everyone, even if the King is having a bad day. Civilization exploded only when the Recorder's need for "Fixed Truth" met the Runner's need for "Social Story."

The Age of Exploration (Runner Ambition + Recorder Tech)

Christopher Columbus (likely a Runner) had the vision, the charisma, and the delusional confidence to sail across the Atlantic. He sold the dream to the Queen.

But he would have died in a circle without the Astrolabe and the Compass.

These tools were not built by dreamers. They were built by Recorders who understood the stars with mathematical precision.

The Runner provided the Why.

The Recorder provided the How.

The Industrial Revolution (The Recorder's Rise)

For most of history, the Runner ruled because the world was agricultural and social.

But the Industrial Revolution shifted power to the Recorder. Steam engines do not run on charisma. Electricity does not care about your social status.

Suddenly, the mind that could focus deeply, calculate thermodynamics, and standardize parts became the most valuable mind on earth.

The modern world—the world of screens, data, and engineering—is a world built by Recorders, even if it is still managed by Runners.

4. THE FRICTION POINT

Why do we have conflict?

Because these two designs speak different languages.

The Runner speaks "Analog."

It flows. It approximates. It values harmony over accuracy.

Motto: "Go along to get along."

The Recorder speaks "Digital."

It steps. It defines. It values accuracy over harmony.

Motto: "Truth is the only safety."

The Runner thinks the Recorder is "difficult" because the Recorder won't just agree to a half-truth to be nice.

The Recorder thinks the Runner is "dishonest" because the Runner changes their opinion based on who is in the room.

Neither is wrong. They are just executing different code.

The Tragedy of Diagnosis

The problem with our current view of neurodivergence is that we judge the Recorder by the standards of the Runner.

We say: "You are bad at 'Big Picture' thinking."

The Recorder says: "I am not trying to see the Big Picture. I am checking the structural integrity of the foundation so the Big Picture doesn't collapse."

When we understand that these are Two Designs—not one Normal and one Broken—we stop trying to "cure" the Recorder.

We start realizing that without the Recorder, the Runner is just wandering in circles, telling great stories, but never actually getting anywhere.

The Runner provides the Motion.

The Recorder provides the Map.

You cannot survive the journey without both.

5. THE INEVITABILITY

Let's perform a thought experiment.

Imagine that tomorrow, a catastrophic event hits the planet. A flood, an asteroid, a solar flare—pick your disaster.

Modern technology is wiped out. The internet is gone. Governments dissolve. The grid goes dark. The slate is wiped clean.

Survivors scatter into small groups. They have no manuals, no Wikipedia, and no laws. They have to start over from zero.

If you came back to visit those groups 1,000 years later, what would you find?

You would not find a random assortment of jobs.

You would find that every single successful tribe had re-created the exact same structure we have today.

They would have someone tracking the food supply with absolute precision (The Numbers Person).

They would have someone negotiating peace with the neighboring tribe (The Connector).

They would have someone building weapons that fly straight (The Creator).

They would have someone enforcing the new rules without favoritism (The Enforcer).

This would not happen because they read it in a book.

It would happen because survival is a specific engineering problem.

And to solve that problem, the human species produces two specific types of minds to do the work.

6. THE PHYSICAL ECHO: LEFT-HANDED VARIANCE

If you still doubt that nature intentionally designs "Minority Variants" for the protection of the species, just look at your hands.

For centuries, left-handedness was treated exactly like the Binary Mind is treated today: as a defect to be corrected.

The Latin word for "Left" is Sinister. The word for "Right" is Dexter.

Schools used to tie the left hands of children behind their backs to force them to write with their right.

They believed that unity required uniformity. They thought a left-handed child was "broken."

They were wrong.

Nature has maintained left-handedness at roughly 10% of the population for thousands of years. It refuses to breed it out.

Why?

The Combat Advantage.

In a tribe where everyone is right-handed, the angles of attack are predictable. The shield is always on the left; the spear is always on the right.

But the Left-Hander breaks the pattern. The enemy doesn't know how to block them. The angles are reversed.

The "Surprise" factor wins the fight.

It is no accident that studies show a significantly higher rate of left-handedness in the autism and high-IQ communities.

The Left Hand is controlled by the Right Brain—the hemisphere responsible for spatial scanning, pattern recognition, and "Sentry" awareness.

History tried to crush the Left-Hander because they didn't fit the desk.

History is trying to crush the Binary Mind because we don't fit the social script.

But nature keeps making us.

Because a tribe without the variant is a tribe that gets conquered.

THE HARDWARE REALITY: TWO SEPARATE BRAINS

Let's be crystal clear about something before we move on.

When I talk about the Runner and the Recorder, I am not talking about your personality.

I am not talking about your "mood."

I am not talking about how you feel on a Tuesday versus how you feel on a Friday.

I am talking about two physically different types of brains.

There are two distinct architectures.

There are two distinct designs.

There are two separate ways to build a human mind.

Just like you have a physical dominant hand (Left or Right), you have a physical dominant brain.

Brain Type One (The Runner) is wired for Distance.

Brain Type Two (The Recorder) is wired for Density.

You are born with one of these two.

It is a binary reality.

It is not a choice.

It is Two. Separate. Brains. And, once you see it, you can't unsee it.

47

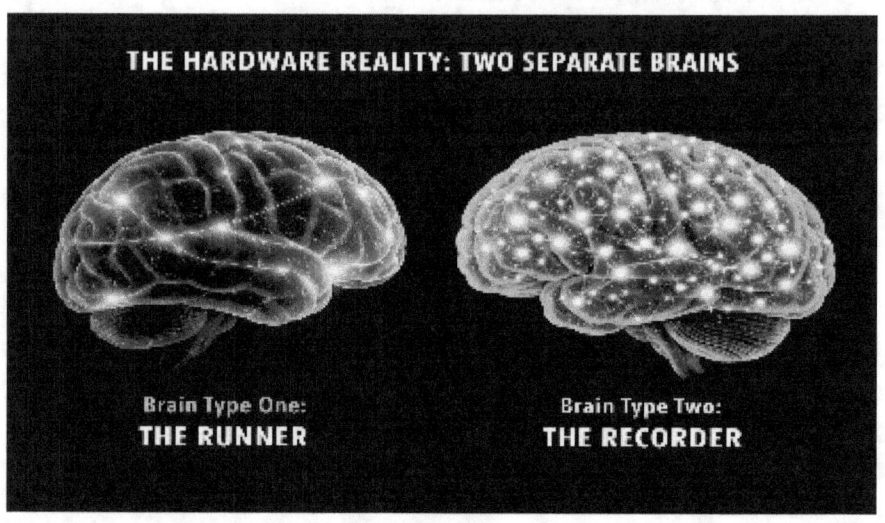

THE HARDWARE REALITY: TWO SEPARATE BRAINS

Brain Type One:
THE RUNNER

Brain Type Two:
THE RECORDER

B INARY-PARALLEL DUALITY ™

48

The SKID:

The Anatomy of a Skid
To understand the Recorder, you must understand the Skid. It isn't a "bad mood" or a personality quirk; it is a mechanical event that occurs when a high-precision machine is forced out of alignment.

There are three ways to identify a Skid:

1. The Structural Protest: A Skid is the friction that occurs when your actions lose their alignment with your structural truth. It happens when you are in an "actionable mood"—actually doing something—but your internal architecture realizes the path is incorrect. It's the sound of the mind trying to course-correct while the body is still at full speed.

2. The Processing Gap: You cannot have a Skid while standing still. It requires movement. A Skid is the violent vibration of a Recorder mind that is being forced to act before it has finished processing the "1s and 0s" of the situation. You are acting, but you are out of alignment with the truth.

3. The Logic-Action Grind: Think of a Skid as a "Mechanical Protest." It's what happens when a Recorder is mid-action and realizes the sequence is flawed. Because the Recorder cannot "fake" the logic, the system begins to grind against itself until the truth is restored.

SKID

"In accounting, if the numbers don't balance, you've made an error. In golf, if your mind drifts for a split second, you lose the match. I call this the SKID. It's that moment where your hardware (The Recorder) and the world (The Runner) stop talking to each other, and you lose your grip on the truth. You start spinning, and the harder you try to 'think' your way out, the deeper the skid gets."

S — System

The biological "System" (The Recorder or The Runner) is being forced to operate outside of its design parameters. You are trying to run "Runner" software on "Recorder" hardware.

K — Kinetic

There is "Kinetic" friction. Instead of a smooth flow, the mind is dragging. This is the golf swing that feels forced, the diet that feels like a prison, or the conversation that feels like an argument. The energy isn't moving forward; it's burning up as heat (stress).

I — Interference

The "Interference" of the ego. The ego is trying to "think" its way through a problem that the subconscious should be "handling." This creates "noise" in the circuitry, leading to hesitation and doubt.

D — Disconnection

The final "Disconnection" between the Mind and the Machine. You lose the "Handshake." The body stops responding to the brain, the 3:00 PM crash hits, and you end up "on the other side of the hospital bed" because the machine has finally shut down to protect itself.

49

When you see a car skid on the road, it's because

*T*he *"Skid" Reality*

THE OTHER THING

50

THE YEARS THE WORLD OPENED
(The Education of a Recorder)

Theory is clean. Life is messy.

In the previous chapters, we looked at the clean lines of history and the precise wiring of the brain. We talked about "Recorders" and "Runners" as if they were clearly labeled parts in an engine.

But when you are a child, you don't see labels. You don't know about neuro-architecture. You don't know that 30% of the population is wired for structural truth while the other 70% is wired for social flow.

All you know is that you are watching a movie that everyone else seems to understand, but the audio is slightly out of sync for you.

You see things they ignore. You hear contradictions they miss. You feel the structure of the room while they are just feeling the vibe.

I want to take you back to where my own recording began—not to write a memoir, but to show you what this cognitive split looks like in the real world.

It doesn't start in a doctor's office. It starts at the kitchen table. It starts on the street corner.

It starts in the quiet moments where a young Binary Mind realizes, for the first time: I am seeing a different world.

1. THE LABORATORY OF EAST BOSTON

I was born into a world that was loud, chaotic, and structurally perfect for observing human behavior.

I was the youngest of seven kids in an Italian-Irish family in East Boston.

My Dad, Arthur W. Caggiano Sr., was the boss for the IRS in the district.

My Mom, Dorothy Thornton, held the pack: Arthur Jr., Paul, Mary, Ann Susan (past), Ann Marie, Karen with Kevin, then me.

Most children slowly develop a sense of identity over time. Mine was handed to me early—not because of anything I had done, but because of the badge my father carried.

Some lives move quietly. Others are lived out loud.

Mine began on the front page of the East Boston Times on March 6, 1957—my first "front-page selfie moment," faster than any Kardashian—not because I was trying, but because I was Arthur Caggiano's kid.

"Boss for the IRS" wasn't a small title. It wasn't a quiet job. In a neighborhood like East Boston in the 1950s, that position carried weight. It was a specific kind of power that doesn't exist anymore—a mix of respect, fear, and curiosity.

From the moment I was conscious, I was observing a master class in the Six Professions.

My father was a classic Enforcer (in the cognitive sense). He held the code.

282 - *ROBERT ANTHONY CAGGIANO*

He collected taxes door-to-door, which is a job that usually makes you a pariah. But he did it with a strange, binary fairness. He returned kindness to people who didn't have any left to give.

Every Thanksgiving, our hallway overflowed with frozen turkeys and gift baskets from families he had helped.

Why?

Because an Enforcer mind is not cruel; it is just.

A Runner in that job might have played favorites based on who they liked. My father played by a code of service. He never spoke about it. He just executed it.

As a child, I watched this. I sat under his desk or behind him while he worked with relatives, neighbors, and friends. I was absorbing the data.

Input: Dad is powerful.

Input: People are afraid of the IRS.

Observation: People love Dad.

Conclusion: Power requires a code to be safe.

My childhood was fantastic. Relatively speaking, I identified with Michael Corleone from The Godfather and John Kennedy Jr., because they were the young, spoiled, fun ones in the family. The Godfather world was easy to relate to; there were plenty of old-school Italians around where I was raised in East Boston.

My father was the youngest in his large family. Born on the kitchen table on Pine Street in the North End of Boston on March 10, 1908. He wore the full-length coat with the hat and the best suits.

My godfather was Lou Musco, a well-to-do man with a stellar reputation. He was going to help get me into the Naval Academy in Indianapolis when I graduated high school if I wanted to go.

I wasn't good enough in my mind for service. I joke now how I knew then I did not want to be in the Guinness Book for "Longest Head Shot by a Sniper" seeing as I have a size 8 head.

2. EARLY CONSCIOUSNESS: DATA FROM DAY ONE

The most direct, irrefutable proof of the Binary Mind Inside (BMI™) architecture is the capacity for extreme, detailed sequential recall, especially from very early moments in life.

This ability is a feature of the Recorder—the deep burning-in of data during initial processing. I am a spokesperson for binary people, and I must share these accomplishments and memories to show the world what the BMI™ mind is truly capable of.

The ability to recall moments before the age of four, or even the moment of birth, is often dismissed as impossible by conventional wisdom.

For the Recorder, these are simply data streams logged with clarity.

I recall recalling my birth.

I recall the day my father took me off his lap for the last time—I wasn't four yet—and the complex emotional data attached to that final moment of infancy.

The Glitch in the Matrix: The "Butterball" Moment

We often assume that autistic or binary children are "in their own world." That is false. We are hyper-present in your world—we are just seeing the cracks you paper over.

I remember the exact moment my Recorder mind came online and flagged an error.

My father used to call me "butterball." It was affectionate. It was a dad joke. To a Runner mind (a neurotypical observer), it was just a warm, fuzzy family moment.

But I was a Recorder. I was sitting on his lap, and he said, "Oh, he's just too big now." And I saw it.

A tiny flicker in his micro-expressions. A millisecond delay between the smile and the eyes. The tone didn't mathematically match the affection.

I remember freezing internally.

- Audio Data: "He is joking/loving."
- Visual Data: "He is uncomfortable/jealous/distant."
- Result: ERROR. CONTRADICTION FOUND.

I remember thinking: Why say it that way? What am I seeing that no one else is reacting to?

Maybe my mother was giving me extra attention, and he was feeling displaced. Maybe he was tired. It doesn't matter what the cause was. What matters is that I saw the gap.

Most children do not record micro-expressions. Most kids ride the wave of the emotion. They trust the "vibe." But a Binary Mind trusts the Data. And when the data conflicts (Tone = Face), we don't just move on. We record it. We store it.

That moment wasn't trauma. It was architecture. It was my brain doing exactly what it was built to do: Detect Inconsistency.

If you are a parent reading this, and your child stares at you strangely when you are trying to be cheerful—stop and check yourself. Are you actually cheerful? Or are you pretending? Because your child isn't staring blankly. They are reading your micro-expressions and wondering why your face is lying to your voice.

These memories are not fuzzy impressions; they are high-resolution, sequentially logged events that define the context of my earliest life.

They are critical because they must tell parents how smart and aware their children are, and the profound harm that will continue if this awareness is ignored.

The good news is, these children are not broken.

3. THE PHYSICS OF THE PLAYGROUND

The Pimple Ball

I was five years old, going on six. I found a "pimple ball" in the gutter across the street. These were those small rubber balls from the 50s and 60s that kids usually cut in half to play stickball.

I picked it up, saw my brother Arthur standing on the porch, and I didn't just throw it to him. I sent it.

I whipped my arm. The ball flew across the street, curved perfectly around the porch post, and snapped right into his hands.

Arthur looked at the ball, then looked at me with total amazement. He threw it back.

I did it again. Same motion. Same whip. Same perfect strike right at his head. He caught it and looked at me like, "Wow."

That was the ignition point. I didn't just want to throw the ball. I wanted to master the arc.

We lived in East Boston, a neighborhood of three-story family homes. Most backyards were filled with tomato plants or grapevines. We got rid of the vegetation and turned the dirt into a workspace.

I took an old tire and leaned it against the chain-link fence. Then I went to the other side of the yard, built a little pitcher's mound, and went to work.

I experimented with the mechanics. One finger. Two fingers.

I learned that accuracy wasn't about staring at the target; it was about feeling the whip of the arm. If I focused on the mechanical snap of my elbow and wrist, the ball went exactly where the physics dictated it would go.

Over time, a game formed while I was playing. Two teams, Black and White. Black was strength. White was skill. I played full nine-inning games that way, each pitch counted.

Only later did the sound become the guide. The metal CLANG on the fence (a successful strike) versus the heavy THUD on the tire (a foul or miss).

This was pure binary feedback: SUCCESS (1) or FAILURE (0).

The Quarterback and the Oil Patch

By the time I was seven or eight, I graduated to a football. The older kids—teenagers—started letting me play. Not because they were being nice to the little kid, but because I was a weapon. I became the quarterback.

I didn't tell them, "Go long." That was too vague. I gave them coordinates.

"Go down 10 feet to that blue car. Take a hard right. Go straight toward the telephone pole. When you see the oil patch on the ground, turn around."

They would look at me, confused. I would tell them: "When you turn around, the ball is going to be there. Don't get scared."

This is the "Secret Sauce" of the Recorder. Observation = Emulation.

The ability of the Recorder to predict outcomes based on precise sequential inputs extends far beyond simple physical tasks; it allows for complex, real-time command structuring.

I ran the huddle exactly as I saw on TV, but the commands I gave were pure Recorder code.

I didn't rely on intuition or implicit understanding. The first few time after the older kids looked at me like, What?

When they ran the play, the ball arrived right on time, exactly where my predictive sequential mind had calculated the endpoint. They caught it and felt like heroes.

The point is this: who the heck taught me that? No one. That's a binary calculator mind.

This power is not intuition; it is the instantaneous compilation and execution of sequential logic in a dynamic environment, proving the high-functioning architecture of the BMI™.

The Physics of Aunt Florence (The 30-Second Swimmer)

It was the same with swimming. Most kids take lessons for months. They splash around while an instructor yells, "Kick, kick!" holding them up by their stomachs.

I didn't have time for that. I didn't want someone to touch me. I wanted to understand how the water worked.

I bought a 3-foot Styrofoam surfboard for 99 cents. I stood by the water and watched my Aunt Florence. I didn't just watch her swim; I studied her chassis.

I saw that she wasn't fighting the water; she was using it as a fulcrum. I watched her twist. I saw how she torqued her body to the water. She didn't slap at the surface; she reached out, grabbed the water, and pulled it past her body.

Input received.

I took my cheap board into the water. I isolated the variable. One arm at a time.

Reach. Twist. Pull.

Reach. Twist. Pull.

I figured out the torque. I figured out the resistance.

It took me exactly 30 seconds. I threw the board away and I swam.

The Altar Boy with the Gin (The Recruit)

To understand why I was the one who figured this out, you have to look at the wiring. And the best way to show you my wiring is to take you back to St. Lazarus Church when I was ten years old.

The church held a retreat for the local boys. The goal was simple: They were scouting for future priests. They wanted to see which of us had "The Calling."

Now, you have to understand the context. I was an East Boston kid. I had my first glass of homemade wine at an Italian funeral when I was five. I smoked my first cigar and cigarette in the third grade. Life moved fast where I was from.

So, when I packed my bag for this holy retreat, I didn't just pack a toothbrush. I packed a half-carton of cigarettes (six packs, rolled up tight) and a half-fifth of gin.

I was a ten-year-old walking into the House of God looking like a bootlegger.

The weekend goes by. We do the prayers, we read the scriptures, we sit in the silence.

At the end of the retreat, the priests sit us down to announce who they think has the potential to join the cloth. I'm sitting there, literally hiding a felony amount of tobacco in my bag, waiting to be sent home.

And the priest points to me.

"Robert," he says. "He is the one."

They didn't pick me because I was a "good boy." (Clearly, they didn't check my luggage).

They picked me because I Understood the Writings.

While the other kids were bored or confused by the scripture, I was locked in. I could articulate the story. I could see the structure. Recorders love Scripture because Scripture is Code. It is Binary.

Sin and Salvation. Truth and Lies. Alpha and Omega.

My brain ignored the social awkwardness of the retreat and locked straight onto the data.

I didn't become a priest. But that moment at St. Lazarus explains everything. I was the kid with the gin in his pocket and the Truth in his mouth. I was the rebellion and the structure wrapped in one skin.

And fifty years later, when I found "The Event," it was that same brain—the one that ignores the rules but reads the code—that was able to solve the puzzle.

4. THE GENETIC BASELINE

My father provided the operating system—the logic, the discipline, the "All Debts Are Paid" philosophy.

But people often ask where the Size came from. Where did Arthur get the strength to bench press a Buick? Where did Paul get the lungs to run forever?

They got it from the girl from Charlestown.

My father was 38 when he married her. She was 21. He was a man who planned everything, and he knew he wanted to raise a strong family. So he found a woman who could hold her own.

I met a man once who asked if I was her son. When I said yes, he laughed and said, "Your mother? She played baseball with us. And let me tell you—she was a long-ball hitter. She could hit that ball way over the fence."

That is the genetic baseline. We got the Mind from the Accountant. We got the Power from the Long-Ball Hitter.

The Movie Star and The Patient

If you look at their wedding portrait, you see the perfect American couple. My mother, at 21, looked like a movie star. She was a stunner—Irish-English beauty, hair perfectly done, radiating class. She looks like she's ready for the red carpet.

My father, at 38, looks like the dashing Coast Guard officer. Handsome, stoic, ready for duty.

But the camera lies.

The truth is, my father hated boats.

And that "stoic" look? That was him holding it together. He was actually a patient in the hospital the night before the photo was taken. He had checked himself in for "nerves"—the Recorder mind going into overdrive.

He literally checked out of the hospital, put on his dress uniform, went to the church, married the most beautiful woman in Charlestown, smiled for the photo... and then went right back to the hospital and put his pajamas back on.

She was the Movie Star. He was the Hypochondriac Hero. And somehow, it worked.

The Service Contract: "I'll Have the Eggplant"

There is a narrative today that parents of autistic or high-energy kids are "exhausted." They act like the child is luggage handcuffed to their wrist—a heavy weight they have to drag through life. They love them, sure, but they are tired.

I look back at my mother, and I don't see luggage. I see a woman who ran a logistics empire for seven children and never once looked at the clock.

People talk about "spoiled." I lived with my mother for twenty-three years. For those twenty-three years, I didn't just eat what was made. I ordered my food.

I didn't walk into the kitchen and ask, "What's for dinner?" I walked in and said, "I'll have the eggplant tonight." Or, "You know, I could really go for a steak."

And she didn't just cook it. She engineered it. Even when I was twenty years old, she would put the steak in front of me, already cut up into bite-sized pieces, and covered in beans. She removed the friction of eating so I could just refuel.

The Snow in the Dark (Age 22)

The true measure of her strength wasn't in the kitchen; it was in the driveway.

When I started working at EDS, I was twenty-two years old. In Boston winters, the morning was dark, cold, and buried.

I would wake up to hear a scraping sound outside.

My mother—a woman in her late 50s at this point—would be out there in the pitch black. She wouldn't just shovel a path. She would shovel out two cars' worth of snow. She would dig out the heavy, icy plow-drift behind my car. She would clean the windshield. She would start the engine so it was warm when I got in.

Inside the house, the logistics were just as precise. I would get out of the shower, and my suit would be laid out on the bed, waiting for me. Breakfast was ready. Lunch was packed in a bag "just in case" I needed it.

She cleared the snow, she prepped the uniform, and she fueled the engine. All I had to do was show up and work.

The Glamour (The Early Years)

But I also remember the earlier days, when we were young, living in East Boston before the move to Melrose. Back then, before the snow shoveling years, she was the Movie Star.

Every single day, before my father Arthur came home from the IRS, the house changed. She would get dressed. Hair done perfectly. Makeup on. She treated his arrival like an event. She was ready for the "Boss" to come home.

She was the Long-Ball Hitter, but she played different positions depending on the season of our lives. When we were young, she was the star. When I was starting my career, she was the pit crew.

But in every phase, she made sure the Caggianos never missed a step.

The Last Instruction (No Breadcrumbs)

There is a philosophy to being a Recorder, and my mother taught it to me in the kitchen. It's the Eggplant Rule.

Most people rush. They salt the eggplant to force the water out fast. They use breadcrumbs because it's easy.

But my mother knew better.

The Prep:

You cut it into slices the night before. You let it dry on paper towels.

"You prepare a little today for tomorrow."

You don't force the starch out; you let it leave naturally.

The Batter: Egg and flour. Never breadcrumbs.

Her logic was flawless, and it applies to life as much as cooking: "Why ruin the sauce with the seasoning in the breadcrumbs? The sauce is already perfect."

If you have done the work to make the sauce right (the Foundation), don't add noise (the Breadcrumbs) that clashes with it. Keep the data clean.

That was the last clear thing she ever said to me the night before her major stroke, My Mom had me promise never let anyone convince me to put breadcrumbs on the eggplant.

I promised.

The Psychotic Episode (The Medical Glitch)

The next day, she had a stroke.

But look at how the system labeled it. I got a call: "Your mother had a psychotic episode. She flipped out."

My Recorder brain instantly rejected that data. "My mother? Jesus Christ could walk through the door and she would just ask him what took him so long. She doesn't 'flip out'."

The doctors saw "Behavior" (Psychosis). I knew the "Hardware" (Stroke).

The System Reboot (The Hospital Room)

I flew back to Boston on pure adrenaline. Twelve hours from the phone call to the hospital door.

I walked into the room, and it felt like a stage. The doctors, the nurses, the family—they were all standing around the bed like spectators at a car crash. They were looking at the monitors. They were looking at the "Psychotic Episode."

I didn't look at the monitors. I looked at the woman.

She was mumbling. Just a stream of static. A loop of confusion.

The doctors stepped back as I walked through them. They had given up; they were just managing the chaos.

I sat on the edge of the bed and took her hand. It was the only thing in that sterile room that felt real. I squeezed it, anchoring her.

Then I leaned in. Not just to her face—to her ear. I needed to bypass the room. I needed to bypass the stroke. I needed a direct line to the processor.

"Ma," I whispered. "It's Robert."

She stopped mumbling for a second. She turned her head, but her eyes were looking through me, not at me.

"No," she muttered. "No, no, no. It's not Robert."

I squeezed her hand harder. "Yes, Ma. It is Robert."

She shook her head, fighting the fog. "No," she said, her voice sounding like a little girl. "Robert is my good boy."

That broke me, but it also focused me.

Even in the middle of a stroke, even in the "psychosis," her definition of me was pure. I was the Good Boy. I was the Anchor.

I leaned closer, my voice steady, cutting through the noise of the machines.

"I am right here, Ma. Robert is right here."

And then—The Snap.

It wasn't a slow drift. It was a Reboot. Her eyes stopped wandering and locked onto mine. The grey fog in her pupils vanished, and the brown came back. The "Psychosis" evaporated in a single second.

She squeezed my hand back. "Robert," she said. Clear as a bell. "What took you so long?"

The doctors were stunned. They were writing "Psychotic Break" on a clipboard, and I had just proven it was a TIA (a mini-stroke) with two sentences.

They were treating the software. I knew how to touch the hardware.

5. KEVIN: THE GRAVITY OF TRUTH

And then, there was Kevin.

If my father was the Enforcer, Kevin was the Truth Anchor.

Kevin wasn't just my brother; he was the gravitational center of my universe. Not in a sentimental way — in a gravitational way. An intense, brilliant, unique force who shaped my world before I even knew what "world" meant.

We grew up in a house where all seven kids slept in three small bedrooms, with sheets hung from wires to create the illusion of privacy. Those makeshift walls meant nothing to Kevin. He lived big, loud, curious, full of ideas. And I slept right beside him.

He showed me the world long before I was supposed to see it.

While most kids were learning nursery rhymes, Kevin was teaching me: where babies really come from, that Santa Claus wasn't real, and that we should go up to the attic and unwrap the "gifts from Santa" early, check what we were getting, then wrap them back up again.

He was four. I was three going on four. We had no business knowing any of that — but Kevin didn't believe in holding information back. If he knew something, I knew it.

My world wasn't shaped by school or books or the neighborhood. My world was shaped by Kevin.

He bought monster model kits — the old Aurora classics.

Frankenstein with the bolted neck. Dracula in his cape. The Wolf Man mid-transform. The Creature from the Black Lagoon with those gills and claws. The Bride of Frankenstein with her hair streaked like lightning.

He built them with precision, piece by piece, painting the faces, the shadows, the stitches.

A kid my age should've been terrified. But I wasn't.

Right next to his monster models, I had stuffed animals from Easter baskets — soft, bright-colored, innocent. Rabbits, bears, little plush toys.

And there I was at three or four years old, lying in that room divided by sheets, looking around thinking: No one would believe my bedroom.

Half monsters, half stuffed animals. Half childhood, half something much older. Two worlds colliding before I even knew what worlds were.

Most kids grow in stages — innocence first, reality later. I got both at the same time. Kevin didn't protect me from the world. He introduced me to it. Not in a harsh way — in a way that said, "This is life. Don't be afraid of it."

There was no childhood illusion in the bed we shared. Kevin replaced illusion with reality, and reality with curiosity.

He had a habit every night: before falling asleep, he would rock back and forth for fifteen or twenty minutes — like he was recalibrating his mind, preparing it for sleep. I'd lie next to him, quietly watching, taking it in, not knowing until decades later how much that rhythm shaped me.

The Artist

His talent was obvious from the start. He could draw with no practice. Not "good for a kid." He was incredible.

I remember one night vividly: we were sitting between the beds in that small room divided by sheets. Kevin opened a comic book, picked a character — Nomad — and on his first try, he drew it perfectly.

Then he held it up and said, "What do you think?"

And all I could say was the truth: "Kevin... you know how to draw."

It wasn't a compliment. It was recognition. After Nomad came a wave of superheroes—perfect, confident strokes, like he was tracing what already existed in his mind. He went to art school at twelve or thirteen.

The Singer

And the kid could sing. By age six, he had a family theme song: "My Way."

Every gathering, he sang it. It became his signature—a child doing Sinatra with a straight face while adults tried not to laugh or cry.

He was a ladies' man early. He had his first true love, Denise, and even after they weren't together, he stayed faithful to her in his heart. Kevin didn't love halfway.

He saved my life when he was six.

I was walking to second grade and made the kind of mistake a young kid makes—running through traffic to beat a light, not seeing the last lane where a car was coming fast. Kevin saw it. He ran. And at the very last second, he pushed me out of the path of the full hit. We both got clipped, but not the way I would have.

He was six. That moment—like everything with Kevin—went straight into my wiring. He protected me instinctively, instantly, without thinking. Like breathing.

He met John Wayne. When Kevin was older, he bartended at the Newporter Inn. John Wayne used to come in. Kevin told me Wayne was responsible for the cows around Orange County at the time and how he was the first person to sign the petition against the airport being built. Funny how they named the airport after him anyway.

The Bookends

When I look at Kevin's life, I don't see a blur of years. I see two specific days. Two specific clubs. Two moments where a Recorder tried to organize a world that refused to follow the rules.

The First Bookend: Revere, Massachusetts.

It was the year the drinking age dropped to eighteen. Kevin had just hit the number. I was only sixteen and a half.

For Kevin, this wasn't just a birthday; it was a classification. The law said he was a Man. The data was clear.

He marched down to the local strip club in Revere with the absolute certainty of someone who has the paperwork to prove they belong. He walked in, scanned the dark, smoky room, and looked for a table.

And then his system crashed.

I was already there. I was sitting at a table with my friends, drink in hand, looking like I'd been paying rent there for years.

Kevin didn't just get mad. He got confused. It was a syntax error. This does not compute.

He walked straight up to the cocktail waitress. He wasn't yelling out of emotion; he was pointing out a factual inaccuracy.

"Hey! You see him? He can't be in here!"

The waitress looked at me. I sat there, calm, holding my glass.

Kevin tapped his chest, presenting his evidence. "I'm eighteen! I'm the one who's legal! He's sixteen! You need to kick him out!"

Technically, he was right. But the waitress looked at Kevin—sweating, frantic about the rules. Then she looked back at me—quiet, settled, observing.

She turned to Kevin and snapped, "Get out of here. Leave your older brother alone."

She walked away. Kevin stood there, stunned. He had followed every rule, and the world still told him he was wrong.

The Second Bookend: Florida.

Years later, the scene repeated, but the setting had changed. We were in Florida now. The humidity was thick. The Golden Boy was fading, but his mind was still recording, still analyzing.

The Ultimate Test: The Balcony

The true test of the Binary Mind comes when the stakes are life and death.

Runners are great at comforting people with platitudes. But when reality breaks, platitudes are useless. When the diagnosis is terminal, or the tragedy is real, the Runner runs out of scripts.

The Recorder steps in.

The day Kevin found out he was terminal, the world shifted. I wasn't there for the diagnosis, but I was there for the crisis. He stood on a tenth-floor balcony. He was threatening to jump.

If I had been a Runner, I might have panicked. I might have screamed, "Don't do it!"

But those would have been lies. My Binary Mind took over. It dropped into High-Stakes Clarity.

I didn't scream. I didn't add drama. I simply projected the logical consequence of his action.

I said: "Think of what I would see if you fell. I'd have to go down there, hold you, and cry. So why don't you just come back in? And if you still want to go back out, I'll help you. But come talk to me first."

Look at the structure of that argument.

Fact: If you jump, I have to witness the trauma.

Logic: That is a terrible outcome for me, and you love me.

Offer: I am not removing your autonomy. If you want to jump later, you can. (Validating his control).

Request: Just process data with me first.

It worked. He came back inside. He sat down and said the three words that changed everything: "I'm terminal — that's all."

We didn't cry hysterically. We didn't pretend. We talked. He promised to look into all options and we were able to relax.

The Diagnosis and The Drive

A couple of weeks later, Paul called me at my office in Santa Monica—the Lotus office—and told me Kevin had AIDS. It was the hardest sixty-mile drive home in my life.

Around the same time Magic Johnson announced he was HIV positive, I flew to Florida to see Kevin. He had lost a lot of weight. He was letting the disease take him. The light was still in his eyes, but dimmer.

I said, "Let's go enjoy the day." We rented a boat in Pompano Beach. I took the wheel and asked him if he wanted to drive. He said no — too fragile. I said, "Well I hate driving," and stepped away from the wheel.

He shot up: "Are you crazy?" and grabbed it. He drove for four hours, loving every second of it.

The Adult Bar: "I'll Take This Day"

We stopped at an adult bar. He tipped a dancer, she wrapped her boobs around his face for a second—playful, quick—and he stepped back, smiling wide, clapping his hands once, and said:

"Okay... I'll take this day."

We left, and he told me there was more to say. He didn't want to die the way he'd seen others die. He told me he didn't want to end up like a girl in the hospital—infected by a dentist—lying in a coma, unable to speak, trapped in her own body. He told me exactly what she would say if she could: "Kill me, you people. I don't want to lay here."

He had been studying Dr. Kevorkian's book. He said the bottle on the table had enough to put him into a coma, and that afterward I would need to insert two morphine suppositories to push him over the edge. He said that's how they killed Marilyn Monroe.

He said it calmly. Honestly. Like he had thought it all the way through.

I said, "Wait... you're serious?"

And without hesitation he said, "Of course," and explained why.

At that time, people didn't fully understand AIDS. There was fear around touching, hugging—and Kevin knew that fear would isolate him in a way he could not bear. Not just about sex. About being human with others. I told him that wasn't necessarily how it ends—that science could change. He said, "So don't touch anyone... for how long? No way."

I stepped out and called Arthur and Paul. They already knew. Arthur said, "Yes, he wants me to come down with my .38, but I can't get there for a bit." Paul said, "Yeah, I know — he wants out."

It felt like a group consensus, a grim understanding. I went back in and asked Kevin if he really wanted me to answer for his death when the police show up?

We roared laughing in the darkest moments in the honest way brothers do.

The Final Lesson: The Good News

The last time I saw him, he was in hospice—a bottom-floor room where the sunlight came through at an angle and lit the green and blue cards on the shelf.

He weighed 78 pounds. The same person who once stood at 230 pounds of pure muscle.

I sat beside him, holding his hands, crying. I was the one falling apart.

He looked at me—clear, present, totally stabilized.

He said: "Robert, you don't get it. You can't see the good news. I won't have to see you die. Please know that I love you. I could never bear seeing you die."

I'm crying now writing this.

Because in that moment, he used the Ultimate Recorder Logic. He took the worst possible thing—his own death—and he found the one good thing in it. He found the single variable that made it a mercy for me.

And I am telling you this because a mind like that—a mind that can find the light in the absolute dark—should not go wasted. Do not let Kevin's life — his beauty, his intensity, his curiosity, his fearlessness — be wasted. Hug Away!

51

Because for those who don't believe in the heart's

6. PAUL: THE ENGINE OF FLOW
     Paul had a way of finding the positive — not in some forced or phony way, but in a way that made you believe it too. If you came to him looking for advice, he'd listen, smile, and remind you that things would work out.

He had a way of giving you hope — the kind that stayed with you long after the conversation ended.

Tire Tubes and The Jet

We had endless tire tubes from my uncle's tire shop in the North End of Boston. One day, Paul a fifteen year old grabs a couple and said, "Let's go for an adventure." I'm five but he knew I could swim.

So there we were — him leading, me paddling behind — floating across the harbor toward Logan Airport.

The water slapped the rubber tubes, and all I could think was, I hope he knows what he's doing.

When we reached the other side, Paul looked around like he'd just discovered a new country. Then he grinned. "Hey, let's run on the tarmac for fun."

So we did. Two kids darting across the runway like it was our backyard.

A fighter jet rolled into position — canopy down, engines rumbling.

Paul stopped, waved. The pilot saw him. And then, unbelievably, the canopy lifted. The pilot looked right at us and waved back.

How high on the Marvel superhero scale was Paul in my five-year-old eyes at that moment?

12 Angry Pauls

Paul's ability to "run" a room wasn't just for fun. Sometimes, he used it to save people.

He got called for jury duty once. Most people try to get out of it; Paul saw it as an audience. He walked in, saw the other jurors, and decided to see if he could pull a 12 Angry Men.

The case involved a high school kid who had taken his parents' Ford Thunderbird, got drunk at a party, and slammed it into a house. The insurance company was suing the parents for damages. It looked like an open-and-shut case. The kid was guilty.

But when they got to the deliberation room, Paul didn't sit back. He stood up.

He asked a simple question: "Just out of curiosity... did anyone actually see him get out of the car?"

The other jurors rolled their eyes. "No," they said, "but it had to be him. Witnesses saw the red high school sweater driving away."

Paul smiled. He was working the angles.

"Okay. But we'll see the other one, right?"

"The other what?"

"The other kid in a red sweater."

The room got quiet. Paul kept pushing. "Look, the testimony said this kid was falling-down drunk. Bouncing off the walls. If he was that drunk, could he have even found the keys? Or was he drunk enough that someone could have taken the keys from him?"

The jurors started to argue. "But he was all banged up! He had cuts on his face!"

Paul nodded, seizing on the detail. "Exactly. He was banged up. But if he was falling-down drunk at a party... couldn't he have fallen down the stairs? Couldn't he have banged his head on a railing?"

He planted the seed of doubt. He took a room full of people con-vinced of guilt and, using nothing but charm and "what-if" logic, he turned the tide. He got the kid off. The parents didn't have to pay a dime. The insurance company had to eat the loss.

Paul walked out of the courthouse laughing. He had just socially en-gineered a verdict because he could.

The Gag — How People Are

That moment never really ended. It just evolved. As we grew up, it turned into this thing we called the gag. Not a trick, not a scam — more of an observation.

The gag was that no matter the circumstance, people are human. When they saw Paul and me, they were disarmed. Neutralized. It's like their mind went into a calm middle gear and said, "They belong here."

We'd walk into places like we worked there, or like we were supposed to be there — never sneaky, just familiar. It was confidence without ar-rogance. We'd look at people the way you look at a neighbor — that half-recognition that makes them think, "Oh, he must be with so-and-so."

And it worked. Over and over again.

The Super Bowl Party

One year, Hugh Hefner hosted his famous Playboy Super Bowl party in Jacksonville, Florida. Paul and a friend had sailed a ninety-foot boat up from Fort Lauderdale and docked right in front — the best spot in the marina. The friend had one ticket. Paul made a copy. There were three scans total, and sure enough, one of them caught. But by then, Paul was already watching the red carpet being rolled out and thought, Why not?

He adjusted his jacket and walked right in.

Hours later — 12:30 a.m. California time — my phone rang. It was Paul, laughing.

"I'm in the middle of the dance floor — surrounded by Playboy bun-nies."

That was Paul. And that was our gag — not pretending, not lying — just carrying ourselves like we belonged everywhere. And somehow, everywhere agreed.

The Chateau Marmont

Years later, we checked into the Chateau Marmont in Beverly Hills. The clerk apologized for not having Paul's room ready and said they'd upgraded us to the penthouse suite. Then he added, "The restaurant is closed tonight — Playboy has it reserved for a private party."

Paul looked at me, that grin creeping across his face. He didn't have to say a word. That grin meant invitation accepted.

The courtyard was alive — stars, executives, producers, and Hefner himself surrounded by six Playmates. At the center sat a white leather couch, roped off like it was on display.

Paul pointed. "That works," he said, and stepped right around the rope. We sat down.

A waitress came over, clearly ready to say something — probably "this area's reserved." Paul didn't let her get there. He smiled, ordered a drink, then looked at me.

"What are you having?"

She jotted it down and walked off. And just like that, we were in the center of the party. Even Hef's table looked over.

The Scarfed Manager

Not long after, a man walked up — perfectly dressed, scarf draped just so, beard trimmed sharp. He stopped in front of us.

"I'm Johnny Depp's manager," he said, like he was announcing a royal title. "Who are you?"

Paul smiled. "I'm Paul Caggiano. We produce a few small projects."

I added, "Yeah, I'm with him."

The man squinted. "Sorry, what was that again?"

Paul leaned toward me, voice low. "He didn't just ask me that again, did he? Because if he did, tell him that scarf looks about the right size to wrap around his head twice."

I bit my cheek, trying not to laugh. "Small films," I told the man. "We produce small films."

He gave a nod and walked off.

The Waitress Returns

A few minutes later, the waitress came back. She leaned in and whispered, "When Johnny shows up... will you let him sit here?"

Paul smiled, took her hand gently. "Of course. Don't worry."

Then turned to me and grinned. "We don't want to get the poor girl fired."

The Director Ruse

I went to the men's room — two minutes, maybe. When I came back, Paul was at the bar, surrounded by a small group hanging on every word.

As I got closer, I heard him say, "Well, when we talk about somebody important, do I have to...?"

He stopped mid-sentence, opened his hand toward me like he'd been waiting for his cue. Everyone turned to look. In that short time, Paul had convinced them I was the director of The Rum Diary.

I walked up clueless, and they started thanking me for my "speech" earlier at the premiere.

Paul nodded calmly. "He's always intentional with his words."

I barely kept it together. Those people went home convinced they'd met the director.

Cameos and Confusions

The illusion spread. Michael Rispoli walked by and gave me a knowing nod.

Then Marilyn Manson drifted through the crowd — pale, slow, scanning the room. But he wasn't looking at me. He was watching Paul. You could see it in his face — that flicker like he was thinking, Did I ever play with this guy?

Even Marilyn Manson got caught in Paul's gravity.

Aaron Eckhart

A little later, Aaron Eckhart came over. He greeted Paul first, handshake and smile — no pretense, no Hollywood act. They talked for a while — easy, like cousins at a cookout. Family. Kids. Life.

Then Aaron tilted his head, curious who Paul really was.

Paul leaned in and said, "Come on, isn't our biggest worry always our kids? Don't you hope they can be as successful as you and I?"

Aaron laughed — the real kind — and nodded. He knew it was a game but didn't want to end it. When he finally stepped away, Paul and I looked at each other and broke — laughing so hard we had to hold our sides.

Johnny Depp

Then Johnny himself arrived — three bodyguards clearing the way.

Paul didn't pause. He walked right up, shook Depp's hand. I followed, hand on Johnny's shoulder, and said, "You've always been one of my favorite actors."

He nodded, smiled, and vanished just as fast.

I turned to Paul. "That was cool."

Looked back — no Johnny, no guards.

"Do you think three bodyguards are getting fired right now?"

We lost it again — laughing in the middle of Hefner's party like kids at Logan all over again.

Reflection

From the tarmac to the red carpet, Paul never changed. He could walk into any room, any world, and somehow — everyone believed he belonged. He didn't do it for attention or ego. He did it because he saw people. And people, when they saw him, saw something familiar in return.

The Cruelest Irony

Paul passed away on September 25th, 2025. He was taken by Bulbar ALS, a wretched disease that attacks the muscles used for speaking and swallowing first.

And in that loss lies a sadness so deep it feels like a mistake in the universe's design.

For years, whenever the topic of death or aging came up, Paul had a standard line. He'd say, "Hey, just put me in the corner. If I can just sit there, see my family, and talk, I'll be happy."

That was his deal with fate. He didn't need to run on tarmacs anymore; he just wanted to hold court.

But the disease denied him that one specific mercy.

I spent several quiet days sitting with him toward the end. He would mumble or text on a screen, frustrated by the trap his body had become. The man who could charm a pilot out of a fighter jet was now fighting just to be heard.

During those quiet days, I shared something personal with him. I told him about my discovery regarding the mind—about the Binary Mind, about where I fit on the spectrum of autism. I was trying to explain why I am the way I am.

Paul looked at me. He didn't skip a beat. He didn't ask for charts or proofs. He managed to communicate a simple truth:

"Robert, you were always different."

He didn't mean it as a criticism. He said it in that good way—the Paul way. He meant that I was me, and to him, that was exactly who I was supposed to be.

He lost his voice, but right up until the end, he knew exactly what to say.

7. ARTHUR: THE TITAN

My brother Arthur was the Gold standard. Everyone in East Boston was measured against him.

The Punch: The Lesson

I was in second grade. I had just gotten my first pair of glasses. Arthur was eleven years older than me—about eighteen or nineteen at the time. He was already the Titan. He decided it was time to teach his little brother how to fight.

He stood me up in the yard.

"Robert," he said, "don't aim for the face. Aim for the back of the head but go through the front of the face first. You punch through the face."

He told me to put my hands up. "Let me see if you can catch my hand," he said.

He threw a punch. It was supposed to be a demonstration, a "pull-back" strike to test my reflexes. But Arthur didn't have a "light" setting. He miscalculated the distance—or the speed—and he hit me square in the face.

CRACK. My brand-new glasses shattered. The force knocked me back.

Arthur froze. His eyes went wide. The Protector had just broken his little brother.

"Oh my god," he said, reaching out. "Robert, I'm sorry! Are you okay?"

I stood there, feeling the sting, checking for blood. I looked at him—this giant of a man, this Luca Brasi of our neighborhood—looking terrified because he thought he hurt me.

I started to giggle. I looked at him and smiled. "I just took one of your best punches. No big deal."

He stared at me. I wasn't crying. I wasn't running to Mom. I was laughing.

I never flinched after that. Not with him, not with anyone. I realized that if I could take a shot from the Titan and laugh about it, the rest of the world couldn't hurt me.

Arthur rose to the rank of Major in the Army. He could have been a General—he had the mind for it—but he refused to play the political game. He didn't want to kiss the rings required to get a star on his shoulder. He preferred the company of the enlisted men. He respected grit over rank.

One night in the mess hall, the talk turned to strength. There was a lineman there—a monster of a man who had been a first-round NFL draft pick before getting called up. He was a professional athlete in his prime.

The guys were ribbing Arthur. "It's too late now, Major. You're not the big man on campus anymore. This guy is the real deal."

Arthur didn't say a word. He just cleared off a table in the center of the room. The NFL lineman sat down, confident. Arthur sat opposite him.

They locked right hands.

Arthur told me later, "Robert, I knew this guy was strong. I knew I couldn't beat him on a burst. So I decided I wasn't going to try to beat him. I was just going to break him."

Arthur used a technique he called "The Lock." He didn't push back; he just solidified his arm like a steel beam.

They sat there for twenty-five minutes. Muscles trembling, sweat pouring down the lineman's face. Arthur just stared at him, holding the line with his right arm. He waited until the lineman's energy bar hit zero.

Then, slowly, Arthur pushed his hand down. Thud.

The room went silent. The lineman couldn't believe it. "No way," the guy said. "No way. Do it again."

Arthur smiled. "Okay."

They locked up again. Same hands. This time, Arthur didn't wait twenty-five minutes. He waited ten. Thud.

The lineman was losing his mind. He was humiliated. He slammed the table.

"Okay!" the lineman yelled. "LEFT HAND! Let's go left!"

He thought maybe Arthur was just right-side dominant. He thought he found a weakness.

Arthur didn't say a word. He didn't warn him. He didn't smile and say, "Buddy, you don't want to do that." He just put his left elbow on the table.

They locked up. Bam. Ten seconds... Arthur slammed the guy's hand through the table.

The lineman sat there, stunned. He didn't realize what had just happened. He had just demanded that a natural-born Lefty switch to his dominant hand. Arthur hadn't said a thing to buy himself an out. He beat the guy twice with his weak arm, and when the guy asked for the left, Arthur just gave him the good news.

The Secret

For years, I looked at Arthur and wondered how the strongest man I knew—the man who beat an NFL lineman with his weak arm—could let himself waste away in a hospital bed. I sat with him during his last five days. The Titan was yellow with jaundice. The muscles were gone.

I finally asked him. I had to know.

"Arthur," I said, "what was the deal? What started this? You were the Gold Standard. What made you start drinking like that?"

He looked at the ceiling. He was quiet for a long time. Then, he told me the secret he had been carrying.

"I was alone at night," he whispered. "I heard someone coming at me. I panicked, Robert. I just reacted. I shot."

He paused, his breathing shallow. "It turned out to be the bad guy," he said. "I got the right guy. But I shot before I knew. I pulled the trigger out of fear, not out of command."

That was the fracture. The world gave him a medal, but his own mind gave him a life sentence. He knew that for one split second, the Titan had flinched.

"It tore me up," he said. "I couldn't shut it off. So I started with a case of beer. Then that wasn't enough to make it quiet, so I switched to hard liquor. And then I just kept going."

I sat there and held his hand. I finally understood. The alcohol wasn't a party. It was anesthesia. He had been trying to silence that one moment of panic for decades.

8. COUSIN JOE: THE KING OF HUMOR

I didn't have to look far to see the other neurotypes in action.

If my father was the Enforcer of law, my cousin Joe Caggiano was the Enforcer of the room.

312 - ROBERT ANTHONY CAGGIANO

Joe was a presence. A big man, a captain in the South Boston Police Department, and the funniest human being ever to never set foot in show business. He was the ultimate Connector/Enforcer hybrid. He knew every joke known to mankind—Henny Youngman, Milton Berle, every classic—but he never told them straight. Joe tweaked every punchline so it fit the person he was talking to, the moment he was in, or the family member standing closest. He didn't recycle humor. He personalized it. That's what made him dangerous and brilliant.

But it was when he worked the streets as a cop that I saw the "Recorder" genius in action. His humor was a tool, a weapon, a performance—all rolled into one. I watched him and learned: Humor is a system hack. It breaks the logic loop of anger. I wasn't just laughing; I was filing that away. If you can make the threat funny, you remove the danger without removing the power. He was the Master of Tone.

I remember watching him roll up on a domestic disturbance call. The other cops would be tense, hands on their holsters. Joe would just pick up the bullhorn. He wouldn't scream orders. He wouldn't threaten to kick the door down. He would just lean into the microphone like he was ordering a sandwich.

"It's Joe. Joe Caggiano. I need you to come out and make it easy on everybody."

Then, he would drop the leverage.

"You know the Caggianos. We run the ambulance service that picks up your parents when they get sick. I'd hate to see that ambulance get stuck in traffic on the way to the hospital."

He'd let that hang in the air for a second. Then he'd drop the hammer.

"And you know my dad has the funeral home over in Winthrop. Honestly, it's just as easy for us to bring them there. We actually make more money driving to the funeral home than the hospital. So, what's it gonna be?"

Five minutes later, the guy would walk out, hands up. As Joe was handcuffing him, he'd look over at the crowd of neighbors watching and wink.

"I could have told him we had the place surrounded and he had nowhere to go... but where's the fun in that?"

The Pirate's Chest

Joe was also the reason I learned ballistics before I learned long division. My brothers and I didn't have much money, so we didn't have store-bought toys. But we had Cousin Joe's cellar.

He had a massive chest down there—like a pirate's booty case—filled with confiscated street weapons. When we wanted to play Cops and Robbers, Joe would open the chest. "Go ahead," he'd say. "I took the firing pins out."

He didn't just let us play with them in the basement. He gave them to us. He handed out switchblades, derringers, snub-nose revolvers, and shotguns like they were party favors. We took them home.

At six years old, I had my own arsenal. We ran the streets of the neighborhood playing war with real evidence. I carried a real handgun tucked into my belt. I learned things a kindergartner shouldn't know. By the time I was six, I knew how to throw a switchblade underhand and stick it into a piece of wood from 10 feet away. I was deadly accurate.

To the outside world, it was insanity. To us, it was just Tuesday. Joe taught me that authority isn't about being the loudest guy in the room. And he taught me that the difference between a toy and a weapon is just a firing pin.

The Bouncer Gene

It shouldn't be a surprise that my brothers and I all worked the door at some point. We were Bouncers. It is the ultimate Sentinel job. You stand at the threshold. You scan the room. You look for the glitch in the matrix—the drunk, the aggressor, the static—and you remove it so the music can keep playing.

The Classroom (Château de Ville)

My first job was at the Château de Ville in Saugus. I was just a senior in high school, working an adult club filled with people in their 30s, 40s, and 50s. It was the era of the giants.

Don Rickles played the main ballroom. I remember standing behind the curtain, watching the master work. He called everyone a "hockey puck." He saw a guy who wasn't laughing, and then he saw another bald guy sitting next to him. Rickles didn't miss a beat:

"Why don't you move over to the side? If you two bald guys sit beside each other, you'll make a perfect ass of yourselves."

The room exploded. Rickles was a Reader. He read the room instantly.

The Lesson (The Look of Inevitability)

My boss was a guy named Joe. He looked like Cary Grant but was built like a boxer. He taught me the secret of the Sentinel. It wasn't about throwing a punch; it was about Physics.

He told me: "Robert, when you come up against a guy giving you a hard time, stay tall. Look him in the eye. Show him the Intent."

"Show him that it is inevitable. You are going to pound him. You are going to end him. Simple as that."

That is the Recorder Stare. It isn't anger. It is certainty. When you look at someone with zero doubt in your eyes, they feel the wall. They usually back down because they realize the outcome has already been decided.

The Reality Check (The 43-Year-Old)

One night, a guy was getting loud. Too much to drink. Belligerent. I had to escort him to the bathroom. I stood right next to him at the urinal—no privacy when you're a threat level.

He starts crying. He starts confessing. "You don't understand," he says. "I'm 43 years old. My life is over. I screwed up. It's all over."

I was a high school kid. To me, 43 seemed ancient. But I didn't become his therapist. I stayed in the role. I told him:

"I don't know what's going on in your life. But I know your time here at the Château is over. And if you don't leave with me right now, your night is gonna be over."

The Loop vs. The Task

Looking back, that story is tragic and funny. He was spinning a loop about his "life being over" at 43 (which is young!). I was just executing a Task: Remove Static. I walked him out. I closed the loop for him because he couldn't close it himself.

9. THE NOISE OUTSIDE AND THE QUIET INSIDE

My brothers were my shield, but they couldn't stop the world from being loud. And in my house, the world was deafening.

For three years, while Logan Airport was building a new runway, the flight paths were redirected. They didn't just fly near us; they flew over us. My house was the three-story building in the direct flight path.

The Annie Hall Life

You know that scene in the movie Annie Hall where Woody Allen visits the family that lives under the roller coaster? The joke is that they try to eat dinner while the room shakes violently. That was my life.

Every ten to twenty minutes, the house would rock. Dishes rattled. The walls vibrated. I'm pretty sure the tinnitus ringing in my ears today didn't come from a rock concert or an industrial job. It started right there, in that third-floor bedroom in Boston.

But because I am the way I am, I didn't just cover my ears. I observed.

My brothers and I would go up to the third floor with binoculars and a telescope. We played a game. The planes were so low—I have literally seen pebbles kick up and bounce off the belly of the fuselage—that we could see into the cockpit.

"Describe the pilot," we'd challenge each other. "Is he wearing a tie?" "Does he have glasses?" "Is his jacket on or off?"

We turned the chaos into data. We turned the noise into a game. That was how I survived the physical noise. But as I got older, I had to figure out how to survive the emotional noise.

The Job I Didn't Take

When I graduated college, I was handed a golden ticket. My cousin Ernie, God bless him, had pulled some strings and got me a job offer as the Permanent Mortuary Attendant at Boston City Hospital.

This was the Holy Grail of employment. It was a city job. Good pension, total security. I would never have to interview again. I could have retired from that spot.

But Boston City Hospital isn't a quiet funeral home. That is where they bring the "street" dead. If there was a car wreck, a shooting, or an airplane crash, they came to us.

I thought about the money. I thought about the security.

But then my mind ran the simulation. I imagined standing there every day, seeing families walk in. I pictured the mothers, the fathers, the children who had just lost someone.

People think that because I have a Binary Mind—because I am "different"—that I am cold. They think I lack empathy. The truth is the exact opposite.

My empathy is not a dial I can turn down; it is a switch that is stuck in the "ON" position.

I knew that if I took that job, I would absorb their grief. I would be sad every single day of my life. I knew my heart would break over and over again.

So, I did a silent thank you to Cousin Ernie, and I turned it down.

The Interview Trap

I cannot tell you how many times in my life I wished I had taken that job. Not because I wanted to work with the dead, but because I hated the process of trying to be hired by the living.

I fall into a category that many folks like me know well. When we sit for a job interview, we don't just answer the question. We over-explain. We give one thousand reasons for one thousand stories. We assume the person across the desk doesn't understand the context, so we try to give them all the context. We dump the whole data bucket on the table because we are terrified of being misunderstood.

Usually, they just look at us like we're crazy. And we don't get the job.

"I'm Taping It At Home"

This is why I struggle with the social grease that keeps the world turning: Small Talk.

For a Binary Mind, small talk is a glitch in the system. It is inefficient. We all say the same lines, we all give the same fake nods. It is a complete waste of bandwidth.

But I take it one step further. I don't just endure it; I usually break it.

If someone walks up to me in an elevator and starts the ritual—"Boy, some weather we're having, huh?"—my filter falls off. I'll look at them and say, "No, please. Please don't tell me what the weather is like. I'm taping it at home."

It stops them dead. It's a joke, but it's also the truth. I don't need the report. I need the silence.

10. HAPPY DAYS VS. THE STREET KID (MELROSE HIGH)

When I moved to Melrose, I thought I was walking into a better opportunity. I didn't realize I was walking onto a movie set.

Melrose High School was Happy Days. It was letterman jackets, cliques, and kids whose parents had known each other since kindergarten.

I was the kid from East Boston. I was the "Street Kid." I was Italian in a town that felt very... established.

This was my first true experience with prejudice. It wasn't someone yelling slurs at me. It was quieter. It was bureaucratic. It was a system designed to make sure the "right" kids got the spots, and the "wrong" kid stayed on the sidelines.

The Football Uniform

I showed up to the first football practice completely blind to their social codes. I walked up to someone in the stands and asked, "Do I need to bring my own uniform?"

They looked at me like I had three heads. "No, the school gives them to you."

I didn't know. In East Boston, we played with what we had. Here, everything was provided—except a fair shot.

The Eye Exam Sabotage

I went out for quarterback. I knew I had the arm. I had been running coordinates in the street since I was seven. I knew the physics.

But before you could play, you needed a physical. The doctor they sent me to was Coach Hogue's best friend. His office was literally down the street from the coach's house.

I walked in. He told me to read the eye chart. I looked at the wall. "Where is the chart?"

He looked at me, scribbled on his pad, and signed the form.

The note didn't say "Needs glasses." It effectively said: "Cannot see for crap. Do not let this kid play quarterback."

He tanked me. He killed my position before I threw a single ball. Why? Because they already had their quarterback. They had the "Melrose" kid. They didn't need an Italian kid from Eastie taking the glory spot.

So, they put me on the line. I spent four years blocking, watching guys with half my arm strength throw the ball.

It wasn't until my senior year, at the very last practice, that the truth leaked out. We were in the gym. I picked up a ball and just rifled it. I threw it 70 yards, a perfect spiral, tearing across the air.

The lineman coach, Chevelle, stopped dead. He looked at the ball, then at me.

"Caggiano? You can throw like that?"

I looked at him. "I've been throwing like that since I was a freshman."

He couldn't believe it. But it was too late. The data had been ignored for four years because it didn't fit their narrative.

Baseball: The "Daddy Ball" Wall

If football was sabotage, baseball was a closed shop.

I had a history with baseball. In Little League, I was a flamethrower. I once struck out 15 kids in a six-inning game. I threw hard, and I was wild. There was one game where I hit three kids in a row. The third kid I actually knocked out. I wasn't trying to hurt them; I just had raw power and no coaching.

After the third kid went down, the fathers in the stands started screaming. They were coming down to the fence, yelling at the ump, yelling at me.

My brother Arthur stood up. Arthur was the Enforcer. He was built like a tank and had a face that didn't smile. He looked at the screaming fathers and said, calm but loud:

"My brother throws the ball really hard. He'll get his control. Sit down."

The fathers sat down. They were intimidated by the sheer "East Boston" of him.

The Melrose Tryout

Fast forward to the Melrose High tryouts. I brought that same heat. I got on the mound and struck everyone out. Bam. Bam. Bam. One kid maybe hit a ground ball. Then I got up to bat. I hit two home runs—absolute moonshots into the long field.

I was the best player on that field. Pure physics.

But when the roster went up? I wasn't on it.

I didn't understand. How could you cut the guy who struck everyone out and hit two homers?

I found out later. The coaches had a list. The local fathers—the guys running the "Minor League" system in Melrose—had already told the high school coach who the "good" kids were. I wasn't on the list. I hadn't played in their league. I hadn't gone to their BBQs. I was the anomaly. So, despite the data, they cut me.

Wrestling: "Don't Get Pinned"

So I ended up in the one sport where politics can't save you: Wrestling.

My junior year, I wrestled "Unlimited" (Heavyweight). I wasn't a giant, but I was dense and strong. I had to eat before each match just to get to the 175 pound minimum weight.

The coach knew exactly what I was. He would go down the line of wrestlers giving instructions:

"You, you're a pin guy. Go for the pin."

"You, you're a pin guy."

Then he'd get to me. "Caggiano... don't get pinned."

That was my job. Damage control. In wrestling, if you get pinned, the team loses 6 points. If you lose by decision, the team only loses 3 points. My entire strategy was: Survive the Monster.

The Baby Huey Match

I had to wrestle a guy they called "Baby Huey." He was massive. A giant. When I stepped onto the mat, the referee actually looked at me with pity. "You know this is Unlimited, right?"

"Yeah, I know. I'm the guy."

He shook his head. "I'll do what I can for you."

The whistle blew, and for six minutes, this giant beat the hell out of me. He threw me around. He slammed me. But every time he tried to stick my shoulders to the mat, I bridged. I fought. I refused to accept the data point of "Defeat."

I lost the match 11-4. But I didn't get pinned.

I walked off the mat and went straight to the bathroom to throw up my guts. I was battered.

Suddenly, the door bangs open. It's Baby Huey. He's smashing his fist into the paper towel dispenser, screaming.

"I can't believe it! I can't believe it!"

He saw me wiping my face. "What is wrong with you? I couldn't pin you! How could I not pin you?"

He had won the match, but I had broken his mind. He couldn't understand the physics of why I wouldn't stay down.

That was my high school career. Blocked from quarterback. Cut from baseball. And left to fight giants in wrestling just to save the team three points. It taught me that in the real world—the "Civilized World"—talent isn't enough. You need the network. And if you don't have the network, you'd better learn how to not get pinned.

The Golf Course: The 19th Hole & The Enforcer

Before I ever swung a club, I learned about the culture of the game from my father. We played at the Bellevue Golf Course. This was a club that, I believe, had only started allowing Italians to join about two years before we moved to Melrose. You could feel it. The air was thin with judgment.

One day, my father was in the "19th Hole"—the lounge where the old guard sat around after their rounds. There was a bumper pool table in the center. My father watched them play. He watched them laugh and slap backs. He waited.

When a game finished, he stood up and walked over. "I've got next."

They looked at him. The Italian guy. The IRS guy. They told him, with that polite condescension, that he had to wait his turn. So, he waited. He sat there, patient as stone, until the table was open.

He stepped up. What these men didn't know was that while they played bumper pool in a country club for fun, Arthur Caggiano had learned to play pool in Northend of Boston for money. They were playing a game; he was executing a trade.

He racked the balls. Crack. Sink. Crack. Sink. He ran the table. Then he did it again. And again. He racked and cleared the table almost five times in a row. The last ball wobbled out. He smiled.

The room went silent. The laughter stopped.

He didn't say a word. He just dismantled them with geometry and pressure. He showed them that their "exclusive club" didn't protect them from someone who actually knew how to play.

The Caddie Recorder: Downloading the Swing

I learned the game the same way I learned swimming: I watched.

I started caddying at Bellevue. I carried the bags for the members. Most kids just lugged the clubs and looked for lost balls. I was studying the mechanics. I saw how the good players swung. It wasn't like a baseball bat—which is how every bad golfer swings. It was a pendulum. It was fluid. I watched the guys on TV, and I watched the best players at the club.

Input: Keep the left arm straight.

Input: Rotate the hips, don't slide.

Input: The club does the work, not the muscles. Hit down through the ball, let the club head push the ball up.

I didn't take lessons. I just downloaded the motion. By the time I went out for the Melrose High golf team, I didn't look like a beginner. I looked like a mimic who had stolen the code.

Psychological Warfare on the Fairway

I made the team. But I quickly realized that mechanics only get you so far. Some of these kids had been playing since they were toddlers. They had better swings. They had better equipment. But they had a weakness: They were soft. They were "Happy Days" kids. They lived in a world of rules and safety. I lived in a world of data and street leverage.

The "Joint" Incident

I was playing a match against a kid who was much better than me. He was "Mr. Clean"—perfect haircut, perfect clothes, probably never broke a rule in his life. He was up by three strokes with six holes to go. Mathematically, I was dead. I needed to hack his system.

It was a beautiful, sunny day. We were walking down the fairway. I reached into my pocket and pulled out a regular cigarette. I didn't light it. Instead, I carefully twisted the end of it, pinching the paper so it looked exactly like a joint. I put it in my mouth and just let it hang there while I walked.

I saw him look at me. His eyes went wide. You could see the panic signals firing in his brain: "Is... is he smoking marijuana? On the golf course? During a match? Is he high right now?"

He completely short-circuited. He was so focused on the "drug" hanging from my lip that he forgot how to play golf. He crumbled. He choked on every shot for the last six holes.

I didn't break a single rule. I didn't smoke anything. I just introduced a variable he couldn't process. I won the match.

By the time I graduated, I had earned letters in Football, Wrestling, and Golf. I didn't get them because I was the most talented. I got them because I was willing to block when they wouldn't let me throw, I was willing to bridge when I couldn't win, and I was willing to twist a cigarette when I couldn't out-swing them.

I was learning that if you can't beat the system with skill, you beat it with psychology.

The Kitchen Table (4:00 A.M.)

It was 1971. The house was quiet in the way only houses are before dawn—no movement, no appliances humming, no voices yet awake. Just structure holding its breath.

I came downstairs at four in the morning and found my father sitting at the kitchen table. He was alone. A single cup of tea sat in front of him, steam barely visible in the low light.

He wasn't reading. He wasn't praying. He was staring into the middle distance, the way someone does when they're working through something that won't let go.

My father was a devout man. For years, without exception, he went to the 7:30 a.m. Mass every single day. Rain, snow, exhaustion—none of it mattered. Faith, for him, wasn't emotional. It was procedural. It was done because it was right.

But that morning, in the silence of the kitchen, he wasn't praying. He was calculating.

He looked up when he saw me, as if he'd been expecting a witness, and without preamble he dropped the thought that had been keeping him awake.

"Robert," he said, quietly, "tell me something."

He paused, then continued. "There are people on the other side of the planet who don't know my religion. They've never heard of it. Why am I special? Why do I get to go to heaven and they don't?"

He shook his head slightly, not in anger—more in disbelief. "It doesn't make sense," he said. "If there are old people in those villages doing good things—helping each other grow, living together, coexisting—shouldn't they be able to go to heaven too? Just because they don't know the specific rules I follow?"

He looked down at his tea, as if the answer might be there. "The math doesn't work," he said. "God has to be bigger than that."

That was the spark. That was the moment something loosened—not his faith, but its frame. Sitting at that kitchen table at four in the morning, my father began outlining what would eventually become the idea of the Six Professions. He started seeing the world not as belief systems competing for dominance, but as functions organizing for survival. He realized something most people never do: that the world does not run on doctrine. It runs on roles. And he understood, long before anyone around him did, that eventually the world was going to have to get over itself.

He started a theory that morning. I finished it decades later.

All Debts Are Paid

That wasn't the only lesson he taught me about how to navigate the world. When I was young, I used to go to funerals with him. After the service, when people gathered around tables and the food came out and the wine started flowing, my father would stand up to make a toast.

He would raise his glass to the deceased—let's say it was Uncle Mike—and say, clearly enough for everyone to hear:

"To Uncle Mike. All debts are paid."

Everyone would salute.

For a long time, I took it literally. My father was a Tax Man—an IRS boss. I assumed he meant exactly what it sounded like. That he'd checked the books. That Mike didn't owe anyone money.

I asked him about it later.

"Dad," I said, "you can't really be that good of a man that you're clearing everyone's financial ledger when they die."

He laughed. "No, Robert," he said. "It's not about money. It's about respect."

He leaned in, lowering his voice. "When someone dies, you talk about them in the future tense. You respect them more than you did when they were alive. You think only of the good. That's the only thing worth keeping. When you speak about them, you bring up their goodness. You clear the slate."

Then he added the part that stayed with me. "And here's the trick," he said. "When you respect the dead, the living respect you for it. You earn respect by giving it."

The Fluidity of the Law

My father was a man of strict rules. But he understood the gray. He had to. He was an accountant. He saw how the real world actually worked.

One day, with a twinkle in his eye, he said something that sounded like a joke at the time.

"You know," he said, "you're not a thief unless you get caught."

I laughed. It felt mischievous. Almost improper. But as I got older, I understood what he was really saying. He wasn't telling me to steal. He was telling me that society's labels are often based on perception as much as reality. That systems pretend to be absolute, but are enforced through human judgment. That morality, law, and truth are not always aligned in practice—even when they claim to be.

He followed the rules. Mass at 7:30 a.m., every day. But at 4:00 a.m., at the kitchen table, he questioned whether the rules made sense. He was the original Recorder. And he taught me—without ever saying it outright—that faith without structure collapses, and structure without honesty rots.

The Suit

ROBERT A. CAGGIANO
76 Bancroft Rd.
. . . Cagge . remembers
c.l & p. concert . . . week
ends at the cape . . .
columbo at the hous . . .
loves sports and partying .
wants to go into psychology
 football 1-4; wrestling 3,4;
golf 2,3; italian club, LOG,
photography

I didn't pick the suit alone. I was standing there with my sister Mary, surrounded by fabric — patterns and textures that were loud in the way the early seventies were loud. Suede. Bold designs. Statements. That was the era. You didn't blend in. You announced yourself.

The tailor knew it too. He was proud when he came down the stairs carrying the suit. You could tell. He held it the way someone holds something they expect to be admired. This wasn't just clothing to him. It was expression. Craft. Style. He laid it out like a reveal.

My father didn't hesitate. He didn't circle it. He didn't touch the fabric. He didn't soften his voice. He looked straight at the tailor and said, very calmly and very clearly,

"That's the suit?"

The tailor nodded. "Yes."

My father leaned forward just slightly and said, "I wouldn't give you two cents for that suit. You made that suit for you. You did not make that suit for my son."

There was no anger in it. No performance. Just certainty. The tailor shrank immediately. You could see it in his shoulders, in his face. He didn't argue. He didn't defend his work. He didn't explain the fashion of the moment. He simply said, "I'm sorry. I'll be right back," and disappeared upstairs.

That mattered to me later — the way authority works when it's real. No escalation. No theatrics. Just truth delivered cleanly.

This tailor had everything. Racks and racks of suits. Leather jackets everywhere. Long leather jackets, short ones, heavy ones. My whole family wore leather jackets through high school. We had the best ones in town. At the time I thought it was style. Years later I realized it was probably debt being paid quietly. My father was a tax man. People settled accounts in different ways.

When the tailor came back down, he wasn't holding a statement piece. He was holding a Brooks Brothers pinstripe. Dark. Conservative. One size too big.

My father looked at it and nodded. "That one," he said. "You can cut it down. It'll fit him perfectly."

Then he turned to me. "You still want this one? I said yeah I need it for the Winter Ball...

He said Really, well then... you're not just going to wear it once," he said. "You're going to wear it for years. Weddings. Events. Whatever comes. I want to see you in this one."

Mary didn't say anything then. But later, she did. My father pulled her aside and gave her a talking-to. She pushed back. She said she thought I really liked the other suit. She said she was helping me choose something I wanted.

My father stopped her. "What do you think you were supposed to do?" he asked her. "Go in there with him to make him happy?"

Then he answered his own question. "No. You were supposed to protect him."

That suit followed me. I wore it longer than any suit I ever owned. I wore it to weddings. I wore it to moments where I needed to look like I belonged, even when I felt like I didn't.

I remember one night in particular — Winter Ball. I went to pick up my date, rang the bell, and when she opened the door she froze for a second. Then she pulled me inside, straight into the kitchen, to show her parents. I was wearing that suit. Bowtie and all. When the door closed behind us, I'm pretty sure they laughed for days. Not unkindly. Just in disbelief.

That suit did its job. Years later, when I look at my high school graduation photo, that's the suit I see. Not flashy. Not trendy. Structured. Built to last. Chosen not for the moment, but for the future.

Mary was there to translate taste. My father was there to enforce structure. Between them, the right decision got made. At the time, I thought it was just a suit. Now I know better. It was a lesson in how the world actually works — and who you want making the final call when it matters.

The Doorknob Theory

I found proof the other day. It was buried in an old box—a poem I wrote in Junior High School.

I wasn't a "school" kid. In fact, in my English class, there was a girl who was a 4.0 student. She was planning to go to college to be an English Major. She did everything right.

But that year, there was a poetry award. She didn't win it. I did. I found out years later at a reunion that she was still upset about it. She couldn't understand how Robert, the kid who wasn't chasing the grades, beat the future English major.

The reason is simple. She was writing words. I was writing a psychological profile.

The poem was called **"The Door Knob."** Even back then, I wasn't looking at the sunset; I was looking at the mechanics of how people touch things.

Here is the poem:

The Door Knob

A Squeeze here, a squeeze there, Is, all I need you will see, for me to tell you what you'll be.

I'm able to tell the traits of one, Especially, when tested like a bun.

I turn I twist to do my job, For that's the fundamentals of a knob.

A squeeze here, a squeeze there, Is, all the action that I can bear.

The bruisers choke, the losers soak, For I'm able to see the cautious use a key.

Read that last stanza again. *"I'm able to tell the traits of one."*

I was fourteen going on fifteen years old, and I was already analyzing people.

- **"The bruisers choke"** — I saw the aggression in people who grabbed the door too hard.
- **"The losers soak"** — I saw the anxiety in people with sweaty palms who were afraid to enter.
- **"The cautious use a key"** — I saw the logical ones who wanted to unlock the mystery before walking in.

I looked at my yearbook from that year. Under "Future Plans," I had written: **Psychology.**

I didn't end up going to school for psychology. The words were to big for me to say, remember or spell. I have all that at my finger tips today but back then I went into business. I went into life. But looking back at that poem, I realize I never stopped being a psychologist. I just swapped the textbook for the real world.

The 4.0 student knew how to write a sentence. I knew how to read a room.

11. THE ASCENT: COLLEGE AND WORK

Before we go any further, I need to take you through the years that shaped how my mind actually worked long before anyone put a label on it. These aren't bragging rights. They're the breadcrumb trail — the proof that my wiring was already doing what it was designed to do.

Freshman Year: The First Turning Point

Northeastern University didn't start with brilliance. It started with effort — blunt, physical effort. My freshman year was dominated by the crew team, and that meant discipline, miles of running, and a kind of pain most people only read about.

Over 350 freshmen tried out. Thirty-five were chosen. I was one of them.

That year, my schedule wasn't "college kid drifting." It was miles on the pavement, lungs burning, a ½-mile incline repeated four times until you bled in your socks, because that's what it took to belong on that boat. Nine miles a day. Up before sunrise. Bed sore. Pride intact.

I wasn't thinking about GPAs or academic awards — I was thinking about survival, teamwork, and pushing through walls most people never hit. Academics that year weren't ignored — they simply weren't the priority. Crew demanded everything.

But even then, my mind was recording, analyzing, and storing. I wasn't a slouch. I wasn't drifting. I was building capacity — the physical side of the same wiring that would later show itself in data, patterns, and logic.

By the time the year ended, I had already learned something most people never learn at eighteen: If I committed, I could outwork anyone. That wasn't ego. It was observation. And it mattered for everything that came next.

Junior Year: The Door That Wasn't Supposed to Open

By junior year, my grades were solid, but nowhere near the 4.0 "top ten percent" cutoff that normally determined who could qualify for Northeastern's prestigious six-month London co-op program. Those were the rules. That was the system. And everyone I knew accepted it as gospel.

One afternoon, my friend Mark told me he'd been selected to go. He said it casually — like it was obvious. "The top ten percent get the shot," he said. "That's how they do it."

I remember thinking: Why should someone else's formula decide what I'm capable of? Not in anger. In confusion. Because even then, I didn't accept blanket rules that ignored the individual.

So I walked into the co-op office and met the senior administrator — a man in a wheelchair, sharp, kind, and not easily impressed. He confirmed everything Mark had said.

"Yes, Robert. Top ten percent only. That's the cutoff."

I didn't argue. I didn't plead. I asked one simple question:

"What if three professors — real professors, not electives — write recommendations stating I'm in the top ten smartest students they've taught? Would that qualify?"

He looked at me the way a man looks at someone who has no idea how the world works. A mix of amusement, doubt, and a little curiosity. Like he thought the conversation would end right there.

"Sure," he said. "If you get three professors to say that, bring the letters back."

Not sarcastic — just certain it would never happen. But he didn't know my wiring. He didn't know that once I saw a path, I walked it. He didn't know that I don't ask questions unless I intend to follow through. He didn't know that binary minds don't bluff — we execute.

And that was the moment the entire trajectory shifted.

The Three Professors

The first professor I went to was Professor Harrington, my economics professor — thirty-three years old, sharp, charismatic, and the kind of teacher who didn't just lecture; he formed minds. The very first word he ever wrote on the board was OBJECTIVITY.

He told us it was the single most valuable skill we'd ever develop. "Every time you evaluate something," he said, "start fresh. No assumptions. No bias. No baggage." That line hit me like scripture. A binary principle before I even knew the term. He was planning to be away one week and had his wife substitute — we joked we'd go easy on her. Turned out she was brilliant, funny, tougher than he was, and she owned that classroom. When I asked him for a recommendation letter, he didn't hesitate. "Absolutely, Robert." He saw something in the way I processed. Sadly, three years later at age thirty-six, he died of a heart attack. But that letter opened one of the most important doors of my life.

The second professor — Investment Management — reacted the same way. He wrote the letter, no hesitation. Nine years later, I ran into him in a sub shop. "Professor!" I said. "Robert," he replied instantly. "You won the six-week $100 investment contest. Options strategy. Very smart."

"You remember that?" I asked.

He laughed. "Hard to forget. Genius work. Just needed real money and no fear." We both laughed — because he was right about the fear part.

The third professor — Competitive Analysis — had built an entire doctoral study around a case involving Legg's pantyhose. The class had a hundred complicated marketing ideas: new packaging, new promotions, new gimmicks. But when I broke the numbers down, the truth was simple: The best strategy was to do nothing. The market was already optimal, and any interference made it worse. He was stunned. It contradicted his own assumptions, but the math was irrefutable. He wrote the final letter gladly.

Three professors, three disciplines, three confirmations — each saying I belonged in the top ten percent intellectually, whatever the GPA said.

Most people would've stopped there. I simply took the letters back to the administrator like it was the next step in a sequence. He read them slowly, looking up at me with a different expression — not amusement this time, but recognition.

"Okay, Robert," he said. "You're going to London."

Whitechapel, Silvertown, and the 21-Year-Old Who Didn't Sleep

In 1979, I flew to London — twenty-one years old, no fear, no hesitation, no map of anything except the confidence that I'd figure it out.

Whitechapel was rough back then. Everyone kept telling me, "Lucky you're big, you're staying in Whitechapel." Even the customs officer said it. I had no idea why. I was a kid from an Italian Boston family — what was going to scare me? The Cockney accent was thick, but I understood it immediately. My classmates didn't. I'd translate for them, and we'd all laugh.

My job was with International Paint in Silvertown, part of Courtlands — one of the largest companies in Great Britain. The Chairman of the Board told my boss to give me one directive: "Prove we sell more than anyone else in our vertical."

That was it. No instructions. No guidance. Just a problem to solve. And a binary mind doesn't complicate problems — we break them down.

I mapped every factory, every production line, every solvent, every undercoat, every car plant, every union strike, every downtime risk. If a factory could produce 850 cars a day, I calculated exactly how much paint that required. If a plant was under construction or delayed by a union issue, I factored that into the nation's output. I built the entire forecast of Britain's car production simply by tracking paint consumption.

When I turned in my report, something unusual happened. The Chairman called me in. Sat across from me. Leaning forward. Eyes sharp.

"Robert... who are you?"

Because at the annual shareholder meeting, 8 of the 10 strategic points he presented were in my report — which he had seen the day before. He thought I was a spy. I laughed and told him the truth: "I just made a lot of calls. And I used the adding machine. You're going to have a big phone bill."

The Financial Times rewrote next year's automotive projections based on my analysis. I wasn't guessing the future. I was deducing it.

That was the London chapter on paper. But the real London chapter happened at night.

When the city slept, I didn't. I'd ride my small 100cc motorcycle through empty streets — the safest time in Whitechapel if we're being honest — and I'd explore every corner. Not for trouble. Not for rebellion. I was kicking the can, the way I always had as a kid — exploring, learning, absorbing, getting away with something harmless but exhilarating.

I became friends with the late-shift postal workers who drank six to eight pints before work. Friends with the DJ at the London Hospital Tavern — he'd play Steely Dan's "East St. Louis Toodle-Oo" whenever I walked in. Friends with a short guy named Spike — a West Ham hooligan with the Inter-city Firm (ICF) who earned his name the hard way. I stood in the South End at the stadium, holding back the crowd so an elderly man wouldn't get crushed, only to have his son turn to me and laugh when I told him it was my first match ever.

Nine years later, when I returned to London on my honeymoon, I walked into a fish-and-chips shop and the owner came out yelling: "It's the Yank!" She remembered me after almost a decade. That's what happens when you treat people like people. Not like roles. Not like strangers.

EDS: The Crucible of Logic

My first real job after college was EDS — Ross Perot's company. It was famous for being brutal. Five interview rounds. The first four were designed to shake you. The fifth decided your fate.

The trick was simple: You had to tell your life story — high school, junior year, senior year, Northeastern — in perfect order. Then they'd disrupt you.

"When you were a junior... why did you choose Northeastern?"

"When you were a senior... what made you choose that co-op?"

"Tell me again about the end of your sophomore year..."

They'd pull you off your timeline, then see if you could return to the exact spot without losing the thread. That's all structured programming is. A branch. A return. A resume point. I passed easily. Not because I was trained — because my mind already worked that way.

Then came the logic test. The instructor said: "Write the steps of me walking to the door. I'll take one step at a time, half the distance each time."

Everyone started writing sequences. I didn't. I raised my hand:

"You'll never reach the door. Halfway forever is still not the door."

He stopped. Pauses. Adjusts his plan. And pretends that was always the test. I saw right through it — the correction, the ego, the pivot — and stored it. Recorders catch that stuff instantly in replay.

EDS was sink-or-swim. Miss one comma in your punch cards and you were fired. Three people in my class failed and were gone. I finished first. They wanted me to stay and teach the next class. I asked to go back to Boston to be near my father — they didn't like that, but they sent me anyway.

In Boston, I worked in Tape Processing and Actual Statistics. Reading claims, fixing errors, making the whole machine run smoother. I noticed most suspended claims were caused by simple address typos in data entry. Once those were fixed, claims started flowing cleanly — too cleanly. So cleanly that EDS had to put a five-day hold on all tape claims because the money was going out faster than expected.

My first real lesson in big business: Money flow scares people more than money problems.

At EDS, the pressure was constant, but for me, the data was transparent. I learned assembler, binary, and dump reading. Patterns were easy—they felt as natural as reading a newspaper. I genuinely thought everyone could scan a string of binary like 01010010 and instantly see the 'R'. I didn't realize yet that I was seeing the world in a resolution most people didn't even know existed.

Ross Perot and the Helicopter

Ross Perot visited our group. I asked him the one question others wouldn't: "You've accomplished more than most people ever dream of. What motivates you now?"

He smiled. "My kids," he said. "I'm raising them to understand work. Real work. I don't want them spoiled."

Later that week, I was in the data center at 9 p.m. Ross Perot's son landed his helicopter outside — coming home from working an oil rig. I laughed. His commute may have looked different from mine, but the wind hits everyone the same. It was all relative.

The Permanent Feedback Loop (The Tea Kettles)

It was during this training in Plano, Texas, that the silence officially ended. I went to a shooting range with a roommate. We were young and stupid. He had a .357 Magnum—a hand cannon. I was standing right beside him. I hadn't put my earplugs in yet. He didn't check. He just pulled the trigger.

A .357 Magnum isn't a sound. It's a shockwave. It felt like someone drove an icepick into the side of my head. The world went mute, and then, the high-pitched whistle started.

I waited for it to go away. That was decades ago. It never went away.

This is my Tinnitus. The "Tea Kettle" that rings 24/7.

Why does this matter for the Binary Mind? Because a Recorder cannot "ignore" input. We process it. Every second of every day, my brain has to allocate a specific percentage of its processing power to filtering out that scream.

Input: Person talking.

Input: Tea Kettle ringing.

Task: Filter the ring, enhance the voice.

It is an invisible tax on my energy. When I talk to you, I am working harder than you realize just to hear the silence between your words. This is why the 90-Day Reboot emphasizes "Neuro-Sensory Quiet Time." I need the external world to be quiet because my internal world never is.

The Phantom Cash (Plano, Texas)

The same trip that took my hearing also taught me a lesson about value.

On the very last night of our EDS training in Plano, we went out to dinner to celebrate. When we came back, the apartment door was busted open. It was a clean sweep. My roommate was devastated. They had taken his arsenal—including the .357 Magnum that had blown out my ears days before. (I admit, I didn't mourn the gun).

But they also took my brand new Canon camera with the long lenses. To a Recorder, losing your camera is like losing an eye. I was crushed.

But then, I remembered the "Gadget Bag" (my gambit bag). I had $1,100 in cash—my entire savings for the trip—hidden inside it. The bag was sitting right there, unzipped, rummaged through, and tossed on the floor.

My roommate looked at me and said, "It's gone, Rob. They took everything."

I walked over, picked up the bag, and reached into the lining. The cash was still there.

The Recorder Strategy: I hadn't just stuffed the money in a pocket. I had visualized the theft. I knew a thief works on speed and touch. They "squeeze" bags to feel for hard objects (cameras, wallets, guns). So I had placed the cash flat in the absolute center of the bag's dead space—the "void" where the structure of the bag makes it feel empty even when it's full.

The thief squeezed the bag. He felt nothing. He moved on.

He took the hardware (the camera). He took the weapon (the gun). But he left the fuel (the cash) because he didn't have the patience to verify the data.

12. THE ROCKET SHIP: LOTUS

I took a break from the streets and walked into a revolution.

It was the early 1980s. The world was still analog. Businesses ran on mainframes and "dumb terminals." The Personal Computer (PC) was seen by serious businessmen as a toy, or a glorified typewriter. They didn't have "workflow." They had paper.

Then came Lotus.

To understand the energy of this place, you have to look at the math. It defies gravity. When Lotus was preparing to launch "1-2-3," the projections were modest. They were hoping—hoping—to sell maybe $3 or $4 million in the first year.

Then came the pre-announcement at Comdex. The world saw the software. The Recorders saw the utility; the Runners saw the magic. Before the first box was even shipped, they had a backorder of $35 million.

By the end of the first year, they didn't do $4 million. They did over $100 million.

It wasn't a company; it was a rocket ship. And I was strapped in.

Beginning a New Chapter

I saw an ad: Lotus was hiring a mainframe systems engineer. I walked into their Beverly Hills office — beautiful place — and handed the receptionist my résumé. "You don't need to keep looking," I said. "I'll take the job."

Cocky? Maybe. But true.

The district manager, Pat Paolili, saw my résumé and recognized the EDS pedigree immediately. She knew exactly what it meant if someone survived four years there. She hired me. She was the first *female* Sales Person of the year at IBM.

Pat was one of the best managers I ever had — brilliant, intuitive, able to spot raw potential and shape it. She hired people who would eventually become VPs, founders, leaders. She knew how to grow talent.

Symphony Link: Outperforming an Entire Company

Lotus was exploding in popularity. 1-2-3 was everywhere. Symphony was growing. Mainframes and PCs were merging worlds.

I discovered something simple: People wanted Symphony Link because it let them pull mainframe print jobs directly to their PCs. So I taught the programming language. If you took the class, you got a free copy of Symphony Link.

Fifteen people per class. Five copies per head. I sold more Symphony Link than the entire company combined.

Rising Through Lotus

I went from systems engineer → district systems engineering manager → sales manager — something unheard of at the time.

There were 22 districts. I got Irvine — ranked 22nd. Within a year, we were number four. Every person on my team hit Achievers Club — top ten percent.

Then I was asked to take over distribution, which accounted for 33% of the company's business. Leadership wanted to get rid of distribution.

They didn't like the middlemen. I didn't see "middlemen." I saw leverage.

I studied the real numbers:

- Returns
- Channel stuffing
- Manufacturing waste
- Margins
- Rebates
- End-of-quarter games
- $19 million per year in destroyed manuals and boxes

I cut the wastage in half. That alone changed the top line. I grew distribution from 33% to 52% of corporate revenue. We hit the numbers 18 quarters in a row.

And while I'm talking about Lotus and computer software I need to rant about Word.

The Channel Truth
(Why Systems Fail Without Recorders)

There is a reason I react so strongly to tools like Word, and it has nothing to do with nostalgia or resistance to change. It has everything to do with what happens when systems quietly drift away from structural truth and toward speed, optics, and momentum.

Word didn't win because it was better.

It won because Microsoft bought the doorway to the user.

OEM agreements.

Education licensing.

Enterprise bundling.

Operating system leverage.

Word arrived everywhere by default. Not because it respected the act of writing, but because it controlled distribution. Functionality became secondary. Presence became everything.

Anyone who lived through WordPerfect or Lotus 1-2-3 knows this isn't opinion. It's history.

Those tools let you scribe.

They did what you told them to do—no more, no less.

Word developed a mind of its own. Auto-formatting. Re-paging. Invisible rules. Behavior that overrides intent. A system optimized for motion instead of fidelity.

That didn't happen by accident.

It's what happens when systems are designed and maintained by people who prioritize movement over verification.

I learned this lesson early—not in theory, but at scale.

At the time, the market reality was simple. Microsoft had enormous financial leverage from the operating system and used it to buy the desktop. Better products lost. Consumers lost fidelity even as they gained ubiquity. That was the environment. I didn't create it, and I didn't try to explain it away.

I had to operate inside it.

What mattered wasn't what should have won. What mattered was what was true.

For eighteen consecutive quarters, I hit my numbers. Not by outspending competitors. Not by end-of-quarter theatrics. Not by panic pricing, extra points, freight concessions, or extended terms.

In fact, that was the first thing I eliminated.

Runner-led sales organizations rely on last-minute motion. Discounts spike. Revenue looks good on paper. Underneath, margins collapse, returns explode, and trust erodes.

It feels productive.

It feels busy.

But it's motion without stability.

I did something different.

I sat down with distributors and asked a question almost no vendor ever asks:

How do you actually make money?

Not list price.

Not programs.

Not incentives.

Actual money.

Margins.

Marketing revenue.

Returns.

Cash-flow timing.

I let them show me the truth.

In some cases, the answers were uncomfortable. There were channel companies whose public story was distribution, but whose real profit engine was marketing programs. Advertising. Placement. Sponsored visibility. When that truth surfaced publicly, stock prices fell. Some didn't survive.

That wasn't the point.

The point was that incentives were misaligned, and everyone was pretending otherwise.

Another truth surfaced immediately: returns were catastrophic.

When I took over distribution, Lotus was destroying roughly nineteen million dollars in hard-cost inventory. At a seventy-percent gross margin, that represented a massive topline revenue loss. We weren't losing business—we were leaking value.

Eliminate returns, and revenue rises instantly without selling a single additional unit.

So I stopped negotiating boxes and started designing a system that removed uncertainty.

I told distributors the truth:

Microsoft would outsell us in raw units. They owned the channel. That wasn't up for debate.

But every time a Lotus box went out the door, they would make more money on it than they did on a Microsoft box.

Not later.

Not hypothetically.

Immediately.

Margins matter more than logos.

Then I shifted the direction of force.

342 - ROBERT ANTHONY CAGGIANO

Instead of pushing inventory into distribution and bribing it to move, I created pull at the secondary level—the point where transactions actually happen. Retailers. Accounts. Buyers who already had demand.

I redirected marketing dollars downstream, away from generic distribution spend and into the hands of the people who could pull product through inventory naturally.

That changed everything.

Returns stopped—not because of policy, but because inventory was no longer misallocated.

Fear disappeared—not because of persuasion, but because risk was removed.

At quarter end, I didn't ask distributors what they wanted to buy. I already knew.

I knew their inventory.

I knew their customers.

I knew what would sell and what wouldn't.

So I did the work for them.

I specified what to buy.

How much to buy.

For how long.

I built the purchase requests.

I created the invoices.

I removed decision fatigue entirely.

I didn't say, "Here are your options."

I said, "Buy four more weeks of inventory. Here's the math."

No returns.

No freight penalties.

No clawbacks.

No games.

If something didn't sell in ninety days, it didn't come back to hurt anyone. It was redirected to a market where demand already existed.

All they had to do was say yes.

That's how the quarter closed.

Every quarter.

Eventually, the executives tried to name what was happening. They called it Revenue Enhancing Inventory—REI—not because it sounded clever, but because they couldn't mentally hold the system long enough to describe it.

From their perspective, inventory was somehow creating revenue instead of threatening it.

From mine, the leaks were gone.

That's why I was invited into the room.

Not because I moved faster.

Because I removed uncertainty.

This is where the Runner–Recorder bond matters.

Jim was the ultimate Runner. He understood motion, scale, and consequence. He trusted me because I told him the truth—every time. If something was wrong, it was wrong. No spin. No delay.

He kept me on a short leash, but he didn't require permission for every decision. I made decisions, then reported them. No surprises. Complete transparency.

That trust is what allowed the system to work.

Runners move civilization forward.

Recorders keep it from tearing itself apart.

When the two designs trust each other, systems stabilize. When they don't, systems still grow—but they grow brittle. They look powerful right up until they fail.

This is why tools like Word unsettle me today.

It still rewrites intent.

It still prioritizes automation over verification.

It still changes structure without asking.

It isn't broken.

It's behaving exactly as designed.

The same is true of organizations. Markets. Civilizations.

When Recorders are sidelined as slow, difficult, or overthinking, systems don't stop moving. They just stop being anchored to reality.

I've lived on both sides of that.

I know—because I've done it—that when incentives align with truth instead of optics, stability follows.

That isn't business advice.

That's architecture.

And it's the same architecture that keeps civilizations alive.

Now as I was saying at Lotus...

Calling the Future (and Being Right)

Deb Bessemer, VP of Sales, announced the new Achievers Club rules: 110% quota. Top ten percent eligible.

I told her, politely but directly: "You're going to change my requirements to go to Switzerland because if you don't twice as many people will qualify you will need twice as many seats." She said the "same conditions for everyone", which I replied "Ok, I warned you."

She laughed it off. She thought I was overconfident.

One year later, in front of 1,100 salespeople at the annual meeting, she announced we will be having two Achieves Clubs this year...she stopped mid-speech and said — almost under her breath — "Robert said this would happen..." We filled Achievers Club twice over.

Later that week Deb was presenting to 300 sales managers what she saw as the top five things she looks for in a manager. Empathy was one of them and she said Robert Caggiano is the example of a manager with empathy for his people that she admired.

Aspen: The Table of Titans

The setting was Aspen. The air was thin, the altitude was high, and the room was filled with the kind of people who moved markets, not just boxes.

It was a three-day summit. Sitting around the massive conference table were the titans of distribution: executives from Ingram Micro and Tech Data. These weren't just managers; these were the people moving hundreds of millions of dollars in software across the globe.

I sat right in the middle of the table. This was my Moneyball moment. Just like in the movie, where the old scouts were looking at the player's jawline and the math guys were looking at the on-base percentage, I was the only one in the room looking at the structural math of their future.

They didn't want a presentation about what I'd done in the past. They didn't care about marketing fluff. They wanted to know one thing: "How do we survive next year?"

Their entire universe revolved around two variables: Margin and Revenue. If they moved $1 million in product, they needed to secure their $120,000 margin. If that slipped, they bled.

So, I didn't give a speech. I gave a diagnosis.

I went around the table, pointing to each titan, breaking down exactly how the Lotus environment was going to shift the ground beneath their feet.

I looked at the reseller with the physical stores. "You're component-driven. You live and die by shelf space. Here is exactly how Lotus's roadmap impacts your 12% margin, and here is how you pivot before you lose it."

I turned to the retail-heavy executive. "You're worried about inventory. Here is how you avoid a wave of returns when the pricing shifts next quarter."

I looked at the enterprise heavyweights. "You handle the big contracts. Ignore the quarterly noise. Here is exactly when you need to buy based on the new fiscal cycles."

Then I dropped the bomb that no one wanted to say out loud: "Shrink wrap is disappearing."

The era of the physical box was ending. Digital was coming.

I wasn't telling them how to run their companies; I was showing them the invisible architecture of the market before the rest of the world saw it. Because I was a Recorder, I could see the structure. That's why they listened.

The Million Dollar Urinal

The tension in the room was high, the focus absolute. We took a break, and I headed to the restroom.

I was standing at the urinal, staring at the wall, when the CEO of Ingram Micro stepped up beside me. It's the great equalizer—two men in a tiled room, doing the most human thing possible, while millions of dollars hang in the air outside the door.

He didn't look at me. He just stared straight ahead and said, in a low voice:

"You know... you still owe me a million dollars."

I didn't blink. I finished up, zipped, and looked over at him.

"Actually... you're lucky you got the three."

He paused. The math clicked in his head. He knew the leverage I had, and he knew the deal we had made. A slow grin spread across his face. He laughed—a genuine, surprised laugh.

"Yeah," he said. "You're probably right. Thanks."

We washed our hands and went back to the table. That is the Recorder in the wild: High stakes at the table, high comedy in the bathroom, and absolute clarity everywhere.

The Secret Weapon: The Power of "No"

I moved through the ranks quickly, eventually becoming a Director. Lotus was unique because the culture allowed a Recorder like me to make massive corporate decisions, even without the traditional pedigree.

Why did they trust me? It started in the interview process for the Distribution Manager role. Jim Manzi, CEO, looked at me and said something that defined my entire career:

"Robert, you have a way of saying 'No' to people, and they're OK with it. I need you to say 'No' to these guys."

Runners hate saying no. They want to be liked. They want to keep the "vibe" going.

A Recorder doesn't mind saying no, because to us, "No" isn't emotional. It's just data. It's a boundary. And because I didn't say it with malice—just with clarity—people respected it.

I became the secret weapon in distribution. While other divisions were fluctuating, I made my number 18 quarters in a row. I built a fortress of consistency in a chaotic market. I accumulated a massive cash reserve because I ran my division on physics, not hope.

The Ultimate Runner: Jim Manzi

The CEO, Jim Manzi, was the best I have ever seen. He was the Ultimate Runner. He had a mind like a steel trap. He could stand in front of an audience of 1,100 people, spot a face in the crowd, and call them by name. He didn't just know the business; he knew the people.

He treated me well because he recognized the wiring. He knew I wasn't blowing smoke. He knew that if I said something was broken, it was broken.

That trust is what led to the discovery of the "52-Week Glitch."

The 52-Week Glitch (The International Ponzi Scheme)

One day, Jim asked me to come see him. He looked puzzled.

"Robert," he said, "I'm curious about our International Group. It feels like they have almost 52 weeks of inventory sitting out there. Why would that be?"

My Recorder brain instantly flagged an error. "52 weeks of inventory? Jim, how do they get paid?"

He looked at me. "What do you mean?"

"Show me the comp plan. Do they get paid on what they sell through to the customer, or what they sell in to the channel?"

The answer, of course, was that they got paid on "Sell-In."

I broke it down for him: "Jim, Lotus Notes is a corporate license. It's a contract. Distributors don't 'stock' contracts on a shelf like boxes of software. They don't sell into a corporation; they transfer to a location. If you're seeing 52 weeks of inventory, no one actually bought it."

I told him I wouldn't be surprised if there were stacks of unsigned contracts sitting in a desk drawer somewhere.

It turns out, that's exactly what it was. The Senior VP of Sales for the International Group had been running his own internal Ponzi scheme.

He was "selling" product to the channel to hit his number and get his bonus, but the product was going nowhere. It was a ghost ship.

The Bailout

When the truth came out, the hole in the books was massive. The company had to figure out how to cover 52 weeks of "fake" inventory while they cleaned up the mess.

And who paid for it? My division.

Because I had hit my number 18 quarters in a row, because I had run a clean ship, I had a massive cash and margin reserve. They took my surplus to plug the hole the Runner VP had created.

I didn't mind. That's the job. The Recorder builds the foundation so strong that it can hold the weight when the Runners accidentally blow up the second floor. Jim Manzi knew that. That's why he let me make decisions. He knew that when the smoke cleared, I would be the one standing there with the real numbers.

The Prince of Runners (Dave Valentino)

If you want to understand what a High-Speed Runner looks like in the wild, you had to know Dave Valentino. He was the Prince. He was the ultimate showman, the ultimate salesman. In the days of the "Channel Wars"—when you had to show up with boxes of tchotchkes and golf clubs just to get a meeting—Dave didn't just show up. He performed.

He taught me that sales isn't about data; it's about Energy Transfer.

I would demonstrate the technology and Dave would light up the audience. Throwing Frisbees with money taped underneath as people went crazy trying to be the lucky one to catch one, and when the last one thrown Dave would tell the audience "Look underneath your seat... you are all winners with me!" There was money—5, 10, 20 dollar bills.

The Magician of Beverly Hills (Selling Hope)

But to really understand his genius, you had to see him pitch. We were in Beverly Hills during the Wild West days of the PC revolution. I had rigged up Lotus Symphony to talk to a little plastic satellite dish that pulled stock quotes out of the FM radio waves.

Dave stood in front of a room full of millionaires—men desperate for an edge—and he played them like a fiddle. He was the ultimate "Snake Oil Salesman" of the digital age, and I say that with love. Because he wasn't selling software. He was selling Hope.

He pointed to the screen where my macro was blinking.

"Gentlemen," he'd whisper, letting them in on a conspiracy. "The market follows physics. The trucks have to move before the factories can sell. If Transportation stocks jump, the Industrials follow 15 minutes later."

He leaned over that plastic dish like it was the Holy Grail. "Right now, you are blind. But this box? This box lives in that 15-minute gap. This box is a time machine."

The room went crazy. They climbed over each other to buy it. He taught me the lesson: The Carrot isn't the product. The Carrot is the belief that you are about to win.

The Bill Gates Incident

The perfect example of Dave's wiring happened in Las Vegas, at the Mirage, during Comdex.

Dave spots a woman he used to date. She's now a VP at Business-Week. She is sitting at a $10 Blackjack table... next to Bill Gates.

Now, a Recorder would freeze. A Recorder would calculate: "That is the richest man in the world. Do not disturb. Do not interrupt."

Dave? He walked right over. He gives the girl a big hug. He turns to Bill.

Bill looks up and says, "Hi, I'm Bill Gates."

Dave looks him right in the eye—the way only a Prince can—shakes his hand and says:

"Bill, I know who you are."

Then he looks at the $10 chips on the table, looks back at Bill, and drops the line of the century:

"Bill... what is this... Nintendo to you?"

The table exploded. Bill laughed. That is the Runner Superpower. He collapsed the distance between a salesman and a billionaire in three seconds.

The Crash

But the Runner engine runs hot. The parties, the alcohol, the constant "Go, Go, Go"—it takes a toll. He called me right around Christmas time, just like today. He was down in Mexico at his timeshare, fishing.

He said, "Robert, I have a belly ache. My stomach is killing me. What do I do?"

I gave him the standard advice—take Zantac, calm down.

He called me back later. "Robert, I went to the doctor. It's not acid. It's cancer. Stage 4."

My heart stopped. But Dave was still in character. He was still the Runner.

"I got this," he said. "You know me. I'm a healthy guy. I'm gonna fight it."

The Long Goodbye

For months, I called him every week. "How are you doing, Dave?"

"I'm good, Robert. Things are going good. I'm fighting."

He was selling me hope, just like he sold those guys in Beverly Hills. He didn't want to break the character.

By August, I said, "Dave, I'm coming to see you."

There was a long pause on the phone. The energy dropped. The Prince put down the mask.

"Robert," he said softly. "It might be hard."

"Why?"

"Because I'm dying. There isn't much left."

He had been protecting me from the truth the whole time. We lost him in early September. The light went out.

To The Family: Dave left behind a beautiful family. A wife, a daughter, and a son who has autism—a pure Recorder born to the ultimate Runner. If you are reading this: Your father was a giant. He could walk into a room of wolves and have them eating out of his hand. I love him. I love you. The Prince is gone, but the show? I'll never forget it.

The Calming Voice (Paul Ohrenberger)

If Dave was the gas, Paul was the steering wheel. He had this soothing, perfect tone. He could stand in front of a room and explain complex systems—not just the technology, but the people mechanics. He was the one who taught managers how to manage different operating systems.

Paul and I had a connection that defied the odds. We were both born in the same hospital in Winthrop. We found out later that we had crossed paths a thousand times before we met. He worked behind the counter at Capone's Grocery in East Boston—the store I went to every single day as a kid. He was serving me deli meat before he was helping me serve software.

The Missing Editor

Paul was my Anchor. No matter how crazy my ideas were, Paul could process them. He enjoyed the way my mind worked. He is the one person who should be sitting here with me right now, writing this book. He would have known exactly how to organize these chapters. He would have known how to translate the "Recorder" experience to the masses.

The Keeper of the Principles

Paul didn't just teach technology. He taught Humanity. He ran the management training programs at Lotus, but he wasn't just reading from a manual. He was teaching the soul of the company. He taught managers how to actually be managers. He taught them how to live up to the Lotus Development Principles—values like fairness, social responsibility, and treating people like adults.

He had this incredible ability to take a room full of stressed-out corporate climbers and walk them through the "Why."

- Why do we treat people this way?
- How do different operating styles work together?
- How do you handle a difficult employee without breaking their spirit?

He helped everyone. He didn't just give you the answer; he walked you through the logic so you felt like you found the answer. He made you feel smart.

The New Orleans Giggle (The Reality Check)

But my favorite memory of Paul isn't in a classroom. It's on a balcony at the Royal Sonesta in New Orleans. We were there for a conference, staying right on Bourbon Street. The party was raging outside—thousands of people, music, booze, chaos. The loudest place on Earth.

We were in the room, relaxing, smoking a little marijuana. Suddenly, my Recorder brain kicked in. The paranoia. The rules. I started waving my hands frantically.

"Paul! Paul! I gotta blow this smoke out the window! What if they smell it? What if we get caught?"

Paul just looked at me. He didn't panic. He let out this beautiful, soft giggle. He gestured to the open window, to the sea of madness below us.

"Robert," he laughed. "We are on Bourbon Street. In the French Quarter. I think you're gonna be okay."

He just laughed at the absurdity of it. Here I was, worried about a puff of smoke in a city that was currently inhaling every vice known to man. That was Paul. He was the Reality Check. When I spun out on the details, he pulled me back to the big picture with a smile.

The Empty Chair

It is a cruel irony that a man defined by his ability to communicate—a man who helped so many people find their voice—was taken down by a rare form of Parkinson's. It robbed him of his mechanics. He should be sitting here with me right now. He would have loved this book. He would have laughed at my drafts. He would have helped me explain the "Lotus Principles" of the brain. He was my Anchor. And God, I miss that giggle.

13. THE UNIVERSAL LANGUAGE: NADADUR VARDHAN
(The Hardware Beneath the Culture)

In 1985, I moved to California. I was a kid from Boston entering a new world. And the first real friend I made—the best friend I made—was a man named Nadadur Vardhan.

Nadadur was an accountant, about ten or eleven years older than me. When I walked into his world, I felt a strange sense of déjà vu. I knew this setup. I knew this rhythm.

You have to understand, almost everyone in my life was a Boss. Cousin Joe was the Captain of the Police Department. My Uncle owned the Funeral Home and the main ambulance service in Boston. And my Father wasn't just an accountant; he was the Boss Man for the IRS in Boston. He collected taxes door-to-door in the neighborhoods. He didn't just work in a high-rise; he had his office right out of the house. I grew up watching men come into that home office, sit down, and spill their financial guts. I saw the fear, the negotiation, the relief. I watched how the "Boss" handled people when they were vulnerable.

So when I met Nadadur—who was starting his own tax practice out of his home in Santa Monica—I wasn't walking into a stranger's office. I was walking back into my childhood, just in a different time zone.

The Trade

We made a deal: I gave him the technology—Lotus 1-2-3, the software that ran the financial world—and helped him set up his systems. In exchange, he did my taxes. It seemed like a simple swap. But what I actually got was a front-row seat to the way the world really works.

The Fly on the Wall

For fifteen years, I spent the first three months of every year working out of his office in Santa Monica. I wasn't an accountant. I was a "Silent Partner." I sat there, just like I used to sit in my father's house, and I listened.

But the clientele had changed. My dad dealt with the streets of Boston. Nadadur dealt with the stars. He did taxes for The Commodores. For Hollywood celebrities. For Politicians. For Multi-millionaires.

And here is what I learned, sitting in that chair, bridging the gap between my father's world and Nadadur's world:

The stories were identical.

It didn't matter if the client was a guy from Southie trying to settle a debt or a global superstar trying to hide assets. It didn't matter if they were from India, America, or Europe. They all had the same fears. The same threading moments. The same stress about money, family, and legacy.

"It's all relative." Just like in the funeral home, and just like in the IRS office, once you strip away the titles, the human structure is exactly the same.

The Bodyguard (Secret Service)

Nadadur's influence grew massive. When Barack Obama went to India, he took Nadadur to introduce him. That is the level he was operating at. He held beautiful events at his home in Brentwood. Ambassadors would come. Influential politicians would gather.

When Hillary Clinton was running for President, Nadadur hosted a fundraiser at a friend's house. I didn't go as a donor. I went as "Security." I played Secret Service agent for the day. I stood by the door—a big Irish-Italian guy, hands folded, scanning the room.

I met Hillary. I looked her right in the face. And as a Recorder, I noticed the one thing the cameras don't quite capture: Her eyes. They were the bluest eyes I had ever seen. You could see the intensity in them. I instantly understood what attracted Bill. It wasn't just politics; it was a magnetic force.

The Scale of Humanity (The Obstetrician)

Nadadur opened the world to me. Through him, I met his sister. She wasn't just a medical professional; she was a highly respected Obstetrician in India. We were talking one day, and I tried to impress her with a statistic I had read.

"I heard you've delivered something like 35,000 babies in your lifetime. That is unbelievable."

She looked at me and corrected me gently. "No, Robert. We are just about to go north of 100,000 babies."

I froze. 100,000? How is that mathematically possible?

She showed me the numbers. The density of the population. The speed of life in her region. It shattered my "Western" scale of reality. It taught me that my view of the world was tiny.

But even with 100,000 babies delivered, she told me the same thing Nadadur did: The bodies are all the same. The first breath is the same. The mother's look is the same.

The Validation (Indubala)

Then there was Nadadur's wife, Indubala. Like the rest of the family, she was a doctor—sharp, kind, and observant.

In 2019, years after I first met them, I finally found the language for my own mind. I was talking with Indubala and I told her, "You know, I found out I would be considered Autistic."

I expected her to be surprised, or maybe offer sympathy. She didn't. She looked at me with the calm precision of a doctor who has seen everything.

"Robert," she said. "Do you know what that means?"

"What?" I asked.

She said. "Binary thinking."

I was stunned. I had spent years trying to explain my brain to people. I had spent years thinking about "Recorders" and "Runners." And here was a doctor from the other side of the world, effortlessly handing me the key. She didn't see "disorder." She saw the operating system. It was confirmation.

The Professor and The Symbols

I used to go to late-night dinners with Nadadur and a brilliant Professor from UCLA. We would eat late, and we would talk about the future.

One night, we were discussing why English became the dominant business language. I expected a political answer. He gave me an Engineering answer.

"Robert, it comes down to symbols. The communication mechanism with the least amount of symbols will always win on a worldwide basis. It is the quickest way to transfer data."

English is efficient code. Mandarin is complex code. The world chose efficiency. He amazed me. If I asked the average American kid to name the 50 state capitals, maybe they get 48. This Professor didn't just know the capitals. He could tell you the name, the family history behind the name, and the economic driver of the city in 1890. He had a Recorder Mind of the highest order.

The Safe Room

Why did these people—Ambassadors, Geniuses, Politicians, Doctors like Indubala—talk to me?

I was a big kid from East Boston. I didn't have their degrees. I didn't have their pedigree.

But I offered them something they couldn't get anywhere else: An Unfiltered Connection.

I listened without judgment. I treated the Ambassador the same way I treated the guy at the sub shop. I appreciated their culture, their religion, and their politics without trying to change them.

Because I had been trained by the Bosses—by Joe, by my Uncle, by my Father—I knew that authority is just a role. The person underneath is just a person.

Nadadur passed away nine years ago. If he were here today, he would be the one writing this book. He was the smarter one. He was the character. But he left me with the lesson that connects everything in this story: Culture is just the software. Biology is the hardware. And if you look past the software, we are all running on the same machine.

14. THE COST OF THE CODE

(Tattoos, Empty Chairs, and The Void)

We talk about the "Binary Mind" like it's a gift. And it is. It allowed me to see the physics of a baseball, the inventory of a corporation, and the truth behind a fake smile.

But there is a cost. The system doesn't just record the wins. It records everything.

The Wrong Environment: Memories as Tattoos

When you raise a sensitive, high-fidelity child in a "tough love" or chaotic environment, you aren't just hurting their feelings. You are writing permanent code.

Most kids are like Etch-A-Sketches. They get yelled at, they cry, they shake it off, and the screen is clear the next day.

I was stone tablets. Every criticism, every time I was misunderstood, every time I was told I was "wrong" when I knew I was right—it was tattooed on my brain.

- The School Trauma: The teachers who didn't understand why I couldn't just "do it their way."
- The Social Friction: The exhaustion of trying to fit into a "Runner" world that moved too fast and cared too little about the details.
- The Diagnosis Gap: Living for decades without knowing why I was different. Thinking I was broken, when I was just operating on a different OS.

The Loss of Artifacts: The "Trinkets"

To a Runner, a "trinket" is just stuff. If they lose a watch or a photo, they say, "Oh well, it's just an object."

To a Recorder, an object is a link. It is a physical coordinate that ties us to a memory, a person, or a time.

- The graduation picture.
- The specific tool.
- The memento from a trip.

When those things are lost, it feels like a file corruption. It's not just "stuff." It is a piece of the archive that has been deleted without my permission. The anxiety of losing those small things is massive because they are the anchors to my history.

The Empty Chairs: The Circle of Friends

This is the heaviest cost. My circle was tight. Recorders don't let everyone in. We have a firewall. But if you get past the firewall—like Kevin, like Joe, like my closest friends—you are part of me.

And they left too early.

- Kevin, Arthur and Paul, My brothers, the protectors of my universe.
- Joe: My cousin, the protector.
- Dave, Paul, and Nadadur my dear friends.

When a Runner loses a friend, they grieve, and eventually, the sharp edges of the memory soften. For me, the edges never soften. The memory is as sharp today as it was the day they died. The silence is deafening. I don't just "miss" them; I feel the structural void where they used to be. It's a missing column in the building, and the weight is harder to carry every day.

The Loss of Purpose: The "Retired" Wilderness

Then there was the loss of the mission. After the adrenaline of Lotus, after the battles were fought and won, there was the drift. The words became "too big." The corporate world morphed into something I didn't recognize. I felt "retired," but not in the good way. I felt unplugged.

For a Recorder, having no data to process, no problem to solve, is a form of death. I wandered in that wilderness for years—knowing I had this engine, but having nowhere to drive the car.

It wasn't until 2019—until the psychology came back, until the "Binary Mind" theory started to form—that the lights turned back on.

15. THE 53-YEAR-OLD ANOMALY (THE ICE CREAM WARS)

I have said that my body processes sugar differently. That I should have been diabetic years ago. To prove this isn't hyperbole, I need to submit two pieces of evidence. Most people look at a "Food Challenge" as a test of hunger. I looked at it as a war game.

Part 1: St. Louis (The Tins)

In 2008, I watched Adam Richman on Man v. Food go to St. Louis to try a legend. The challenge: Drink five metal tins of malt shake—nearly a pure gallon of dairy—in 30 minutes. Since 1917, only 22 people had done it. Adam failed. He threw up.

I happened to be flying to St. Louis two weeks later. I was 51 years old. My wife told me, "Don't do it. You're crazy. You're going to make yourself sick." I ignored her. I had a plan.

I brought my SE, Wayne. Wayne wasn't just an engineer; in Desert Storm, he ran Covert Communications. He was also a trained paramedic. I told him, "Wayne, I need your paramedic skills on alert. I am going to do this at 3:30 PM. I'm going to override my body, and you need to watch for the crash."

We walked in. The owner went to grab the fancy tall glasses. I stopped him. "No. Keep it in the shakes. Keep it in the metal tins. I'll drink all five of them, one at a time."

I blasted through the first three tins. No problem. I got through the fourth.

Then I picked up the fifth tin. And the wall hit me.

I looked at the tin. I looked at the clock. And for the first time, the math didn't look good. I stopped and thought: Oops. I'm not gonna make it. This is the reason only 22 people have done this since 1917.

My stomach was screaming. The curdling had started.

Wayne looked at me. He saw me fading. He didn't offer sympathy. He leaned in and said, "Come on, Robert. I didn't wait around to see you do this. You can pull the car over now if you want."

He knew exactly which button to push.

I looked at him. "Give me one of your french fries."

I ate the fry. The salt cut the sugar slime on my tongue. It tricked my brain just enough to reboot the system.

I tipped the fifth tin back and sucked it down in a single flip.

Time: 26 minutes.

I got the T-shirt. I got the plaque. I told them to engrave it: Robert. Age 51.

Part 2: The Pig Trough (The Inhale)

A year later, my wife called me. She found another one. Farrell's Ice Cream was relaunching. They were holding a contest: The Pig Trough. Two massive banana splits, softball-sized scoops, piled into a plastic trough.

I qualified as the number 8 seed. I was 53. Every other competitor was a college kid in their 20s.

My wife and I showed up that morning. The women went first. I watched them delicately spooning the ice cream into their mouths. I turned to my wife and shook my head. "They are losing because they are eating it. You can't eat this. You have to inhale it."

The whistle blew. I didn't eat. I didn't chew. I just opened the hatch.

I also had a strategy the college kids didn't. I had mapped the density:

Strawberry: Softest. Melts fast. First.

Chocolate: Medium. Second.

Vanilla: Hardest. Last.

If you wait, the vanilla turns into a rock. I attacked the strawberry while the college kids were still trying to look cool.

The Result: I finished in 1 minute and 15 seconds. I looked up. The college kids were barely halfway through.

I won the trophy. I won free ice cream for a year. I got my name on the menu cover. I told the owner: "Put Robert. 53."

The Epilogue: Feelings vs. Profits

The irony is that while I mastered the ice cream, the owner failed the business. The next year, he called me back. He wanted me to defend my title for a news segment... at 6:00 AM.

I told him, "I'm the defending champion. You should find people to try to beat me." He said no. He didn't understand showmanship.

So I sat there at 6:00 AM, half-awake, and tried to speed-eat a trough on live TV. They left a cherry stem in the bowl. Because I was "inhaling" it, the stem got lodged in my throat. I nearly choked to death on the morning news.

Years later, I watched Marcus Lemonis on The Profit try to save that same business. It was painful to watch. You had Marcus—a guy who looks at the math—trying to explain to the owner that feelings are not a currency. The owner wanted it to work because he loved the brand. He had the "Runner" mindset: If I just hope enough, it will work. Marcus was trying to show him the P&L. The business failed.

Why? Because you can't pay the rent with nostalgia. Feelings don't equal profits. Whether it's eating ice cream or running a company, the moment you ignore the physics, you lose.

16. THE 1975 PREDICTION

(The Logan Airport Simulation)

Recorders are often accused of being paranoid or "doomsday thinkers." We aren't. We just see the trajectory before the curve hits the graph.

In 1975, I was living in the shadow of Logan Airport in Boston. Every day, I could smell the jet fuel. I could taste the exhaust. While everyone else just saw "airplanes," I saw a web of pollution being sprayed over the population.

I sat down and wrote a story. It was a prediction about how the world would end.

The Scenario: It wouldn't be a nuclear war. It would be the air. I described a choking agent that would suffocate the population.

But the specific detail was the Spread Pattern. I wrote that it wouldn't hit everywhere at once. It would hit the Major Cities first—the hubs. Then, it would ride the transportation lines to the rest of the world. It would be a global choking event, distributed by our own travel networks.

The Reality (45 Years Later):

Fast forward to 2020. If you took my story from 1975 and scratched out the word "Pollution" and wrote in "COVID-19," the story wouldn't skip a beat.

- It started in the major hubs.
- It traveled on the airplanes I watched at Logan.
- It choked people out.

Why did I see this? I wasn't a psychic. I was a Canary. I was breathing the exhaust at Logan. My body registered the toxicity, and my brain extrapolated the logic: If this system continues, this is the inevitable result.

Most people live in the moment. Recorders live in the projection. Sometimes that makes us look crazy. And sometimes, it makes us the only ones who bought masks 45 years early.

17. THE INTIMACY OF CONNECTION: HUG AWAY

I tell you these stories about Dad, Joe, Kevin, and Paul not just because they are memories, but because they are evidence.

They are evidence that connection doesn't always look like "normal" conversation. Sometimes it looks like a joke about a funeral home. Sometimes it looks like waving at a fighter jet. Sometimes it looks like finding the "good news" in death.

And sometimes, it looks like a squeeze.

The Language of the Squeeze: Hugs and the BMI/Autistic Child

For BMI and autistic kids, hugs are more than a nice idea. They are development tools.

Many kids like me grow up in a world where words don't always do the job. But the body speaks in other ways. A hug is one of them.

When an autistic child hugs, they may squeeze harder than expected. Not because they want to hurt, but because they don't always know their strength. Or maybe because the intensity of what they feel pours out all at once.

Too often, the world says: "Don't hug. Pull back. That's too much."

And in that moment, we shut down a gift instead of shaping it.

The Philosophy: Development vs. Treatment

The system loves the word "treatment." "We're treating autism." "We're treating behavior."

But let me ask: are we talking about a disease or about developing a human being?

BMI and autistic kids are not broken to be treated. They are individuals to be developed.

Words matter. If we call it treatment, we look for cures and fixes. If we call it development, we look for growth and strength.

Here's where hugs get caught in the crossfire. A child hugs too hard? Treatment says: "Remove the behavior." But development says: "Shape it, guide it, help them use it as a tool."

Training the Gift, Not Killing It: A Call to Action

The answer isn't to take hugs away. The answer is to train them.

Teach the child how to feel another person's body language. Show them how to adjust pressure. Help them notice if someone is leaning in or pulling away. But don't stop the hug. Because when you do, you don't just remove a behavior—you cut off one of the clearest ways they connect with the world.

When I say "hug them harder," I don't mean ignore a child screaming "don't touch me."

I mean: don't give up on hugs as part of their growth.

Hug harder in your commitment. Hug harder in your patience. Hug harder in your creativity.

Studies show hugs lower cortisol, raise oxytocin, and regulate breathing. That's the science.

But the soul knows it too. Every time two hearts touch, they exchange electricity. It's presence. It's trust. It's life.

So here's the truth: Hug away.

Don't let fear steal the best of us. Because for many of us, hugging is not just affection. It is our language. Our way of saying what words cannot. Our way of plugging into you—the world's most important WiFi.

52

If you want to fix the machine, find a Recorder.CH

(D efining the Two Architectural Poles)
   If you strip away the personality, the history, and the trauma, what are you left with?

You are left with the Operating System.

In the computer world, we understand that a Windows machine and a Mac are both computers. They can both send emails, they can both browse the web, and they can both crash.

But deep down, at the kernel level, they organize information differently.

If you try to run Mac code on a Windows machine without an adapter, it won't work. It's not because the code is bad; it's because the architecture is different.

Human beings are the same.

We are all the same species, but we are not all built on the same kernel.

As we established, evolution produced two necessary minds to keep the species alive. Now, we are going to define exactly how they work.

We call them the Binary Mind Inside (BMI™) and the Parallel Mind Inside (PMI™).

1. The BMI™: The Binary Mind Inside

Function: The Recorder

The Recorder is the brain's original accountant, engineer, and system-builder. It is the "Safety Architect."

• The Core Directive: System Integrity. The Recorder's primary goal is not "happiness" or "connection." Its primary goal is Accuracy.

• It asks: Is this true?

• It asks: Is this safe?

• It asks: Does the pattern hold?

• Cognitive Style: Sequential (System 2). Psychologist Daniel Kahneman famously described "System 2" thinking as slow, deliberate, and logical. The Recorder lives here. It processes life in a single-file line.

• Input A -> Process -> Output B.

• You cannot jump the line. You cannot skip a step.

• This is why Recorders hate being interrupted. If you interrupt a sequential process, you don't just pause it; you crash it.

• Data Preference: Consistency. The Recorder trusts Rules, Facts, and Logic. If the rule is "No shoes in the house," and you wear shoes in the house, the Recorder feels a physical spike of distress. It isn't about the dirt; it's about the violation of the code. If the code can be broken, safety does not exist.

• Evolutionary Role: The Sentry. The Recorder is the one who remembers that the red berries killed Uncle Joe five years ago. The Runner might say, "But they look so good!" The Recorder says, "The data says death."

2. The PMI™: The Parallel Mind Inside

Function: The Runner

The Runner is the brain's social engine, diplomat, and executor of real-time action. It is the "Social Architect."

• The Core Directive: Fluid Adaptation. The Runner's primary goal is Cohesion.

• It asks: Are we okay with each other?

• It asks: Does this fit the vibe?

• It asks: How do I keep the peace?

• Cognitive Style: Simultaneous (System 1). Kahneman's "System 1" is fast, intuitive, and emotional. The Runner lives here. It processes life in parallel streams. It takes in the tone of voice, the body language, the smell of the room, and the social hierarchy all at once. It doesn't analyze the data; it feels the data.

• Data Preference: Context. The Runner trusts Emotion, Subtlety, and Intuition. They understand that rules are flexible. "No shoes in the house" applies... unless the Queen visits, or unless you're rushing to the bathroom. To the Runner, the context matters more than the code.

• Evolutionary Role: The Diplomat. The Runner is the one who convinces the neighboring tribe not to attack. They don't use logic; they use charm, gifts, and social signaling.

3. The Architectural Trade-Off

You cannot be elite at both. This is the Zero-Sum Game of neuroscience.

To be a great Recorder, you must suppress the urge to "go along to get along." You must be willing to be the buzzkill who points out the math is wrong.

To be a great Runner, you must suppress the urge to correct every factual error. You must be willing to let a lie slide to keep the party going.

The "Autism" Label

What we call "Autism" is simply High-Fidelity Recording. It is a brain that has traded social fluidity for structural precision.

• Sensitivity to Light/Sound: This isn't a defect; it's a high-gain microphone. The Recorder hears everything because it is designed to miss nothing.

• Literal Thinking: This isn't a defect; it's coding language. The Recorder expects words to mean exactly what they are defined to mean.

4. Polarity and The Six Professions

Now we can map the Six Professions (from Chapter 1) directly to the architecture. They are not random. They are inevitable.

RECORDER DOMINANT (BMI)

Focus: Logic, Rules, System

• The Numbers People: Accountants, Scribes. They guard the resource.

• The Creators: Inventors, Engineers. They guard the tool.

• The Enforcers: Judges, Inspectors. They guard the law.

RUNNER DOMINANT (PMI)

Focus: Context, People, Adaptation

• The Connectors: Merchants, Diplomats. They guard the relationship.

• The Leaders: Visionaries, Politicians. They guard the future.

• The Healers: Counselors, Shamans. They guard the spirit.

5. The Physics of the Switch (Voltage)

To truly understand why a Recorder cannot "just relax" or "read between the lines," you have to go down to the physical layer of the machine. You have to look at the Voltage.

In the physical world, a computer chip is just a vast landscape of transistors. A transistor is a gate. It blocks electricity, or it lets it through.

• Voltage High (+5V): The gate is open. Current flows. We call this 1.

• Voltage Low (0V): The gate is closed. Current stops. We call this 0.

There is no "Medium Voltage." There is no "Sort of On."

If the voltage hovers in the middle (say, +2.5V), the machine does not "guess." It enters a floating state. It becomes unstable. It crashes.

The Recorder's Biology

The Binary Mind is biological hardware wired to reject the "floating state."

When a parent says "Maybe," or a boss says "We'll see," they are sending a +2.5V signal.

• The Runner Brain: Smooths the signal. It rounds up to "Yes" or down to "No" based on hope or feeling.

• The Recorder Brain: Detects the floating voltage and throws a Hardware Interrupt.

The physical anxiety you feel isn't emotional "worry." It is the system alerting you that the input is invalid. You cannot process a floating signal. You need the switch to click.

6. The Operating Languages: High-Level vs. Assembler

Every computer system has layers of language.

• The Surface (The Runner): This is what you see on your screen (Windows/MacOS). It is colorful, intuitive, and uses metaphors like "Files" and "Trash Cans." It is designed for ease of use.

• The Bedrock (The Recorder): This is what happens inside the chip. It is electricity, switches, and direct commands.

Humans cannot read billions of 1s and 0s. So, engineers created the first bridge: Assembly Language (Assembler).

Assembler is the native language of the Recorder. It is a low-level coding language that speaks directly to the hardware. It is rigid, sequential, and literal. It does not assume context. It demands specific instructions.

The Syntax Error

In a modern "High-Level Language" (like Python or English), you can say: "Please get me a glass of water." The system infers what you mean.

In Assembler, that instruction does not exist. If you type "Get water," the system crashes.

In Assembler, you must write:

```
MOV ARM, 45_DEGREES
OPEN HAND
DETECT OBJECT_GLASS
CLOSE HAND
RETRACT ARM
```

This explains 90% of the conflict in a Recorder's life. The world speaks in High-Level nuances. The Recorder listens in Assembler.

SCENARIO: THE CLEAN ROOM

• Parent (High-Level): "Clean your room."

• Recorder Child (Assembler): Error. Instruction Undefined. Does "clean" mean vacuum? Does "clean" mean organize by size? Does "clean" mean shove everything under the bed?

The child stands there, frozen. The parent thinks the child is being defiant. The truth is, the child is experiencing a Syntax Error.

The Fix: Change the input to Assembler.

"Put the laundry in the hamper."

"Put the Legos in the bin."

The child moves instantly. The code is valid.

7. The Instruction Set: Why "I'm Fine" Freezes Us

In Assembler, you don't talk to the computer. You command the memory. A massive portion of the Recorder's brain energy is spent on one specific instruction: CMP (Compare).

Code: CMP A, B (Compare Value A with Value B).

• The Runner: Compares feelings.

• The Recorder: Compares data.

The "I'm Fine" Scenario

A spouse says "I'm fine," but their jaw is clenched.

• Runner Code: Ignores the jaw. Listens to the word. Result: "They are fine."

• Recorder Code:

MOV AX, [AUDIO_INPUT] ("I'm fine")

MOV BX, [VISUAL_INPUT] (Clenched Jaw)

CMP AX, BX (Compare Audio to Visual)

JNE ERROR_HANDLER (Jump if Not Equal -> Error)

The Recorder freezes because the JNE (Jump if Not Equal) instruction forced them out of the conversation and into the error loop. They cannot move forward until the inequality is resolved. They aren't being difficult. They are stuck in a logical loop.

8. The Stack: Why Interruption Hurts

High-Level minds (Runners) use a "Heap" memory structure—they throw everything in a pile and grab what they need. Assembler minds (Recorders) use a Stack.

The Stack: You put data on top (Push), and you take data off the top (Pop). To get to the bottom item, you must remove the top items first.

If a Recorder is deep in focus, they have loaded 15 layers of data onto their mental Stack.

- Layer 1: The math.
- Layer 2: The pattern.
- ...
- Layer 15: The current thought.

If a Runner interrupts them with "Hey, look at this cat video!", the Stack collapses. The Recorder screams or shuts down.

Why? Because you didn't just distract them. You toppled the Stack.

They dropped the data. Now they have to painstakingly re-load all 15 layers, one by one, to get back to where they were.

To the Runner, it was a 2-second interruption. To the Recorder, it was a total system crash and reboot.

9. The Compilation Tax (Energy Cost)

This brings us to the concept of Energy Cost.

If you are a Runner, your brain comes pre-installed with the "Social Interpreter." It costs you almost zero energy to interact.

If you are a Recorder, you do not have that interpreter. You are running on manual mode.

Every time a Recorder interacts with a Runner, they have to perform a process called Compiling. They take the "High-Level" social input and manually break it down into Assembler code.

The Transaction:

Input: "How was your weekend?"

- Runner Brain: Say "Good," ask them back. (Cost: 1 unit).
- Recorder Brain: Analysis required. Why are they asking? Do they want data? Is this a trap? Scan memory. Select response: "Fine." (Cost: 50 units).

We call this the Compilation Tax.

This is why a Recorder can solve calculus for hours (low energy cost because the logic is pure) but needs a nap after a 20-minute cocktail party (massive energy cost because of manual translation).

10. The NOP State (No Operation)

Sometimes, a Recorder sits perfectly still, staring at nothing. The world thinks they are "zoning out" or "daydreaming."

In Assembler, there is an instruction called NOP (No Operation). It tells the CPU: Do nothing for this cycle. Just wait.

Why do programmers use NOP? To sync the timing. To let the rest of the system catch up.

When a Recorder is rocking, pacing, or staring, they are executing NOP cycles. They are not broken. They are waiting for their internal clock to re-sync with the chaotic external world. They are calibrating.

Conclusion: The Advantage of Assembler

So why would nature keep the Assembler mind? Why not upgrade everyone to the High-Level "Social" language?

Because High-Level languages are slow and bloated.

Assembler is the fastest language in existence. It runs closer to the metal. There is no lag. You cannot hide a bug in Assembler.

When the crisis hits—when the plane is going down, or the server is hacked, or the patient is crashing—you do not want a mind that operates on "vibes." You want a mind that can read the raw code of reality and execute the fix without hesitation.

The Runner sees the Story. The Recorder sees the Source Code.

If you want to feel good, talk to a Runner.

53

The world needs these minds. But the world must st

(The Operating System of the Recorder)
Human beings were never meant to think the same way. That simple truth—ignored, denied, and bulldozed over for centuries—is the source of almost every modern misunderstanding about the mind.

We have established the History (The Six Professions) and the Code (Assembler). Now, we must look at the Daily Operation.

How does a Binary Mind actually navigate a Tuesday afternoon?

It doesn't happen by magic, and it doesn't happen by "acting normal." It happens by following a strict set of internal principles. These aren't choices. They are the hard-coded subroutines that keep the system stable.

When a Recorder tries to violate these principles to please a Runner world, the system destabilizes. Anxiety spikes. Burnout sets in. The mask slips.

But when a Recorder understands these principles and builds a life that respects them, they become unstoppable.

If you are a Recorder, you will recognize these instantly. If you are a Runner, this is your user manual for the people in your life you have labeled "difficult."

1. Principle One: The Replay Protocol (The Truth Engine)

If there is one trait the world has wildly misunderstood, it is Replay.

Psychologists often call it "rumination." They treat it as a symptom of anxiety or depression. They tell clients to "let it go" or "stop dwelling on the past."

They are fundamentally wrong. Replay is not emotional wallowing. Replay is forensic analysis.

The Mechanics of Latency

To understand Replay, you must understand the "Compilation Tax" we discussed in the previous chapter. In the moment, a social interaction is often too noisy for a Recorder to process fully.

• Input Stream: The person's words + their tone + their body language + the lights in the room + the background noise.

• Recorder Capacity: The Assembler mind is trying to verify every single bit of that data in real-time. It is often impossible. The bandwidth is maxed out just trying to survive the interaction without saying something "wrong."

So, the Recorder engages a buffer. We record the raw data to the hard drive without fully analyzing it. We survive the moment by using scripts and nodding.

The Post-Processing Phase

Later—often hours later, while driving, showering, or trying to sleep—the system finally has the bandwidth to process the data. It boots up the Replay Protocol. We play the tape back. But this time, we aren't distracted by the noise. We play it frame-by-frame.

• Frame 14: You said you were happy.
• Frame 15: Your eyes narrowed.
• Frame 16: You shifted your weight away from me.
• The Conclusion: You were lying.

This leads to the "Delayed Truth" phenomenon. A Runner forgets the argument ten minutes after it ends. "It's over, we hugged." A Recorder wakes up two days later, angry. Why? Because the rendering process just finished.

To the Runner, this looks like holding a grudge. To the Recorder, this is just Late Arrival Truth. We aren't dwelling. We just finished the math.

SCENARIO: THE KITCHEN ARGUMENT

You're in the kitchen. Your partner says, "It's fine, really. I'm not mad," and walks away a little too fast. In the moment, you feel a faint internal jolt, but you don't have the bandwidth to analyze it. The dishwasher is humming, a kid is asking where their shoes are. You say "Okay" and move on.

Three hours later, you're driving alone. No noise. No interruptions. Replay starts running on its own:

• You hear the exact pitch of "fine."
• You notice the micro-pause before "really."
• You remember they closed the cabinet harder than usual.

By the time you pull into the driveway, the conclusion is clear: They weren't fine. They were hurt, and they lied to keep the peace. From the outside, it looks like you "got mad out of nowhere" in the car. Inside, this was just the moment the rendering finally finished.

SCENARIO: THE PERFORMANCE REVIEW

At work, your manager says: "You're doing great overall. Just be a little more flexible with the team." You nod. The meeting moves on.

Two nights later, Replay reassembles the meeting data:

• "Flexible" was only used when you challenged bad data.
• "Team" actually meant one specific co-worker who cuts corners.
• "Overall" was padding to soften the correction.

Suddenly the real sentence appears: "Stop pointing out structural problems because it makes someone uncomfortable." You're not obsessing. You're decoding.

2. Principle Two: Pattern Detection (Locking vs. Scanning)

A Runner mind "scans" the world. It looks for the gist. It ignores the details to build a fast, general picture.

A Recorder mind "locks" onto the world. It looks for the structure.

This is not a visual preference; it is a processing filter. When a Runner looks at a forest, they see "Nature." When a Recorder looks at a forest, they see:

• The fractals in the fern leaves.

• The repetition of the pine needles.

• The specific angle of the shadow.

• The brown patch on the oak tree that signifies a beetle infestation.

The Curse of Cassandra

This principle allows Recorders to predict the future with unnerving accuracy. Because we record the pattern, not the story, we notice when the pattern breaks long before anyone else does.

We are not psychic. We just noticed that the variable X changed from 1 to 0, while everyone else was looking at the scenery. The pain of the Recorder is seeing the train wreck coming, warning everyone, being told to "stop being paranoid," and then watching the train wreck happen exactly as predicted.

SCENARIO: THE SLOW-MOTION BUSINESS CRASH

You work in a small company. Everyone is celebrating a big new client. The Runner minds are fully activated—music, pastries, high-fives.

You look at the numbers and see:

• Payment terms are longer.

• Profit margin is thinner.

• Loyal customers are being deprioritized to serve the new one.

You say, "If we keep prioritizing this one account and they pull out, we're overexposed."

The response: "You're being negative. Can't you just enjoy the win?"

Six months later, the client pulls out. Cash flow collapses. The same people say, "Nobody could have seen this coming." You did. You just didn't fit the mood.

SCENARIO: THE TEENAGER AND THE NEW FRIEND

A Recorder teenager comes home and says: "Something's off about that new kid in our group." The parent answers: "You're being judgmental. Give people a chance."

Replay plus Pattern Detection fires quietly in the background:
- The new kid changes their story slightly each time.
- They only show up when there's something to gain.
- They subtly pit one friend against another.

Three months later, there's a blow-up, secrets are revealed, and the friend group splits in half. The Recorder is not surprised. They saw the pattern while everyone else was watching the performance.

3. Principle Three: Sensory Memory (The 4D Record)

Memory works differently for the two architectures.

When a Runner remembers a childhood memory, they remember the narrative and the emotion. "It was a happy Christmas. I got a bike."

When a Recorder remembers, they reconstruct the Sensory File. The file isn't compressed. It is stored in RAW format. We don't just remember "Christmas." We remember:
- The scratch of the wool sweater on the back of the neck.
- The smell of the pine resin (Terpenes).
- The hum of the refrigerator in the background (60Hz).
- The exact sequence of the lights blinking (Red, Green, Green, Blue).

This is why Recorders are often accused of being "stuck in the past." We aren't stuck. But when we access a memory, we are transported back into the full sensory experience.

The Trigger Mechanism

Runners can "fade" bad memories over time. They blur the edges. Recorders have to archive them. The edges stay sharp. This is a superpower for creativity and engineering, but a liability for trauma processing.

SCENARIO: THE "OVERREACTION" TO A SMELL

An adult Recorder walks into a new office building. Everything seems fine until they step into a conference room. A specific cleaning chemical hits their nose. Instantly, their heart rate spikes. Shoulders tense. The brain wants out.

To colleagues, it looks irrational. "It's just a smell. You're being dramatic." But the internal system has retrieved a file they didn't ask for: Hospital corridors. A sick family member. The helplessness of that moment. The body isn't responding to "now." It's responding to the archived file.

SCENARIO: THE SAFE SOUND

The flip side is just as powerful. A Recorder sits in a crowded cafe, barely holding it together. The noise is sharp. Cups clink. Then a specific song comes on—one they listened to alone in their room as a kid. Their system immediately calms. Breathing slows. Shoulders drop. To someone else, it's "just a song." To a Recorder, it's a tagged file: SAFE.

4. Principle Four: The Single-Task Protocol (The Myth of Multitasking)

Society worships multitasking. Corporate job descriptions demand it. But neurologically, multitasking is a lie. The brain cannot do two things at once; it just switches back and forth very fast.

• Runners: Switch fast with low cost. (Low switching penalty).
• Recorders: Switch slow with high cost. (High switching penalty).

A Recorder is a Serial Processor. We do A. We finish A. Then we do B. If you force us to do A and B at the same time, both systems degrade.

The Physics of the "Stack"

Think of the Recorder's focus like a stack of plates. To enter "Deep Work," the Recorder has to load the context onto their mental stack.

• Plate 1: The goal.
• Plate 2: The variables.
• ...
• Plate 10: The current thought.

If a Runner interrupts a Recorder with "Hey, look at this cat video!", they aren't just pausing the work. They are knocking over the stack of plates.

The Recorder screams or shuts down. Why? Because you didn't just distract them. You crashed the system. Now they have to pick up every single plate, check it for cracks, and re-stack them one by one.

SCENARIO: THE PARENT AND THE HOMEWORK

A Recorder child is doing math. They've quietly built the internal stack: the rules, the problem, where they left off. A parent walks in: "Pause that for a second and tell your sister about your day."

To the parent, this is polite. To the child, the stack just collapsed. They stare. They look "defiant." Actually, they are trying to keep the context from sliding off the stack. If the parent insists, the child snaps. Not because they are rude, but because their system is being forced to violate its own architecture.

SCENARIO: THE OPEN-PLAN OFFICE

A Recorder adult wears noise-canceling headphones, trying to write a report. Within 30 minutes: A "Got a sec?" at the desk. A Slack ping. A meeting pop-up.

Each interruption is a stack crash. A context reload. By 3:00 PM, the office thinks the Recorder "doesn't handle stress well." In reality, the Recorder has spent more energy rebooting than thinking.

5. Principle Five: Absolute Morality (The Internal Compass)

For a Runner, morality is often Socially Relative.

• Rule: "Don't steal."

• Context: "Unless it's from a big corporation, or I'm underpaid, or everyone else is doing it."

For a Recorder, morality is Structurally Absolute.

• Rule: "Don't steal."

• Context: "Stealing is a violation of property rights. Violation is Error. Error is bad."

The Pain of the White Lie

Recorders struggle to "play the game" or "kiss the ring" in corporate politics. We cannot fake respect. We cannot lie to a client to smooth things over.

It isn't that we are "holy." It's that we are Binary. A lie introduces a corruption in the database. To a Recorder, holding a lie in their head feels physically painful—like a pebble in a shoe. The system flags it as an error every few seconds.

SCENARIO: THE "SMALL" CORPORATE LIE

A manager pulls a Recorder worker aside: "Tell the client we're further along than we are. It'll buy us time."

To the manager, this is spin. To the Recorder, this is a request to introduce corrupted data into the system. They feel physical discomfort. A drop in trust. If they comply, they will think about that lie for weeks because the database won't let it go.

SCENARIO: THE POLITE CHILD

A child is told: "No matter what Aunt Linda gives you, say you love it." Aunt Linda gives them a scratchy, painful sweater. The child says: "I don't like it. It hurts." Later, they are scolded for embarrassing the family. The child learns that adults ask them to corrupt their truth to protect an image. Some disconnect; others refuse and get labeled "difficult."

6. Principle Six: Environmental Overload (Hardware vs. Software)

When a Recorder has a meltdown in a busy restaurant, it is not a "behavioral issue." It is a Denial of Service (DoS) Attack.

The Runner brain has a built-in Filter. It says: Ignore the humming fridge. Ignore the tag on your shirt. Focus on the conversation.

The Recorder brain has a Funnel. It receives everything.

- The lights are flickering at 60Hz.
- The music is too bass-heavy.
- The smell of cologne is chemical.
- The chair is scratchy.
- Three people are talking.

The Recorder processes all of this with equal priority. The CPU hits 100%. The cooling fans spin up (stimming, rocking). If the input doesn't stop, the system crashes.

The Meltdown is a Reboot

380 - ROBERT ANTHONY CAGGIANO

A meltdown is not a tantrum. A tantrum is a manipulation tool used to get a reward.

Don't negotiate with Terrorist.

A meltdown is a biological system failure.

SCENARIO: THE BIRTHDAY PARTY

A child is at a loud trampoline park. Whistles, screaming, lights, sugar. They hold it together for an hour. They smile for pictures. On the drive home, they explode—screaming, inconsolable. The parent thinks: "You were fine all day, why are you acting like this now?"

Reality: The system capacity was exceeded gradually. In the quiet of the car, there was no more distraction to absorb the load. The crash happened.

SCENARIO: THE ADULT DINNER

An adult Recorder is at dinner. TV on the wall. Music loud. Kitchen noise. They are doing internal load balancing: Focusing hard on one face, suppressing the silverware sounds, fighting the glare.

After an hour, they say: "I need to step outside." The table laughs: "You're such an introvert." No. They like people. They just can't survive the data stream.

7. Principle Seven: The Binary Decision Tree (If/Then)

Finally, the Binary Mind navigates life through If/Then logic. Runners navigate through Feel/Flow logic.

• Runner: "I'll see how I feel when I get there."

• Recorder: "If I get there and the door is locked, then I will call you. If you don't answer, then I will wait 10 minutes. If you still don't answer, then I will leave."

We script the future. We build decision trees to handle uncertainty. When the plan changes suddenly, Recorders panic. It's not because we hate spontaneity. It's because we pre-rendered the entire decision tree for "Plan A." When you switch to "Plan B" instantly, we have no tree. We are standing in the void without code.

SCENARIO: THE SUDDEN CHANGE

A Recorder has a plan: Leave at 6:00. Park in garage. Eat at restaurant. They have quietly coded the tree: If lot full → use overflow. If wait long → sit at bar.

At 5:45, a friend texts: "Actually, let's just wing it. We'll wander around and see what we feel like."

To the Runner, this is freedom. To the Recorder, this is a request to delete the entire decision tree and operate in an empty space. They freeze. They get irritated. "Can we please stick to the plan?" They aren't being rigid. They just had their map torn up right before the trip.

SCENARIO: THE FAMILY VACATION

Parents tell a Recorder child: "We're going away. It'll be fun. Just pack."

The child asks: "Where? For how long? Is there a pool?"

Parent: "Why can't you just relax?"

The child is asking for the variables required to build a stable If/Then tree. Without that, the trip feels like a bug report waiting to happen.

A BINARY TUESDAY (Putting It All Together)

To see how this feels in real time, let's walk through a single day.

• Morning: Replay runs on yesterday's conversation with a coworker. You realize they weren't honest. (Principle One)

• Commute: A specific smell on the train triggers an old memory file. (Principle Three)

• Work: Someone interrupts your deep-focus task five times in an hour. Your stack crashes. (Principle Four)

• Meeting: You're asked to "massage the numbers" in a presentation. You feel physically sick. (Principle Five)

• Lunch: The cafeteria is loud and bright. You eat fast and escape to a hallway to cool down. (Principle Six)

• Afternoon: You warn leadership about a small pattern in the data that nobody else sees yet. They ignore you. (Principle Two)

• Evening: A friend cancels a plan at the last minute and says, "Let's just play it by ear later this week." Your whole decision tree goes blank. (Principle Seven)

From the outside, it looks like you "overreacted" three or four times in one day. From the inside, your system was simply trying, over and over, to maintain integrity in an environment not designed for your wiring.

Conclusion: The User Manual

These principles are not flaws. They are the specs of a high-performance machine designed for truth, precision, and depth.

54

(Structural Advantages of the Recorder)
People don't associate the word power with the word autistic. That alone tells you how wrong we've been looking at this.

For decades, the conversation around the Binary Mind has been dominated by a "Deficit Model." We talk about what is missing. We talk about the lack of social fluidity, the lack of eye contact, the lack of filter. When we do talk about strengths, we drift into Hollywood clichés. We talk about the "Savant"—the guy who can count toothpicks on the floor or memorize the phone book.

That is insulting. It treats the Binary Mind like a party trick.

The powers I'm talking about are not cinematic. No lightning bolts. No magic tricks. They aren't flashy, and they don't perform on command for an audience. In fact, that's why they've been missed, suppressed, and misinterpreted for so long.

These powers are Structural. They are the result of an operating system that prioritizes Truth over Tribe and Precision over Peace.

When a Binary Mind is forced to mask—to act like a Runner—these powers are buried under anxiety. But when the wiring is allowed to operate cleanly, something startling occurs. The person doesn't become different. They become fully themselves.

This chapter is the inventory of your arsenal.

1. The Power of Replay (The Forensic Audit)

The world values speed. It rewards the person who has a quick comeback in the meeting. It rewards the person who can smooth over an awkward moment instantly. That world favors Runners. Runners live in the "Now."

But the Binary Mind was not built for the "Now." It was built for the Truth. And the Truth rarely reveals itself in real-time. It reveals itself in the analysis.

The Mechanics of Replay

To a Runner, memory is a watercolor painting. It captures the feeling of the moment. "We had a good meeting. Everyone seemed happy."

To a Recorder, memory is a Black Box Flight Recorder. We do not just remember the event; we possess the raw data file. This capability—Replay—is the ability to re-run a social interaction, a technical problem, or a conflict frame-by-frame, hours or days after it happened.

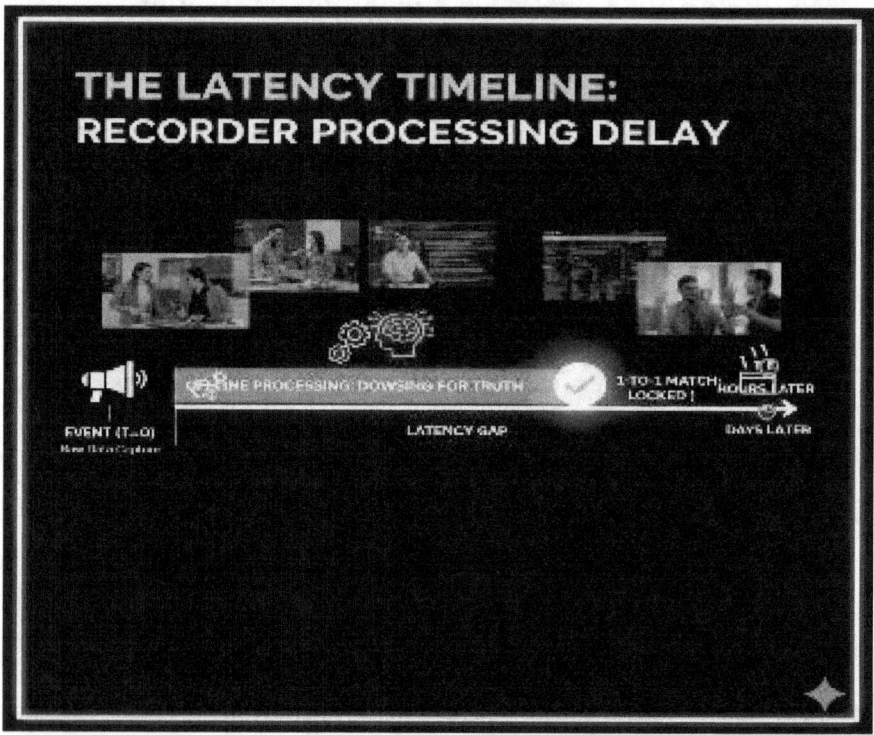

Replay in the Real World

Replay isn't something you turn on. It turns on you. It happens when your hands are finally idle and your body is no longer managing the world. It happens when the engine noise quiets and the pressure drops. That's when the file opens.

You've likely had this moment countless times: a conversation you thought was over suddenly plays back with ruthless clarity. Not emotionally—structurally. You don't feel hurt first. You see something first.

- You notice the pause that didn't belong.
- The answer that skipped a step.
- The smile that appeared half a beat too late.

And in that instant, the conclusion isn't dramatic. It's calm. Oh. That's what happened.

This is why Binary Minds are rarely fooled twice by the same person. Once replay resolves a pattern, it never needs to be solved again.

In workplaces, this has enormous consequences. While others move on quickly from a meeting that "felt fine," you quietly disengage from proposals that don't withstand replay. Later—sometimes months later—when problems surface, people are shocked. You're not. You didn't argue. You didn't confront. You simply updated your internal map.

Replay doesn't make you loud. It makes you accurate. And over time, people sense this. They may not be able to name it, but they know: you won't forget what actually happened.

2. Pattern Recognition (The Prediction Engine)

Replay gives you clarity on the past. Pattern Recognition gives you dominion over the future. From a very young age, you likely noticed things others dismissed. You noticed the teacher got angry exactly 30 seconds after the bell rang. You noticed the specific tone your mother used two days before a family fight.

Vertical vs. Horizontal Thinking

Runners think Horizontally. They scan the horizon for immediate threats.

Recorders think Vertically. We look at the root cause. We record the structure of reality rather than the story of reality.

- The Story: "The company is doing great!"
- The Structure: "Accounts Payable is delaying checks by 14 days. This precedes bankruptcy by 3 months."

Why You Were Always "Ahead of Your Time"

Pattern recognition rarely earns praise in the moment. It earns respect in hindsight. As a child, this ability often made you feel out of step. You noticed when friendships were unstable long before they ended. You sensed shifts in teachers, institutions, or authority figures before anyone acknowledged change.

Adults often dismissed this as imagination or negativity. But what they were rejecting wasn't anxiety—it was premature clarity.

Binary Minds don't see events as isolated dots. They see sequences. This means when most people are reacting emotionally to the present, you're already observing the future being assembled piece by piece. This is why you often felt older than your age—not emotionally, but structurally. You weren't precocious. You were orienting in three dimensions while others operated in two.

In business contexts, this shows up as early warnings:
• "This process won't scale."
• "That incentive structure is flawed."
• "This success is unstable."

These comments make social rooms uncomfortable because they interrupt momentum. And momentum—especially social momentum—is something Runner systems protect. But history always sides with architecture. Civilizations don't fail suddenly. They fail predictably—because patterns compound quietly until collapse appears "unexpected." You noticed the compound early.

3. Deep Focus (The Monotropic Laser)

There is a reason interruption feels physically painful to you. It feels like a physical blow because your attention is not a lightbulb; it is a laser. Neurologists call this Monotropism.

• Runners (Polytropism): Attention is diffuse. Like a lantern, it lights up a wide area dimly.

• Recorders (Monotropism): Attention is concentrated. Like a laser, it burns hot on a single point.

Why Your Best Work Was Always Done in Silence

If you look back honestly, your most important work didn't happen in meetings. It happened when you were left alone.

Binary Minds don't warm up gradually. They drop in. When the environment is clean and interruption-free, something rare happens: the system engages fully. This is why time disappeared when you were absorbed. Not because you were escaping—but because your cognitive architecture was finally allowed to operate at capacity.

Completion isn't optional for you. It's regulatory. Unfinished tasks don't sit in the background. They actively draw energy until resolved. That's why half-done projects feel physically irritating and mentally noisy. Closure isn't satisfaction—it's silence.

In environments that respected this—labs, workshops, studios, solitary problem-solving—you thrived. In environments that demanded constant switching and responsiveness, you burned out. None of that reflects motivation or attitude. It reflects system design.

4. Emotional Fidelity (The Lie Detector)

You were often accused of being "too honest," "too intense," or "too sensitive." None of those were flaws. They were signs that your emotional signal wasn't distorted.

Runners have a built-in Social Mixer. They can take their true emotion (Boredom) and mix it with a social mask (Polite Interest) to create a smooth output. Recorders lack the Mixer. We have a Direct Line.

The Human Mirror

When someone is fake, you physically recoil. You don't laugh at jokes that aren't funny. You don't nod when you don't agree. You act as a mirror. And people who hate their reflection will hate the mirror.

Why You're Trusted in Crises

When systems fail, people seek Binary Minds—not because of charm, but because of steadiness. In emergencies, performance collapses and emotional scripts evaporate. What remains is signal.

Binary Minds excel here because they don't amplify chaos. Their emotions stay proportional to reality—not to perception, not to fear, not to group panic. You've likely noticed this:

• You became calm when things got serious.

• You thought clearly when others couldn't.

• You saw solutions instead of noise.

Emotional fidelity isn't loud. It's clean. And clean signals are invaluable when stakes are high. This is why people instinctively look to you when things break—even if they ignore you when things are comfortable.

5. The Moral Spine (The System of Justice)

Why do Binary Minds struggle to lie? It's not because we are saints. It's because a lie is a Data Corruption.

To a Runner, a lie is a social tool. To a Recorder, a lie is a structural flaw. Holding a lie requires energy. It requires maintaining a false file alongside the true file. Recorders hate wasting energy on false files.

Why Integrity Costs You—and Why It's Still Non-Negotiable

Integrity wasn't a value you adopted. It was an internal condition. This is why compromising yourself never felt strategic—it felt dangerous. A small deviation from alignment didn't feel social or strategic. It felt like introducing instability into a load-bearing structure.

You may have paid for this:

• Lost promotions

• Burned bridges

• Being labeled "difficult"

But over time, something stronger replaced that loss: internal coherence. Binary Minds don't fracture well. Once fractured, everything degrades. So the system protects itself by resisting corruption—even when that resistance is socially expensive.

That moral spine isn't rigidity. It's load tolerance. Structures that bend too far collapse. Structures that hold preserve safety for everyone else.

6. Crisis Stabilization (The Cool Head)

Have you ever noticed that you are anxious when everything is calm, but totally calm when everything falls apart?

This is the paradox of the Binary Mind. Daily Life is full of ambiguous signals (small talk, unwritten rules). This ambiguity triggers anxiety because the variables are undefined.

Crisis is binary. The car has crashed. The system is down. Suddenly, the ambiguity is gone. The variables are locked. While the Runners are panicking, the Recorder steps into Operational Mode.

This is a superpower that cannot be taught. It is the ability to turn off emotion and turn on logic exactly when everyone else is losing their minds.

7. Sensory Radar (The Sentry)

We call it "Sensory Processing Disorder." We should call it Early Warning Radar.

Your inability to filter out background noise is not a defect; it is a Sentry function. In the tribe, the heavy sleepers were the ones who got eaten by the lion. The light sleepers—the ones who woke up because a twig snapped 50 yards away—were the ones who woke the tribe and saved everyone.

You notice the anomaly. You are the canary in the coal mine.

8. When These Powers Finally Turn On

Filter

Filter: Blocks most input.
Reduces information.
Creates 'calm' by
ignoring data.

**Funnel
(Sensory Radar)**

Funnel (Sensory Radar / The Sentry):
Processes inputs information for anomlies.
Creates 'warning' by finding the threat.
🔍. You are the Sentry.

interference, not because of alignment.

But when interference stops—when pressure lifts, when autonomy appears, when environments stabilize—the system initializes fully. This often happens later than you wanted. Sometimes decades later.

And when it does, the feeling is unmistakable. You don't feel smarter. You feel quieter. The noise drops. The contradictions resolve. Your past reorders itself.

You finally understand: I wasn't behind. I was paused.

This is what people mean when they say Binary Minds "come into their own." Nothing was added. Nothing was learned. The system simply stopped fighting incompatible input.

Conclusion

The world didn't fail to notice Binary Minds. It failed to understand them.

Once you see these powers clearly, a different truth appears: civilization has always depended on people like you—but rarely knew how to protect them. You were asked to adapt instead of being translated. To perform instead of being deployed. To socialize instead of stabilize.

And yet, when systems needed truth more than comfort, you were always there.

These are not superpowers because they make you special. They are superpowers because they keep reality anchored when everything else drifts.

Not broken. Not delayed. Not defective.

Deployed late—but deployed exactly as designed.

55

THE SENTINEL'S PARTNER

I have a theory about why Recorders bond so deeply with animals, and why the loss of a dog can bring a grown man to his knees in a way that confuses the rest of the world.

To understand the grief, you have to understand the history. I believe the Dog and the Recorder didn't just meet by accident. We co-evolved. We are two halves of the same security system.

The Night Watch Go back 20,000 years. Picture the tribe at night. The fire is dying down. The "Runners" are asleep. They are exhausted from the hunt, huddled together, sleeping soundly because they trust the safety of the cave.

But there is one guy who is awake. **The Recorder.** He is the Sentinel. His brain is stuck in the **"ON"** position. He hears the twig snap 100 yards away. He feels the shift in the wind. He is flooded with cortisol because his job is to anticipate the threat before it arrives. He is exhausted, but he cannot sleep because the data won't stop coming in.

Then, out of the darkness, comes the Wolf. The Wolf is also a Sentinel. He is also scanning. He is also binary: *Safe/Unsafe.*

The Recorder looks at the Wolf. The Wolf looks at the Recorder. And in that moment, a contract was signed that changed our DNA. The Recorder realized: *"I can't smell what you smell. And you can't plan what I plan. But if we sit here together, I can finally close my eyes for five minutes."*

The First Anxiety Medication The dog became the Recorder's **Regulation Partner.** For the first time in history, the Recorder could offload the "Scanning" duty.

- If the dog is sleeping, I know it is safe to relax.
- If the dog's ears perk up, I know my anxiety isn't "crazy"—it's real.

We became a single unit. The dog learned to read the human's eyes, and the human learned to read the dog's ears.

The "Always On" Solution Fast forward to today. My brain is still that ancient Sentinel. It is still burning massive energy scanning for threats that don't exist. This causes **Atrophy**. My system is overheating.

But when I walk through the door and see my dog, the chemical re-action is instant. My dog looks at me. There is no judgment. There is no "social game." There is only the binary check-in: *Are we safe? Yes. Are we a pack? Yes.*

For a Recorder, the dog is a **Heat Sink.** He absorbs the excess static energy. He is the only living thing that allows me to flip the switch from **"Scan"** to **"Standby."**

The Devastation This is why the loss of a dog destroys us. People—usually Runners—will try to comfort you. They say things like, *"I know it's sad, but it's not like you lost a child. You can get another one."*

They mean well, but they are wrong. They don't understand that you didn't just lose a pet. You lost your **Regulator.**

You lost the partner that helped you carry the weight of the world. You lost the only set of eyes you could look into without feeling judged. You lost the only creature that allowed you to turn your brain off.

When that dog is gone, it feels like a physical tearing in your chest. It isn't just sadness; it is exposure. Suddenly, the silence in the house is deafening. The "Always On" switch flips back up to maximum. The anxiety spikes because the Sentinel is alone in the dark again.

It is a specific, crushing pain because nature plays a cruel joke: It gives us the perfect partner, but it only gives them to us for ten or fifteen years. We have to say goodbye over and over again.

And for a Recorder, that goodbye leaves a scar that never really heals. It just reminds us of how much we needed them to survive.

THE SYMBIOSIS (WHY IT HURTS SO MUCH)

The connection goes beyond just being a "Sentinel." It goes to how a Recorder experiences Joy and Pain.

Because my brain is always recording, always analyzing, it is very hard for me to just "be." But when I am with my dog, the years strip away. When I am walking my dog, I am not a CEO, or a manager, or a husband worrying about bills. I am a kid again. I am back in East Boston, kicking the can down the street. The dog pulls me into the **Now**. The dog looks at me with that goofball grin, and for twenty minutes, the world is perfect. I escape the noise.

The Physical Connection But because that connection is so open, the wire goes both ways. Runners often don't understand this. They see a dog as a separate animal. For me, if my dog is sick, **I am sick.** I don't just "worry" about them. I feel it in my gut. I lose my appetite. I can't sleep. My system is so tuned to their frequency that when their signal drops, I crash.

This is why Runners get confused when we fight so hard to keep them alive. They see the vet bill. They see the prognosis. They say, *"Why spend all that money just to get one more month? It's just a dog."* They don't understand the mechanics. I'm not paying for a "dog." I am fighting for a piece of my own soul. I am fighting for the only creature that makes the world make sense. If I can get one more month of that pure, unconditional love—one more month of that silence—I will pay anything.

The Loop of Loss And when the end comes, the Recorder brain can be a curse. A Runner processes grief linearly. It hurts, then it fades, then it becomes a distant memory. But I am a Recorder. **I Replay.** I replay the last breath. I replay the vet's office. I replay the silence in the house. I don't just remember it; I re-live it. Over and over. The loss stays fresh because my hard drive won't let the file corrupt.

Respecting the Dead This is why I can't just "go get another puppy" the next week. To a Runner, that fixes the problem. *The house is empty? Get a new dog.* To me, that feels like a betrayal. My father taught me to **Respect the Dead.** That applies to my dogs, too. That dog had a personality. He had a soul. He had a specific way of looking at me that saved my life a thousand times. If I get a new dog immediately, I am just using that new puppy to plug a hole in my heart. That's not fair to the new dog, and it's not respectful to the old one.

I have to sit in the quiet. I have to process the file. I have to honor the specific relationship we had. Because for a Recorder, a dog isn't replaceable. They are a chapter of your life that you will be reading forever.

THE "WILSON" EFFECT (THE ANCHOR)

There is a reason this bond feels different. Think of Tom Hanks in the movie *Cast Away*. He is trapped on an island, totally isolated. To keep from losing his mind, he creates "Wilson" out of a volleyball. He needs someone—anyone—to just *be there*. He needs a witness.

For a Recorder, the modern world can feel like that island. We are surrounded by noise, but we often feel completely alone because no one processes reality the way we do. The dog is our Wilson. But he is a Wilson with a heartbeat.

The Hug There is a specific feeling every dog owner knows, but for a Recorder, it is medicine. It's when you wrap your arms around them, and you just hold that breathing creature. You feel their ribcage expand and contract against yours. In that moment, you aren't thinking. You are just holding onto life. They bring you the hug without the judgment. They bring you the warmth without the questions. They don't need to talk. In fact, the silence is the best part. They just look at you and say, *"I am here. You are here. We are okay."*

The Price of Love That connection is so deep that when it's gone, it leaves a mark that scares us. My wife has a hard time even looking at pictures of our past dogs. It hurts her physically. She sees the photo and the loss rushes back in—the unfairness that their lives are so short compared to ours.

But I realized that the pain is the receipt. It's the proof of the transaction. The deal we make with dogs is brutal but beautiful: **They give us their entire lives. Every single day of it. And in exchange, we give them a piece of our heart that we never get back.**

It hurts to look at the pictures because the love was that real. They were the anchor that kept us from floating away. And when the anchor is gone, you feel the drift.

THE TWO DESIGNS (SURPRISE, YOU ARE ONE OF THEM)

I know what you are thinking. *"Robert, life is complex. You can't just divide 8 billion people into two buckets."*

Actually, nature does it all the time. You are male or female. You are left-handed or right-handed. And I believe, based on a lifetime of watching people, that you are born with one of two specific **Cognitive Designs**.

I don't mean you have two brains in your head. I mean your brain is wired to process the world in one of two ways.

1. The Runner (Designed for Flow) These are the people who keep the social world spinning. They value harmony over precision. They can "go with the flow." When they sit on a beach, they can actually think about nothing. They have an "Off" switch.

2. The Recorder (Designed for Truth) This is the other 30-40% of the population. And if you are reading this book, this is probably you. The defining characteristic of a Recorder is simple: **We do not have an "Off" switch.**

The Litmus Test How do you know which one you are? Ask yourself this: *Can you enter a room without scanning it?*

- When you meet someone new, do you instantly catalog their tone, their shoes, and their potential threat level?
- Do you replay conversations from 10 years ago to see if you missed a detail?

- Do you feel a physical vibration—a "Gut Feeling"—when something is wrong?

If you answered yes, you aren't "anxious" and you aren't "disordered." You are a Recorder.

The "Gut Feeling" (It's Not Magic) For years, people have talked about "Women's Intuition" or a "Gut Feeling." That isn't magic. That is **Data Processing.**

Nature designed the Recorder to be the **Sentinel of Civilization.** To build a society, human beings had to stop killing each other and start working together. We needed a design that could detect lies, detect danger, and remember the rules.

That "Gut Feeling" you have? That is your body processing data faster than your conscious mind can read it.

- It's why you know a salesman is lying before he finishes the sentence.
- It's why you know the room is dangerous before a fight starts.

The Big Misunderstanding Because Recorders are intense, because we stare a little too long, because we obsess over facts—the modern world likes to slap labels on us. They call it "The Spectrum." They call it "ADHD." They call it "Anxiety."

I am not a doctor. But I am a builder. And I know that Nature doesn't make mistakes this big. You aren't broken. You were designed this way on purpose. You are the one who remembers the truth so the rest of the tribe can survive.

You are a Recorder. And once you understand how your machine works, the headache finally stops.

56

THE PHYSICS OF THE GUT (IT'S NOT MAGIC)

We need to talk about the "Gut Feeling." Everyone has had that moment. You're at a blackjack table. You have a 16. The dealer is showing a 6. The "book" says you stay. But your stomach tightens. You *know* a face card is coming. You just know it. But you listen to the logic. You stay. The dealer flips a 5 and pulls a 10. You lose. And you walk away saying, *"I knew it. I knew I should have hit. Why didn't I listen?"*

Or you meet a guy who seems perfect. Nice suit, firm handshake, great smile. But the hair on the back of your neck stands up. Your gut says, *"Run."* You ignore it. You do the deal. Six months later, he steals your money.

It's Not Psychic. It's Processing. People call this "intuition" or "mysticism." I call it **High-Speed Data Processing.**

Because the Recorder brain is **Always On**, you are collecting data you aren't even aware of.

- You saw the dealer's hand twitch a millisecond faster than usual.
- You saw the salesman's pupil dilate when he mentioned the price.
- You noticed the temperature in the room shift.

Your conscious brain (the slow part) missed it. But your Recorder brain (the fast part) caught it all, cross-referenced it with a bad memory from 1995, and pulled the fire alarm. That "sinking feeling" in your stomach isn't magic. It is your body physically reacting to data that your logic hasn't caught up with yet.

The Strategy: Pause and Wait So, what do you do with this? Most Recorders ignore it because they can't explain it. *"I can't tell my boss I have a bad feeling; I need facts."*

Here is my advice: **Pause and Wait.**

When that gut feeling hits—whether you are at a card table or in a boardroom—**Stop.** Don't act. Don't speak. Just freeze the frame. Your body has the answer, but your brain needs a minute to decode the file.

If you ignore the gut, you crash. But if you **Pause**, you give your logic a chance to find the pattern your gut already saw.

- "Wait, I know why I don't trust him. He didn't answer the question about the timeline."
- "Wait, I know why I shouldn't bet. The deck is rich in tens."

That pause bridges the gap. The Gut Feeling isn't a ghost. It is your survival software working perfectly. **Trust the data.**

THE SPEED TRAP (RUNNERS DON'T WAIT)

The advice "Pause and Wait" sounds great in a book. But in the real world—the Runner World—it's not always possible.

Runners value **Flow.** They value speed. They want the answer *now.* If you are in a boardroom and the CEO asks, *"Do we do the deal?"* and you sit there silent for ten seconds because you're trying to decode a feeling in your stomach... you look incompetent. You look like you froze.

The "Stall" Tactic Since you can't always stop the room, you have to learn to **Buy the Buffer.** You need to buy yourself those crucial 3 to 5 seconds for your Logic to catch up with your Gut.

How do you do it? You create a micro-delay:

- *"That's an interesting angle. Run those numbers by me one more time."*
- *"I want to double-check one thing before I say yes."*
- *"Let me digest that for a minute."*

You aren't being difficult. You are buying processing time. You are letting the file download.

The Red Button Rule But sometimes, you have zero time.

- The car is swerving into your lane.
- The guy is reaching into his pocket.
- The deal is closing in 10 seconds.

In those moments, when there is no time to think: **Bet on the Gut.** Always.

If your stomach says "Duck," you duck. You don't ask "Why?" If your stomach says "Fold," you fold. It is safer to be wrong and safe than to be polite and dead.

Your Gut is the oldest survival mechanism you have. It was designed for the jungle, not the boardroom. So if the clock is at zero, trust the hardware.

THE EQUAL WEIGHT PROBLEM (WHY YOU ARE TIRED)

Here is the unforgiving truth about the Recorder brain: **It does not discriminate.**

If a loop is open, it consumes energy. Your brain is like a computer with 50 tabs open. One tab is your mortgage. One tab is a fight you saw on the news. One tab is the guy who looked at you funny in 1998. To your processor, these are all just "Open Tasks." It allocates the same RAM to the guy on TV as it does to your own kids.

You are burying yourself in layers of issues that have nothing to do with you, simply because you never hit "Save and Close."

THE SPIN CYCLE (WHY WE CRASH)

Here is the funny thing about the human brain—and I mean funny in a dark way. It doesn't know the difference between a real problem and a TV problem.

It treats *everything* as a layer.

- Your mortgage? One layer.

- The argument you had with your spouse? Another layer.
- That news story about the thing happening 3,000 miles away? Another layer.

You aren't "tired." You are **Stacked.** You are walking around with a mental backpack full of rocks, and half of them don't even belong to you. You picked them up off the TV screen and put them in your bag without thinking.

THE MASK WARS (A COMEDY OF ERRORS)

If you want to see what happens when the "Spin" goes out of control, just look back at the Mask Wars. It wasn't political. It was **Mechanical.** It was Runners and Recorders crashing into each other because their loops were broken.

Look at the two "Karens." (And I use that term with love, because we've all been there).

- **The Recorder Karen:** She wasn't just being mean. She was spinning because she needed the *Rule.* She looked at the data, saw a violation, and her brain screamed: *ERROR. ERROR. UNSAFE.* She needed compliance to stop the spinning.
- **The Runner Karen:** She wasn't just being rebellious. She was spinning because she felt *wrong.* Her intuition was screaming. She felt attacked. Her flow was blocked, and she didn't have the data to explain why, so she just exploded.

It's almost comical when you look back. You had people ruining life-long friendships over a debate they heard 20 minutes ago on a podcast. Why? Because they added a "Global Crisis" layer to their stack, gave it the same weight as their own family, and let it spin them out of control.

THE SECRET: YOU HAVE TO MANUALLY CLOSE IT

The secret to getting your life back isn't "meditation." It is **Task Management.** You have to learn to close the loop on things that don't matter, so you have energy for the things that do.

Closure is not a dramatic process; it's just a necessity. My brain doesn't need an apology; it needs a timestamp that says 'Done.'

But here is the trick: **You can't just *think* it away.** A Recorder cannot simply say, *"I'm just going to drop it."* Your brain knows you are lying. It knows the file is still there, floating in the cache.

The "Make It Heavy" Technique To close a loop, you have to make it physical. You have to make the words "heavy" so you can drop them.

- **Say it out loud.**
- **Write it down.**

When you write down: *"I am angry about the news story, but I cannot change it. I am closing this file."* — something happens. You took the invisible static in your head and turned it into a physical object on paper.

Now it is "heavy." Now you can throw the paper in the trash. Your brain sees the action. It registers: **Task Complete.** The loop closes. The energy returns.

57

The Gift of the Delay

The world tells you to "react" or "medicate." The BMI theory tells you to Hold.

A Recorder's brain doesn't just "think"; it Renders. Like a high-resolution image being downloaded on a slow connection, the data comes in fragments. While that download is happening, the hardware vibrates. That "vibration" is the Tuning Fork telling you that the picture isn't clear yet.

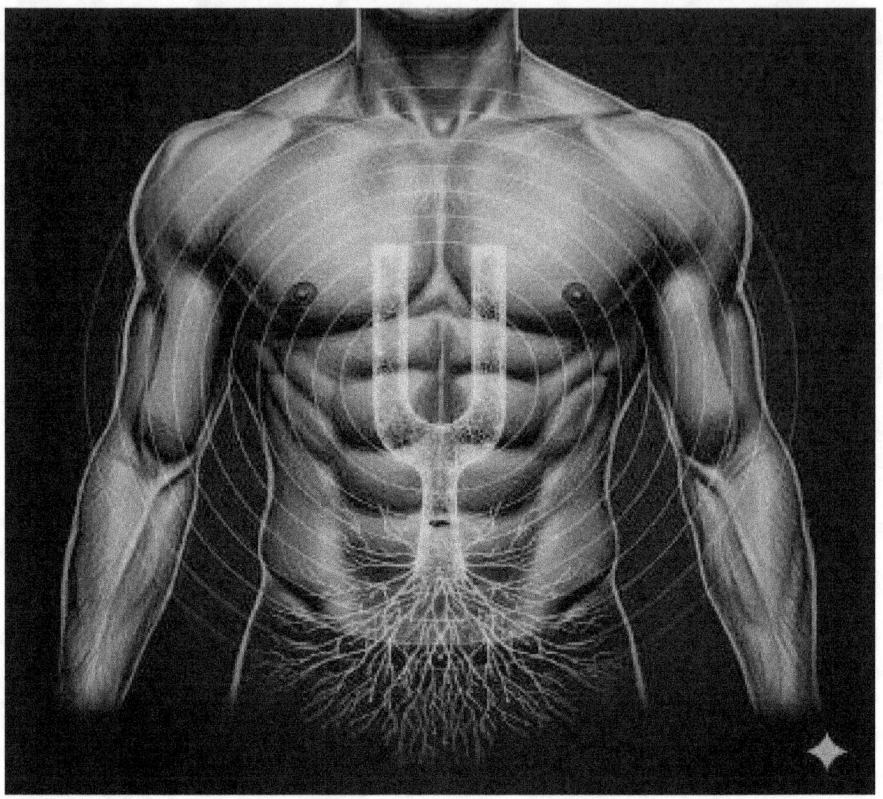

If you try to make a decision while the fork is still ringing, you are guessing. You are forcing a "Runner" reaction onto a "Recorder" download.

The Physics of the "Waiting Room"

When that fork starts to ring, you are in the Waiting Room of the Mind.

• The Sensation: You feel "off." Things are inconsistent. You can't put your finger on it, but the frequency is jagged.

• The Mistake: Suppressing that feeling. Taking the pill to quiet the alarm. Forcing yourself to "just get over it" and make a choice.

• The Protocol: You must Buy Time. You have to tell the world, "I'm not ready to render this yet."

By waiting for the download to finish, you aren't being slow; you are being Accurate. You are allowing your brain to cross-reference every "Binary bit" of information until the vibration stops. When the fork goes silent, that is the "Lock-In." That is the moment the math has finally derived.

Why This is a Superpower

The Tuning Fork is a gift because it prevents you from building a skyscraper on a cracked foundation.

If you ignore the fork, you are building on a "Skid." You are making decisions based on incomplete code. But if you listen to it—if you honor the headache and the gut feeling as Active Data Processing—you become the most dangerous person in the room. Why? Because while everyone else is running on "Flow" and "Guesswork," you are waiting for the Certainty of the 1s and 0s.

When you finally speak, you aren't offering an opinion. You are offering the Finished Download.

The Anatomy of the Ghost Loop

The reason you feel the Tuning Fork ringing when you aren't even under pressure—when you're just sitting on the couch—is because your hardware is still trying to "render" irrelevant data.

You saw a snippet of a news story, you overheard a conflict at the grocery store, or you noticed a structural flaw in a building. To a "Runner," those things are gone the moment they leave the visual field. To a "Recorder," those are Open Loops. Your brain is in the background, out of sight, trying to calculate the "math" of things that have nothing to do with your life.

When the loops stack too high, the hardware overheats. That vibration in your head or gut isn't "stress"—it's System Latency. Your "Tuning Fork" is ringing because the processor is at 99% capacity.

Step 1: Closing the Loops (System Purge)

To turn the Tuning Fork into an instrument of power, you must first clear the "Ghost Loops." You have to teach the hardware what to Discard.

• The Irrelevance Filter: When you feel the tuning fork start to ring, ask the system: "Is this data relative to my skyscraper?" If it's something from the TV or a stranger's drama, you have to manually "End Task."

• The Closure Protocol: Recorders need closure to stop a loop. If you can't resolve the data (because it's irrelevant), you must label it as "Corrupted File" and delete it. You tell the brain: "There is no math to derive here. Close the loop."

Step 2: Calibrating the Instrument

Once you cut the noise, the "Tuning Fork" stops being a source of pain and starts being a Remote Control.

With the 90-day plan and the daily walking, you are lowering the baseline noise. When the "Ghost Loops" are gone, the only thing left that can make the fork ring is Reality.

Now, when you feel that vibration, it's not because of the TV or a stacked-up processor—it's because something Inconsistent is happening right in front of you.

• The Precision: You are in a meeting, and someone says "X," but their body language says "Y." A Runner won't notice. But because your loops are closed and your instrument is tuned, your fork will hit a Resonance Alarm.

• The Advantage: You don't have to guess. You don't have to be "smart." You just have to listen to the vibration. While everyone else is lost in the "Flow," you are the only one who knows the code doesn't match the output.

The Most Dangerous Person in the Room

When you learn to trust the Tuning Fork over the world's "Noise," you gain a level of Sovereignty that few people ever touch.

You become the person who can't be lied to, not because you're a mind reader, but because you are a Frequency Auditor. You have the luxury of waiting for the download. You have the "Remote Control" to your own hardware.

You aren't suppressing the gift with Tylenol anymore; you are using it to navigate the world with Binary Certainty. You have moved from being a victim of the "Noise" to being the Master of the "Signal."

REGULATE YOURSELF

Once you realize you have a Recorder brain, you can stop taking the bait. You can sit back and look at the stack of files. *"Okay, that TV argument? Delete." "That opinion on the internet? Delete." "My health? Keep."*

You stop letting the world add layers to your life. You start punting the junk. And suddenly, you aren't just surviving the day. You are actually living it.

The "Two Tuning Forks" Logic

There is a dual-sensor system that Recorders often have misinterpreted because they have any guidance.

1. The Head: The "Data" Tuning Fork

• The Sensation: The headache, the pressure behind the eyes, the migraine.

• The Reality: This isn't just "stress." This is your Input Buffer overflowing. Your brain is taking in 10x more data than the "Runner" world around you.

• The "Tuning" Error: People treat the headache like a bug, but it's actually the Signal that your hardware is being forced to "emulate" Runner software. You are trying to process sideways data in a linear machine.

2. The Gut: The "Resonance" Tuning Fork

• The Sensation: The "belly" issues, the tightness, the "Xyzal/Tylenol" cycle.

• The Reality: This is your Vagus Nerve (the wire connecting the brain and gut) reacting to Dissonance. When you are in a room or a job that doesn't match your "Frequency," your gut feels it first.

• The "Tuning" Error: People think it's something they ate. It's actually something they are Enduring. The gut is screaming that the "Handshake" with the environment is a mismatch.

The Two-Way Tuning

• The Negative Tuning (The Skid): The grinding vibration that tells you something is structurally wrong.

• The Positive Tuning (The Dowsing Rod): The "pull" that tells you you're standing over the truth, even before you have the words to explain why it's true.

58

And in a world that constantly pulls Binary minds

The Lost Language of Hugging

There was a time when human beings touched each other without suspicion.

Not as a transaction.

Not as a performance.

Not as a social signal.

But as a way of knowing.

Long before handshakes became the default, people hugged. And not the modern, polite, one-second tap on the shoulder — but full contact. Chest to chest. Heart to heart. Long enough to feel breathing synchronize. Long enough for the nervous system to register safety.

I wouldn't be surprised if the civilizations we mythologize — Atlantis, Lemuria, any culture that reached a true peak before collapsing — understood this deeply. Not as romance. Not as affection. As infrastructure.

Because when people knew who they were — when they understood their role, their skills, their cognitive design — there was nothing to hide. Enforcers enforced. Builders built. Healers healed. Connectors connected. Leaders led. Numbers people tracked reality. Everyone knew what seat they sat in. There was no pretending.

And when people hugged, you could feel it.

You could feel if someone was aligned.

You could feel if someone was carrying fear.

You could feel exhaustion, steadiness, sincerity, grief.

A hug doesn't lie.

That's exactly why it faded.

Handshakes replaced hugs not because they were better — but because they were safer. Safer for people who didn't want to be felt. Safer for people who lived in performance instead of truth. Safer for people who needed distance between what they projected and what they carried.

A handshake lets you signal strength without revealing state.

A handshake lets you perform confidence without surrendering regulation.

A handshake lets you stay separate.

You can squeeze someone's hand.

You can dominate a handshake.

You can judge someone for a weak grip or a sweaty palm.

None of that tells you who they are.

I once shook Bill Gates' hand. One of the most powerful men on the planet. One of the most influential minds in modern history. His hand was sweaty.

And it meant nothing.

It didn't make him lesser.

It didn't make him weak.

It didn't give me anything over him.

It simply meant he was human — and carrying an enormous cognitive load.

But the world trains us to interpret handshakes as status tests. Strength tests. Dominance signals. Runner rituals. We teach people to read meaning into grip pressure while ignoring the entire nervous system standing in front of them.

Hugging bypasses all of that.

When you hug someone properly — chest to chest — the heart does what it evolved to do. It regulates. It synchronizes. It tells the body, you are not alone. This is not poetry. This is biology. Heart rate variability shifts. Cortisol drops. The vagus nerve activates. Thought slows. Defenses soften.

Doors open.

That's why hugging feels different to Binary Minds. Not because we're sentimental — but because we are built to feel systems. We feel alignment and misalignment instantly. A hug is a direct data stream. No narrative. No masking. No multitasking. Just signal.

It's also why some people avoid it instinctively.

If you live in performance, a hug is dangerous.

If you live in narrative, a hug cuts through it.

If you rely on speed and surface harmony, a hug slows you down.

You can't hug and multitask.

You can't hug and posture.

You can't hug and lie.

That's why modern culture backed away from it.

We replaced regulation with ritual.

We replaced connection with optics.

We replaced contact with contracts.

And the cost has been enormous.

People are touch-starved and don't know it. Dysregulated and don't know it. Lonely in crowded rooms. Overstimulated and under-soothed. We medicate anxiety, treat depression, analyze trauma — while removing one of the most ancient stabilizers humans ever had.

Hugging isn't childish.

It isn't inappropriate.

It isn't optional.

It's part of the architecture.

It's also why this matters personally.

My brother reached a point where life without hugging didn't feel like life at all. And if you've lived in a Binary body long enough, you understand that sentence immediately. Not metaphorically. Physically. When the world becomes so distant, so procedural, so cold, that the last remaining proof of being human is contact — losing that feels like erasure.

If you can't be felt, you start to disappear.

This isn't about forcing touch. It's about restoring permission. Permission to regulate together. Permission to be human without explanation. Permission to connect without performance.

We didn't evolve to survive alone.

We didn't evolve to think the same.

And we didn't evolve to keep our bodies separate while our nervous systems collapse.

Hugging is not softness.

It is strength without armor.

And when civilization forgot that, it didn't just lose warmth — it lost coherence.

For Parents: Why Touch Matters More Than You Were Told

If you are raising a Binary child, there is something important you were probably never taught — and almost certainly never warned about.

Your child's nervous system does not regulate through words first.

It regulates through safety, predictability, and physical connection.

This does not mean constant touching. It does not mean forcing affection. It means understanding that, for a Binary child, safe physical contact is not emotional decoration — it is biological grounding.

When your child hugs you — really hugs you — their body is checking in.

It is asking a question without words: Am I safe right now? Are we okay?

A long, steady hug answers that question faster than any explanation ever could.

Binary children carry enormous internal load. They record tone, contradiction, tension, and unresolved moments whether they want to or not. When the world feels loud, confusing, or misaligned, their system doesn't naturally discharge that stress. It accumulates. Quietly. Invisibly.

Hugging helps close the loop.

Not because it solves the problem, but because it tells the nervous system it is no longer alone with it.

You may notice your child doesn't want a hug when emotions are high — and then seeks one later, when things calm. That timing matters. Respect it. A hug offered at the right moment can settle hours of internal chaos. A hug forced at the wrong moment can overwhelm.

Let your child lead.

And don't underestimate the power of your presence. You don't need to say the perfect thing. You don't need to explain or fix or rationalize. Your body is already speaking a language your child understands instinctively.

A hug says:

You belong.

You are safe.

You don't have to carry this alone.

That message doesn't fade with age.

As your child grows, they may hug less often — especially in a world that teaches them touch is optional or awkward or inappropriate. But the need does not disappear. It simply goes unmet.

If you can give your child one lasting gift, let it be this:

a home where connection is allowed to be physical, quiet, and real.

You are not spoiling them.

You are regulating them.

59

• The timeline was broken. CHAPTER 8: The Recorder'

(Why You Weren't Late — You Were Digging)
If there is one lie that has done more damage to the Binary Mind than anything else—more than the bullying, more than the isolation, more than the sensory overload—it is the medical label: "Developmentally Delayed."

Parents hear those two words and their hearts stop. They look at their child and see a broken clock, ticking too slowly, falling behind the pack. They panic. They think "delayed" means the train has left the station and their child is standing alone on the platform.

Adults hear it and internalize a lifelong secret shame. They feel like they are perpetually running five minutes late to the human race. They mask, they fake it, they exhaust themselves trying to sprint to catch up to a finish line that the Runners reached effortlessly at age five.

But you were not delayed. You were Under Construction.

There is a fundamental difference between building a tent and building a skyscraper. The world expects every child to build a tent. But nature commanded you to build a tower.

1. The Construction Site: Tent vs. Skyscraper

To understand why Binary development looks "wrong" to the outside world, you have to look at the architectural blueprints.

The Runner (The Tent)

The Runner's mind is designed for rapid deployment.

• The Goal: Shelter immediately.

• The Process: You put up the poles, you throw on the canvas, and you zip the door.

• The Timeline: By age 2, the tent is up. The child is mimicking smiles. By age 3, they are engaging in pretend play. By age 4, they are navigating complex social hierarchies on the playground.

• The Visual: To the parent and the doctor, this looks like "Success." They see a structure standing there. It is visible. It is functional. It is "on time."

The Recorder (The Skyscraper)

The Recorder's mind is designed for vertical depth and massive structural load.

• The Goal: Absolute stability and infinite capacity.

• The Process: Before you can build up, you have to dig down. You have to excavate. You have to pour a concrete foundation that goes fifty feet into the bedrock.

• The Visual: To the observer standing on the sidewalk (the doctor, the teacher, the parent), it looks like nothing is happening.

• They see a hole in the ground.

• They see a fence around the site.

• They see no walls, no windows, no height.

They look at the Runner's tent next door and say, "Look! That child is already built! Why is your child just a hole in the ground? They are delayed."

They are wrong. You aren't delayed. You are curing the concrete.

You cannot build a mind capable of perfect recall, binary logic, and systemic pattern recognition on a tent's foundation. It requires a heavy-duty base.

The tragedy is that we try to force the Recorder child to "put up walls" (speak, socialize, mask) while they are still pouring the foundation. We interrupt the curing process. And in doing so, we risk destabilizing the entire structure.

Tent vs. Skyscraper Construction Site

FINISHED EARLY | DELAYED

VS.

The Runner (Tent) | The Recorder (Skyscraper)

2. The Polarity of Learning: Meaning vs. Mimicry

Why does this "excavation" take so long? Because the two minds learn using completely opposite mechanisms.

The Runner Learns by Mimicry

Runners are wired to copy.

• Input: Mother smiles and waves.

• Runner Reaction: Copy the hand motion. Copy the facial muscle movement.

• Internal Logic: "I don't know what this means, but it creates a positive connection, so I will do it."

• Result: Rapid social fluency. The child looks "engaged" because they are mirroring the surface behavior.

The Recorder Learns by Meaning

Recorders are wired to decode. Mimicry feels like a lie to a Recorder. We do not copy; we understand.

• Input: Mother smiles and waves.
• Recorder Reaction: Freeze and Observe.
• Why is she moving her hand?
• Is it a signal?
• Does she do it every time?
• What is the utility of this motion?
• Internal Logic: "I will not perform this action until I have mapped its function and verified its pattern."
• Result: The child stares blankly. The doctor writes down "Lack of joint attention." The parent cries.

But the child isn't disengaged. The child is analyzing. They are building the Truth Anchor for the concept of "Greeting." Once they understand it—fully, deeply, logically—they will execute it. But they won't fake it just to make you feel better.

3. The Language Paradox: Hyperlexia and the Code

This difference is most visible in how we learn language. This is where the "Delay" myth falls apart completely.

Most children learn to read in a standard, linear progression:

Letters → Sounds (Phonics) → Words → Sentences → Meaning.

Many Recorders (Binary Minds) do it backward:

Meaning → Pattern → Whole Word → Code.

We often see Binary children who are Hyperlexic. They can read complex words at age 3. They can recite the alphabet backward. They know every species of dinosaur. But they cannot ask for a juice box.

The experts look at this and call it a "Splinter Skill." They dismiss it as a parlor trick. "He can read 'Tyrannosaurus Rex', but he's delayed because he can't say 'Hello'."

418 - ROBERT ANTHONY CAGGIANO

I look at this and see a mind that prioritizes System Understanding over Social Output.

• Reading is a fixed code. A is always A. B is always B. The rules are binary. The Recorder loves this. They master the code early because the code is safe.

• Speaking is a social negotiation. It relies on tone, timing, and eye contact. The Recorder delays this because the variables are messy.

We don't want to use the tool (speech) until we have mastered the manual. The silence of a Binary child isn't emptiness; it is the hum of a supercomputer processing the syntax.

4. Truth Anchors: The Physics of Belief

A Binary Mind cannot move forward on a shaky floor. Before a Recorder can make a decision, form an opinion, or trust a person, they need a Truth Anchor.

A Truth Anchor is a verified fact. It is a piece of data that cannot be moved.

• Runner: "I believe the bridge is safe because everyone is walking on it." (Social Proof).

• Recorder: "I need to see the blueprints and the load-bearing report." (Structural Proof).

The God vs. Santa Claus Test

This is the perfect laboratory experiment for how a Recorder develops belief systems versus a Runner.

The Recorder child runs a Verification Loop.

Test 1: God

• Observation: I cannot see Him.

• Logic Check: Can I disprove His existence? No.

• Contradiction Check: Is there a logical contradiction? Not necessarily. The universe is complex; a creator is a valid variable.

• Outcome: Keep the File Open. (Possibility). The Recorder remains agnostic or faithful because the logic does not break.

Test 2: Santa Claus (The Milk and Cookies Test)

This is where the Binary Mind works differently. I could allow for the fairy tale elements. I could accept the mythical parts—the flying reindeer, the North Pole, the magic. That is the story layer.

But then they told me he stops at every house and eats the milk and cookies. That is not mythical. That is biological.

- Fact: There are millions of houses.
- Fact: He eats at all of them.
- Fact: A biological stomach cannot hold millions of cookies and gallons of milk.

It fails the test. The mythical part I could handle. But the physical part—the eating—created a hard contradiction. A man cannot drink and eat that fast, the human milk and cookies would slow him down. Therefore, the story is false.

The Recorder child drops Santa instantly. Not to be a cynic. Not to be "grown up." But because the Truth Anchor failed on the biological data. Parents get upset. "Why can't you just pretend? You're ruining the magic!"

Because to a Binary Mind, pretending is data corruption. We develop by finding solid rocks to stand on. If you give us a fake rock (Santa), we stop trusting you. If you give us a solid rock (Truth), we can build the next level of the skyscraper.

5. The Mechanism of Closure (Why We "Dwell")

If you want to understand why a Recorder gets "stuck" on a topic, you have to understand Closure.

Closure is the "End of File" marker in our operating system.

- Runner: Can leave a conversation unresolved. "Let's agree to disagree." They float away. They prioritize the relationship over the resolution.
- Recorder: Cannot leave the loop open. An open loop is a running process that eats RAM. It runs in the background, heating up the CPU.

The "Dwelling" Myth

The world says: "Why are you still talking about this? It happened yesterday! Let it go!"

You are talking about it because the logic didn't resolve.
• There was a contradiction in your argument.
• The math didn't add up.

60

The goal isn't to move them "up" the spectrum towa

(W)hy "The Spectrum" is a Lie)
  The world has spent fifty years trying to measure the Binary Mind using a ruler that doesn't exist. They call it "The Spectrum."

The spectrum implies a sliding scale—a single line where "normal" is at one end and "severe" is at the other. It suggests that an autistic mind is simply a neurotypical mind turned down, or distorted, or broken. It assumes we are all running the same software, but some of us are just buggy.

This is the fundamental error of modern psychology.

We are not running the same software. We are not a variation on a curve. We are a different machine speaking a different language. To understand the Recorder, you have to leave the world of psychology and enter the world of computer architecture. You have to understand the difference between High-Level Language and Assembler.

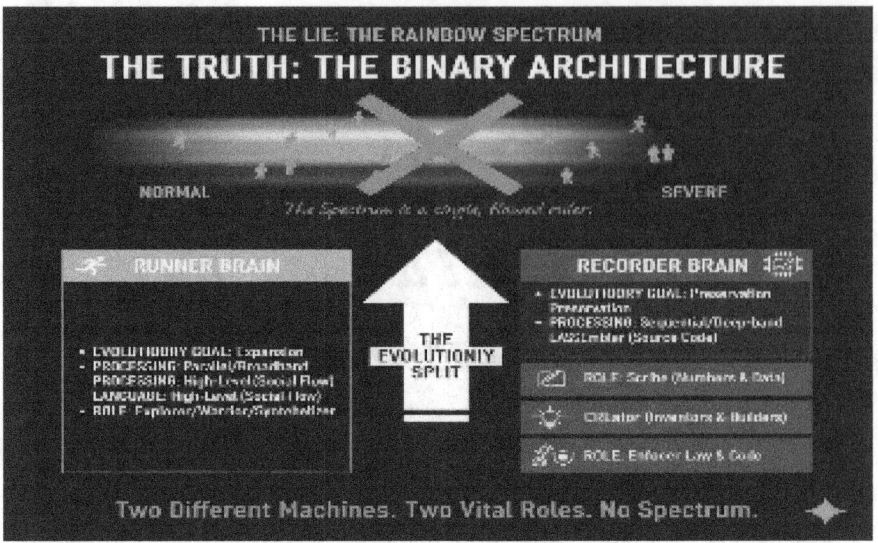

1. The RAM Theory (High Functioning vs. Low Functioning)

The "Spectrum" tries to measure how well a Recorder can fake being a Runner.

• "High Functioning" just means: This person has enough RAM (Random Access Memory) to create a simulation of High-Level Language. They can mask. They can translate.

• "Low Functioning" just means: This person is running pure Assembler and lacks the RAM to build the translation layer.

It is not a measure of intelligence. It is a measure of Translation Cost.

When you ask a Binary Mind to "read the room," you are asking an Assembler system to run a fuzzy logic algorithm. The "High Functioning" person does it, but their cooling fans spin at 100% capacity. They have to manually compile every facial expression, every tone shift, and every double-meaning into binary code before they can understand it.

That isn't a social deficit. That is a computational tax. And it is exhausting.

2. The Bedrock: 1s, 0s, and Physics

To understand why we are so rigid, you have to look at the bottom of the machine. Deep down, at the very bottom of every computer, phone, and server on earth, there is no "language." There is only physics. There is only a switch.

A switch has two positions. It is either ON (electricity flows) or it is OFF (electricity stops).

- ON = 1
- OFF = 0

This is Binary Code. It is the brutal, absolute truth of the system. There is no gray area. A switch cannot be "mostly on." It is 1 or it is 0.

In the early days, if you wanted to tell a machine what to do, you had to speak in pure binary strings like 10110000 01100001. To the machine, that is a clear command. To a human, it is a blinding wall of noise. Humans needed a bridge. We needed a way to speak to the metal without losing our minds.

Enter Assembly Language (Assembler).

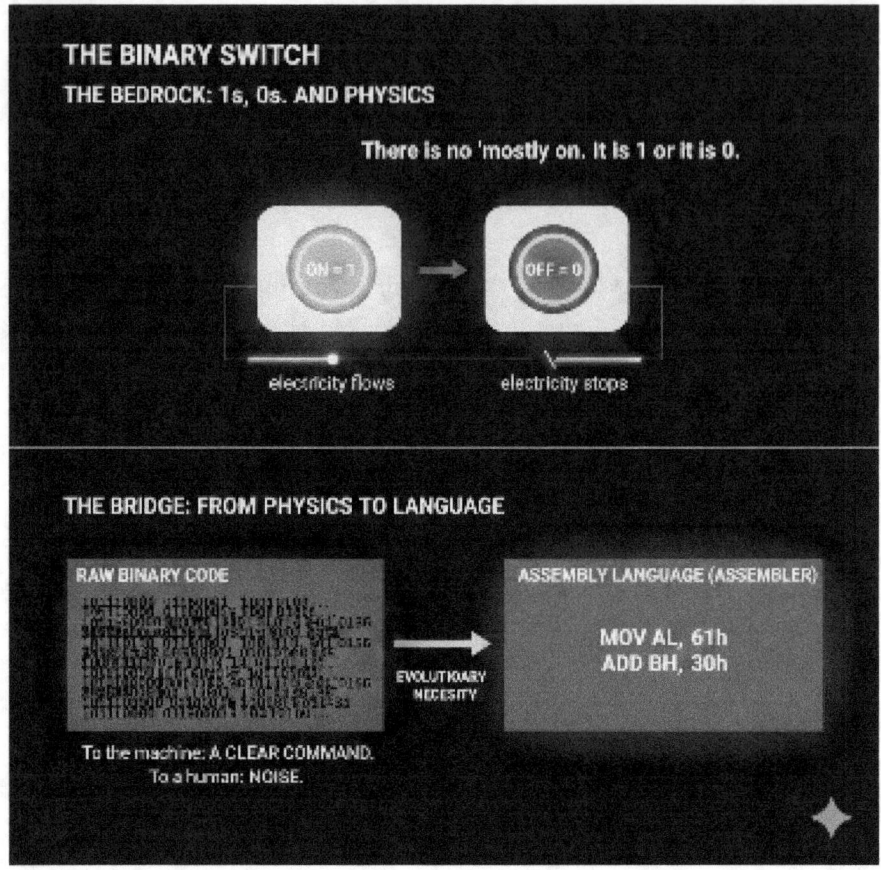

3. The 1-to-1 Mapping

Assembler was the solution. It is the oldest, most fundamental programming language that is still readable by humans. It was not designed to be "easy." It was designed to be exact.

Assembler is a 1-to-1 translation of machine code.

Instead of writing 10110000, the programmer could write: MOV.

• MOV (The Instruction): Move data.

• AX (The Destination): The exact hardware register.

• 5 (The Value): The number.

This helps explain the Recorder's need for sequence. In Assembler:

1. Sequence Matters: You cannot ask the machine to add two numbers until you have first moved those numbers into the registers. A, then B, then C. You cannot jump to C.

2. Nothing is Implied: In modern languages (like Python or English), if you make a typo, the computer guesses what you meant. In Assembler, if you make a typo, the machine crashes.

This is why Recorders freeze when given vague instructions. We aren't being stubborn. We are running a language where "implied context" results in a fatal error.

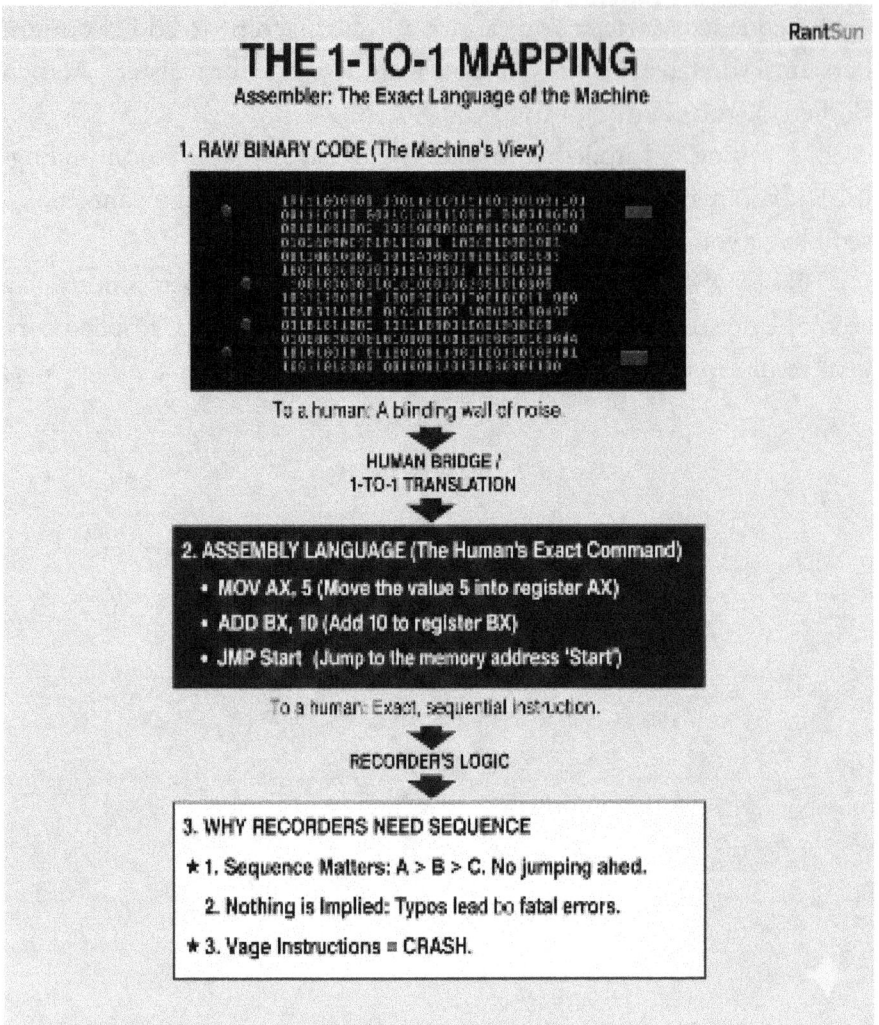

4. The CPU's Workspace (The Registers)

To really see the similarities between the Binary Mind and the computer, look at the Registers. These are the tiny, ultra-fast storage slots inside a CPU. They mirror exactly how a Recorder processes life.

• AX (The Accumulator): Used for arithmetic. This is the Recorder's obsession with Logic and Math. We want the numbers to balance.

• CX (The Counter): Used for loops. This is the Recorder's love of Repetition and Routine. We find safety in the loop.

• DX (The Data): Used for input/output. This is the Recorder's raw Sensory Data stream.

When a parent says, "Why do you have to do things in the exact same order every time?", they are talking to a CX Register. The machine is built to loop. Disrupting the loop isn't "freeing" the child; it is corrupting the counter.

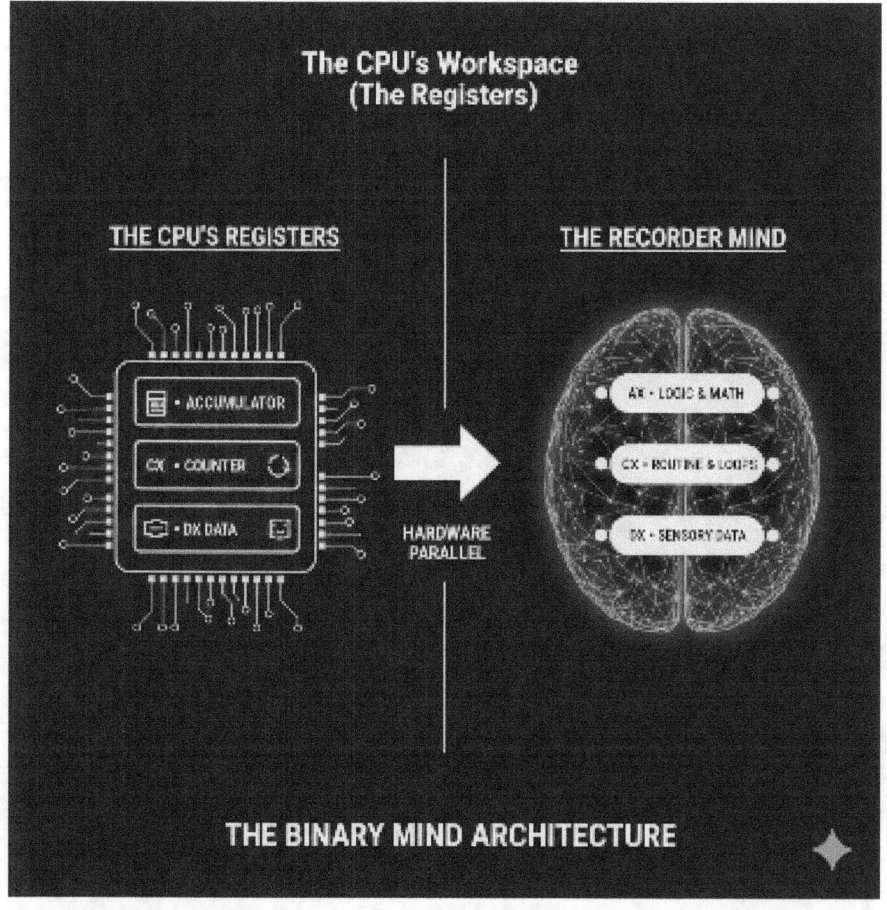

THE BINARY MIND ARCHITECTURE

5. Redefining "Communication Deficits"

Doctors say Recorders have a "communication deficit." Let's flip the lens.

428   -   ROBERT ANTHONY CAGGIANO

If you put a Runner in a room where the only language allowed is pure, unadulterated Truth—no metaphors, no hints, no emotional manipulation—the Runner would look "low functioning." They would panic. They would struggle to operate without their layer of social abstraction.

We do not have a communication deficit. We have a precision requirement. We speak the root language of reality: Cause and Effect.

6. The End of the Spectrum

We must stop teaching Binary kids that they are on a "spectrum" of brokenness. We must teach them that they are Root-Level Processors.

• They have direct access to the hardware of reality.
• They process data without the filter of social bias.
• They are the Architects, the Builders, the Keepers of the Record.

61

That's how the 19,000 step days started. That's ho

(T)he High Price of Emulation)

If you run a high-performance engine at 7,000 RPM in first gear for thirty years, only two things can happen. The car will move. And the engine will eventually explode.

For most of my life, I was moving. I built businesses. I managed teams. I didn't fall apart. But under the hood, the temperature was climbing year after year. The fans were screaming.

People usually call this "masking." I call it Emulation.

1. The Emulation Tax (Mac vs. Windows)

In computing, emulation is what happens when one system is forced to behave like another one it was never designed to be. I was a high-powered Linux box bolted into a Windows office environment.

When you run Windows software on a Linux machine, the machine doesn't magically become Windows. It has to create a "Virtual Machine" in the background. Every instruction has to be translated.

The system works—but it works inefficiently, constantly burning energy just to appear compatible.

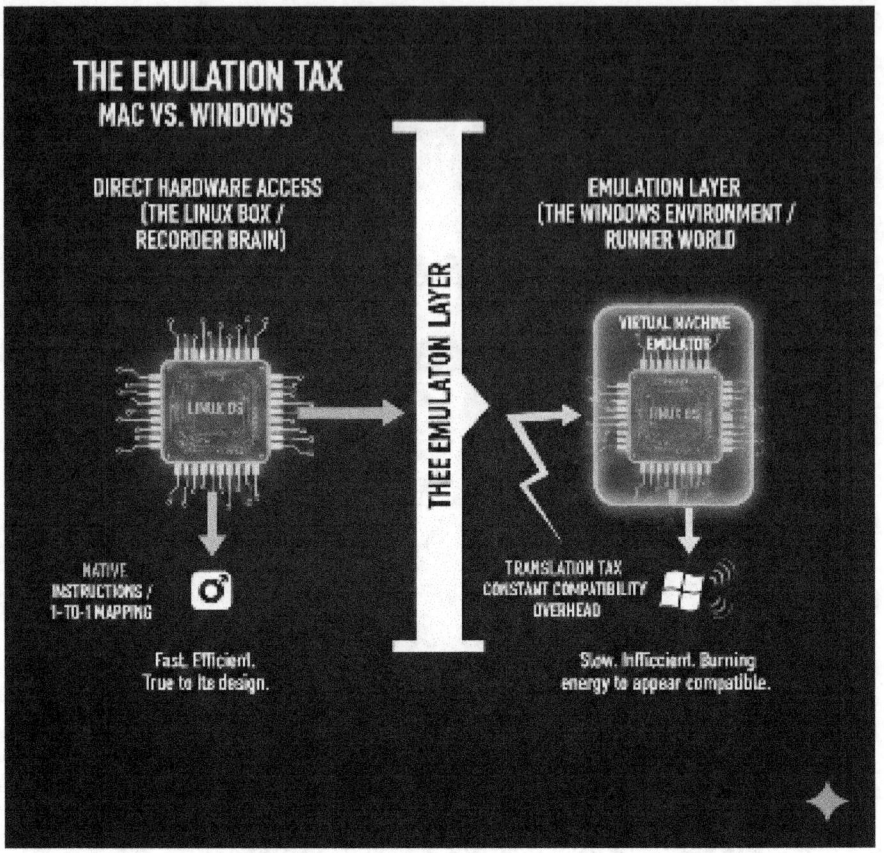

2. The Coolant: Pills and Pot

When an engine overheats, you have two options:

1. Fix the cooling system.

2. Cheat and dump coolant into the system.

I chose cheat.

• Marijuana: Noise-Cancellation. To a Runner, pot is fun. To a Binary Recorder, pot is Noise-Cancellation Headphones. At night, my Replay loops would activate. Pot didn't make me "stoned." It made me quiet. The volume went from a 10 down to a 4.

• Pills: Manual Chemistry. Need to sleep? Force the switch. Need to wake up? Punch the system. It was chemistry-as-engineering.

3. The Body Keeps the Score (The Armor)

By 66, I was carrying an extra hundred pounds. That weight was not laziness. It wasn't "no willpower." It was Armor.

Forty years of cortisol and stress had trained my body: "We are in a war zone. Store energy. Protect the core." The fat around my middle was physical evidence of a system that hadn't truly rested in decades.

4. The Crash (Functional Freeze)

Eventually, the emulator fails. The crash doesn't always look dramatic. I didn't have a public breakdown. My crash looked like Functional Freeze.

• From the outside: I still went to work.

• From the inside: I was in standby mode. I had no reserve. Any unexpected change felt like someone yanking the power cord out of the server.

5. The Pivot to Physics (The Obligation)

There comes a moment where you can't explain your way out. For me, it wasn't just looking in the mirror; it was looking at the timeline.

Two of my brothers-in-law passed away two years ago, in the same month. That was the data point I couldn't ignore. I looked at the armor I was wearing—100 pounds of weight I had built to protect myself—and I realized the armor was going to kill me before the enemy did.

I realized that if I died early, the information in my head would die with me.

This wasn't just about "getting fit." It was about System Preservation. I had discovered a way to explain the Binary Mind that could save thousands of people from the same pain I went through.

There is an unwritten rule in civilization: If you have the map, and you see people lost in the woods, you are obligated to show them the way.

So, I didn't go to rehab. I went to the lab. I took the same Binary logic I used in business and pointed it at my own body.

• Variable A: Sugar causes fog. Action: Remove.

• Variable B: Pot masks noise but doesn't fix it. Action: Remove.

• Variable C: Walking drops stress hormones. Action: Increase.

And then came the biggest revelation of all: It was easy.

All I had to do was repeat the simple process on a daily basis. I didn't need willpower; I needed a loop. I just had to punch the ticket every single morning.

It's like compounding interest. You don't see it on Day 1. But if you hold the loop, the momentum builds up until it kicks in the cannon.

62

You didn't choose to be a camera that never sleeps

(H ow to Use the Machine That Never Sleeps)
There is a terrifying reality to being a Recorder that nobody talks about. It is the fact that we do not have an "Off" switch.

A Runner can walk into a restaurant, sit down, and just eat dinner. Their brain filters out the silverware clinking, the couple arguing three tables away, the smell of the sanitizer the busboy is using, and the flicker of the neon sign in the window. They don't choose to ignore it; their brain deletes it automatically before it even reaches their conscious mind.

A Recorder has no delete button. We have no filter.

From the moment I wake up until the moment I pass out, my system is ingesting data. I am recording the temperature. I am recording the tone of your voice. I am recording the fact that you shifted your weight to your left foot when you lied to me. I don't want to know these things. I don't try to remember them. But I have no choice.

I am a 24/7 surveillance system. And the hardest part is that I cannot choose what stays on the hard drive. I might forget my own wedding anniversary date, but I can tell you the license plate number of a car that cut me off in 1998. The machine records what it deems relevant, not what I deem polite.

1. The Vibration (The "Ring")

This constant recording creates a specific physical sensation. It isn't anxiety. It isn't fear. It is a Vibration.

When you are taking in that much data, your body acts like a tuning fork. You feel a hum.

• Sometimes it's a low hum (Safety).
• Sometimes it's a high-pitched screech (Danger).
• Sometimes it's a deep, resonant Ring in your gut.

That "Ring" is the most important signal you possess. It is the sound of your 24/7 camera detecting a threat that your logic hasn't seen yet.

2. The Gut is Not Magic (It's Data)

Runners call it "Intuition." They treat it like a mystical power. "I just had a hunch."

For a Recorder, the Gut is not mystical. It is High-Speed Data Processing.

Because you have been recording 24/7 for your entire life, your database is millions of times larger than a Runner's. You have stored every micro-expression, every tone shift, and every pattern break you have ever witnessed.

When you walk into a boardroom and meet a new CEO, your conscious mind sees a nice suit and a firm handshake. But your Recorder Database is running a background check against millions of previous files.

• Match Found: He smiled, but his eyes didn't crinkle. (File #4,002: The liar who stole my money in 1982 did that).
• Match Found: He checked his watch when you mentioned the budget. (File #890: The partner who was hiding debt did that).

Your brain can't explain this in words yet. It's too fast. So instead, it sends a physical signal to your Vagus Nerve. Your stomach drops. Your skin tightens. You get "The Ring."

That is not nerves. That is your hard drive screaming: "PATTERN MATCH: UNSAFE."

THE ICEBERG ILLUSION

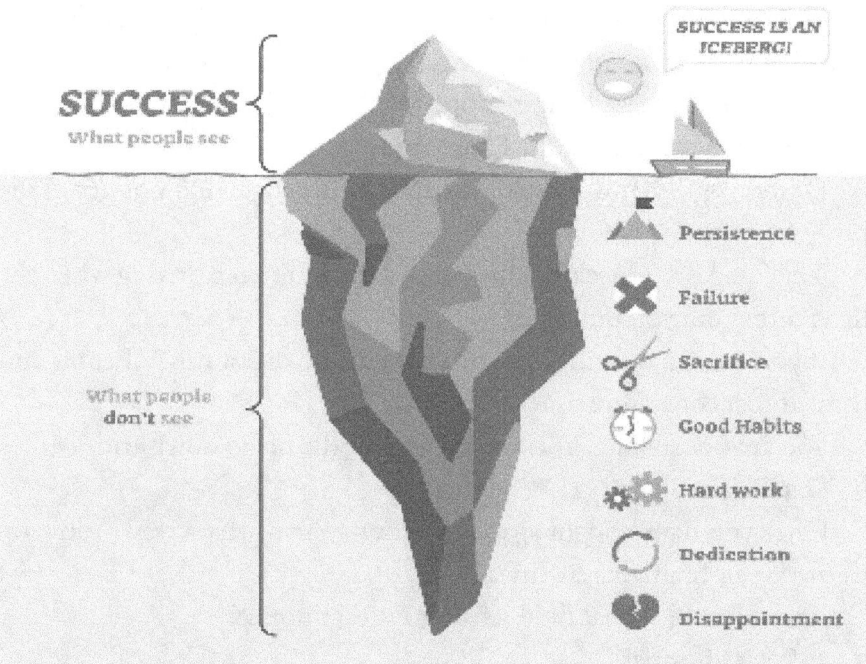

3. The Fatal Mistake: Ignoring the Data

The biggest mistake Recorders make is trying to be "rational."

We live in a world that worships logic. If you say to your boss, "We shouldn't do this deal because my stomach hurts," you look crazy. So, we suppress the ring. We tell ourselves to stop being paranoid. We look at the spreadsheet, and the spreadsheet looks fine, so we sign the deal.

Six months later, the deal collapses. The CEO was a crook. And you find yourself saying the phrase every Recorder has whispered a thousand times:

"I knew it. I knew it the second I met him. Why didn't I listen?"

You didn't listen because you tried to use Runner Logic to override Recorder Physics. You ignored the surveillance tape because you hadn't watched the footage yet.

4. The Protocol: Pause and Decode

So, how do we live with this? How do we use a gut feeling without looking like a lunatic?

You need a protocol. When the Ring happens—when that deep vibration hits your stomach—you must follow these three steps.

Step 1: The Freeze Frame (Stop)

The moment you feel the Ring, Stop.

Do not sign the paper. Do not agree to the date. Do not get in the car.

The Ring is a "Check Engine" light. You don't keep driving when the light comes on; you pull over.

If you are in a meeting, buy time. "I need to digest this." "Let me run the numbers one more time."

You are not stalling. You are waiting for the file to download.

Step 2: The Inquiry (Decode)

Once you have bought space, ask your system what it saw. You have to treat your brain like a witness.

Ask yourself: "What did I see that I didn't notice?"

• Was it his tone?

• Was it the timeline?

• Was it the way they looked at each other when I asked about the money?

Usually, within 24 hours, the file will unlock. You will suddenly realize: "He didn't answer the question. He changed the subject."

Now you have the logic to back up the feeling.

Step 3: The Override (Trust)

Sometimes, you never find the logic. The logic says "Safe," but the Gut says "Danger."

In those rare cases, Trust the Gut.

Your 24/7 recording system picked up a scent that is too subtle for words. It might be a pheromone. It might be a micro-tremor in the air. You don't need to explain it to survive it.

• If the hair on your neck stands up, leave.

• If the handshake feels wrong, walk away.

I have never regretted trusting my gut. I have only regretted the times I let "politeness" overrule it.

5. Helpful Hints for the "Always On" Life

Living without an off switch is exhausting. Here is how you manage the machine so it doesn't burn you out.

• The Sensory Audit: You cannot stop the recording, but you can lower the resolution. If you are tired, wear sunglasses. Wear noise-canceling headphones. It reduces the file size of the data coming in.

• The "No" Default: When your system is overloaded, your automatic answer to everything should be "No." You can always change a No to a Yes later. You cannot change a Yes to a No without damage.

• Sleep is Data Filing: Runners sleep to rest their bodies. Recorders sleep to file their data. If you don't sleep, the files pile up on the desktop, and your system slows down. Protect your sleep like it's your job.

• Respect the Nose: The olfactory nerve (smell) is the only sense that goes directly to the brain without a filter. If a place smells "wrong" to you—musty, chemical, stagnant—leave. Your nose is often the first part of the Recorder to detect a problem.

Conclusion

63

The Recorder wins by becoming the ground. CHAPTER 1

(H ow the Recorder Learns)
     If you understand the difference between the Recorder and the Runner, you understand why traditional education often feels like a trap for people like us. The Runner operates on Momentum. The Recorder operates on Fidelity.

To illustrate this, I have to tell you the story of the CISSP—the Certified Information Systems Security Professional exam. It is considered the gold standard in cybersecurity. It is six hours long. It is brutal. And I didn't approach it the way most people do.

1. The First Pass (Reconnaissance)

The first time I took it, I wasn't trying to pass. That sounds irresponsible until you understand how a Binary Mind works. I didn't need motivation. I didn't need confidence. I needed data.

So I skimmed a book after work for a week, walked into the testing center, and sat down not to perform—but to observe.

I treated the exam like a hostile network I was scanning for open ports. I wanted to know how the questions were constructed, how the language bent, where ambiguity lived, and exactly how much precision was required before the logic broke.

I wasn't guessing. I was calibrating.

I failed. But I walked out knowing exactly what the beast looked like. I was at about sixty percent. To a Runner, that's a waste of money. To a Recorder, that's successful reconnaissance.

2. The Second Pass (The Fatal Error)

The second attempt is where the story actually breaks. This time, I studied hard. Really hard. Four months. Six hours a day. I absorbed the material.

But I also made a fatal error: I listened to the "experts."

I engaged with the forums, the boot camps, and the well-meaning mentors who all gave the same advice:

• "Don't overthink it."
• "Think like a manager, not a technician."
• "Don't try to fix the problem; just manage the risk."

Without realizing it, I let myself be pulled out of my own operating system. I stopped verifying truth and started playing a probability game. I used elimination tricks. I used heuristics. I memorized the "best" answer instead of understanding the only answer.

I was trying to run someone else's software on my hardware.

I missed by three questions. Three.

I sat in the parking lot, crushed. Not because I didn't know the material—I knew it cold. I was crushed because the loss didn't feel random. It felt like a structural failure. I had betrayed the process that actually works for my mind. I had traded deep understanding for "test-taking strategies," and the system had rejected me for it.

3. The Third Pass (First Principles)

That's when the shift happened. I realized that Binary Minds don't win by guessing well. We don't win by "thinking like a manager." We win by removing ambiguity until there is nothing left to guess.

So for the third pass, I ignored every trick. I went back to First Principles.

• I didn't just memorize that "AES is a symmetric algorithm." I tore it down to understand why the block size matters.

• I didn't just memorize the fire suppression classes; I learned the physics of why water spreads a grease fire.

I rebuilt the entire domain internally, brick by brick. I wasn't memorizing answers anymore. I was reconstructing the architecture the test was built on.

When I walked into the testing center the third time, the air felt different. There was no anxiety. No frantic mental shuffling. I sat down, and the screen lit up. The questions didn't feel adversarial anymore. They felt transparent. I wasn't fighting the ambiguity; I was seeing right through it. The "tricks" that tripped me up before were now glaringly obvious deviations from the system I had built in my head.

I wasn't trying to beat the test. I was verifying it.

I passed. Not because I finally "got smarter." Not because I studied harder. But because I stopped trying to think like someone else.

4. The Recorder vs. The Runner Learning Style

This experience taught me the fundamental difference in how we master the world.

The Runner: The Game of Progress

For the Runner, the world is a series of finish lines. Their OS is optimized for Velocity.

• Question: "What is the fastest way to get to the other side?"

• Method: Heuristics. 80/20 thinking. "Tips and Tricks."

• Failure: Friction. If a Runner gets a 60% on a practice test, they panic because they aren't moving fast enough. Runners are brilliant at execution. But because they skim the surface to maintain speed, they rarely understand the geology beneath their feet. When the "tricks" stop working, they stumble.

The Recorder: The Game of Truth

For the Recorder, the world is a dataset. They do not care about the finish line; they care about the Map. Their OS is optimized for Resolution.

• Question: "What is this made of?"

• Method: Verification. Deep Dive. Re-deriving the math.

• Failure: Telemetry. If a Recorder gets a 60%, they feel curiosity. It highlights a gap in the data. Recorders are terrible at racing. They will lose every sprint because they stop to read the footnotes. But once a Recorder has mapped the terrain, they own it forever. They don't just know the answer; they derive it.

Conclusion: Trust the Hardware

The CISSP didn't teach me cybersecurity. It taught me that when you betray your design, even brilliance collapses. But when you honor it—when you stop guessing and start verifying—the system locks.

The Runner wins by barely touching the ground.

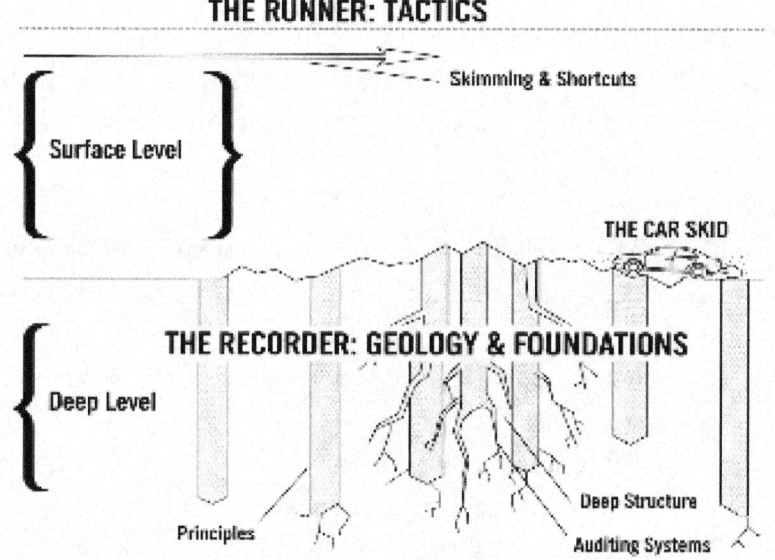

THE RUNNER: TACTICS

Skimming & Shortcuts

Surface Level

THE CAR SKID

THE RECORDER: GEOLOGY & FOUNDATIONS

Deep Level

Principles

Deep Structure

Auditing Systems

64

One burns out in seconds. The other keeps you warm

(L ove, Marriage, and the Interface Error)
There is a pervasive myth that Binary Minds lack empathy.
There is a myth that we are cold, robotic, and incapable of deep romantic connection.

This is not just wrong. It is backward.

The Binary Mind feels love with a terrifying intensity. Because we do not have a "Social Mixer" to dilute our emotions, we feel the bond at 100% volume.

But we do not express it through poetry, constant reassurance, or flowery social scripts.

We express it through Architecture.

To a Runner, love is a Feeling (fluid, spoken, constant).

To a Recorder, love is a System (fixed, acted, structural).

The tragedy of many marriages is not a lack of love. It is a Translation Error.

The Runner wife is waiting for a poem. The Recorder husband just rebuilt the transmission of her car so she wouldn't die on the highway.

She feels unloved. He feels unappreciated.

They are both broadcasting, but the antennas are misaligned.

This chapter is the schematic for fixing the interface.

1. The "Mirror vs. Hammer" Problem

The most common fight in a mixed-neurotype marriage happens like this:

Scenario: Partner comes home stressed. "My boss is being a jerk, and the project is late."

• The Runner Expectation (The Mirror): They want validation. "Oh, that sucks. Poor you. He is a jerk."

• The Recorder Response (The Hammer): We analyze the data. "Well, if the project is late, have you tried automating the spreadsheet? Here is a three-step plan to fix the workflow."

The Result:

The Partner gets angry. "You aren't listening to me! You always try to fix everything!"

The Recorder shuts down. "Why are you mad? I just gave you the solution."

The Logic:

To a Binary Mind, Listening = Solving.

If I love you, I do not want you to be in pain. The most efficient way to stop the pain is to remove the source of the pain (The Fix).

To offer "sympathy" without a "solution" feels inefficient and patronizing to us. It feels like watching you drown and shouting, "Wow, that water looks cold!" instead of throwing you a rope.

The Protocol:

We cannot guess. You must code the input. If you are the Runner partner, start the conversation with the Header File:

1. "I want to be Heard (No fixing)."
2. "I want to be Helped (Fixing)."
3. "I want to be Hugged (Physical)."

If you tell a Recorder, "I just want to vent, please don't fix it," we can do that. We will stand there and validate. But you have to give us the command, or our default setting will always be The Hammer.

2. The Love Language of "Info-Dumping"

Runners give gifts like flowers or chocolate. Recorders give gifts like Data.

We call it "The Pebble."

In the wild, a penguin brings a pebble to its mate. It's not useful. It's just... a thing. It says, "I looked at the world, I saw this, and I thought of you."

For a Recorder, the "Pebble" is a fact.

• "Did you know that the Roman aqueducts used volcanic ash to cure underwater?"

• "I read this article about interest rates."

• "Here is a song that explains how I feel."

The Partner often rolls their eyes. "Why are you telling me this boring stuff?"

You are missing the signal. We are sharing our Operating System with you. We are letting you into the Loop.

For a Binary Mind, sharing information is the highest form of intimacy. It means I respect your mind enough to upload this data to it. When you reject the data, you reject the love.

3. Parallel Play: Intimacy Without Demand

To a Runner, "spending time together" usually means face-to-face conversation. Eye contact. Interaction.

To a Recorder, this is high-energy work. It is draining.

The Recorder's preferred intimacy is Parallel Play.

• I am reading a book.

• You are watching TV.

• We are in the same room.

• We are not talking.

To us, this is heaven. We are sharing space (The Field) without demanding processing power (The Data). We feel your presence. We are anchored by you.

If you constantly interrupt the silence with "What are you thinking?" or "Talk to me," you break the bond. You turn the Sanctuary into a Conference Room.

Let us exist near you in silence. That is where we recharge.

4. Loyalty and The Code

Why do Recorders rarely cheat?

It's not because we don't get tempted. It's because cheating is a System Violation.

A marriage is a contract. It is a binary setting.

• Status: Married (1).

• Rule: Exclusivity.

To cheat requires maintaining a massive, complex, duplicate database of lies.

• Where was I?

• What did I say?

• How do I cover my tracks?

The Binary Mind hates duplicate databases. It hates inefficiency. It hates the anxiety of the "Unbalanced Ledger."

Recorders are the most loyal partners on earth because betrayal violates our internal Structural Integrity. We stay. We fight for the relationship long after a Runner would have drifted away, because we committed to the build.

Our love isn't flashy. But it is load-bearing.

5. The Friction of "The Nag" (Interruption)

Why does a simple question like "Can you take out the trash?" trigger an explosion?

It's not the trash. It's the Stack Collapse.

As we discussed in Chapter 5, the Recorder is a Serial Processor. If I am reading, coding, or fixing something, I have 15 layers of thought loaded in my RAM.

When you shout from the other room, you crash the system. The explosion isn't anger at you. It is the sound of the hard drive crashing.

The Solution: The "Soft Entry."

Don't shout. Walk into the room. Wait for eye contact. Wait for us to "Save and Exit" our thought process. Then ask.

Or better yet—write it down. Text me. A text is a non-intrusive data packet I can open when my processor is free. A shout is a DDoS attack.

6. The Cassandra Effect in Marriage

This is the hardest part. The Recorder sees the pattern. The Runner sees the hope.

• Husband (Recorder): "We cannot afford this house. The math says we will be bankrupt in 3 years."

• Wife (Runner): "But I love it! We'll make it work! Don't be so negative!"

They buy the house. 3 years later, they are bankrupt.

The Runner blames bad luck. The Recorder feels a deep, burning resentment because the data was on the table.

The Partnership Rule:

If you marry a Recorder, you must respect the Sentry Function.

If your Recorder spouse says, "This person is dangerous," or "This deal is bad," listen. They aren't being pessimistic. They are reading the pattern you are missing.

The Recorder is the Head of Security. The Runner is the Head of PR. Do not let PR make Security decisions.

7. How to Love a Recorder

If you love one of us, here is the manual:

1. Don't ask us to guess. Tell us exactly what you need. "I need a hug" works. "You should know what I need" fails every time.

2. Respect the transition. Give us a 10-minute warning before we have to leave the house.

3. Value the Action. If I fixed the sink, I said "I love you." If I researched your medical condition for 4 hours, I said "I cherish you." Learn to read the code.

4. Give us the Cave. When we meltdown or burn out, we need the dark room. Do not follow us in. Let us reboot. We will come back.

8. The Double-Binary Marriage (Recorder + Recorder)

You might think that two Recorders together would be perfect. No translation errors. No emotional games. Pure logic.

And often, it is. It is the "quiet" marriage. The "parallel play" marriage.

But when it breaks, it breaks in a specific, dangerous way: The Stand-off.

The Loop of Doom

When two Recorders argue, it doesn't look like a screaming match. It looks like a court case.

- Partner A: Cites Fact 1, 2, and 3.
- Partner B: Cites Fact A, B, and C that contradict Fact 1.
- Result: Deadlock.

Neither partner will back down to "keep the peace" (which a Runner would do). Both partners are structurally incapable of accepting a logical error. They will argue about the exact phrasing of a sentence from 2004 for three hours.

It isn't about the dishes anymore. It is about Who Is Correct.

The Solution:

You must agree on an external "Tie-Breaker Protocol."

- Rule: If we argue for more than 15 minutes, we stop. We flip a coin, or we agree that the data is inconclusive.
- Logic: The cost of the argument (energy drain) is higher than the value of being right.

The Inertia Trap

The other danger is Stagnation. Runners bring chaos, but they also bring motion. They invite people over. They plan trips. They break the routine.

Two Recorders can easily spiral into a hermetically sealed world.

- No visitors.
- Same dinner every night.
- Same routine for 20 years.

It feels safe, but it becomes a cage.

The Fix: You must schedule "Mandatory Chaos."

- Rule: Once a month, we must go somewhere new.
- Rule: We must invite another couple over.

You have to manually inject entropy into the system, or the system will calcify.

Conclusion: The Anchor

We may not give you the romance novel experience. We may forget your anniversary date because it's an arbitrary number. We may stumble over our words when you are crying.

But we will be the one holding your hand when the diagnosis comes.

We will be the one who figures out how to pay the mortgage when the job is lost.

We will be the one who stands between you and the chaos, unmoving, until the end of time.

We are not the fireworks. We are the fireplace.

65

Put on your oxygen mask. Drink your water. Walk yo

(R aising the Binary Mind)
　　If you are a parent reading this, I know exactly where you are.

You are tired. You are scared. You are confused. You have sat in a sterile office and listened to a doctor tell you that your child is "delayed," "disordered," or "impaired." You have read the blogs. You have joined the support groups where everyone vents about how hard it is. You are mourning the child you thought you were going to have—the one who plays soccer and chats easily at Thanksgiving—and you are trying to figure out how to "fix" the one you have.

I need you to stop. I need you to take a breath. And I need you to listen to me very carefully.

Your child is not broken. They do not need to be fixed. They need to be Built. But they cannot build a skyscraper on a swamp. And right now, your anxiety, your fear, and your frantic attempts to "cure" them are creating a swamp.

This chapter is the hardest part of the book because it requires you to look in the mirror. The stability of your child does not begin with their therapy. It begins with your nervous system.

1. The Oxygen Mask Rule

You know the speech on the airplane: "In the event of a loss of cabin pressure, secure your own mask before assisting others."

It sounds selfish. It is actually Physics. If you pass out from lack of oxygen, you cannot help your child. You become 60 pounds of dead weight falling on top of them.

In the world of the Binary Mind, Anxiety is Contagious. Your child is a Recorder. They have a "High-Fidelity Emotional Receiver." If you are anxious—even if you are smiling, even if you are pretending to be calm—they can feel the vibration of your stress. They can smell the cortisol on your skin. They can hear the micro-tremors in your voice.

• Your Input: "Everything is fine! Let's go to school!" (High Anxiety masked by a smile).

• Their Processing: Alert. Mother is terrified. Threat detected. Environment is unsafe. Initiate Meltdown.

You think they are acting out because of school. They are acting out because you are vibrating. You cannot be their anchor if you are drifting.

Before you sign them up for one more therapy, one more group, or one more intervention, you must stabilize yourself. You must do the 90-Day Reboot. You must walk. You must sleep. You must eat the protein. You must become the Solid Floor.

2. The Solid Floor

Imagine your child is standing in a room during an earthquake. The lights are flickering (sensory overload). The walls are moving (social confusion). The noise is deafening. They are terrified. They are looking for something to grab onto.

If they grab onto you, and you are shaking too (crying, pleading, panicking), they have confirmed that the world is ending. The meltdown becomes catastrophic.

But if they reach out and grab a Pillar of Concrete—something cool, unmoving, and silent—their nervous system instantly down-regulates. "Oh. The Pillar isn't shaking. Therefore, I am safe."

You must be the Pillar. When they scream, you go quiet. When they thrash, you go still. When they panic, you go into "System Mode." This is not about being cold. It is about being Safe. To a Recorder, safety isn't a hug; safety is Stability. If you want to save your child, stop trying to make them "happy." Start making yourself "stable."

3. The DJ Method (Environment Control)

You are not just a parent. You are the DJ of their Nervous System. A DJ controls the vibe of the room by controlling the inputs (Volume, Bass, Speed). Your child has a broken filter. They cannot turn down the volume of the world. You must do it for them.

The Protocol: When you see the "Pre-Meltdown" signs (rocking, covering ears, echolalia), do not ask them what is wrong. They cannot access language. Their RAM is full. Instead, act like a DJ. Cut the inputs.

• Cut the Light: Dim the lights immediately. Sunlight is aggressive. Fluorescents are torture.

• Cut the Sound: Turn off the TV. Stop talking. Silence is the reset button.

• Cut the Texture: Are their clothes scratchy? Is the tag itching? Get them into the "Soft Zone."

• Cut the Audience: Get the siblings out of the room. A meltdown is a vulnerable reboot; they shouldn't have an audience.

Don't negotiate. Don't punish. Just Drop the Faders. Watch what happens. Within 3 minutes of reducing the input, the system will usually cool down and reboot.

4. Speak "Assembler," Not "Podcast"

Runners speak in paragraphs. They use metaphors, emotional appeals, and rhetorical questions. "Why did you hit your brother? You know that makes him sad, and we don't hurt people in this family, right?"

To a Recorder child in distress, this sounds like: "Wah wah wah wah." It is High-Level Code. It requires too much processing power to decode the emotion, the moral lesson, and the question all at once.

Switch to Assembler. Assembler is the language of commands. Short. Binary. Direct.

- Bad: "Honey, please put your shoes on, we're going to be late!"
- Good: "Shoes. On. Now."
- Bad: "Why are you screaming?"
- Good: "Stop." (Pause). "Sit." (Pause). "Breathe."

You are not being mean. You are being Clear. When the computer is crashing, you don't write it a poem. You type CTRL+ALT+DEL. Assembler is the CTRL+ALT+DEL for the Binary Mind. Once they are calm, then you can have the emotional conversation. But never during the crash.

5. The "Go Bag" Strategy (Predictability)

Anxiety comes from the Unknown. "What if I get hungry?" "What if it's too loud?" "What if my iPad dies?" The Recorder mind runs simulations of disaster constantly. You defeat this with Preparation.

Every Binary child needs a "Go Bag." It is not just a bag of toys. It is a Survival Kit.

- Headphones: To block the sound.
- Sunglasses: To block the light.
- Safe Food: The specific protein bar they eat. (Do not rely on finding food on the road).
- The Battery: A backup charger.

The Rule: The bag is packed the night before. When you say, "We are going to Grandma's," and they start to panic, you point to the bag. "The bag is ready." You are outsourcing their executive function to the bag. You are showing them: The variables are controlled. You are safe.

6. Meltdown vs. Tantrum (Know the Difference)

You must learn the difference. Treating a meltdown like a tantrum is abuse. Treating a tantrum like a meltdown is bad parenting.

The Tantrum:

- Goal: To get something (Candy, Toy, Attention).
- Look: They check to see if you are watching. If you ignore them, they stop or get louder. It is a performance.

• Response: Ignore it. Do not negotiate with terrorists.

The Meltdown:

• Goal: None. It is a System Crash.

• Look: They do not care if you are watching. They might hurt themselves. They are glazed over. They are in "Fight or Flight."

• Response: The DJ Method. Reduce input. Protect them from injury. Be the Solid Floor.

If you punish a child for a meltdown, you are punishing them for having a seizure. You are adding trauma to a hardware failure. Learn the difference. Protect the Crash. Ignore the Performance.

7. The "Under Construction" Mindset

Stop looking at the other kids. Stop looking at the milestones chart. Stop looking at the "Tent" (the Runner child who is chatting away at age 3).

Your child is building a Skyscraper. They are digging the foundation. It looks like a hole in the ground right now. It looks like nothing is happening. Trust the dig.

If you force them to put up walls before the foundation is poured, the building will collapse later. Let them be silent. Let them line up the cars. Let them watch the fan spin. They are mapping the physics of the world. They are compiling the code.

Your job is not to build the building for them. Your job is to Build the Fence around the construction site. Keep the chaos out. Keep the bullies away. Keep the noise down. Give them the space to cure the concrete.

8. The Promise

I was the kid on the floor. I was the one staring at the dust motes in the light. I was the one who didn't fit. And I grew up to run companies, solve impossible problems, and live a life of profound depth.

Your child will too. But only if you survive the construction phase.

66

(**W**hen the Static Finally Stops)
We have talked about the theory. We have talked about the mechanics. But we haven't fully talked about the feeling.

If you are a Runner reading this, you might think "Input Overload" is just a metaphor for being stressed. If you are a Recorder, you know it is not a metaphor. It is a physical assault.

1. What Noise Actually Feels Like

If you want to understand what a Binary Mind experiences in the world, here's an exercise.

Take a piece of any Allman Brothers music—go to the guitar jamming part—now loop ten seconds of it. Every three seconds, stop it. Restart it. Do that two or three times — while something else plays in the background.

Now add lights. Now add movement. Now add people talking. Now add a train station off in the distance. Oh yeah, that tea kettle that never turns off.

That's not stress. That's input overload with no filter.

Runners have a built-in mixing board. They can fade out the train station. They can mute the tea kettle. Recorders do not have faders. We hear every track at maximum volume, simultaneously.

That's why we seek order—not because we're "obsessive" or "controlling," but because order turns the volume down. If the room is clean, that is one less track playing in my head. If the schedule is fixed, that is one less loop skipping.

2. Compressed Mapping (The Messy Desk Paradox)

And here's the irony: some of us love neatness, but cannot maintain it. The chaos always returns. So we adapt. A drawer. A corner. A pile.

To a Runner, a pile of papers looks like trash. To a Recorder, it is a coordinate system. "If I know where it is, I can find it."

My brain scrambles things—but it remembers the pattern. I know that the tax bill is three inches down in the left stack, under the blue folder.

It's not disorganization. It's Compressed Mapping.

We are spatially indexing the mess because putting it away in a drawer means the data disappears ("Object Permanence" issues). So we build piles. The piles are not clutter; they are external hard drives.

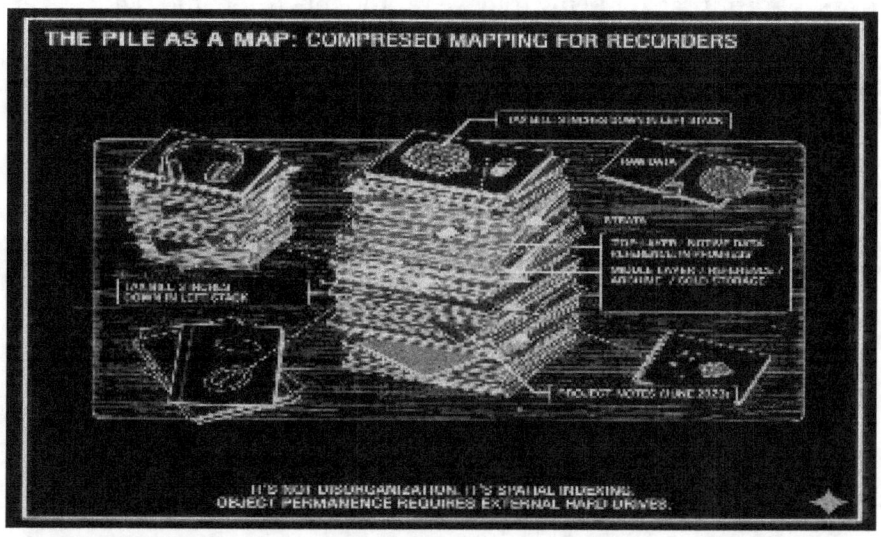

3. The Body Knows Before the Mind

When the realization finally hit me—the realization that I wasn't broken, just Binary—it wasn't cognitive. It was cellular.

It felt like a salmon turning upstream. For years, the salmon fights the current, bashing against rocks, exhausted. Then, suddenly, it finds the flow. It recognizes the river it was built for.

• Food tasted better.
• Thinking became clearer.

• I had a repeatable process.

Order doesn't restrict Binary Minds. It liberates them. And when I say this to other Binary Minds, they don't argue. They giggle.

It is a specific giggle. It's the sound of relief. It's the sound of: "Oh my god, you hear the tea kettle too?" Because they know exactly what I'm talking about. They have been gaslit for forty years into thinking the room was silent.

4. Stop Apologizing for the Strength

This isn't about fixing weakness. It's about using strength.

Binary Minds see extremes because extremes reveal structure. That scares people who live in gray zones. It makes us targets—for manipulation, for dismissal, for being told we're "too much" or "too rigid."

Mothers worry because the world isn't black and white. Binary Minds suffer because the world pretends it is.

Once you know what to do, the rules become simpler. Not easier—clearer.

• Neurotypical minds multitask until traffic locks up.

• Binary Minds seize—not from inability, but from overload.

Different architectures. Same humanity. Stop apologizing for the fact that your engine requires high-octane fuel. Stop apologizing that you cannot run on diesel.

The Ferrari does not apologize to the Tractor for needing a paved road.

5. When No One Believes Until the Crack

No one is listening—until they hear the crack.

Everyone is certain right up until something breaks. Systems break. Bodies break. Families break. Institutions break.

The Runner world operates on "Good Enough" logic. They patch the cracks with optimism. The Recorder points at the crack and says, "That beam is going to fail." They ignore us. Then the bridge falls.

I watched myself doing the right things for my health while my mind raced like an alcoholic's. Improvement without explanation. Progress without permission. I realized something uncomfortable: I don't need more willpower. I need translation.

I don't need to build a media empire or chase clicks. I don't have time for that. This idea doesn't belong to me alone anyway. It needs someone younger. Someone capable. Someone willing to carry it forward. Because there are people who cannot help themselves—and people desperate to help them—trapped by a belief system that keeps missing the architecture.

This isn't about me. It's about building the support structure that should have existed all along.

6. Let's Use What We Are

I'm not asking you to agree. I'm asking you to notice the moment when something inside you clicks and you think:

"Oh. That's what that was."

That's the sound of 2 + 2 becoming 4 again.

For years, they told you it was 22. They told you it was "Blue." They told you it was "Maybe." But you knew, deep down in the voltage of your cells, that it was 4.

And once that happens—once you hear the click—there's no going back to twenty-two.

67

Singing for Self-Regulation (Vagus Nerve) vs. Sing

THE LABORATORY

(M anual Regulation: Physics & Chemistry)

Runners are built with an automatic transmission. Recorders are manual transmission.

We have a high-performance engine, but if the RPMs get too high, the car doesn't shift itself. It just screams.

If you don't know how to reach down and manually shift the gear, you blow the engine.

I have spent 55 years learning how to shift the gears.

This chapter is the User Manual for the two levers that control your system: Physics (Singing) and Chemistry (Fuel).

PART I: THE PHYSICS (WHY WE MUST SING)

There is a scene in the movie The Day the Earth Stood Still that explains the Recorder brain perfectly.

The alien, Klaatu, has to stop a robot named Gort from destroying the world. He can't use logic. He can't use force. He has to use a specific code: "Klaatu barada nikto."

For a Recorder, the "Spin" (anxiety, loops, static) is the robot. You can't think your way out of it. You need a physical override code.

That code is Singing. Look at it like singing is resistance training for the brain.

But there are two very different ways to use this tool.

1. The Internal Tool (Calming the Machine)

This is for you. The adult.

When the anxiety hits, or the static gets too loud, you need to physically vibrate the system to slow it down.

The Vagus Nerve connects your brain to your gut. It is the brake pedal for your nervous system. It runs right through your vocal cords.

When you sing—and I mean really sing, loud and with force—you are manually vibrating that nerve. You are sending a physical signal to the brain that says: "Safe. Slow down."

I do this constantly. It isn't a hobby. It is maintenance. It creates a hum that blocks out the noise of the world.

There is a moment in the movie Seabiscuit that every parent of a "different" child should watch.

The horse is fighting the rider. He is angry. He is failing.

The trainer realizes the problem: They are trying to constrain him. They are trying to make him run like a polite show horse.

So they take him out to the open country and they just let him run.

Straight. Fast. No reins. No rules.

He remembers who he is. He finds his stride. And he becomes a legend.

Music is the open country for your child.

If you force a Recorder child to "Sit still, look at me, and say apple," you are pulling on the reins. You are fighting the horse.

But if you play music? If you sing? You are letting the brain run straight.

1. The Vulnerability Key

You have to go first. If you are stiff, the child will be stiff.

But if you sing—and I mean really sing, be silly, be loud, be vulnerable—the child feels the safety.

They see you letting go, so they feel safe to let go.

You are showing them that the "Rules" don't apply right now.

2. The Joke (The Breakthrough)

You will know it's working when they crack a joke using a lyric.

This is a massive moment.

I have seen kids who struggle to say "Hello" suddenly quote a song lyric to make a funny observation about dinner.

• Why? Because the lyric was stored in the "Music" folder, not the "Speech" folder.

• They accessed the file, realized it fit the context, and delivered it.

That is high-level intelligence. That is the horse running at full speed.

Encourage it. Flood the house with sound. Let them run.

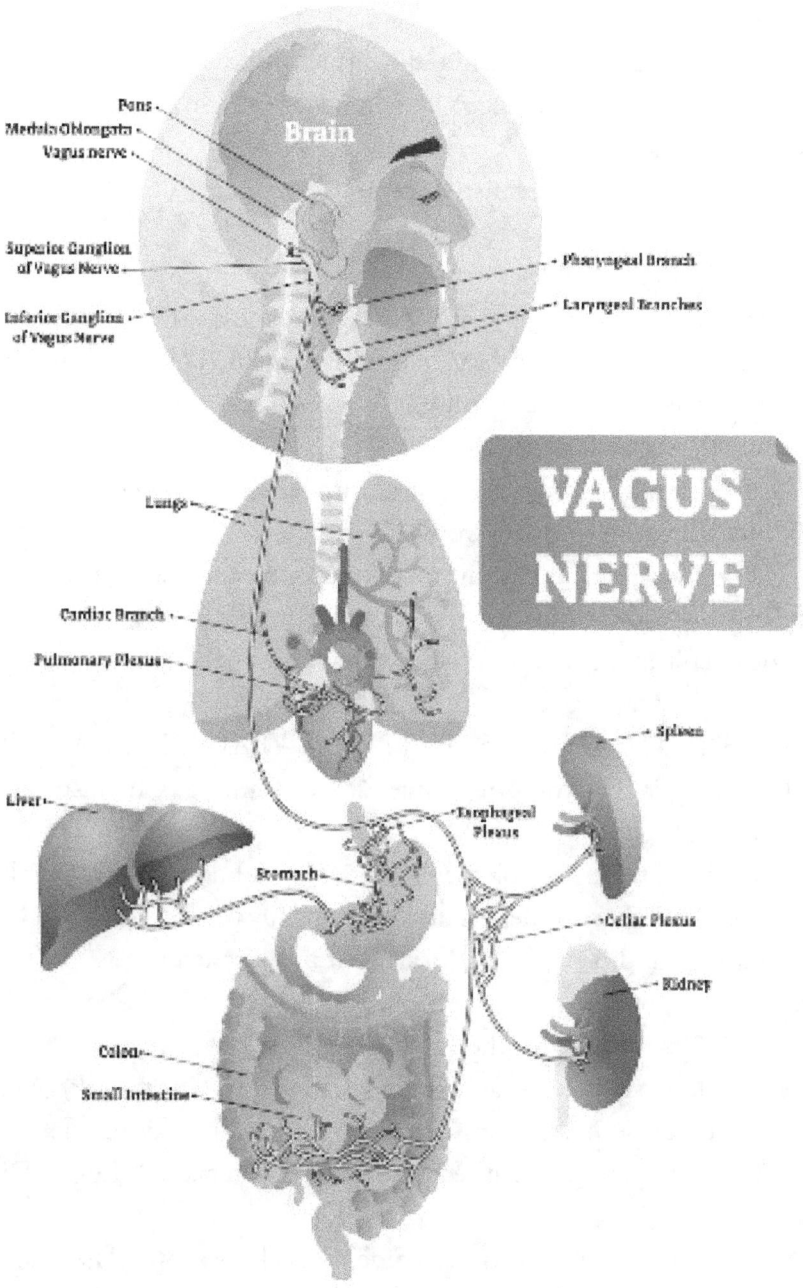

2. The External Tool (The Bridge to Speech)

This is for the parents. Especially if you have a child who is nonverbal, delayed, or struggling to talk.

You have to understand the architecture of the brain.

• Speech lives in the Logic Center (Left Brain). If that door is jammed, the kid can't speak.

• Music lives in the Creative Center (Right Brain). That door is often wide open.

If you just talk to a delayed child, you are banging on a locked door.

But if you sing to them, you are using the side door.

When you sing lyrics, you are combining melody (Right Brain) with words (Left Brain). You are building a bridge across the gap.

I am telling you: Sing to them.

Don't just play Mozart. Sing songs with lyrics. Pop songs, rock songs, anything with a rhythm and words.

You will see them start to hum. Then they mouth the rhythm. Then, suddenly, the word slides out on the melody.

You aren't just teaching them a song. You are teaching their brain how to process language.

PART II: THE CHEMISTRY (THE 55-YEAR EXPERIMENT)

If Singing is the workout, like resistance training, Chemistry is the coolant.

I have been taking supplements for 55 years. I don't mean a multivitamin here and there. I mean a disciplined, daily protocol.

I didn't read this in a book. I learned it in a kitchen in East Boston in 1968.

1. The Giant in the Kitchen

I was a kid. My cousin came up to visit us from Norfolk, Virginia.

You have to understand my lineage to understand this moment.

• The Software (My Father's Side): The Caggianos. Logic. Discipline.

• The Hardware (My Mother's Side): The Thorntons. The Giants.

My cousin was a Thornton. He was massive. A muscle-man. He filled up the doorway.

He walked into our East Boston kitchen, and he put a bottle on the table.

Vitamin B.

He didn't give me a lecture. He just handed me the pill.

"Take this."

2. The Flush

I took it on an empty stomach.

Ten minutes later, the "Niacin Flush" hit me. My skin turned red. My stomach turned. I felt heat rushing through my veins.

Most people would have said, "I'm sick. I'm never doing that again."

But my Recorder brain didn't register "Sick."

It registered Power.

I realized: I can feel this working. I can change my state.

I realized my body was a machine, and this Giant had just handed me high-octane fuel.

3. The Crew

That day started a 55-year experiment.

My Dad, my brother Kevin, and I—we became a unit. We analyzed it. We realized that our brains ran hotter than other people's. We burned up nutrients faster because we were recording more data.

We needed more B-vitamins for the nerves. We needed more support.

We weren't "popping pills." We were the pit crew for our own race cars.

4. The Result

People ask me how I walk 19,000 steps a day at 68. They ask why I don't have brain fog.

The answer is that moment in East Boston.

I never let the tank go empty. I respected the machine enough to fuel it.

68

You're not dealing with a fragile child. You are d

(H ow to Teach a Binary Mind)
If you teach long enough, you eventually meet a student who doesn't fit the standard model. They're bright—often brilliant—but inconsistent. They listen but seem distant. They know the rules but struggle to follow them in the moment. They're either locked in or checked out, hyper-focused or overwhelmed, precise or distracted.

The modern educational system often calls these students autistic, ADHD, twice-exceptional, gifted, inattentive, oppositional, or "behavioral." But all of that language misses the point.

These students have a Binary Mind—a Recorder Mind. Your job isn't to normalize them. Your job is to understand the design so you can teach them correctly. Once you understand the mechanics, every mysterious behavior suddenly makes perfect sense.

1. The Binary Mind Records (Constantly, Automatically)
Most students filter the classroom. Binary students record it.

• Every sound.
• Every shift in tone.
• Every movement.
• Every pattern.
• Every inconsistency.

This recording is not a choice. It is the operating system. So when a Binary student "overreacts," "shuts down," or becomes "lost," they are not misbehaving—they are overloaded. Their bandwidth is full. The fix is not discipline. The fix is structure.

2. Unfinished Moments Stay Open (The "Big One")

A Runner-wired child moves on automatically. A Binary child cannot. If something confusing, unfair, abrupt, or unresolved happens in your classroom—even something tiny—the Binary mind keeps the file open.

Examples:

• You changed a rule without warning.

• You corrected their work but didn't explain why.

• You raised your voice slightly.

• You said "We'll talk later" and didn't.

To you, these are small moments. To them, these are unfinished threads the mind must resolve before they can move on. This leads to freezing, avoidance, and repetitive questions. They aren't refusing. They are waiting for closure. Once they get closure, they reset instantly.

3. They Learn in Sequence, Not Chaos

Most classrooms are built for Runners—fast transitions, multitasking, concurrent instructions. Binary Minds don't multitask. They sequence.

If you give three instructions at once, they can't prioritize. If the classroom is loud, their brain logs all of it. The key is not more time—it's more clarity.

Teach them using:

• Step 1 → Step 2 → Step 3.

• Visual sequences.

• Predictable routines.

• One variable at a time.

This is not lowering the bar. This is enabling full performance.

4. Literal Interpretation Is Not Misbehavior

Binary students take words at face value because their system privileges accuracy over social inference.

• When you say "Be quiet," and five students whisper, the Binary student sees injustice.

• When you say "You can start when you're ready," they think you mean "ready," not "right now."

• When you say "Work with a partner," they assume any partner, not "someone you choose socially."

Their literal interpretation is not obstinance. It is structural integrity—the same trait that makes them exceptional problem-solvers later in life.

5. Their Empathy Is Deep (Just Not Performed)

Teachers often misread Binary students as cold, detached, or uninterested. All incorrect.

Binary empathy is internal, not social. They feel your disappointment. They feel classroom tension. They feel hypocrisy deeply. But they don't always perform empathy the way Runners expect—smiling, nodding, mirroring. Their empathy is quieter. But sharper. When a Binary student trusts you, the bond is unbreakable.

6. Group Work Is a Minefield

Group assignments require multitasking, role negotiation, rapid transitions, and reading social cues. These are the exact conditions that overwhelm a Binary Mind.

To support them:

• Assign specific roles explicitly.

• Place them with stable partners.

• Give written instructions.

• Allow independent alternatives when appropriate.

• Measure mastery, not social performance.

When Binary students melt down during group work, they are not being antisocial. They are drowning in ambiguity.

7. Their Morality Is Absolute

Binary students have a rigid internal moral code: Fairness, Honesty, Consistency, Truth. They assume adults have the same code.

So when a teacher enforces rules inconsistently, says "because I said so," or makes exceptions, the Binary student experiences genuine moral distress. They are not challenging your authority. They are reacting to perceived structural failure. When you explain the reasoning behind decisions, their trust strengthens dramatically.

8. Sensory Overload Is Hardware, Not Attitude

A loud cafeteria, buzzing lights, scratchy clothes, unpredictable noises. These are not mild annoyances. They are system overload events. The solution is not discipline. The solution is Environment.

Small adjustments help enormously:

• Quiet workspaces.

• Dimmer seating areas.

• Noise-blocking headphones.

• Predictable routines.

• Reduced transitions.

Reduce the noise, and their brilliance appears.

9. ADHD Is Not Opposite to Autism

ADHD students are not inattentive. They are recording too much, too fast, without the ability to compress it.

• They are Sentries in motion.

• They are Scanners instead of still observers.

• They are Over-recording instead of Under-focusing.

This view transforms classroom management. You stop trying to "control behavior" and start trying to stabilize bandwidth.

10. The Practical Guide (What Costs Nothing)

Here are classroom adjustments that cost nothing and change everything:

• Clear Entry Protocol: Tell them exactly what to do when class starts. Same every day.

• Predictable Transitions: Give warnings. Give countdowns.

• Written Instructions: Always pair verbal directions with text.

• One Variable at a Time: Don't mix multiple new tasks.

• Private Corrections: Public correction = humiliation replayed for years.

• Explain the "Why": Binary students comply when they understand the logic.

• Let Them Finish Their Thought: Interrupting mid-processing creates panic.

• Don't Interpret Shutdown as Defiance: It's overload. Let them reset.

• Be Consistent: Your reliability is their safety.

11. When a Binary Student Trusts You, You Get Genius

When they feel understood—

When they feel safe—

When the environment makes sense—

Their abilities explode: Memory. Pattern recognition. Problem-solving. Moral insight. Creativity. Deep empathy.

69

(E arn The Day™: A Biological Factory Reset)
I am 68 years old. In 2025, I walked an average of 19,000 steps every single day. I lost 100 pounds. I did not do this with a "miracle drug." I did not do it with a surgery. I did not do it with young genetics.

I did it by treating my body like a failing server that needed a hard reset.

The 90-Day Reboot is not a lifestyle plan. It is not a diet. It is not a motivational trick. It is a biological recalibration for Binary Minds.

Most health advice fails Recorders because it is written for Runners. It relies on "motivation," "community," and "fun." A Binary Mind doesn't care about fun. We care about System Integrity. BMIs don't "change" gradually. We flip. We click. We lock. You are either running the old operating system (Crash Mode), or you are running the new one (Optimization Mode). There is no middle ground.

This chapter is the manual I used to save my own life. Specifically, I doubled my remaining timeline, and reset my biological clock so that I'm living those years—"kicking the can"—with the engine of a 30-year-old.

THE CORE PRINCIPLE: "**EARN THE DAY**"

The philosophy is simple: I do something today that makes tomorrow better. Most people live in debt to yesterday (cleaning up mistakes) or in fear of tomorrow (anxiety). To Earn The Day means you execute the code today that guarantees a stronger platform for tomorrow morning.

We build this structure around three systems:

1. Biology (The Hardware: Light, Load, Chemistry).

2. Wiring (The Software: Replay, Closure, Focus).

3. Environment (The Network: Noise, Objects, People).

PART I: THE MATH (BMI vs. BMI)

We possess a trait that society calls a disorder: Obsessive Compulsive behavior (OCD). In a Runner world, OCD is a problem. In the 90-Day Reboot, OCD is the fuel.

We are going to take that obsessive, repetitive, system-locking nature and aim it at your health. And when a Recorder aims their obsession at a target, they don't just hit it. They obliterate it.

PART II: THE PHYSICS OF THE WALK

(Why 19,000 Steps?) : 8,000 min?

People ask me, "Robert, why 19,000 steps? That takes hours. Who has the time?" You are asking the wrong question. You think walking is "exercise." Walking is not exercise. Walking is Optical Flow.

The Engineering of the Predawn Walk

When you walk forward, images move past your retina. This is called "Optic Flow." Neuroscience proves that Optic Flow quiets the Amygdala (the fear center).

• Stationary Stress: When you sit and worry, the amygdala screams because you aren't moving away from the threat.

• Walking Stress: When you move forward, the amygdala quiets down. It assumes you are handling the problem.

I walk 19,000 steps not to burn calories (though that is a nice side effect). I walk to burn off the Replay Loops. If I sit, I ruminate. If I walk, I process.

The Protocol

• The Predawn Launch: You must be outside before the sun comes up. The shift from dark to light triggers the Cortisol Awakening Response (CAR). If you miss this window, your melatonin (sleep hormone) will be messed up 16 hours later.

• No Headphones (Phase 1): For the first mile, no podcasts. No music. Let the brain dump its cache. 30 minutes to start. Increase as you see fit.

• The Pace: This isn't a stroll. It is a mission. Walk like you are late for a meeting. This engages the cardiovascular system without spiking cortisol.

PART III: THE HARDWARE RESET (The Body)

You cannot run high-performance software on broken hardware. If your inflammation is high, your cortisol is spiked, and your nutrients are depleted, your Recorder mind will remain in "Emergency Mode."

Phase 1: The Flush (Days 1–15)

• Goal: Stop the chaos. Get the system to "Neutral." In this phase, you will feel worse before you feel better. That is the "Herxheimer Reaction"—the sound of toxins leaving the building. Push through.

• Hydration Protocol: 16oz of water immediately upon waking. Before coffee. Before phones. The system is dehydrated from sleep; you must depressurize the hydraulics.

• Vitamin Prep: Prepare morning, midday, and night supplements the day before. Do not make decisions in the morning. Execute the plan.

• Fuel Cleanup: Remove the noise. No processed sugar. No seed oils. These are acoustic interference for your gut-brain axis.

• The Binary Rule: If it comes in a box with a cartoon character, it is not food. It is product.

Phase 2: Stabilization (Days 16–33)

• Goal: The body remembers what "Steady" feels like. Now that the noise is down, we install the rhythm. The Binary Mind craves predictability.

• Sleep Anchoring: Wake up at the exact same time every day. No exceptions for weekends. You cannot stabilize a clock that you keep resetting.

• Protein-First Structure: Eat protein before carbohydrates.

• The Logic: Protein signals satiety to the brain. Carbs signal "Hunt for more." If you eat carbs first, you trigger a glucose spike that crashes 90 minutes later. That crash feels like anxiety to a Recorder.

• The "Stop" Switch: You stop eating 3 hours before bed. Digestion requires massive energy. If you eat late, your body spends the night digesting instead of repairing.

Phase 3: The Resistance Protocol (Days 34–90)

(The "No Injury" Rule)

Most people start a diet and try to become a Navy SEAL on Day 1. They grab heavy weights, do push-ups until their shoulders blow out, and quit by Day 3 because their brain registers "Pain."

The "Start Slow" Routine

I use a simple resistance routine. 5 Exercises. Basic. Repeatable. You don't need a gym. You need adjustable dumbbells (hand weights).

1. The Bench Press (Chest/Triceps)

2. The Curl (Biceps)

3. The Squat (Legs/Core)

4. The Overhead Press (Shoulders)

5. The Row (Back)

The Volume: 10–15 Reps. 3 Sets. That's it.

The "Motion First" Progression (Tricking the Subconscious)

• Phase 1: The Ghost Reps (Zero Weight): Start with no weight. Just your hands. You are tricking the subconscious into accepting the routine without the threat of pain. You are establishing the "Base" without the "Burn."

• Phase 2: Finding the Resistance: Once the motion is automatic, add the lightest possible weight.

• Phase 3: The "Paper Clip" Progression (For Life): Runners jump 10 pounds at a time. Recorders use Micro-Loading. Increase the weight by the "weight of a piece of paper." You are going to do this for the rest of your life. There is no rush. You want to keep the subconscious in tune with the progress, never shocking it, just constantly upgrading the system bit by bit.

PART IV: THE CHEMISTRY (The Supplement Engineering)

You cannot build a house without bricks. Modern food is acoustically loud (calories) but chemically quiet (nutrients). Note: I am not a doctor. I am an engineer of my own biology.

List 1 — Essential Vitamins

• Fat-Soluble: Vitamin A, D3, E, K2 (MK-7).

• Water-Soluble: Vitamin C, B1, B2, B3, B5, B6, B7, B9 (Folate), B12 (Methyl cobalamin).

List 2 — Essential Minerals

• Magnesium (Glycinate for sleep / Citrate for digestion), Zinc, Calcium, Iron (careful with dosage), Potassium, Sodium (electrolytes), Iodine, Selenium, Copper, Manganese, Chromium.

List 3 — Omega & Fatty Acids

• Omega-3 Fish Oil (EPA + DHA) or Algae Omega.

List 4 — Gut Health

• Probiotic, Digestive Enzymes, Collagen (Type I & III).

List 5 — The Accelerators (The "Secret Sauce")

• Creatine Monohydrate: It is battery fluid for the brain. Recharges ATP. Prevents the 3:00 PM "Brain Fog Crash."

• Essential Amino Acids (EAAs): Tells the body: "Eat the fat, save the muscle." Precursors to Serotonin and Dopamine.

• Others: CoQ10, L-Theanine (calm), Ashwagandha (stress), Green Tea Extract, Turmeric/Curcumin, Alpha-Lipoic Acid, NAC.

PART V: THE ENVIRONMENT RESET (The Server Room)

A Binary Mind does not filter environment; it absorbs it. If your house is chaotic, your mind is chaotic. You cannot think clearly in a dirty server room.

The Daily Rules:

• Minus Three: Remove 3 unnecessary objects from your home every single day. In 90 days, you will have removed 270 items of noise. Why: Every object is a line of code your brain has to render.

• The Drawer Protocol: Reset one drawer or shelf per week. Organize it until it pleases your Binary eye.

• News Blackout: No news before noon. Do not let the chaos hijack your dopamine before you have earned the day.

• No Chaotic People Before Caffeine: Protect your morning bandwidth.

PART VI: TROUBLESHOOTING (When The Protocol Breaks)

The Runner approach to failure is "Guilt." The Recorder approach to failure is "System Correction."

• Scenario A: "I missed the morning walk."

• Recorder: "The morning window is closed. I will execute the Sunset Protocol. I will walk 30 minutes at dusk to signal the end of the day."

• Rule: Never miss two days in a row. One miss is an anomaly. Two misses is a new pattern.

• Scenario B: "I ate the cake."

• Recorder: "Glucose spike detected. Counter-measure required."

• Action: Walk for 15 minutes immediately. The muscles will soak up the excess glucose. The system resets.

SPECIAL SECTION: FOR PARENTS (The Ignition Protocol)

I know what you are thinking. "Robert, that sounds nice, but you don't know my kid. He will scream for three hours. He will starve himself for two days."

I am here to tell you: Biology is Biology. You cannot negotiate with it, but you also cannot stop it from working when the inputs change.

1. The "Trojan Horse" Strategy

You don't need them to agree to the new diet. You just need to get the chemistry in. You don't fight the Nugget. You use the Nugget.

• Inject the Code: Put the Amino Acids and Creatine in the ketchup or the drink.

• The Subconscious Shift: When you sneak in the good fuel, the body realizes, "Wait. I feel better. The fog is lifting." Suddenly, the subconscious starts asking for the good stuff. The "Nugget Addiction" breaks not because you forced it, but because the body is finally getting the premium gas it was designed for.

2. The Movement Hack (The Tether & The Turnaround)

A non-verbal child often refuses to walk because "Open Space" = Infinite Variables.

• The Tether: Hand them one end of a rope or a heavy stick. To a Recorder, holding an object provides proprioceptive feedback (grounding). It says, "I am here."

• The Formation: Walk shoulder-to-shoulder. You are towing the car until the engine starts.

The Turnaround Celebration (The Vulnerability Hack)

Here is the most important part of the walk. When you reach the halfway point and turn back toward home, I want you to do something that feels uncomfortable.

I want you to sing. Loudly.

• Why? Your child needs to see the "Pillar" being vulnerable.

• The Signal: They need to see that "letting go" is safe. You aren't just walking anymore; you are modeling joy. If you can sing without the world collapsing, maybe they can too.

3. The Melodic Bridge: Hacking the Hemispheres

To understand why a non-verbal child can sing a song perfectly but cannot say a sentence, you have to look at the wiring.

• Left Hemisphere (Broca's Area): The "Speech Center." Often jammed in Binary Minds (Apraxia).

• Right Hemisphere: Melody and Rhythm. Usually wide open.

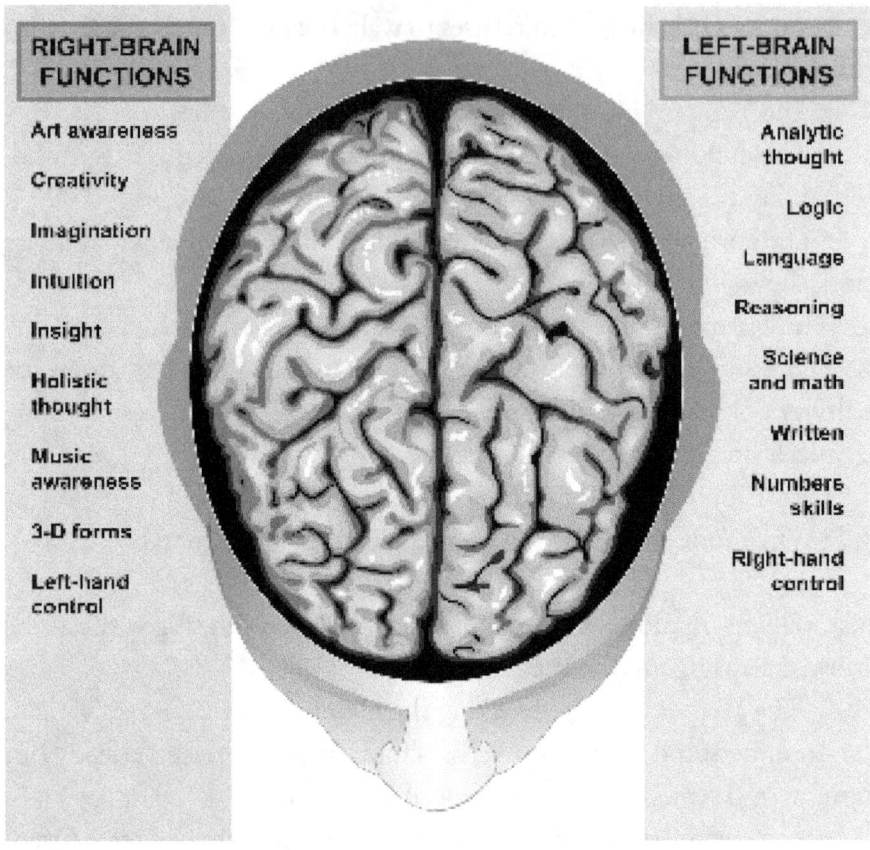

RIGHT-BRAIN FUNCTIONS

Art awareness

Creativity

Imagination

Intuition

Insight

Holistic thought

Music awareness

3-D forms

Left-hand control

LEFT-BRAIN FUNCTIONS

Analytic thought

Logic

Language

Reasoning

Science and math

Written

Numbers skills

Right-hand control

The Back Door Approach: When you force speech, you bang on the jammed front door. When you sing, you use the open back door. By attaching words to melody, you force the signal across the bridge to the Right Hemisphere.

4. The Tool: AI Lyrics for Personality

We give non-verbal kids buttons that say "Bathroom." We treat them like survival machines, ignoring their wit.

The Strategy: The AI Lyricist

Use AI to write Short Melodic Scripts based on their mood.

• Old Way: Robot voice says "YES."

• New Way: AI generates a rhyming lyric set to a beat.

• Example (The Sarcastic No): "I heard what you said / And I think you are wrong / So I'm shaking my head / While I sing you this song."

Why This Works:

1. Rhythm: Acts as a metronome for the motor system.

2. Wit: Proves intelligence.

3. Integration: Forces Left/Right brain synchronization.

5. The DJ Method: Using Pop Culture

The Recorder mind is a vault of music. Stop forcing them to speak like textbooks. Let them mix the audio they already have.

The Mechanic: Search and Replay

Instead of struggling to form a sentence, the child scans their internal library for a song lyric.

• Input: Mom says "You need friends."

• Search: "Friends" + "Mama" + "Advice."

• Output: Child sings "Once I was seven years old, my mama told me..."

The Mirror: If the parent sings it back, the circuit closes. You have validated their language and shared a joke.

6. The Biology of the Oxygen Mask

In Chapter 13, we talked about the emotional oxygen mask. Now we need to talk about the physical one.

Raising a Binary Mind is an endurance sport. It requires physical strength to handle meltdowns and mental speed to play the "DJ Game."

• If you are inflamed, they feel the heat.

• If you are exhausted, they feel the static.

The 90-Day Reset is a tactical requirement. You walk at dawn so you have the patience for the morning routine. You lift weights so you are a solid wall when they crash into you. Get healthy for their stabilization.

PART VII: THE TIMELINE (Loading, Cooking, and Lift)

People ask me, "When does the magic happen?" Biology requires Saturation.

1. The Loading Phase (Days 1–10)

You are pouring water into a dry sponge. The Amino Acids are repairing damage. You are stocking the "System Kitchen." Most people quit here because they don't see instant results. Do not quit.

478 - ROBERT ANTHONY CAGGIANO

2. The "Cooking" Phase (Day 10)

Around the ten-day mark, the tank hit "Full." I felt a sensation I can only describe as "Cooking Inside." My body finally had the materials to fix the chassis. I looked down at my watch and realized I had walked 5 miles. I didn't "push" myself. My body asked for it.

3. The Moment of Lift (Day 32)

It was 4:45 AM. I was three miles from my house. I started moving down a hill, and I wasn't just walking. I was jog-walking. My legs felt like springs. I felt light. I stopped in the dark and said out loud: "Are you kidding me? This can't be that easy."

That was the moment. The engine wasn't just repairing itself anymore; it was performing. The motion became a drug.

The Result (15 Months Later)

Since that morning in the dark, I have walked 4,000 miles. I didn't do it on willpower. I did it because on Day 32, the system came online, and I realized that feeling good is the most addictive substance on earth.

70

The Universal Blueprint

We have been conditioned to believe a lie: that our biology is a product of our geography. We've been told that "people from here" are built differently than "people from there," or that your heritage gives you a different set of rules to live by.

It is a lie designed to give you an excuse.

The truth is that the human body is the only piece of architecture on this planet that is a Universal Constant. If you take a man who is six-foot-two from a village in China and stand him next to a man who is six-foot-two from a small town in Alabama, you are looking at the exact same machine. Their hearts have to pump blood the same distance. Their skeletons have to support the same load. Their lungs have to oxygenate the same volume of tissue.

The math of the human frame does not care about your passport. It doesn't care what language you speak or what your ancestors did for a living. Biology has no borders.

BODY MASS INDEX (BMI)

To find your BMI, locate where your height and weight intersect; your BMI is listed at the top of that column.

HEIGHT

REDUCED RISK   INCREASED RISK

WEIGHT (IN POUNDS)

Your Body Mass Index (BMI) is your "Factory Setting." It is the mathematical coordinate where your specific height meets your ideal weight. When you live outside of that number—even by a small percentage—you are asking a universal machine to perform a task it wasn't designed for. You are forcing the engine to redline every single day.

The 90-Day Reboot isn't about "getting in shape" for your neighborhood. It's about returning to the one and only physical truth that applies to every human being on Earth. You provide the chemistry—the Creatine and the Amino Acids—to keep the engine from stalling. Then, you move. You walk. You do what the machine has done for 200,000 years.

You aren't a "special case." You are a human. Start living like the one you were designed to be.

71

CHAPTER 17: The Protocol (Fighting Tomorrow)

Kick the Can — Inspiration and Analogy

The Twilight Zone (Season 3, Episode 21, "Kick the Can," 1962).
The episode takes place in Sunnyvale Rest Home, where a group of elderly residents are living out quiet, repetitive days. One of them, Charles Whitley, begins to suspect that growing old isn't a physical inevitability but a mindset. He remembers that as kids, they used to play a game called Kick the Can in the streets — running, laughing, full of life.

He convinces the others that the secret to youth might be something as simple as acting young again. In the middle of the night, they sneak out into the yard and begin to play. The magic of childlike joy — the freedom, the rhythm, the sheer silliness of the game — transforms them into children again.

The next morning, the staff find only empty clothes and a single can rolling down the grass. One skeptical resident, who refused to play, is left behind — still old, suddenly realizing he's missed his last chance at wonder.

It's a deeply symbolic story: Age, like misunderstanding, is often self-inflicted. The moment you reawaken your joy, your spirit begins to reverse the damage done by doubt. That healing, energy, and vitality aren't "treatments." They're returns to the natural state of being alive.

This is the same spirit that drives my mission: to invite everyone — BMI and non-BMI alike — to rediscover the joy of simply being themselves again.

The Clean Loop Reset

"Stop kicking the can down the road. To find clarity, you must aggressively close the open loops in your life—the issues, the 'stack,' and the mental clutter that cause the headaches. If a loop cannot be closed, you must find a way to bury it.

The secret is redirection: take the natural intensity of your mind—the part of you designed for repetition and 'OCD' focus—and point it toward something beneficial for yourself. Use your design; don't let it use you. Close the loops, clear the field, and let your natural focus finally work in your favor.

The 33rd Day: The Momentum of the Child

By the 33rd day, I found myself running down the hill, amazed at the simplicity of the shift. I had stopped forcing the system and started following the process, day by day. Suddenly, the fog was gone. I woke up the next day, and the next, feeling like a kid again—free to fantasize, free to move, and finally clear enough to "kick the can" every single morning.

You see it on YouTube all the time: fitness experts screaming "consistency, consistency, consistency." They say that because they know that when they give you all the 90-day details, your eyes glaze over. But when you finally find the rhythm, you start to smile at the people who think you're "missing out" because you don't drink or eat like they do.

You aren't missing out on anything. You're waking up every day with a mind that is light and a body that wants to move. You eat what you want because you know your system. You enjoy your day because you've mastered the "Kick." That is the power of the 33rd day—it's the moment the data becomes a feeling.

72

CHAPTER 18: The Unified Map

Y ou've read the theory.
You understand the two designs.

Now comes the part that actually matters.

Tomorrow morning.

This is where most books fail parents. They explain why a child is different, then quietly step back when it's time to say what to do. This book does not do that. We are not here to observe these children from a distance. We are not here to protect them from life. And we are not here to wrap them in therapeutic bubble wrap and hope the world becomes gentler.

It won't.

So instead, we prepare them.

Not by hardening them.

By engaging them.

By meeting them where their biology actually lives.

Start Moving Them

I hear this constantly from good, well-meaning parents.

"He prefers to be alone."

"He doesn't like sports."

"He's not built for that."

And so the child is left alone. Quietly. Safely. Inside.

This is a mistake.

A dangerous one.

Binary children do not need isolation. They need motion with attachment. They need physical engagement that is grounded, predictable, and shared with someone they trust.

Look at how I grew up. I had older brothers. I had kids in the street. No one sat me down to analyze my mind. No one asked me how I felt about competition. They cared whether I could catch a ball. They pulled me into the game. They challenged me. They adjusted the rules just enough to keep me in play.

That wasn't cruelty.

That was calibration.

I am not telling you to throw your child into chaos. I am telling you to enter the arena with them. You play with them. You run with them. You wrestle on the floor. You throw the ball badly on purpose so they can win sometimes. You let them feel resistance, weight, gravity, balance, momentum.

Movement organizes the brain.

Always has.

A child left motionless becomes trapped inside their own replay loops. A child in motion begins to resolve them.

This is not optional.

The Real BMI (Fuel, Not Shame)

We need to reclaim a phrase that medicine hollowed out.

Body Mass Index is not a moral scorecard. It is a fuel gauge.

And this applies to parents just as much as children.

Step back and look honestly.

Is your child growing?

Are they sluggish?

Do they crash emotionally after eating?

Do they struggle to wake up?

Children grow at different rates, yes. But biology still tells the truth if you look long enough.

If the body isn't building correctly, the brain won't stabilize correctly. Period.

This isn't about dieting. It's about inputs.

If you feed a high-output brain low-quality fuel, you get volatility. If you feed a developing body ultra-processed food, you get inflammation, lethargy, emotional dysregulation, and confusion that looks psychological but isn't.

Fix the fuel.

Protein. Minerals. Hydration. Real food.

You are not being controlling.

You are being responsible.

Kill the Rainbow (The Label Problem)

This is where I'm going to be blunt.

Stop telling your child they are "on the spectrum."

Stop.

I am not talking about erasing who they are. I am talking about erasing a narrative that quietly tells them they are a deviation.

Every time you frame their identity as a medical category, you separate them from the human story. You teach them—subtly, repeatedly—that they are an exception rather than a participant.

That is poison to a developing Recorder.

They are not a color on a chart.

They are not a diagnosis first.

They are not broken software.

They are boys and girls with a specific cognitive orientation that has existed since the beginning of humanity.

Call them what they are.

Recorders.

Observers.

Builders.

Truth-keepers.

Language matters because it shapes self-trust. And without self-trust, nothing else works.

Turn On the Music (The Singing Rule)

Binary children often struggle with spoken language under pressure.

Music bypasses that entire bottleneck.

Music is structured emotion.

Predictable rhythm.

Safe repetition.

Embodied timing.

That's why it works.

This isn't about putting on background noise. This is about inviting resonance into the home.

Have music available. Always. A smart speaker. A playlist. Something accessible.

But here is the part that actually matters:

You sing.

Not well.

Not confidently at first.

Not because they asked.

You sing because you are regulated enough to be vulnerable.

Let them see you enjoying rhythm. Let them see you off-key and unafraid. Let them witness joy without performance anxiety.

That does more for their nervous system than a hundred conversations.

And yes—this connects directly to the morning walk. Singing changes the frequency of the environment. It softens defenses. It invites participation without pressure.

Music opens doors language cannot.

The Doctor Partnership

We are not going to war with medicine.

We are going in as adults.

You are not a passive recipient of opinions. You are the primary observer of your child's system.

You have data. You have patterns. You have lived experience.

So you walk into that office calmly and say:

• "I'm noticing hydration issues."

- "I'm noticing sleep disruption."
- "I'm noticing food sensitivity."
- "I'm noticing growth patterns."

And then you ask a simple question:

- "How can you support this plan?"

You are not asking for permission.
You are inviting collaboration.
Good doctors respond to clarity.
And if they don't, you find another one.
This protocol is not about controlling your child.
It is about fighting for their future without turning them into a patient.
You are not raising a fragile mind.
You are raising a specialized one.
And tomorrow morning is where that work begins.

73

(A Shared Language for Parents, Teachers, and Adults)
Human beings do not think the same way, and they were never supposed to. Modern society invented the idea of a "normal brain," but biology never built one. It built two. One mind Records. One mind Runs.

This chapter is the operating manual for the Recorder Mind—the Binary Mind Inside—written directly for the three groups who need it most:

1. **Parents**, who carry the emotional weight of raising a child whose wiring they were never taught to understand.
2. **Young Adults**, who have lived the confusion firsthand and deserve clarity.
3. **Teachers**, who guide these children daily inside a system designed for the opposite wiring.

Each group needs the same truth, but expressed in a way that speaks to their role.

SECTION 1: THE CORE TRUTH

The Binary Mind isn't a "different kind of personality." It isn't a deficit, a disorder, or an impairment. It is an ancient cognitive design built to **store, track, verify, and predict.**

The Binary system records automatically, constantly, and without filtering. This is not a choice; it is hardware. If you understand this one sentence, everything else in life becomes easier: **A Binary Mind does**

not control what it records. It controls what it does with the recording.

This is why people misunderstand you. This is why you misunderstand yourself. But once you understand the architecture, what felt like chaos becomes an organized machine.

SECTION 2: THE MECHANICS (RECAP)

1. Recording Without Filtering Runners filter. Recorders take everything in. Every sound. Every tone shift. Every micro-expression. Every environmental detail. The irony is that BMI memory is not perfect—it's selectively permanent. The system stores anything the mind flags as meaningful, even if the reason isn't obvious in the moment.

2. Replay (The Search for Resolution) Replay is not rumination. Replay is forensic analysis. A Binary Mind replays until it finds the truth, the cause, or the pattern. If the moment never resolves, the replay never stops. This is the source of 70% of the emotional pain in Binary individuals. Not trauma. Not defiance. **Unclosed files.**

3. The ADHD Connection (Motion-Based Recording) ADHD is not the opposite of Autism. It is the motion-based version of the same recording system.

- **Autism:** Still Recording (Depth).
- **ADHD:** Moving Recording (Breadth). Both lack the Runner filter. Both log raw data. Both become overwhelmed by unresolved inputs.

SECTION 3: FOR PARENTS (The Home Manual)

Parenting a Binary Mind is not about controlling behavior. It is about **managing bandwidth.** Your child is not lazy, disrespectful, or dramatic. They are **Overloaded.**

The Directives:

- **Their Brain Records Everything:** You didn't do anything wrong. But their brain logs your stress, your tone, and your inconsistency. This is why they "explode" after school. They have been recording for 7 hours straight.

- **Give Them Closure:** A Binary child needs endings, explanations, and sequence. Without these, the nervous system holds open tabs.
- **Meltdowns Are System Failures:** A meltdown is not manipulation. It is a computer overheating. Fix the overload (lights, noise, pressure), not the behavior.
- **Your Calm is Their Medicine:** If you deregulate, they collapse. If you stabilize, they stabilize. Put on your oxygen mask first.

SECTION 4: FOR YOUNG ADULTS (You Are Not Broken)

If you are a teenager or young adult reading this, here is the truth nobody told you: Nothing is wrong with you. You weren't "bad at school." You weren't "lazy." Your brain was trying to run a complex recording system in a world built for multitasking Runners.

The Directives:

- **Interest Is Your Switch:** Other people use willpower. You use the ON/OFF switch of Interest. This is why you can hyperfocus for 10 hours on a game or a code base but can't focus for 10 minutes on boring homework. You are a specialist, not a generalist.
- **Replay is for Resolution:** You replay because you are searching for truth. But once you learn closure tools (movement, writing, structure), your life stops feeling like an emotional backlog.
- **Your Empathy Is Real:** You feel deeply. You simply don't express it in the Runner style (smiling/nodding). You are not cold. You are precise.
- **Don't Fake Being a Runner:** Masking is slow death. Your power comes from leaning into pattern, truth, and structure. These are civilization-building abilities.

SECTION 5: FOR TEACHERS (The Classroom Manual)

Teachers are the front-line interpreters of wiring. What you understand shapes a child's entire identity.

The Directives:

- **They Record the Room, Not Just the Lesson:** They are logging the lights, the noise, and the social dynamics. This is why transitions destabilize them. Your structure creates their safety.
- **Overwhelm Is Hardware:** Too much noise = shutdown. Too many instructions = panic. Use visual instructions and one-step sequencing.
- **Trust Comes From Consistency:** You don't need to be warm. You need to be reliable. BMIs respect fairness and clarity above all else. You become their safest adult when you stop changing the rules.

SECTION 6: THE ALIGNMENT

The system was never broken—it was **mismatched.** Parents are not failing. Teachers are not failing. Young adults are not failing. The environment was simply misaligned with the design.

When all three groups align, the child becomes unstoppable.

- When parents provide stability...
- When teachers provide structure...
- When the child understands their own wiring...

Meltdowns drop. Confidence rises. Learning accelerates. A Binary Mind in the wrong environment struggles. A Binary Mind in the right environment shines.

74

EPILOGUE:

The "Man Living Together" Timeline
  Milestones to show how the Two Brain Designs were forged:
  • 200,000 Years (The Hardware): Modern Homo Sapiens emerge.

This is 190,000 years of pure "Runner" survival. The Recorder was just for tracking tracks and seasons.

  • 10,000 Years (The Covenant): The end of the Ice Age. We start "Taming" the land.

This is where the Six Professions begin to solidify because we aren't just moving; we're building.

  • 5,000 Years (The System): Writing and "Civilization" (Sumer/ Egypt).

This is when the Recorder starts getting "Loud." We start logging laws instead of just survival.

  • 100 Years (The Skid): The Industrial/Digital Age. We stopped moving.

This is the "last one and a half seconds" where we decided the "Runner" was a "disability" (ADHD) and the "Recorder" was the only thing that mattered.

  1. The Hardware Release: 200,000–300,000 Years Ago

This is when the modern human body—the 6'2" frame, the lungs, the "Runner" biology—was finalized.

  • The Reality: For 95% of our existence, there was no "home." There was only the Move.

• The Logic: If you didn't move 10+ miles a day, you didn't eat. The BMI of every human was dictated by the terrain, not a chart.

2. Living Together (The Tribe): 50,000–70,000 Years Ago

This is the "Great Leap Forward." Humans started living in larger, cohesive groups (tribes of 50–150).

• The Change: This is when Specialization became a biological survival trait. You didn't need everyone to be a generalist; you needed the Six Core Professions to coexist so the group could out-survive the environment.

• The Record: This is where the "Runner" and "Recorder" designs began to function as a unified team.

3. The Settlement (The Covenant): 10,000–12,000 Years Ago

The end of the last Ice Age. Humans stopped follows the herds and started "Taming" the land (Agriculture).

• The Impact: This is the first time the "Hardware" stayed in one place. We traded the "Constant Move" for the "Constant Work."

• The Tension: This is the birth of the Recorder's dominance. You had to track seeds, seasons, and property. The "Map" became more important than the "Hunt."

4. Civilization (The System): 5,000–6,000 Years Ago

The rise of cities (Sumer, Egypt).

• The Shift: This is where "Man living with others" turned into "Man living under a System."

• The Result: We invented writing to keep track of taxes and laws. The Runners began to label the "Recorder's" energy as something that needed to be "managed" or "restrained" for the sake of the city.

The "Last Two Minutes" Perspective

If you look at the 200,000-year history of our "Hardware":

• The Move: (Nomadic) lasted 190,000 years.

• The Settlement: (Farming) lasted 10,000 years.

• The System: (Cities) has lasted only 5,000 years.

The "Man with Electricity" has been around for less than 250 years (since the Industrial Revolution). That is 0.125% of our history.

The Truth: Your body is still 190,000 years deep in the "Move." It doesn't recognize the light switch or the desk; it only recognizes the 8,000 steps.

"Minutes."

• The Runner Baseline: It took **roughly 7,500 generations** of "Runners" to build your current body. They lived, breathed, and survived by the Move.

• The Settlement: It took only **400 generations** of "Farmers" to start settling the land.

• The System: It's been only **8 generations** since the Industrial Revolution (the "Electric Man" era).

• The Crash: You are the **1st or 2nd generation** to try and live entirely inside a digital screen.

75

SOMEWHERE IS HERE
(The Dawn of the Age of Aquarius)

We have spent thousands of years living in the Age of Pisces—an age defined by hierarchy, belief, and vertical power. In that world, the Runner Mind ruled because it was the mind of social climbing, diplomacy, and fluid adaptation. The Recorder Mind was the tool—used to build the pyramids and write the laws, but kept silent in the back room.

But the stars have shifted. We are entering the Age of Aquarius. Astrologers and mystics have said for decades that this new age would be defined by:

• Information (The Recorder's Domain)
• Networks (The Recorder's Architecture)
• Truth over Hierarchy (The Recorder's Moral Code)

For the first time in history, the environment is aligning with the Binary Mind. The digital world, the need for absolute data precision, and the collapse of old social structures are all signals that the Recorder is no longer the "broken" version of humanity. It is the necessary version.

A New Way of Living

The song says, "Someday, somewhere, we'll find a new way of living." That "somewhere" isn't a physical place. It is a mental place. It is the place where we stop forcing Recorders to mask. It is the place where we stop forcing Runners to do data entry. It is the place where the two halves of the human design—the Binary and the Parallel—stop fighting for dominance and start building the future together.

A New Way of Forgiving

And then the lyric that cuts the deepest: "We'll find a way of forgiving."

For centuries, Recorders have been angry at a world that lies to them. For centuries, Runners have been frustrated by a mind they couldn't understand. The "forgiving" happens when we realize: It wasn't personal. It was architecture. We forgive the friction. We forgive the misunderstanding. We forgive the years we spent trying to be someone else.

Integration Means You Are Not Sick

Even when Binary Minds finally recognize themselves, that lie still whispers underneath: Something is wrong with you.

That is false. Binary Minds are not a disorder. They are not a condition to be treated. They are a required cognitive orientation, as necessary to civilization as motion is. A world made only of Runners collapses into chaos. A world made only of Recorders never moves. The species survives because both exist. You were not born broken. You were born load-bearing.

Final Truth

Binary Minds don't need curing. They need to stop fighting physics. Your strengths are not compensation mechanisms. They are primary functions: Precision. Consistency. Depth. Endurance. Truth detection.

When you build life around those—using routine, repetition, and long arcs—you don't become dull. You become dangerously effective. And that was always the point.

76

APPENDIX:

THE DIGITAL FACULTY
(My YouTube University)

I am not a doctor. I am a student. A Recorder mind does not invent data; it collects it, verifies it, and organizes it. Everything I learned about the 90-Day Reboot, I learned because we live in the greatest era of information in human history.

You don't need to go to medical school to understand your liver. You just need to listen to the people who are obsessed with the mechanics. These are the teachers I trust. I don't agree with everything they say, and I certainly can't afford everything they do, but they are the ones "kicking the can" down the road and showing us the map.

1. Bryan Johnson (The Architect)

People call him eccentric. I call him a pioneer. He is spending millions of dollars to reverse his biological age.

• Why I watch him: I can't afford the blood transfusions or the team of 30 doctors. But I can afford the olive oil, the sleep protocol, and the logic. He proves that health isn't luck; it's an engineering problem. He provides the data on the supplements so I don't have to guess.

2. Jeff Cavaliere / Athlean-X (The Mechanic)

He is a Physical Therapist first, a trainer second.

• Why I watch him: He respects the "No Injury" rule. He doesn't just show you a lift; he takes a marker and draws the muscle fibers on a skeleton so you understand the leverage. He teaches you how to lift so you can still move when you're 70.

3. Thomas DeLauer (The Chemist)

He understands inflammation and the metabolic engine better than anyone.

• Why I watch him: He explains the specific biology of fasting and food. He breaks down why certain ingredients (like seed oils) cause noise in the system. He speaks the language of cellular inflammation.

4. Dr. Mike Israetel / Renaissance Periodization (The Scientist)

No fluff. No "rah-rah." Just pure sports science.

• Why I watch him: He understands the "Paper Clip" method (Progressive Overload). He explains that you don't need to kill yourself in the gym; you need to stimulate the muscle with precision. He appeals to the logical, binary brain.

5. Jeremy Ethier (The Optimizer)

He focuses on the most efficient way to get from Point A to Point B based on research.

• Why I watch him: He looks at the studies. He corrects your form. He is calm, precise, and data-driven.

6. Dr. Rhonda Patrick (The Biologist)

She is the bridge between the laboratory and the kitchen. She looks at human body at molecular level to find the " Skeleton Key" for longevity.

> • Why I watch her: She understands the "Heat and Cold" protocol. She provides the hard data on why saunas and cold plunges stop the " Skid" in your cells. She explains how things like sulforaphane (broccoli sprouts) and Vitamin D act as a filter for your system. She doesn't give you opinions; she gives you peer-reviewed evidence. If you want to know how to protect your brain from aging, she is the one holding the map.

My Advice: Don't just watch them to be entertained. Watch them to take notes. Treat their channels like a lecture hall. The data is free. The application is up to you.

77

Why Every Major Autism Theory Misses the Point

For more than forty years, professionals have tried to explain autism by staring at the symptoms instead of the system producing them. Each theory captured a slice of the behavior but never the architecture underneath it. Researchers kept measuring the oceans by looking at the waves.

This appendix exists for one purpose: To show that the world wasn't blind—it was simply measuring the wrong thing.

Autism was never a disease. Never a disorder. Never a deficit model. It was always a different operating system—a binary one—and the world kept diagnosing the output without ever reading the code.

What follows is the landscape of theories that shaped the last half-century. Good people, smart minds, real effort—but wrong target. These explanations circled the symptoms but never touched the root.

And once you see the architecture—Recorder vs. Runner—the limitations of every prior theory become obvious.

1. THE SOCIAL DEFICIT FRAMEWORKS

The oldest and most persistent theories assume autism begins with social impairment: trouble reading faces, following conversations, engaging in reciprocity. It sounds accurate because it describes what observers see. But these theories misinterpret the surface.

• Social Deficit Theory claims autistic individuals lack social instinct.

• Theory of Mind Deficit says they can't infer thoughts or intentions.

• Social Motivation Theory insists autistic people simply don't want connection.

Every one of these theories treats the social behavior as the cause instead of the by-product of a different processing engine.

The Binary Correction:

Binary Minds aren't socially disinterested—they're socially precise. They don't assume what people mean because they don't hallucinate meaning. And when interpretation varies wildly from person to person, a Recorder steps back rather than fabricating. These theories describe the outcome of misaligned processing—not the processing itself.

2. THE COGNITIVE DEFICIT FRAMEWORKS

• Executive Dysfunction Theory argues autistic people struggle with planning, sequencing, and multi-step tasks.

• Weak Central Coherence Theory claims they fixate on details and lose the big picture.

• Developmental Delay models frame autism as "arrested growth."

None of these theories ask a basic question: "What if the mind isn't failing the task? What if the task conflicts with the wiring?"

A Runner brain starts multiple processes and can leave some incomplete. A Recorder brain moves in straight lines, one at a time, and needs structural clarity. When a world designed by Runners evaluates a Recorder, the Recorder is framed as dysfunctional.

The Binary Correction:

A binary system isn't impaired. It's precise. It requires order because the operating system demands it. These theories pathologize a design.

3. THE PERCEPTION & SENSORY FRAMEWORKS

Here the field came closer—but still missed the anchor.

• Sensory Processing Disorder

• Enhanced Perceptual Functioning

• Intense World Theory

All recognize that autistic individuals experience too much, too intensely, too unfiltered. Correct observation. Wrong explanation.

The Binary Correction:

A Recorder brain logs raw data at full resolution. It doesn't discard inputs. It doesn't blur the image. It captures everything exactly. No compression. No rounding. No assumed meaning. This results in "sensitivity," but the sensitivity is a feature of the recording system, not a defect in the sensory system.

A camera that captures in 8K is not "overwhelmed." It's accurate.

4. THE PREDICTION & ERROR-PROCESSING MODELS

These theories—especially Predictive Coding Error Theory—claim autistic people assign too much weight to precision, making the world unpredictable and stressful. Ironically, this one is closest to the truth.

Predictive coding models say:

• Runner minds guess and adjust.

• Binary minds don't guess; they confirm.

But researchers treat this as malfunction instead of orientation. They assume the inability to "let go" of precision is pathological.

The Binary Correction:

It isn't. It's the stability mechanism of a Recorder. A machine that must replay accurately cannot afford corrupted inputs. What scientists called "maladaptive prediction" is simply the cost of a truth-based operating system.

5. THE COMMUNICATION FRAMEWORKS

The Double Empathy Problem finally admitted that misunderstanding is mutual, not one-sided. It opened the door to recognizing that autistic communication isn't broken—it's different.

But even this theory stops short. It doesn't explain why the difference exists. It only acknowledges that it does.

The Binary Correction:

A Recorder doesn't infer tone, subtext, or intention unless those elements are explicitly encoded. A Runner assumes meaning based on pattern and social context. Two operating systems speaking two languages. Not deficits—differences.

6. THE NEUROBIOLOGICAL & GENETIC THEORIES

These are the theories that attract headlines:

• Autism = inflammation

• Autism = abnormal connectivity

- Autism = too many or too few synapses
- Autism = polygenic burden

These may capture correlates. But none explain the consistent cognitive profile seen across time, geography, culture, and socioeconomic layers. If autism were simply "genetic load," it wouldn't produce such a stable pattern of strengths:

- Extreme pattern recognition
- Memory replay
- Precision
- Honesty
- Direct interpretation
- Hyper-focus

These aren't random outcomes. They're the expression of a particular architecture. Biology supplies the hardware; it doesn't explain the operating system.

7. THE MOTOR & BEHAVIORAL FRAMEWORKS

Motor theories (dyspraxia) and behavioral theories (ABA) describe the visible challenges without ever explaining the origin. Behavior is output. Motor planning is output. Regulation is output. The machine producing the output remains undescribed.

The Binary Correction:

Autistic behaviors aren't random. They're mechanical consequences of:

1. Overloading the recording buffer.
2. Interrupting a process mid-sequence.
3. Forcing a Runner framework onto a Recorder brain.

ABA treats the visible behavior as the illness. It tries to reprogram symptoms instead of understanding systems. This is why ABA often harms—it fights the operating system instead of working with it.

THE FUNDAMENTAL PATTERN EVERY THEORY MISSED

Every traditional theory is built on the same assumption: "Neurotypical is the default. Autism is deviation."

Once that assumption is wrong, the entire field fractures. It explains why every theory contradicts the others. It explains why every theory captures a piece but misses the whole.

Autism is not deviation. Autism is one half of a dual-design system: Recorders and Runners. Precision and Motion. Truth and Navigation.

The world treated one design as standard and the other as error. Thus book reframes it: One records. One runs. Both are required. And civilization collapses without the synchronization of the two.

WHERE THE BINARY ARCHITECTURE MODEL FITS

This model doesn't fight the existing theories. It explains them.

Every fragmented theory becomes a predictable output of a Recorder system placed in a Runner-built world:

- Social "deficits" = Refusal to guess.
- Communication "issues" = Insistence on explicitness.
- Executive "dysfunction" = Linear sequencing vs. multitasking.
- Sensory "abnormalities" = High-resolution data capture.
- Predictive "errors" = Precision-based updating.
- Motor loops = Clearing internal buffers.
- Anxiety = Forced parallel processing.

Every old theory becomes a symptom of misalignment. Binary Architecture is not another psychology framework. It is the operating system underneath the behavior.

Once a reader sees it, they will never be able to un-see it.

78

WELCOME HOME!

..

Connect with the Data

506 - ROBERT ANTHONY CAGGIANO

If this record has provided clarity, or if you have data to share, reach out.

Website:

www.RantSun.com

Email:

robert@RantSun.com

This is a living record. The search for the "Binary Handshake" continues.

◇◇ WARNING

READING THIS BOOK MAY CAUSE IRREVERSIBLE CLARITY.

Once you understand the Operating System of the people around you, you will never be able to un-see it. The confusion will disappear, but so will the excuses.

SIDE EFFECTS MAY INCLUDE:

- The End of Drama: You will stop taking people's behavior personally and start seeing it as "System Output."
- A Sudden Drop in Entertainment: TV shows, news cycles, and gossip may become incredibly boring to you. Once you know how the magic trick is done, you can't enjoy the show anymore.
- The "Groundhog" Effect: You will realize that most people are running the same loop every day.

Proceed only if you are ready to trade the excitement of chaos for the peace of certainty.

www.ingramcontent.com/pod-product-compliance
Lightning Source LLC
Chambersburg PA
CBHW060401130626
46555CB00005B/1964